Adri van der Heijden (b. 1951) is one of Holland's greatest and most highly awarded authors. His œuvre consists mainly of two sagas: *The Toothless Time* and *Homo Duplex*. He has also written four other requiems, one of which is about his father's death, *His Father's Ashes*.

Tonio won three of Holland's most prestigious literary awards: the Constantijn Huygens Prize, the 2012 Libris Literature Prize, and the 2012 NS Reader's Award for the Best Book of the Year. It has been a major bestseller in Holland and in Germany, and this edition marks its first appearance in English.

Tonio

a requiem memoir

Adri van der Heijden
translated by Jonathan Reeder

SCRIBE

Melbourne • London

Scribe Publications
18–20 Edward St, Brunswick, Victoria 3056, Australia
2 John St, Clerkenwell, London, WC1N 2ES, United Kingdom

Originally published in Dutch by De Bezige Bij in 2012
First published in English by Scribe in 2015

The publisher gratefully acknowledges the support
of the Dutch Foundation for Literature.

N ederlands
N letterenfonds
dutch foundation
for literature

Typeset in 11.5 / 15 pt Dante MT by the publishers
Printed and bound in China by 1010 Printing Asia Limited

National Library of Australia Cataloguing-in-Publication data

Heijden, Adri van der, author.

Tonio: a requiem memoir / Adri van der Heijden

9781925106732 (AU edition)
9781925228076 (UK edition)
9781925113921 (e-book)

1. Heijden, Tonio van der. 2. Sons–Death–Biography.
3. Traffic accident victims–Netherlands–Biography. 4. Parental grief–Biography.

306.874092

A CIP record for this title is available from the British Library

scribepublications.com.au
scribepublications.co.uk

Give sorrow words: the grief that does not speak
Whispers the o'erfraught heart, and bids it break.

— William Shakespeare, *Macbeth*

Farewell, thou child of my right hand, and joy;
My sin was too much hope of thee, loved boy,
Seven years thou wert lent to me, and I thee pay,
Exacted by thy fate, on the just day.
O, could I lose all father, now. For why
Will man lament the state he should envy?
To have so soon 'scaped world's, and flesh's rage,
And, if no other misery, yet age!
Rest in soft peace, and, asked, say here doth lie
Ben Jonson his best piece of poetry.
For whose sake, henceforth, all his vows be such,
As what he loves may never like too much.

— Ben Jonson, 'On My First Son'

Contents

No middle name

1

'*Tóóóóóó-niii-óóóóó!*'

Never have I called out his name more often than in the scant four months since Black Whitsun. If I add 'at the top of my voice', I am referring to my inner voice, which is infinitely louder and more far-reaching than anything my vocal cords, brought into vibration by a thrust of air, are capable of. There's no sign of it on the outside.

Compare it with crying. Sometimes I'm ashamed of myself in front of Miriam, who, unlike me, is able to surrender completely to the natural force of a sudden fit of sobbing.

'Even though you don't see the tears, Minchen, I *am* crying with you,' I once explained to her (with a choked voice, mind you). 'For me, this damn grief is like internal bleeding. It trickles away, or gushes, on the inside.'

2

At the beginning of Vladimir Nabokov's novel *Lolita*, the narrator savours the name of his lover, syllable by syllable: 'the tip of the tongue taking a trip of three steps down the palate to tap, at three, on the teeth. Lo. Lee. Ta.'

My son's name *begins* with a similar tap of the tongue behind the front teeth ('T ...'), upon which the lips separate in order to render the vowel 'o' in all its fullness. Via the sinuses, higher up, the remaining breath produces a slightly shrieking nasal sound ('niii ...') — little more than a brief interruption of the drawn-out 'ooo', which then further resounds, unhindered, through the still-open mouth.

'Tóóóóóó-niii-óóóóó!'

What a perfect thing to call him, we thought — literally, too, so that later, when he was playing outside, we could call him in to dinner. The swell of the second 'o' could easily reach the end of the street, if need be all the way to the Jacob Obrechtplein, where one day the boy would hang around the synagogue with his chums.

When Miriam was pregnant it never occurred to us to establish the baby's sex via an ultrasound. Even without scientific confirmation, we were both convinced it would be a girl — I don't remember why. We wanted to name her Esmée, after the opera *Esmée* that Theo Loevendie was composing at the time. He regularly kept us up to date on its progress over at Café Welling.

A few weeks before her due date, Miriam came into the bathroom, where I was in the tub nursing a hangover. The door was ajar; she nudged it further open with her pointy belly, which jutted out even more from the way she planted both hands behind her back.

'What if it's a boy?'

My head hurt too much to tackle that one. For months, the house had been littered with sheets of notes for a paper Miriam was writing for her Dutch literature work group: a comparative study of Thomas Mann's novella *Tonio Kröger* and Alfred Kossmann's novel *Smell of Sadness*. I only had to see a page of her notes from a distance, and the name Tonio Kröger caught my eye. Copies of *Tonio Kröger* were strewn around the living room, even the kitchen — a variety of editions, in German and Dutch. Miriam read passages to me from her paper. I heard her discussing it on the phone with the docent, with her fellow students. And always the rounded euphony of that name: '... like it says in *Tonio Kröger* ...'

2

'A boy,' I repeated, extending Miriam a sudsy arm. 'Then we'll have no choice but to name him Tonio.'

A light smack on my hand sent the soapsuds fluttering. 'Okay.' Miriam wobbled out of the bathroom. Case closed, apparently. Esmée still had top billing, but now we had a boy's name on hand, in the unlikely event *that*.

3

A few days after the bathroom scene, our son was born, a good three weeks prematurely. Standing at the incubator, I whispered his name, reading it from the pale-pink bandage stuck to his tiny chest. It was starting to grow on me.

To. Ni. O.

It had the ring of a rolling, breaking, rumbling wave to it. *Ni*. A case of declawed negation.

All right, it was a gamble, but the name 'Tonio' turned out to fit him like a glove. Once the little blindman's eyes opened wide, they looked at you with the same roundness and directness as the boldface o's on the birth announcement.

My nickname for him — Totò — came up more or less by itself. It got a droolier laugh out of him than at his real name, so I guessed he wouldn't murder me for it later. When the mafia don Totò Riina was arrested in Sicily a few years later, a visitor who overheard me call my little one by his nickname said: 'That's pretty bold, naming your kid after a mafioso.'

'Before yesterday I'd never heard of this Riina guy. I was always reminded of Antonio de' Curtis. The Neapolitan comedian. Stage name: Totò. He was in Pasolini's *Uccellacci e uccellini*. Hell of a clown.'

Years later, whenever Tonio pulled one of his pranks, I called him Totò les Héros, after the movie by Jaco Van Dormael. Then he laughed even harder, but a bit nervously once I'd explained I was calling him a 'hero', and he knew you could take that in all sorts of ways.

Miriam's nickname for him at first was, I thought, more Vondel-like: Tonijntje, 'little tuna'. When she spoke it she put so much love in her voice that he knew he had nothing to fear — and, self-satisfied, he was happy to show it.

'Okay, five more minutes, Tonijn, but you have to come sit here with me.'

'I'm sad.'

'About Runner, heh …' (Runner was his Russian dwarf hamster, found dead in his wood shavings months before. Off and on, when it suited him, Tonio would grieve for him. He and his guitar teacher had composed a brief requiem for Runner.)

'I'm so sad he's *dead*.'

'Sad, but you don't feel like crying.'

'I feel tears you can't see.'

4

With all my angst on the subject of his vulnerability, it never occurred to me that the lively pair of o's that smiled at me so eagerly via the name Tonio were typographically identical to those that glowered out from the rigid congruence of the word 'dood' — *death*.

The last time Miriam and I saw him, two surgical drains stuck out of his forehead, a short one and a slightly longer one, like horns. They had been inserted earlier that day to siphon off excess fluid from his swelling brain. Even with everything going through my mind at that moment, my own brain still had room for a scene from the movie *Camille Claudel*, which Miriam and I had seen many years earlier. I wanted to remind her of it, but no, not there, not then.

The sculptor Rodin examines a small statue of a rhinoceros. 'He's called Totò, says one of Claudel's sisters. 'If you look straight at him, you've got his name.'

Two different horns, two identical eyes. Although one of the eyelids was starting to creep upwards, you could safely say Tonio kept his eyes closed, so that the image only partly hit the mark.

5

'Antonio' was taboo, but otherwise he liked his name, with all its nicknames, pet names, and bynames. But when he was required — for registration at school or elsewhere — to supply his other given names, he came home outraged. The irate Tonio crossed his arms over his chest in a sort of incomplete interlock, the wrist joints sticking upwards like angry lumps.

'Why have I only got one name?'

'My boy, Tonio is such a beautiful, such a perfect, name on its own ... why spoil it with a middle name?'

'Adri, *everybody* has a middle name. Some of the kids at school have *two*. I don't even have *one. You've* got two.'

'Yeah, and I can thank my lucky stars they didn't stick another one on. "Maria" was in back then. Especially for boys.'

One day, when he was a bit older, I explained it to him, that lone first name. 'It's my fault, Tonio. My own clumsiness deprived you of more than one name.'

A confession from his father: Tonio wasn't about to pass *that* up. He was keen as mustard, and glowed with anticipation. 'Let's hear it.'

'God, now I'm sunk ... Well, here goes then. What is Mama's and Aunt Hinde's last name? And no cheeky answers now.'

'Rotenstreich.'

'And you, son of Miriam Rotenstreich and grandson of Natan Rotenstreich, what's your last name?'

Laughing: 'Van der Heijden, of course. Just like you.'

Tonio triumphantly flung his security blanket into the air, as always trying to hit the ceiling, which seldom succeeded. It was his favourite teething cloth, white with red polka dots, cut from one of Miriam's old cotton blouses. He had forsworn the pacifier some time ago, and while he was actually too old for a blankie, he couldn't go entirely without. It fell back and landed on his head. 'Oops.'

'How many sons does Grandpa Natan have?'

Tonio pretended to count on his fingers, and then said: 'None. Just two daughters. Mama and Aunt Hinde. They're sisters.'

'Grandpa Natan is in his eighties. He won't live forever. And Miriam and Hinde … of course, we hope the Rotenstreich sisters will be with us for a long time yet. But eventually it'll be over. The name Rotenstreich will die out.'

'Yeah, 'cause if Aunt Hinde and Uncle Frans have children, they'll also be called Van der Heijden. You and Uncle Frans are brothers, married to two sisters, right, Adri?'

'Which is why the family argues twice as much,' I said. 'But that's a whole other story.'

'Doesn't Grandpa Natan have any brothers?'

Tonio swung the knotted fabric in circles like a catapult, and launched an imaginary projectile. Squinting, he followed its path. Bull's eye. He pumped his fist. 'Yesss!'

'No brothers, no. He used to have sisters. They were murdered by the Nazis in World War II. Just like his parents and the rest of the family. Now there are just three people on earth with the name Rotenstreich.'

'Y'know, Adri … at school there's a boy, and his last name is the same as his mother's. He hasn't got a father. So what if Aunt Hinde …'

'Oh? Dunno if Uncle Frans will like that.'

'Oops.'

Tonio draped the cloth over his head, covering his face.

'Oops for me, too, just now,' I said. 'I neglected to mention something. See, years ago, Grandpa Natan did a lot of research, in old registers and such, looking into his family name. All he found were dead Rotenstreichs. With one exception — a Professor Rotenstreich in Jerusalem. So Grandpa Natan rang him up. The man swore up and down they weren't related. He didn't want any more contact. So that was that — another dead end.'

There was a brief silence. Tonio had slid his cloth back on his head so he looked like a miniature pharaoh. 'Adri,' he sang, sweet as pie, 'you were going to tell me why I don't have a middle name.'

'Patience sure isn't your middle name, is it now? Without this detour along the name Rotenstreich, you wouldn't get my drift at all. I'm taking a carefully chosen path to my goal.'

'Okay, sorry.' Laughing, he fell over backwards, and at the same time tossed the balled-up cloth into the air. It noiselessly grazed the ceiling and fell back down with a dull thud. 'Yesss!'

'Listen, Tonio, I'm going to tell you what a numbskull your father is. You'd like to hear that, I'll bet.'

'Yeah! Yeah!'

'From the moment Mama was pregnant, we searched for a way to attach the endangered name … Rotenstreich … to the name of our future child.'

'Huh?'

'With all the exotic pedigrees around these days, no one thinks anything of an unusual, long first name anymore. Especially if it's a middle name. When you were born … I'm not sure if you were allowed to file fantasy-names at the birth registry back then. If you can't follow me, just say so.'

'I don't know what a regis …'

'Where all our names are written down. Everybody who lives in Amsterdam. Where I went the day after you were born to add your name to the list.'

'Like at a hotel.'

'Checking in, yes. Couldn't hurt to try. A publisher suggested we write to the queen. "Your Majesty, have mercy, it is a rare name, etc. etc …" Well, *that* was the last thing on our minds. I just wanted to walk into the registry office and announce: "People, listen up. The new arrival is named Van der Heijden, first name Tonio, middle name Rotenstreich. In full: Tonio Rotenstreich van der Heijden. No hyphen." Just as long as it got written down. If it was a girl, she could have called herself Rotenstreich van der Heijden until she got married, or until she died. A boy could even pass the name Rotenstreich van der Heijden to *his* children.'

'No hyphen. Funny.'

'*If* they fell for it. On 16 June 1988, the day after you were born, I went to the birth registry office on the Herengracht. You and Mama were still in the hospital.'

'Slotervaart,' Tonio said, somewhat absently. 'I had to stay in the incubator.'

'We'd been sold faulty merchandise, as usual. We decided to keep you anyway. So the next day … off I went to the Herengracht. Picture me walking there, the proud young father.'

'*Young* father?' The polka-dot cloth went sailing again. This time, the rag, unfolding on its descent, landed on my head. 'Oops.'

'Brand-new father, then. Whatever you say, ace. I went to see Mama in the maternity ward earlier that day. She must have reminded me twenty times that I had to finagle a way … she didn't care how … to get the name Rotenstreich on that birth certificate.'

'No hyphen.'

'So there I am, walking down the Leidsestraat and Herengracht reciting "Tonio Rotenstreich van der Heijden" to myself, over and over. I started to like it. Not two first names, but a double surname. There was something aristocratic about it. I had just become father to a son. A full-blood prince, that's what you were. There: the entrance to the registry office. Me on the front steps. It was child's play. I would mention it as offhandedly as possible, like I had other things on my mind. "I've come to register the birth of my son. Tonio Rotenstreich van der Heijden. Yesterday, yes, the fifteenth of June. Sixteen minutes past ten in the morning." If the guy at the registry office asked: "Excuse me, is that a name, Rotenstreich?", then I'd answer: "Yes, in the Ukraine, where my father-in-law comes from, it was a common given name." Just a question of putting on the right attitude.'

Tonio laughed. 'I'll bet I know how it ended.' He pulled the cloth back round his neck and pressed the cool fabric against his overheated ears, a sign sleep was at hand.

'Hey, no butting in, you. Well, it did go differently than I'd planned. Behind the door where I needed to be was a kind of hallway, only a metre square, with a plastic chair. Not enough room to swing a cat. There was this small counter with a computer on it, and—'

'You had computers back then?'

'Yeah, wouldn't you know it? Computers, even before you were born. Antique ones, pedal-powered.'

'So how come you still don't know how—'

'You can teach me one day. So there was this young woman at the birth-registry computer, she was all friendly and welcoming. Entirely truthfully, I said: "My wife gave birth to a son yesterday, and now—" This was in the days when civil servants were still encouraged to put the public at ease, so she cried: "Oh, how *gre-e-e-at*! What's his name?" I thought the official part was still to come, so I answered — again, nothing but the truth — well, what do you think I answered?'

Tonio dropped his voice and said, dreamily: 'Tonio.'

'And the young woman, half singing: "What a great *na-a-a-ame!*" I should've noticed her fingernails dancing over the keys, but I was a nervous young … er … brand-new father, and I wasn't on the ball. She glanced at the passport I had laid on the counter and went back to her typing. A sheet of paper came rolling out of the printer, and *bam*, on went the city's official stamp. She folded it in half, slid it into a plastic cover, beamed at me, and said: "I wish you and your wife, and of course baby Tonio, a happy start." Before I knew it, I was standing outside by the canal, reeling slightly from the fast-track process. Something wasn't quite right …'

'Adri, I *said* I knew how it was going to turn out.'

'Yeah, go ahead and laugh. It was first and foremost about you.'

'But how could you—'

'Exactly. That's what being a brand-new dad does to you. You lose your mind. I opened the folder. Van der Heijden, Tonio, born 15 June 1988, registered 16 June 1988. A-OK. Dumb bunny! If she'd just *asked* for a middle name, I'd have pulled it off.'

'Why didn't you go back? You could have said: something has to go in between. Rotenstreich. No hyphen. Huh, Adri?'

His voice sounded soft and childlike. The story had taken a turn for the worse. His hands were stuck into the rolled-up cloth, like in a muff.

'I didn't dare. I was afraid that if she heard that so-called middle name now … that she'd get suspicious.'

'Whoa.'

'I first had to rethink my strategy. Maybe write to the queen after all.'

'Mama was cross, I'll bet.'

'So back to the hospital. She was just breast-feeding you in the maternity ward. She looked at me with … you know … with those big, brown, expectant eyes, which think they know what's coming. That her family name has been rescued for at least a whole generation.'

Tonio slowly shook his head no, and again no. If I detected a whiff of *schadenfreude*, it was directed at me, not at his mother.

'I told Mama what went wrong. A happy start? No, you couldn't call it a happy start.'

'Adri, I can't believe you could be so stupid.'

6

It's time I finally gave him his middle name.

BOOK I

Black Whitsun

CHAPTER ONE

100 days

1

The doorbell, twice: first short and hesitant, then long and emphatic.

The abrasive shrillness always scared the Norwegian forest cats out of their wits, and sent them scampering for cover — the reason Miriam would disconnect the electric bell on weekday mornings, when the postman might ring with a package. The cats always came first. Today, Sunday, the chance that anyone would ring was negligible, certainly this early in the day, so she left it plugged in.

The first tinkle sounded as though a finger was unable to get a grip on the button. Loud enough, however, to send the cats charging up the first flight of stairs. Even from where I was, in bed on the second floor, I could hear the drumroll of their heavy paws on the steps. They probably paused in the bend of the stairs, only to dash up even faster after the second, much more insistent, ring. Their claws scrabbled over the parquet floor on the first-storey landing, after which they took the next flight of stairs by leaps and bounds. The stampede and the doorbell's echo ended simultaneously, so Tygo and Tasha probably came to a halt halfway up the second flight, their ears pricked up and their coarse fur standing on end, alert for further hostilities.

2

Whit Sunday, 23 May 2010. The bell of the Obrechtkerk had just chimed nine times. The intrusive peal calling the parishioners to prayer would only come later, at a quarter to eleven. Classic Sunday morning tranquillity in Amsterdam Oud-Zuid.

I lay on my back in bed. I had raised the head end of the mattress by remote control to reading level. The curtains were open partway, so from my pillow I could see what a fine spring day it was becoming. (The newspaper had predicted a 'summery' day.) The sun was still hidden behind the tall houses, their eaves in stark silhouette against the deep blue sky. Just as the structure of falling rain can often portend much of the same all day, today's sky betrayed its intention of remaining cloudless until evening.

The breeze that wafted into the bedroom through the balcony doors was still cool, raising goosebumps on my bare shoulders, so I slipped on a yellow-and-brown checked flannel shirt.

I wasn't really reading. The book in which I had planned to look up a certain passage lay, skewered on my index finger, on the covers. Flipping through it only made me more aware of the sense of delicious comfort I'd been granted this morning. Lounging here in bed, hunting down that paragraph, counting the church bells ... it all served as an extremely agreeable deferment.

On the long sorting-table in my workroom a floor higher lay a new work schedule for the coming 100 days, starting tomorrow, Whit Monday. According to the outline, today was Day Zero, tomorrow Day One, and 31 August Day 100. September 1: Delivery Day.

Always those 100-day work blocks ... it's been like this for twenty years now. Superstition? An affectation? Compulsive clinging to decimal urges? A bit of all of them, I suspect, and more of the same.

I had discovered by coincidence that a schedule of 100 consecutive workdays (a sizeable yet manageable timespan) fitted me like a glove. At the end of 1989 I went off, wife and child in tow, to live for a year in the

Veluwe, a wooded region in the middle of the province of Gelderland in the east of the country. I had convinced myself that it would benefit my new novel, which was set in Amsterdam, if I were to remove myself from that setting for a while. In fact (although I didn't admit it) I wanted to shelter my little family, including the eighteen-month-old Tonio, in the security of the hinterland. When the little tyke was old enough to go to primary school we would return to the city.

But after only a few months, in the spring of '90, we became involved in a dispute with the landlord, whose house was connected to ours by a glass-enclosed walkway. The quarrel escalated into the kind of psychological (and occasionally physical) warfare I certainly didn't need to leave Amsterdam for. In order to finish my book in time for its autumn publication, I was forced to look for suitable lodgings elsewhere.

I chose De Pauwhof, an old artists' and scientists' colony in Wassenaar, where on 23 June I began the definitive version of *Advocaat van de Hanen*. On 1 October I sat in a taxi with the completed typescript of that cursed book on my lap, heading back to Loenen in the Veluwe, where I would fetch wife and child and take them back to Amsterdam. On the back seat I calculated how long I had worked on the completion of the novel while in Wassenaar. *Nulla dies sine linea* ('Not a day without a line') — panic and a guilty conscience had guaranteed that. I arrived at a total of exactly 100 days, including weekends. An obsessive ritual was born.

For the next twenty years, the rule was: if a novel required two or three versions, then I would mark off that many blocks of 100 days on the calendar. Accordingly, the book I had been working on since the autumn of 2009 (*Kwaadschiks*) had already swallowed up two such time blocks. At the end of April I submitted a draft (but complete) typescript to the publisher. The last eight days of May plus the coming three summer months would be devoted to the definitive version.

Drawing up a schedule like this meant — with the requisite superstition — naming the days. Counting from a diary, I typed out 100 available days, and named them. Day 18, Day 19, Day 20 … Day 92, Day 93, Day 94 … Some of them got nicknames, depending on their contribution to the endeavour, but only after the fact.

Claiming and taking control of dates in advance: wasn't that tempting Fate? Once they were numbered, they were still useful as empty time, but they were definitely no longer neutral. I had annexed them.

Each new schedule began with a Day Zero. In this case it fell on 23 May, today, Whit Sunday. A marvellous kind of temporal no-man's-land. So as to soften the blow of Day One, I always saw to it that the production of Day Zero, expressed in pages, already met the target average. But at the same time, Day Zero was nonbinding and by definition could be a partial or even complete flop. Nothing would be lost.

So there I lay, while half of Amsterdam enjoyed its holiday sleep-in, looking forward to the imminent nonbinding workday, the start of which I could put off for as long as I pleased. Downstairs, in her workroom on the ground floor, Miriam would undoubtedly have already been at her computer for an hour-and-a-half or so. On weekdays, she usually got up at about six to go to the gym, and started working by half past eight, but Sundays she skipped the exercises, which gave her an extra hour in bed as well as an hour's head start on her work. I wasn't in such a hurry. Her concentration usually waned by noon, while mine was then at its best and only started flagging by late afternoon.

I pictured the cats sycophantically weaving figure eights around her legs under the computer table, manoeuvring for her attention, or, if that failed, stretching out ostentatiously across the keyboard. Our deal was that if I felt like coffee I'd phone, and she'd bring breakfast upstairs. I knew how it would go. Side by side, propped up on the pillows, talking over the day's plans. In midweek the weather had suddenly turned warm. As we'd done the past few days, we would meet out on the back terrace at the end of afternoon, under the golden rain, for a glass of fruit juice. No need to cook: Tonio was coming to eat, and he had already placed an order for a portion of chow mein from the Surinamese takeaway.

I picked up my mobile phone from the bed but immediately laid it back down. Breakfast could wait. The only hitch in my wellbeing: my stomach — normally staunch, stout, and reliable — was in rather a bad way, and thus hindered my appetite. It couldn't have anything to do with alcohol: we hadn't touched a drop for several weeks now. I tried to remember what we had eaten the night before. Veal, because there was a marsala sauce — no, for *scaloppine marsala* Miriam had turned to organic chicken these days out of environmental concerns. The first course was spaghetti *aglio olio*, rich in darkly sautéed garlic, and, as a side dish, a salad that had been generously sprinkled with more freshly chopped garlic. Apparently a clove too many, because early that morning, somewhere between four and half past, I'd woken up to a clenching stomach, complete with an unstoppable flood of saliva. I sat upright in bed, continually swallowing, battling the nausea, until it subsided and I was able to lie back down.

3

Now, hours later, my stomach was still not entirely back to normal. Of course I could just ask Miriam for some coffee, a dash of espresso diluted with plenty of milk, but I decided to enjoy the comfy situation a bit longer on my own. It was fine like this. As Japi, from Nescio's *The Sponger*, said: I was always getting myself worked up. Since cutting short a disastrous work visit to Lugano a year ago, I had asserted ownership of my time. I'd share part of it with Miriam (and with Tonio, if he so desired), but otherwise no one could lay any claim to it. Written enough letters, contributed to enough magazines. I was tired of buffing the regulars' tables at assorted pubs with my jacket sleeves, not to mention all the language that evaporated out of your mouth, free of charge, and that could just as well have been written down at home.

And it worked. Every day was a gift. I once remarked to Miriam that 'most people always came to *get* something, never to *bring* it'. It was a burst of pique, no more than that, but once I'd said it I realised it was true. Since then I made certain there was no longer anything to be had. I would continue bringing people things now and again, but all in due course.

My mind drifted back to the work schedule lying on the long wallpaper table upstairs. It lay next to the copy of the draft typescript I had submitted at the end of April. There was also a plastic folder containing 160 pages of the definitive version. I had written it more or less off the cuff, outside every hundred-day schedule. Thus there was a starting balance, so to speak, to compensate for the less productive days.

In short, I had my act together. I sank back onto the pillows, almost purring with pleasure. I would ring Miriam in a minute. After the coffee, and perhaps some lazy lovemaking, I would mount the exercise bike for half an hour, then it was just a matter of showering, getting dressed, and going upstairs. There, I would choose exactly the right moment to release the agreeably wound-up spring for the next 100 days.

4

And then the bell. One short, one long. Loud and invasive. In the echoing silence that followed, the thumping of the cats as they raced upstairs.

As always, the strident buzz of the doorbell irritated me (God, Miriam, weren't we going to have the Brom people install a friendlier bell?), but now it was a sense of unease that made me sit straight up in bed. I turned my head to the right, glanced at my watch on the night table. Ten past nine. It was probably my mother-in-law. Lately she'd taken to showing up on our doorstep, befuddled, delivered by cab. The reason was usually that Miriam didn't answer the phone or offer any other sign of life.

Yes, it had to be Wies. Who else? But … if I was so sure it was her, no more than an annoying incident, why did my already upset stomach tighten in anxiety? I slid out of bed, suppler than my back in reality allowed, and went out to the landing to hear what was going on. I went by way of the bathroom. At first it was as though the quiet had returned to the house. Miriam didn't open the door, and her mother drove back off in the taxi.

My stomach and my heart did not share the relief being coaxed into my head. This wasn't the first time I'd stood there, holding my breath, to see if Miriam opened the door. The mailman — wasn't Miriam home? Should I answer via the intercom?

Something, perhaps the gust of air that blew up through the stairwell, told me the front door was open. I struggled with all my might to recognise my mother-in-law in the voice that rose up indistinctly from down below, but I *knew* that it was a man's voice. The sound of Miriam's brief and heated (but unintelligible) reaction offered the hope that she — as she often did in this kind of situation — was yelling at her mother. My fear spoke another language.

Just above me, Tygo and Tasha stuck their furry heads inquisitively through the balusters of the handrail. Downstairs, the glass doors to the hall rattled. A snippet of an unmistakably male voice, followed by an anguished cry from Miriam. The cats dashed down the stairs, their tails swishing along my bare legs as they crossed the landing and continued their patter down the stairs towards the cry of their mistress.

Through the open bedroom door I could hear my mobile phone ring. It lay on Miriam's half of the bed. I dove at it from the far side. Too late. Just as I pushed the button her voice, loud and panicky, rose up through the stairwell.

'Adri! It's Tonio! He's in the hospital! In a critical condition!'

I was back on the landing in a few steps. In the bend between the first and second floor stood a young policeman, his arm on the handrail, looking up at me impassively. His spotless, white polo-sleeved uniform shirt lit up in the shadows.

'Sir, I'm afraid I've got unpleasant news for you,' he said. 'There's been a traffic accident. Your son, Tonio, is in the Academic Medical Centre in a critical condition. My colleague and I are here to take you there. Our van's waiting outside.'

I felt myself sink into the kind of grainy, teeming semi-darkness that usually precedes fainting. My organs contracted, and I almost threw up. It *could* be that at the same moment Miriam came running up the stairs with an inhuman cry, first squeezing past the policeman and then past me. I do not have a clear recollection of the moment, only a churning sensation,

19

from which a high-pitched wail arose. If it did indeed go like that (Miriam can't confirm it either, for her it is even more of a black hole) then she ran across the landing to Tonio's old room. It is there that I found myself. Miriam sat on the edge of the bed, shuddering with teary cramps, putting on her socks. Her overwrought face.

'Tonio's in a critical condition,' she kept repeating, in a sort of gasping trance. 'He's going to die. Maybe he's *already* dead.'

Those socks. She almost couldn't manage. They kept getting caught on her toenails, and she had to start over. The stark details which, despite the constriction of one's awareness, manage to nestle themselves in you … This bitterly surprised me, in retrospect. Or this: a tripod in the corner of the room, without a camera but instead, a silvery lighting umbrella screwed to it. Snow-white styrofoam panels here and there: the photographer's reflectors.

I stood there in my long work shirt and underwear, as though petrified, perhaps no more than a few seconds, but it felt like much longer.

'Get *dressed*,' Miriam cried, nearly screaming. 'We've got to get to him. He's dying.'

5

I didn't dare look over the banister on the landing to see if the policeman was still standing in the bend in the stairs. Maybe I was hoping he was a figment of my imagination, a vision that had shadowed me beyond slumber. Even out of the corner of my eye, I could not see the glow of his white polo shirt.

In a critical condition. For much too long (however briefly it may have been), I stood in the bedroom at the chair where a few articles of clothing lay, holding a single sock. All I could do was stare at the framed photo above the radiator. A Venetian gondola with a baldachin and a small sign on the side reading AMSTEL HOTEL. It was floating in the Amstel River in front of the Hoge Sluis, at the service of hotel guests, a few of whom were being transported to the opposite side. Judging from their dress, the scene must have dated from the twenties or thirties. Tonio had downloaded the photo from the Internet and enlarged it for me as a gift marking the thirtieth anniversary (in late 2008) of my book *Een gondel in de Herengracht*. He was that kind of kid.

I heard Miriam's hurried footsteps on the landing and, right away, further up the stairs. The gait added a nasty cadence to her high-pitched wailing. I tugged on the faded sweatpants that I'd laid out for the long session at my desk.

Socks. Shoes. Oh God, let him pull through. Not for me. For Miriam. For Tonio himself. And yes, for me, too, even though I didn't deserve it.

A knock at the door. I was just tying the laces of my shabby house-shoes, which I normally wouldn't dare wear in public. The policeman again. 'Sir, are you about ready? Your wife wants you to hurry.'

His young, academy-trained voice, with just that whiff of compassion.

'Coming.' A touch of irritation. I was being forced to get dressed, unshowered, in the rattiest possible clothes, and this kid was hustling me along on top of it. Damn it all, what did they expect? That we'd be standing by the front door, spiffed up and passport in hand, impatiently anticipating this long-awaited bad news? What if we had been out on the town until three or four in the morning, as in past Whitsun weekends, and were still sleeping off our grogginess? Did that ever occur to them?

As I charged toward the door, my eye fell upon a coloured-pencil drawing above the bed. Tonio's double portrait, from 1994, of his parents. He was five, nearly six, and had drawn it in just a few minutes, lying on the floor of a French restaurant while his pasta went cold. Since the man in the drawing wore a hat, which I never did, I asked Tonio who those people were, just to be sure.

'You and Mama.'

'There's a bunch of red hearts flying around our heads.'

'Yeah,' he laughed, 'you're in love, aren't you?'

It had finally happened. I had imagined this a hundred times, ad nauseum. How the police would arrive at the door to bring us the worst news imaginable. *Your son ...* And then we were people capable of regarding our overanxious sacrifice to Fear as a cleansing, forestalling ritual. As though imagining an accident down to the most minute detail would stave it off.

Last summer, for instance, when we had given Tonio money for a trip to Ibiza, I immersed myself in repeated nocturnal fantasies, torturing myself with the most gruesome possible scenarios. The *guardia civil* had found the lifeless body of a young man in a rock crevice. No passport on him, but the night porter at a hotel in Ibiza City recognised him ... could we come identify the body ...

Miriam and I picked him up at Schiphol Airport. I had expected to see a sun-tanned Tonio strut into the arrivals hall, but he was paler than when he'd left, thanks to holiday nightlife and daytime sleep. But it was him, and he was alive. You see? It worked: the perils of reality were no match for the even more perilous power of the imagination.

6

Downstairs in the front hall, I found Miriam, trembling and in tears, in the care of the policeman. The cats, recovered from their initial panic, sat side by side in the hallway, restlessly sweeping the floor with their puffed-up tails. They remained anxiously in the neighbourhood of the open door to the pantry, where their baskets and food were kept and through which, in case of emergency, they could escape through the cat flap into the backyard. Sometimes, if the doorbell rang particularly long and loud, Tygo, the more skittish of the two, would flee into the golden-rain tree — so high he couldn't get himself back down and Miriam had to rescue him with the library ladder.

Under normal circumstances, we would certainly have locked Tygo and Tasha in the kitchen. But now, just clicking the glass door had to suffice, so that they wouldn't follow us.

Although the front of the house was still in the shade, we were nevertheless ambushed by the low, brilliant sunlight that bathed the junction with the Banstraat, and the white police van parked on the corner, in a flood of light. A young female officer who had been waiting at the vehicle approached us with a concerned, almost distressed look on her face, and introduced herself.

'My colleague and I are going to take you to the AMC,' she said. And, pointing: 'There's the van.'

Apparently anticipating a warm day, she, too, wore a short-sleeved shirt, a dark-blue scarf tucked in the open neck. Even now I made a mental note of such details, thinking with almost ulterior motives of *Kwaadschiks*, which featured female police officers. (Note: cleavage covered by scarf. Even when on a mission of mercy, a police officer carries handcuffs on her belt, next to a holstered can of pepper spray.) The van, its sliding door already open, was painted in the familiar red and blue stripes, perhaps intended to suggest speed. As one could read in my manuscript.

'It's best if you get in back,' said the woman.

I turned to her colleague: 'Do you know what happened?'

'Sir, as far as we know your son was hit by a car at approximately four-thirty this morning on the Stadhouderskade. Somewhere near Max Euweplein. We've been told he's in the Intensive Care unit at the AMC. They're operating on him at the moment. That's all we know. The driver of the car is being questioned at the Koninginneweg bureau. We've just come from there.'

'He must have just left Paradiso,' I said, mainly to myself. And then to him: 'Could he have taken that footbridge over the canal, towards the Stadhouderskade?'

'We don't have any details, sir. Only that the driver of the car remained at the scene of the accident. He phoned the police immediately.'

'Adri, just get *in*, will you,' Miriam said. She was already sitting on the back seat. 'Before it's too late.'

I got in next to her.

'We'll get you there as fast as possible,' the policewoman said before slamming the sliding door shut. 'It's still early, the A10 won't be too busy.

Although … with the holiday weekend …'

She got in next to her colleague, who had taken his place at the wheel. I pulled the sobbing Miriam up close to me. She was now crying uncontrollably.

'Our sweet Tonio … he might be *dead* already.'

7

H&NE. For more than thirty years, this was my secret code for the woman — even she didn't know about it — whom I held tight on the back seat of the police van.

'How'd that rice get into the pasta?'

Miriam's question, on a warm summer evening in '79, had set everything in motion. 'Memory is like a dog that lies down wherever he wants,' writes Cees Nooteboom. In this case, it cannot have been purely dog-like that there on the back seat, with this shuddering body in my arms, I thought back on the first time I met her. The two police officers up front had more or less dragged us out of bed because Tonio was badly injured — the son that, nine years after that rice in the pasta, we had made together. The child whose life was now in danger. The boy who we were following a terrible, careening path to be with.

The official story that I had foisted on the world began at her birthday party, 23 November 1979, three days after she turned twenty. Not many people know that she had already come into my viewfinder six months earlier.

I wanted to have a short novel finished by the end of the summer, having started it that spring in Perugia. I had hoped to catch up with a young woman, Mara, whom I'd met the previous year in Sicily. I didn't have her address, but did have a phone number, although I didn't dare ring her — and so it happened that I just bumped into her on a Perugia street. A hasty and sloppy romance ensued, which was at the very least detrimental to my book. I fled to a tiny island in Lake Trasimeno, with

99 or 102 inhabitants, and set to work. I stayed there until the end of July. On Sundays, Mara came over by ferry. It was a good arrangement, until she started to insist that I join her and a small group of friends on Sardinia for the remainder of the summer holidays. I had nothing against Sardinia, but didn't much relish six weeks of enforced loafing, especially while the publisher at home was waiting for his text.

So I took the train back to Amsterdam and my stuffy third-floor walk-up in De Pijp. It was a hot summer. In the evening, I'd sit working at my desk in front of the open balcony doors until dusk, not wanting to turn on lights because of the mosquitoes. I was lucky with late-afternoon sunlight: where, according to the architectural logic of the neighbourhood, one would expect a parallel cross-street between the Van Ostadestraat, where I lived, and the houses on Sarphatipark, there was only an expanse of low-rise sheds belonging to an assortment of shops and small businesses. Two doors further along, behind a squatted building, one such shed had been torn down and a sort of wild garden had sprouted up among all the rusty scrap metal and rotting wood. The squatters barbecued there on warm summer evenings. One of them was Hinde, whom I knew because one day she brought me a huge bunch of pink tea-roses as thanks for having let her tap into my water main. I knew she had a younger sister who also hoped to move into the squat, but until then only visited once in a while.

On one of those never-ending summer evenings, Hinde and her housemates organised another barbecue and invited me along. 'My sister'll be there, too,' she said, but I wasn't sure if it was intended as a fix-up. I politely turned down the invitation. I hadn't come back from Italy to go to parties: shit, if I wanted to party I could have spent the summer with Mara and Ivana and the rest of them on Sardinia. But my work didn't amount to much that evening. The barbecue, a rusty three-legged thing, billowed smoke. My balcony, with its open doors, acted like a fireplace flue, so that I spent most of the evening looking at my papers through watering eyes.

'A rat!' cried one of the fellows. 'I just saw a rat. There, by those crates!'

'Onto the barbecue with him.' Hinde's voice, I recognised it already.

Laughter from down below.

'How'd that rice get into the pasta?' A distant voice that resembled Hinde's: that had to be the sister.

'From the salt shaker,' Hinde called back. 'The cap came unscrewed.'

The wind was apparently blowing my way, so the sausages and drumsticks on the grill made my mouth water, but it was above all the voices cutting clearly through the fading light that made me regret not being down there, too, where it was alive with rats and girls, and where I would have relished spooning up a mouthful of macaroni-and-rice. I sat there, not doing much myself, listening to their talk and laughter, to the tinkle of clinking glasses, until the bats began to circle above the sheds, and it became altogether too dark to put another letter on paper.

It could have been the swerving of the police van that made me feel slightly queasy, but more likely it was the memory of the desires sparked by that summer evening. Later, that desire got itself a future: Miriam and me … me, Miriam, and Tonio … But this, too, was part of that future: us on our way to the hospital to be told just how critical our boy's condition was. If he stood a chance. If he was still alive.

8

H&NE. In the late summer or early fall of '79, one of the backyard barbecue voices got a face.

The squatters' pad, Van Ostadestraat 205, was next door to a primary school with a playground at the back and a widened sidewalk out front where mothers waited to pick up their brood. This is where I saw her, kick-coasting her granny bike, manoeuvring between clusters of chatting women, some of whom cast her a disapproving glance while stepping demonstratively off to one side. With her left foot resting on the pedal and propelling the bike along with her right foot, she caused just as much inconvenience as regular cycling, except this way the police couldn't give her a fine.

I had just closed the door to no. 209, where I lived, behind me. I can't remember if there was a threat or forecast of rain, but the kick-coasting girl wore a raincoat several sizes too big. The garment, in a men's cut, must have been beige once, but was now shockingly filthy — it was an eye-catcher even in this neighbourhood of dilapidated squats and rusted-through bikes lying half in the gutter. The front was particularly grubby, full of random smudges, while the fabric around the buttons was pretty much black, as though the coat had once done service as a coalman's apron.

I would have just shrugged it off, were it not for the very pretty head that stuck out of the equally grimy collar, shiny with grease and buttoned up to the chin. Loose, dark hair framed a lightly tanned face that nevertheless gave the impression of paleness, perhaps because of the dark eyes that weren't even made up (which would have been rather incongruous alongside a coat like that). The oversized garment concealed her figure, but a certain roundness in the chin, neck, and jaw suggested the girl was on the chubby side.

Although there wasn't an obvious resemblance to Hinde, I could tell right away that they must be sisters; this one, the younger of the two, I guessed about eighteen.

When she noticed me, no more than a vague shadow of recognition passed over her face. Maybe she couldn't place me any better than I could her, and she only *thought* she should know who I was because I lived in the house that provided her sister's squat with running water. Her 'hello' was diffident and distant in equal measure; its slightly questioning tone did not tally with the broad, carefree smile (a kind of gentle grin) with which she returned my greeting. It seemed to me that in passing she looked at me just a tad too long (which means I did the same), causing her to overshoot the bike rack, so she ended up propping her bike against the front of no. 207.

When I looked back as I walked along the sidewalk past the school, she was half bent over her bike, pulling the chain lock through the spokes. The front of the too-wide coat — really no more than a coal sack, just as black and just as shapeless — hung all the way to the ground. The chubbiness — well all right, that wasn't her strong point, but she was definitely pretty. But that shabby old rag really had to go. She slighted herself with it — and, by extension, me, although she was far from being H&NE yet.

All the more vexing was that I didn't see her again for the next few months. So like it or not, I was forced to picture her in that filthy raincoat.

9

The Utrechtsebrug. As mucky and murky as the water could look under low cloud cover, in today's morning sunshine the Amstel River glistened as though silver-plated. The brilliant sunlight bleached the surrounding colours, bathing everything in the same milky blue.

The bridge was always the last landmark on the way home from vacations in the south. Tonio used to start talking about it as soon as we left Lugano or the Dordogne: on the other side of the Amstel, a man-sized K'Nex Ferris wheel was waiting for him to complete its construction. For me, the Utrechtsebrug symbolised the imminent reunion with my stationery shop up on the third floor. So for hundreds of kilometres we could all look forward, each in his own way, to this gateway to the city.

For Miriam, the bridge meant an end to many hours of concentrated driving. She never really had an outspoken opinion about post-vacation life. Yes, being home, nothing beat that.

On the front seat of the van, the two police officers focused on the exact route to the AMC — as though they couldn't have done it blindfolded. The woman reminded her colleague that he just had to keep an eye out for the hospital exit, which wouldn't be signposted for a while yet. They were young, fresh from the academy. Having to concentrate on the traffic came in handy: this way they didn't have to worry about us.

Between their seat and ours was an empty middle row whose back regretfully did not offer us complete invisibility. With both arms around

Miriam, I kept a stranglehold on her. I made half-hearted hushing noises, but did not know what to say to her. That everything would be all right? What right did I have?

In a critical condition. I was incessantly, feverishly analysing that phrase. Since Miriam had frantically shouted those four words, and the policeman had repeated them with professional calm, their meaning swung back and forth. At one moment they announced the inevitable, the next moment they took on something reassuring. Recently on the news a casualty was said to be in a critical condition. Two days later the papers reported the injuries to be no longer life-threatening.

'Our Tonio,' Miriam murmured. 'It might already be too late.'

'No, Minchen, you mustn't think that.'

Critical was critical, and nothing else. Critical did not mean: dead. Not even: as good as dead. Critical meant: alive (as long as not proved to the contrary). Critical was something you had to get through.

Miriam sniffed, but it was not hysterical crying. 'We're too late, I can *feel* it.'

'I forbid you to talk like that.'

10

H&NE: Her and No-one Else. All right, now that I had chosen this woman (this girl), I'd have to put my money where my mouth is. Make nice things for her: folding paper boxes filled with images and anecdotes, but I would also have to open real, existing worlds for her. The hedges surrounding the ivy-clad house. The chicken wire of the champagne cork. The salt edge around the pink sirloin.

The boom gate of paradise.

When I learnt from her parents that they had considered naming their second daughter 'Minchen' after her German grandmother, I tried it out on her, at first teasingly. Too often, perhaps, because at a certain point I couldn't shake it off my tongue. She has remained Minchen to this day.

Meanwhile ... something was not right, something that could well backfire one day. Too young. Just turned twenty. She hadn't, to put it officially, had time to sow her wild oats. One day she would realise that she'd spent her youth with *only me* ... and that there were some secret things she had never been able to make the most of ...

I couldn't just put the brakes on the restless life I'd been leading for all these years. Amsterdam meant loafing around, sleeping in, accomplishing little. The discomfort of travelling spurred me to labour. I wrote in night trains, in the cubbyhole of an illegal hostel, on draughty train platforms, seated between two pallets jam-packed with chicks: an uncommon late-evening serenade.

In January 1980, I took a train to Naples, and from there a boat to Ischia. Arriving back at Amsterdam Central Station in February, I made the acquaintance of the paralysis that would overwhelm Miriam after a long absence (a repeat of the farewell-paralysis of a month earlier). It could have something to do with the fear of abandonment that permanently plagued her family, compliments of recent European history.

In late March of that year, I left for Calabria. Starting in the toe of Italy's boot, I travelled northwards along the coast, investigating every village until I found a enchantingly tiled hotel room in Positano, on the Amalfi coast. I thought: *This is the place.* Every telephone call to Miriam cost me ten thousand lire.

'Minchen, I'll come get you at the end of May. Then we'll stay here for another month.'

Was it only about working in seclusion? Or did I, even then, want to view my happiness from time to time from a distance, preferably through reversed binoculars? Whatever the case, it later became a routine.

When I think back on myself in those days ... Always busy with those massive manuscripts. All for her. The conceit and vanity did not end with the written and printed word. The young writer wanted to live better *per book*. He undertook a long march through the architecture of desirable locations, to the palazzo, the country estate, the Spanish castle. I pulled out all the stops for her, but apparently did something wrong. I went over the top. It flustered her, like the child who sees an oversized stuffed bear emerge from the wrapping paper.

With her around, I could do anything. Miriam was a muse down to the smallest domestic detail. Without her contribution we would have never had a better house. She was a master key that opened all doors.

She saw to it that I finished what I started, just by being there. (More than that wasn't necessary.) But having a child — that was out of the question. I could plead and pray as much as I wanted.

'I'm still young, aren't I? How about letting me finish my degree first?'

Although the doctors couldn't find anything, I felt sick and exhausted and, like Mozart on his deathbed, 'the taste of death was on my tongue'. Transferring life into a child gradually become an obsession. Sure, she commiserated, but even if I were to drop dead at her feet, she would not give in.

11

In the spring of 1982, strolling through Vondelpark, we occasionally came upon a young woman I knew by sight, and who apparently recognised me as well. She was pushing a pram and quite emphatically greeted me, not Miriam. Her name eluded me, but I concluded that I must have known her from my student days in Nijmegen. Maybe we had lived in the same block of student housing. It was the baby carriage that did it for me. At one of these chance meetings, seated next to Miriam on a park bench, I saw how the nameless acquaintance bent lovingly over the baby, which was hidden from our view, and stuck her hand under the canopy to rearrange something. I can't rule out that she had intentionally stopped in front of our bench to strike up a conversation that didn't materialise. She nodded at me, smiling, and went on her way, clearly on cloud nine.

Once the woman was out of earshot, it all spilled out: what a wrung-out dishrag I felt the past year-and-a-half, much worse than I had dared admit up until now, and how an unbearable physical urge to become a father was growing in me. Despite my debilitating fatigue, the belief had arisen that a child would rejuvenate me.

'If that's really how you feel,' said Miriam, 'then it's the worst possible reason to become a father.'

I knew that. But I kept at it — until a year later, again in the spring, my health began to improve, and the dips into hellish exhaustion became ever more infrequent. After turning in a manuscript at the publisher on 1 September, I cycled past my house, towards the Amstel. I followed the river all the way to Ouderkerk, kept cycling, and allowed myself to stray into uncharted territory, somewhere where woods meets meadow. Suddenly I realised: I'm better. There wasn't even a trace of the old tiredness in me.

Still, it wasn't until 1987, four years later, that I dared to pester Miriam again with what is called 'wants children' in newspaper personals.

My yearning for progeny was as powerful as my fear of it. This was the kind of dilemma that makes for a good film or novel. My wanting a child was paralysingly on par with the fear of losing it.

12

In early May '87, with summer in sight, I left for the Provence to work out a new idea for a novel (*Advocaat van de Hanen*). I still had the need to 'view my happiness from a distance' occasionally, but did make a deal with Miriam that she would join me a month later.

On the train to Paris, I read a newspaper advertisement for a country house near Aix-en-Provence, available for rent during the summer months. I phoned the number immediately upon arriving in Paris. The woman who answered the phone turned out to be Dutch: Anneke, married to a French singer who specialised in Provençal folksong. Yes, I could rent part of the house. I took an option for June and July, and promised to ring her once I had arrived in the south.

After a few days in Paris, I took the TGV to Arles. Miriam and I had been there the year before. One day, I escaped the blistering heat, taking refuge in the refreshingly cool and quiet old library in the centre of town. There, and nowhere else, would I spend the coming months transforming the documentation I'd dragged with me into a first version of the book.

Every morning, I walked from my hotel at the foot of the amphitheatre to the library on the main square. I worked. I observed my happiness from a distance. I looked forward to Miriam's arrival.

In mid-May, I took the train via Aix to Marseille, where Anneke came to fetch me by car. The blonde woman in the light-blue pantsuit was young. Ten years earlier, still a teenager, she had met her folk singer, twenty years her senior, at the Avignon Festival, where he was performing his Provençal songs. By now they had two young sons.

Their house, Villa Tagora, was situated in what was called the 'green zone', but which, under the southern springtime sun, had already lost much of its colour, and looked dusty, almost arid. The grounds surrounding Villa Tagora were overgrown, with tunnels formed by intertwining thornbush, like rolls of rusty barbed wire. But it also smelt vividly of lavender — a purple field full of white butterflies. The cicadas added to the silence just the sound that went with this heat. The two mouse-grey cats that stalked through the long grass would distract Miriam from the weeds. I paid Anneke the deposit for the apartment annex, which consisted of two rooms and a bathroom that also housed the fridge and gas cooker. June and July were guaranteed, but just to be on the safe side I took out an option for August as well.

At the end of May, I went to Paris to meet up with Miriam. Gare du Nord. She stepped out of the drab train wearing a summer dress I did not recognise. A surge of infatuation — so that's what studying your own happiness from a distance was good for. First to the hotel, then lunch on the steamy sidewalk of the Boulevard St. Germain, just outside the shadow of the awning.

Two days later, the TGV to Arles. At the beginning of June we settled into Villa Tagora. Blissful weeks largely spent in the shade of the neglected garden. Talking, thinking. Reading, writing. When the afternoons became too sultry, we would retire to the bedroom for some languid love-making, ending in a siesta. The blue bedsheets, apparently not very colourfast, became batiked by all the sour sweat we produced in that heat.

13

'Penny for your thoughts,' Miriam said one of those afternoons, when I propped myself on one elbow in preparation to jack myself up to a vertical position.

'Oh, nothing, just a little mind game. Tomorrow we'll probably lie here like this again. Enjoy the tingling while it lasts. But just imagine a world in which a person was only allowed to perform this … mating act, as they call it in the nature films … just once. No second chance. That one time, it would have to embody everything. Love, tenderness. A whole human life in one discharge … Because of its intensity, weaker specimens wouldn't stand a chance of survival. May I speak to the man of the house? No, I'm sorry, he can't come to the telephone. You see, it's like this … sir ejaculated yesterday, and is now confined to his bed for the next fortnight at least.'

'Don't forget fertilisation,' said Miriam. 'That's also got to be bang on that one time, otherwise the poor little species will die out in no time.'

I made a note of this mad notion, and then promptly forgot it. Coming across the sheet of paper later, I saw that the entire conversation had been summarised thus: 'one-day world, one-day people.'

In the morning, when it wasn't so hot, we would occasionally walk down the lane to a suburb of Aix, where we caught the bus to the city centre to have lunch and do some shopping. On the way back we would stop at our favourite supermarket for *gourmandises* that Miriam would only have to heat up for dinner. That is how it went on 29 June, but the next day it was too hot to walk along the searing asphalt. Supplies needn't be replenished, and there was still half a portion of *boeuf à la Normande* with *pâtes fraiches* from the previous evening (what a life). We stayed put in Villa Tagora.

What does a historic day in the life of two lovers look like? Not sensationally remarkable, in this particular case. In my diary, I wrote that on Tuesday, 30 June 1987 we had taken breakfast in the garden at about a quarter after nine. 'We watch the hornets and butterflies flit from one cone-shaped purple flower to the next. The (white) butterflies remind me of white-jacketed lab assistants going from flask to flask with a pointy pipette. At 9:30 I sit down to work at my small military-invalid table in the shadow of the terrace. Documentation folder Hans K. Notes for *Advocaat* ...'

At around midday, I took a walk in the surrounding open fields. Squatting down on a gently rolling, thicketed hillock under the murderous sun, the whole intrigue for the new novel fell into place. Without pen and paper, I simply *had* to stay sitting there, risking sunstroke, until the plot had been worked out in its entirety.

Not that this point made the day such a historic one *per se*. I mentioned *two* lovers.

Overcome by the heat, I walked back to the house, where I scribbled everything down, obstructed by a swarm of *mouches volantes* between my eyes and the paper. I then drank, out of euphoria or to reward myself, nearly a litre of wine at lunch, after which Miriam and I retired to the bedroom-sauna. We woke from a deep sleep only at half past five. Miriam had dreamt about sharks.

Out in the shade, I wrote some letters until Gijs, or Gregory, came over to chat. Gijs was an actor and musician from Amsterdam, who, under the *nom d'artiste* Gregory, had built a career in France. Thanks to his coppery red hair (and his accent), he was cast as Vincent van Gogh in a television series on the painter's life. He married a local politician, and accordingly wound up in Marseilles, where, having appeared on regional broadcasters, he was becoming something of a local celebrity. Additionally he served as the regular accompanist, on guitar and accordion, of Jean Nehr, the Provençal singer. He had come to Villa Tagora to rehearse with Jean for a series of performances. They were planning to record an album soon.

Gregory, so he told me, missed Amsterdam. Whenever he got the chance to go back, no matter how briefly, he would make a beeline for the pool hall above the Hema on the Ferdinand Bolstraat, where he had played since his youth. He promised to bring me one of his LPs the next time he was in Amsterdam. 'If I send one by post, there's a good chance the package'll sit in an overheated van in the sun and arrive at your door two days later as a warped liquorice pancake.'

With that, he disappeared into an annex behind the house for his rehearsal. Soon we could hear a guitar being tuned. Since we had promised to pay the rent for the upcoming period on the last day of the month, I asked Miriam to take Anneke the money. She was gone for some time: Anneke would never pass up the chance of a chat in her mother tongue. I sat at the small table on the terrace, drinking Pays du Var wine from a cardboard carton, listening to Gregory's melancholy accordion, which more or less drowned out Jean's unamplified voice. Miriam's absence made me impatient (I wanted to share with her my story of the novel's plot that had come to me in a brainwave under the scorching midday sun), and at the same time I hoped she'd be away there a while (perhaps I was aware that there was something false and dangerous about my euphoria). The moon, melon-coloured and surreally large, appeared on the horizon. The music, the wine, the moon — what more could a person ask for?

'Empty.' Miriam shook the wine carton; there was nothing left to slosh about. 'Where do you put it, for heaven's sake?'

More wine with dinner. The musicians must have opened a window or door, for Jean's voice now reached us; even the words were clear. He sang, as far as I could tell, a doleful song about ill-fated love. Gregory accompanied him on the mandolin. The music was moving and extremely melancholic.

I tried to relate the intrigue of my *Advocaat* to Miriam. Maybe the copper-headed punk, in teamwork with the plot, had rammed my head full of sunstroke: I couldn't make a sensible yarn of it, but Miriam expressed her enthusiasm for my progress, even if it was hazardous to my health.

The next number, with Gregory back on the accordion, was in a completely unintelligible Occitan dialect. Judging from the profoundly minor-key melody, the text described an even more tragic love than the previous one. During the coffee and cognac, I heard myself suddenly broach an old subject. It hadn't been brought up in so long that it seemed to be weighed down by a heavy taboo.

14

A child. The child. Our child.

'Minchen, I haven't brought up you-know-what in ages. The hush-hush subject.'

If — past difficulties on this issue at the back of my mind — I was trying to raise the subject a bit teasingly, cloak it in light-heartedness, then I apparently did not succeed. Perhaps I had been too ebullient all evening for yet more banter.

'Of course I want a child,' Miriam said. 'But I also want to achieve something. Do something.'

Just like that, all of a sudden. She didn't give in entirely, but this was the first time she openly acknowledged her own desire. I was buoyed. Now just stay the course.

'I'd say ... have the child first. Finish your studies during pregnancy, get on top of your writing and all ... and once you're past the breast-feeding period, get a job. I'll look after the little one during the day.'

Aside from the moon, the only source of light was a candle on the small dining table. Although Miriam did her best to lean back, the flame still illuminated her tears. The candle stem was, for some reason, decorated with strawberries.

'Of course I'd like it,' she said. 'But I'm so afraid ... so afraid that everything, taking care of him, will end up on my shoulders. Especially when you're stressed out by a new book or something. Just try to understand that.'

Now she was crying for real. Between the wails I could hear Jean Nehr singing *a cappella* and nearly bursting out laughing in the process.

'The cooking, Minchen, the washing up, I shamelessly leave that all to you when it suits me. But raising a child … that's something else entirely. Responsibilities. Trust me.'

'Adri, I don't want my life to end once I've had a child. I have to achieve something. So …' (with a comically pleading voice) 'promise you'll help out?'

I gave her my word, in all sincerity, while at the same time my heart skipped a beat. Responsibilities. Miriam sat up next to me, rubbing her face with both hands. She sniffled a bit more and then said: 'We could try as soon as the end of July.'

'And if we waited another month? End of August?' I can't rule out that I was already backpedalling. 'I want to get myself cleaned up a bit inside. Lot of poison been put through the ol' system lately.'

'Then I'll quit smoking,' Miriam said. 'End of July, no, then it'll be an April baby. That's no good. Rather May or June.'

We sat in silence for a while, hand in hand, each with our own thoughts, listening to the drawn-out sighs of Gregory's accordion and Jean's nasal vocals. The organisation of my life suddenly stretched out before me in a different, more rigid configuration than I was accustomed to up until now. Not unappealing, although something like nostalgia began to hum inside me as well. I would, for starters, finish all open projects during Miriam's pregnancy. I would expel all the scoria and sluggishness from my blood, and restore my youth to its former glory, despite my impending fatherhood.

15

'So we're on?' I asked all at once.

'We're on,' Miriam said, smiling.

The elongated flame of the candle, the rising moon, and, in between them, the rugged terrain of Villa Tagora — everything took on the scent, the colour, the sheen of our decision.

'Let's drink to it,' I said. 'While we still can.'

I fetched a new carton of Var wine, and snipped open the spout. Red drops balled up on the scissor blades. 'And no wisecracks about snipping the umbilical cord — from now on everything is symbolic.'

Miriam didn't care for more wine. I knocked back one Duralex tumblerful after the other. Even after the music was finished, we stayed sitting there chatting for so long that our fleeting kisses did not particularly disrupt the conversation.

'So …' I started all over again.

'Yes, we're on.'

'Really?'

'We'll do it. Really.'

'I was just thinking …' I said. 'As soon as it's born I'm going to keep a diary of his, or her, life. Every day. Everything. As a present for his or her eighteenth birthday.'

'Then you should start with the pregnancy,' said Miriam. 'As a prologue.'

'No, with today. The decision. And everything from this moment on. I'll start tomorrow.'

All I can recall from the rest of the evening is that most of our sentences began with: 'I could …' or 'We could …' And the choice of a home birth versus a hospital came up.

'At home, at home,' Miriam said decisively. 'No hospital birth for me.'

'Y'know, Minchen, not to get on your case, but … until now, whenever we talked about having a child you were so intractable. I've often suspected you were secretly afraid of the pain.'

'Oh no, no way. The pain? Then you don't know me.'

16

I had won Miriam over so convincingly that I lost sight of my own doubts and fears about fatherhood. They reared their head now that, even with all her conditions, she had relented. I had created a danger zone for myself, and dragged Miriam and me over the line.

Within two weeks of the decision, we took the express train back to Amsterdam, so impatient were we to cleanse and prepare our bodies for procreation in the intimacy of our own home. Miriam would quit smoking, I would — at least until after a successful conception — stay off the booze. Miriam was such a moderate drinker that she had no trouble forgoing that one glass.

While we felt ourselves becoming more radiant and healthier by the day, my mother-in-law's birthday approached. Wies had lobbied for a grandchild for so long — demanded it, almost — that we figured she'd be delighted with the news that we were bringing our bodily equilibrium into balance in preparation for a perfect copulation and a pure conception.

A misjudgement. I phoned her up.

'No, Wies, we're coming for your birthday, don't worry. The only difference is that won't be drinking on account of —'

'Well, don't bother coming then. Not even a little nip, what a pair of killjoys. Either we celebrate my birthday or we don't.'

Not a word of happiness about the imminent addition to the family. It wasn't, incidentally, her doing that in the 'dry' weeks that followed (abstinence from alcohol, but not from sex: Miriam would only go off the pill once our degenerated bodies had been revitalised), doubts started to creep back into my head. Whether I would be up to the responsibility of raising a child. To placate Wies, we broke down and hit the 45 per cent Polish vodka that friends of Natan in Cracow still sent him. At home, too, we occasionally cheated on our self-imposed regime. I still found, to my relief, emptied blister pill strips in the bathroom wastebasket. Maybe it wouldn't come to parenthood all. Whenever we loosened the reins I'd sneak an extra splash into my glass. Miriam would do the same with each new half-smoked cigarette, and say it would be irresponsible to go off the pill so soon.

<h1 style="text-align:center">17</h1>

Shortly before leaving Aix, we received the news that Miriam's aged cat Baffie had died. Once back in the Netherlands, we stopped off at my parents' in Eindhoven on the way to Amsterdam. We hadn't been there even an hour when I asked my father if there was an animal shelter nearby. Yes, he knew of one, not so far away. Without further ado he drove us there. Miriam glanced at me occasionally, her eyebrows raised, but she, too, refrained from asking anything.

A staff member led us past the hysterically barking dogs, their claws haphazardly playing the harp on the cage fronts, to the cat unit.

'This litter was born in June ... they're less than a month old.'

Miriam promptly fell in love with a tabby with undersized front legs and who allowed herself to be constantly overrun by her siblings. She hadn't even picked the runt up yet, and its claws were already tangled in her hair. 'No getting loose now. I'll have to take her.'

'She's not meant just to replace Baffie,' I said. 'Her job is to be a constant reminder of the pledge we made in Aix—'

'What,' Miriam said, kissing the kitten on the pink heart-shaped spot on its nose. 'Is the poor little thing supposed to go back to the shelter once the promise has been fulfilled?'

So the adoption was sealed. In anticipation of a definitive name, we provisionally baptised her Brilliant-but-with-Undersized-Legs. Back on the Obrechtstraat we temporarily housed her in the bathroom, which proved to be a bad idea. The stunted front legs did not prevent her from clawing her way up the outside of the laundry basket, and jumping from the lid into the tub. She slid all the way down the slippery porcelain and practically into the drain. That's how we found her the next morning: totally bruised, swollen with internal fluids, and bleeding.

She survived it by the skin of her teeth. So when the crisis had passed and she was able to stand on her own uneven legs, she got her new name: Cypri. Considering the result, a scant four months later, it seems she performed her function as reminder admirably indeed.

18

Usually, it's the woman who knows, in retrospect, precisely which act of coupling resulted in conception. In the case of baby Tonio, however, I am the one who maintains: 'the fourth of October 1987. A Sunday afternoon, between four and five.'

Miriam has never challenged me on this. We had returned from a walk through the Jordaan. Jacob Obrechtstraat 67. Huize Oldenhoeck, the place was called. We took the lift up to the fourth floor. The enclosed space had its usual cheesy body-odour smell of the unwashed caretaker. I remember this because Miriam commented on it. A deliveryman had complained to us about the smell a few days earlier.

Once inside, we were apparently in a hurry. We didn't even make it to the bedroom. The two sofas in the living room, with their narrow seats, could not accommodate spread limbs. We kneeled behind one another on the two-seater. The Sunday tranquillity was interrupted only by the *pok-pok* of the tennis court behind the building.

How did I know for sure that Tonio's conception took place then and there? I recall aiming high into her, and that the gratification seemed to come from deeper than usual. Perhaps that last detail points to momentarily heightened fertility. Our calculations six weeks later did not refute the theory that Tonio's foetal existence commenced in the late afternoon of the fourth of October.

19

According to that year's diary, on the morning of Friday the 13th of November 1987 Miriam came to tell me that the pregnancy test she had just performed came up positive. I did not attach any significance to that ominous date back then, and to do so now, some two decades later, in a police van on the way to the hospital, would be unwise, too.

'So I guess I'm pregnant,' Miriam said with a lightness that suggested it was the most normal thing in the world. She had come from the bathroom to the kitchen to deliver me this domestic notice, where (without a hangover, having sworn off alcohol) I was sitting down to a late breakfast.

'Pregnant,' I repeated, chewing and nodding. 'Doesn't sound good.'

We looked at each other for a moment with feigned dejection — until I couldn't contain myself any longer, leapt up, and squeezed her close to me.

'Ow!'

'Oh, Minchen, this is so wonderful ... so wonderful.'

When I relaxed my arms a bit in order to look her in the eye, she put on her customary clown's pout, with wrinkled chin and puffy hamster-cheeks. 'That's just how it is,' she said, her grimace accompanied by crossed eyes.

'Come on, get into that outfit you had on recently. Make-up, too. This is something to be celebrated.'

'Now? It's not even noon.'

'We'll go kit out the nursery first. No time to lose.'

In a furniture boutique on the Rozengracht, I bought her the modern extendable dining table she'd had her eye on. It cost me a fortune, but who cares. The centrepiece of the living room would remind us of this day forever. Fully extended, it could seat ten.

'The test didn't say anything about octuplets,' Miriam said.

'Never can be too careful.'

I rang my brother from Café De Zwart. He reacted rather cautiously.

'Don't you think you should wait a few months,' he said, 'before you go telling everybody? Anything can happen.'

'You're not everybody. But thanks for the tip. I'll keep it under my hat for the time being.'

Inside, Miriam was drinking apple juice. 'I'll have a glass of wine at dinner. Just this once. So … what'd Frans say?'

'He says we should keep mum for the next three months. Till we're sure nothing goes wrong, a miscarriage or something.'

'The heck with him. I'm going to shout it from the rooftops.'

Now that my share of the job was completed, my blood no longer had to be kept alcohol-free. From now on I could drink what I wanted, and did just that. Later that afternoon, we took a tram to Central Station. Whenever we had something to celebrate, we did it at De Bisschop, a restaurant in Leiden. Of everything we ordered, I only remember the bottle of Margaux, which was — minus half a glass — all for me. While the wine warmed me I gazed, speechless, at the girl across from me, who was still my girl, but since this morning with a blissful asset that belonged indivisibly to both of us.

If the foetus proved viable and grew into a full-fledged child, then it must never escape my vigilance. Write? Only as breadwinner for the little one and his obliging parents, and only then during the time-outs from fatherhood. It was a weighty oath I silently made to myself in De Bisschop. Dread and delight struck home in alternation.

'I've heard Theo mention the title of his opera so often,' I said to Miriam, 'that if it's a girl, we'll name her Esmée.'

'Don't let Frans hear you,' she said. 'In three months, we can bring it up again.'

CHAPTER TWO

'So who's the third?'

1

With a child on the way, we thought it best to get married forthwith. The ceremony was scheduled for 24 December 1987. I had read somewhere that in Switzerland they had invented a digital watch whose alarm would go off once a year, showing the telephone number of the local florist in the display, so you knew: today is my anniversary. I figured that putting it on a special date would compensate for my innate forgetfulness — and it was cheaper to boot.

A Christmas Eve wedding: the family was not amused. The 24th of December, damn it, was Christmas-dinner shopping day. We decided to make it an intimate family wedding, giving the hubbub of a reception a pass: my father suffered from emphysema, my sister nearly did, and my brother had burnout. But once confronted with the hostile mood on the day itself, I sorely regretted not having organised a bacchanal for my friends, colleagues, and the pub regulars.

The words that kept cropping up among the guests were *haricots verts*, which had to be procured from a particular Beethovenstraat vegetable shop for Christmas dinner. There was also, among my siblings and sister-in-law at least, a certain lack of empathy with the wedding itself. Surely no one got *married* anymore?

The only one who kept the mood up and running was my mother-in-law, who every half-hour asked for a repeat of the Mendelssohn wedding march, which I had put on for the opening of the first bottle of champagne. Once seated, my mother confessed to having spent the whole week agonising over whether to prepare a humorous speech. She had planned to bring up the cowboy chaps I had received from her sister in Australia for my First Communion: they were open at the back, of course, leaving my legs bare and thus inviting jeers from the neighbourhood scallywags: 'Half of your pants are still caught on the barbed wire.'

The girl who faithfully sped past my parents' house on her white scooter, without it ever having led to an affair, was another of the barbs she looked forward to. Just like my scraping together my vacation money picking strawberries, and my refusal to be caught using my father's Honda moped.

The poor woman was not up to delivering this kind of toast. 'So … that's that,' she said with that stock trivialising gesture of hers, which meant: don't mind me, I'm too stupid for that kind of thing.

I was sorry she didn't, all the more so because no one had taken the trouble to prepare even a modest toast. I looked over at my sister. We had grown up together. At Sinterklaas I had produced long, rhymed epic poems for her, even for the most trifling gifts. She would usually read it out in complete non-metre, and then promptly tear it up. Now that her eldest brother was getting married, she had nothing to say except the customary handful of bitchy gossip. She spent the whole afternoon sitting there with a smug smirk on her face, chain-smoking in an attempt to catch up with my father's emphysema. With each coughing fit, her eyes narrowed into little stripes in her carmine-red face.

It never occurred to me that even our immediate family might be susceptible to outright envy. The 250-square-metre flat, this wedding, a child on the way … Things were going too well for us, and you know what, they were right.

The pregnancy was going fine, and the child's legitimacy was confirmed. Nothing stood in its way, not even my own fears. I feared that which I loved at the same time: the vulnerability of a child.

The responsibility I so dreaded was already manifesting itself. The child was due the first week of July. My fingers trembling, I counted down the days.

2

'What is it with young people these days?', I wondered more and more. 'Aren't they *angry* anymore, or what? Tonio is eighteen, has his high school diploma, studies at university … but is still living with his parents. In his boyhood room. Of course we're secretly glad to postpone the empty nest syndrome … but for *him* …'

Parents in the same situation, with more sociological instinct, would reply: 'What it is, is there's no generation gap anymore. Well, okay, there is, but it's not such a chasm. The generational differences don't lead to insoluble conflicts anymore. Everything can be discussed. Everything can be solved. Why run away from a father who doesn't want to murder you, nor you him? When's the last time Tonio and you argued?'

Never, actually. Our only argument, which never really got off the ground either, was still to come. Since he was a child, until he was at least sixteen, he would ask at the end of the day: 'Work well today?' (Just like, at the end of a meal, he would ask: 'May I be excused?' He would drop his voice an octave, as though wanting to feign the maturity befitting the somewhat affected question. He must have picked up this nicety somewhere and appropriated it, because he didn't learn it from us.) You couldn't argue with this kind of kid even if you tried.

Barely two years after graduating high school, he managed to find a sublet apartment in De Baarsjes with his best friend Jim. Standing on his own feet suddenly outweighed the cushy room and board at home. It was April 2008. I wasn't even able to help him move, as I was in the midst of a series of guest lectures at TU Delft. I do recall the stab in my heart: he had flown the nest after all. I felt a bit slighted, so that the missing generation gap also took its toll. All right, if he really wanted to trade his space, his comfy, well-appointed room on the Johannes Verhulststraat, for half a stuffy flat over in Amsterdam West: fine. Bye-bye, kid, don't let me catch you on our doorstep with your tail between your legs.

He had completed his first year at the Amsterdam Photo Academy, but wanted to switch to the photography department at the Royal Academy of Art in The Hague. Around the time he moved to the De Baarsjes, he broke off his second course of study, grumbling about 'changes' that had been introduced out of the blue. I read him the riot act for his gross lack of ambition. As I said, this confrontation, too, was a dud. He swore he was brimming with ambition, but that he'd rather, after the summer, tackle a proper university major. Until then he was planning to get a job to make ends meet — well, almost … hopefully we would still take care of his rent …

He found work at Dixons, a computer and photography-accessories shop on the Kinkerstraat. We saw very little of him after that. If he came round for a visit, it was usually on Sunday evening, when we would get Surinamese takeaway. Sometimes he would give us advance notice, but more often he just appeared in the living room.

3

I was up on the third floor preparing my lectures, while one flight below Tonio dismantled his room — the room we'd had renovated and furnished for him only a couple of years earlier, far too late. Suddenly the alarming noise of falling objects rose straight through the ceiling. I raced down the stairs.

The space stripped quite bare by now, Tonio stood desperately propping up a set of connected wall cupboards in an attempt to keep them from crashing down for good: the anchors had come loose.

'Stupid me — again,' he moaned. I helped by adding my own clumsiness to his. Once the danger had been averted, I returned to my desk rather than help him finish the job. I made a feeble promise to come see his new place once he'd moved.

We had lived under the same roof with Tonio for nearly twenty years, the last sixteen of them in this house. Perfectly normal that now, two years after his final exams, he would leave the parental nest in order to live on his own. So normal that the drama of it all — for a drama it was — more or less escaped me.

It was during those two-plus years he lived in De Baarsjes that my life, I imagined, became busier than ever. A new book came out, and I started accepting speaking engagements again. And on top of that: a weekly column, the guest teaching, an essay assignment … not to mention the work already on my plate. After his holiday in Ibiza, summer 2009, we fetched him from Schiphol by car, and dropped him off at his house on the Nepveustraat: the only time I saw it, and then only from the outside. We didn't get asked in. He was clearly in a hurry to share his adventures with Jim — the British girls he'd mentioned in passing on the way back. He'd nearly been thrown out of the hotel for letting them stay overnight in his room without checking in.

He left his bag of dirty laundry in the car. 'I'll come by on Sunday to pick it up.'

Nor did I ever write to him at his new address. In the past, if I was working at Château St. Gerlach, I did send him the occasional pep note around exam time. If I was so bent on working with 'old stuff', rather than computers and email, why not write an old-fashioned letter, handwritten and delivered by post?

My publisher asked me a while ago, perhaps not entirely selflessly, how many letters I thought I'd written in the past forty years. I came up with an estimate of ten thousand. Short and long, typed and handwritten, personal and business. During those two years that Tonio lived in De Baarsjes, the copies in my archive numbered a good four hundred — and not a single one of them to him.

It needn't be too late. If Tonio survived his accident and operation, I would write to him every day of his convalescence. At first, if his mind had to recuperate, simple letters that a nurse could read out loud to him. Gradually, more elaborate ones. And once he was back on his feet, I would never stop — even if he didn't write back.

4

'We've lost him, Adri,' came the high, singsong voice beside me. 'I just feel it.'

When had I last seen and spoken to Tonio? Last week, twice in short succession — atypical since his move.

On Wednesday, I worked until four. I went downstairs, hoping to catch some sun out on the veranda: after a chilly first half of the month, the weather had turned the previous day. The French doors leading from the library to the terrace were open. I recognised Miriam's voice; she was talking to someone, but since the curtains, billowing in the breeze, were still closed, I couldn't see to whom. I stepped out onto the veranda. There sat Tonio. More relaxed and self-assured than I was used to seeing him. When he noticed me, a mildly mocking grin spread across his face.

'So, up to your ten pages a day yet?' he asked.

After an overconfident glass some time ago, I expressed this as my target for my current novel. He asked it teasingly, but I thought I also heard in it something of the old polite interest.

'Five's the minimum,' I replied. 'Six, seven is doable. Eight is a banner day. So cut me some slack.'

He had been to visit grandpa Natan, his ninety-seven-year-old grandfather who lived on the Lomanstraat, and since he 'was in the neighbourhood anyway' he took a short detour to drop in on his parents. I suspected there was more to it than that.

'Grandpa Natan's going to have a cataract operation,' he said, suddenly serious.

'Oh?' Miriam and I knew nothing about it.

'Yeah, crazy, actually ... putting an old man through all that.'

'I'm about to take him over to Beth Shalom,' Miriam said, glancing at her watch. 'I'll bring it up with him in the car.'

I had the impression that it somehow did Tonio good to show his concern for his fragile grandfather. Since leaving home, he lived life to the hilt, and his youth, not exactly overflowing with close family anyway, was vanishing rapidly in his wake. No, this wasn't just a casual social call.

'Tonio, your master's degree, that's where we left off.' Miriam got up; it was her turn to go to the Lomanstraat. 'Don't forget to tell Adri.'

After she left, Tonio explained to me that when the time came, he had decided to get his master's in Media Technology.

'How about just getting your bachelor's in Media & Culture first? You're hardly through your first year.'

He grinned. 'Can't hurt to think ahead, now and then.'

Maybe that was his way of erasing the words 'lack of ambition', which had been lingering ever since our first and only real clash. Tonio spelled out what Media Technology involved, and told me the course wasn't offered by the University of Amsterdam. He found out he would have to alternate between Leiden and The Hague.

'That'll mean moving,' I said.

'That'll mean the train,' he said.

There was something different about him, but I couldn't put my finger on it. He dared to look deeper into his future, and there had to be a reason for it. More self-confidence, yes, but his shyness hadn't vanished. Perhaps to avoid having to lower his eyes, he looked up at the laburnum, where the green clusters were starting to show yellow buds.

'Late bloom this year,' I said.

'Yeah, what do you expect,' Tonio replied, 'with such a cold May.'

It dawned on me that we seldom, if ever, discussed nature. At the Ignatius Gymnasium open house, a number of older students who were showing him around gave him a stick insect in a glass jar from the biology lab to take home. The gift thrilled him so much that Vossius and Barlaeus were directly out of the running; Ignatius was his choice. He installed a small terrarium around the stick bug, but not long thereafter asked our permission to let the ghost grasshopper loose in the Vondelpark. This was the extent of his yen for nature. His passion lay with physics. I remember when, at school, he and a classmate gave a demonstration of the internal combustion engine, complete with computer simulation. It was grand to see him so in his element.

When I'd stoked up the fireplace one Christmas Eve and wondered out loud how the flames got their form and colour, the fourteen-year-old Tonio responded with a complete physics lecture, full of facts that had never occurred to me.

'It's all about energy, Adri.'

And now, father and son were earnestly discussing, like a pair of oldies, the late bloom of the laburnum. Fortunately, Tonio soon switched to a topic more in synch with the physical sciences: his photography.

'Adri, a small favour … Miriam has agreed, but I'm supposed to ask you, too. There's this girl, and I promised …'

'Aha.'

'… I'd do a photo shoot with her. For a portfolio. It's like this … she wants to make extra money as a model or an extra, and needs a photo portfolio to take around to casting agencies and such. And, well, I thought … this house, your house, it would be just the place for a photo shoot. It's tomorrow afternoon. Miriam doesn't mind going out for a couple of hours, but she didn't know if you …'

'Oh-ho! You come here to badger me about whether I'm doing my ten pages per day, and then chase me out of my study so you can take pictures of a cute girl. Without an audience.'

If I were to think back now on the slightly uneasy look he gave me, I'd see his clear brown eyes, which radiated more vitality than a person needs for an entire lifetime.

'Great,' he said, getting up. 'I knew you'd say yes.'

5

The motorway was quiet, in both directions. Anyone planning to spend the Whitsun bank holiday elsewhere had already left town on Friday or

Saturday. And as for the Amsterdam day-trippers, they would hit traffic snarls only later in the day.

We knew the route to the Academic Medical Centre better than the police officers up in the front seat. Since autumn 2005 Miriam had driven me there for monthly medical examinations in my role as guinea pig for a new wonder drug that could restore and regulate an imbalanced metabolism. In recent months, Miriam had taken the same route a few times to deliver Tonio to the AMC, where they had lecture halls suitable for the Media & Culture written exams.

Whitsun morning was, in a taunting sort of way, glorious. A haze that had not yet completely cleared sifted the sunlight, making it look as if gold dust was suspended in the air. We speeded straight through that glittering mist, and at the same time were radically closed off from it. *Critical condition.* The police van was moving further and further away from the day I had promised myself. Half an hour ago, I was still lying in bed, seventeen stairs away from my manuscript. At that moment I still had the choice: shower first, or give in to a wholesome impatience and take the bedroom smell upstairs with me.

The doorbell had made choosing superfluous. Work on my novel about the murder of a police officer today? There was a *real* one standing on the doorstep. A van just like in my manuscript was parked at the corner, but without a police squad poised to spring into action. It was empty and real, and would take us to the AMC, where Tonio, in a critical condition ... See, the fact that reality pursues one's fiction, tries to overtake it, and sometimes even passes it, or, worse yet, makes it redundant, is something that every novelist just has to take into account. No point in moaning: it is one of the hazards of the trade. Beautiful, of course: the complete sovereignty of an invented reality, its closed circuit ... but just try to take out an all-risk policy on it.

I never complained. Only today, reality thrust itself with such obscene and devastating directness into my fragilely constructed world that I could only bow my head — or let it hang.

6

Last Thursday, too, it was abundantly spring, almost summery, 19 degrees Celsius and clear skies. When I went downstairs just before one o'clock to drive out to the Amsterdamse Bos with Miriam, I met Tonio in the front hall. He had just brought a folding tripod up from the basement, where he'd been storing some of his things since moving to De Baarsjes. A few white reflectors of framed styrofoam were already leaning against the wall of the passage.

'Check this out,' he said, running his hand over one of the styrofoam sheets, which was pocked with an irregular pattern of tiny holes. 'Totally chewed up by beetles.'

'Come on, styrofoam-eating beetles?'

'Polystyrene beetles, yeah. The storeroom at Dixons was swarming with them. Computers just sank through their own packaging ...'

'Cross your fingers for this afternoon then,' I said. 'Holey reflectors, they'll give a model a moth-eaten face every time.'

'Very funny, Adri. Good day at the typewriter, I see.'

'I don't see any model, by the way. You hiding her from us?'

I noticed he had shaved. He was not wearing his hair in a ponytail; it had obviously been washed, and brushed smooth and glossy. We rarely saw him so kempt at home.

'She just phoned to say she'd be a bit late. Had to stop by the drugstore first. Bladder infection.'

Miriam emerged from her study. She kissed her son and ran the back of her hand across his cheek. 'Mmm, babyface.' She held him at arm's length and inspected him from head to toe. 'Hey, your favourite shirt. I thought I'd washed and ironed it for this weekend ... for if you went out ...'

'I'll change it soon. So it'll stay clean.'

'Okay, we're off,' I said. 'Now Tonio, good luck. Or should I say: good shooting.'

I shouldn't have thrown him such a knowing look, because he cast his eyes down, groaned softly and mumbled: 'Pl-l-lease.'

The trees on our street were now yellow-green, their crowns bursting with seed pods. We drove via sun-drenched Amsterdam-Zuid to Amstelveen.

'Funny,' Miriam said. 'When he photographs, he thinks nothing of stretching out on his stomach in the dust. In the mud, if need be. Now he puts on his best shirt.'

'Sometimes a photo shoot is more than a photo shoot.'

There were considerably more fishermen on the bank of the Bosbaan than the last time we drove here, and they no longer huddled so timorously in their shelters, which resembled something midway between an umbrella resting on its side and a one-man lean-to. Where the Bosbaan's water dead-ended, we could really plunge into the woods — a churning mass of fresh green vegetation, snipped-up sunlight, and lacy shadows.

'Just look at the spring,' Miriam said.

At the goat farm café, we ordered the house classic for lunch: tuna salad on a nearly black multigrain roll. Goat buttermilk. Manure-scented tranquillity.

'Strange to think,' Miriam said, 'that I used to bring Tonio here to see the newborn goats and piglets. Now it's where he shoos us off to so he can have the whole house to himself and that girl. I have to say I rather like it.'

The situation apparently had a rejuvenating effect on us: after lunch we set out on a ramble, each of us holding a cone of goat's milk ice cream. We walked to the blue bridge, under which the rowing lake narrowed, and hung over the railing, dreamily watching the few kayaks and water bikes out this early in the season.

'Gosh, that Tonio,' Miriam said. 'Media Technology ... and then right away he picks up his photography again. He's doing well. I'm so glad. If I think back to two, three years ago ...'

'I was a little hard on him, I guess, chewing him out for his lack of ambition. At his age I was no better.' First one job after the other for a year, then two aborted studies: psychology and law. And after my philosophy bachelor's: two half-doctorates, philosophical anthropology and aesthetics — two halves, unfortunately, don't make a whole. So much for my own goals.

'I've got a hunch Tonio *will* finish his degree.'

'Or else he'll do other amazing things.'

We strolled back towards the parking lot. 'Half past three,' said Miriam, as we passed the goat farm. 'No, we can't do that to him.'

'Oh, Tonio's a pretty efficient photographer. He doesn't go for the scattergun approach. When he had to snap me for *De Groene Amsterdammer* he sat me down at an antique Remington, tossed a few rolls of telex paper around. I heard a few clicks, and assumed he was taking some proofs. "Ready when you are," I said. But he already had what he was after.'

'You just said a photo session is sometimes more than a photo session. Come on, let's go have a drink at the goat place. Grant him this one afternoon.'

8

When we got home at around five, Tonio was packing up his cameras in a large plastic bag. The girl had just left. A whiff of cigarette smoke hung in the house.

'And ... any luck?' I asked.

'We'll see,' he said. 'I can judge the digital shots pretty well on the computer. But I took some analogue ones, too, and for those I'll have to wait for the prints.'

'Pop out back before you go,' I said.

One of the styrofoam reflectors was leaning up against the side of the small arbour that enclosed a wooden loveseat. I settled down on the veranda with the evening papers. A little while later, Tonio placed two square photos on the table in front of me.

'Remember, they're just Polaroids,' he said. 'I always take a couple to test the light.'

They were in black-and-white. A girl, or young woman, Tonio's age, with shoulder-length hair and a pleasant face that looked far too sweet-natured for the aloof business of modelling. She had put herself in a somewhat too deliberately winsome pose, framed by the mini-arbour, its bench apparently removed during the session.

'Pretty girl,' I said, my expert eye far from withered. 'Very pretty. But a professional model ... I dunno.'

I handed him back the Polaroids. I could see on his face that once again, I just didn't get it.

'Professional? Adri, she's a *college* student. That modelling and acting, it's only a side job. Just like me at Dixons.'

'She's awfully attractive, that's for sure.'

Suddenly, his demeanour changed. 'She asked me go to Paradiso with her on Saturday night,' he said, with bashful pride. 'Some kind of Italian blockbuster night, with Italian hits from the '80s.'

'Oh, there'll be lots of Eros Ramazzotti then.'

He pulled a comic face that said: never heard of him. Miriam came out onto the veranda and offered us something to drink. Tonio declined, but sat down anyway, albeit restlessly, on the edge of a chair. Miriam reminded me of two funerals the next day, at more or less the same time. Two close acquaintances, both of whom were equally important to us.

'We still have to choose,' she said. 'And not like: you do one, I'll do the other. Not this time.'

'Too many people dying lately,' I said. 'Cremations, funerals ... The question is: are they all mandatory? People are so quick to make you feel like there's no getting out of it. There's something unfair about it, considering my own—' I turned to Tonio. 'I'm not sure if you know ... well, so now you do ... but when the time comes, I insist on being buried in the absolutely smallest possible company. Not cremated, mind you, buried. A hole in the ground with three people standing around it. Three, no more.'

'Oh,' said Tonio, 'and who's the third one then?'

There was a moment's silence, and then we all burst out laughing in unison. He was right. The third one would be lying in the coffin.

Tonio had a delightfully unassuming laugh, with lively bursts which made his parted lips looked even fuller and the skin on his nose creep upward toward his forehead. (That laugh, too, was in a critical condition. Oh God, save his laugh.)

He got up and, still chuckling, asked his mother: 'Do you still get Surinamese takeaway on Sundays?'

'A tradition since before you were born,' Miriam replied.

'Whitsun, too?'

'We don't do Whitsun.'

'Sunday's on then. Chow mein would be delicious.'

'All right, just don't cancel again because you're so *beat*. Like last Sunday, when we were supposed to go into town.'

'Oh yeah, that watch ... we'll have to make another date.'

In his quick, springy way, his shoulders hunched just a tad, he headed to the door, and said goodbye with his variable salutation, which this time sounded something like: 'Oi.'

'Have fun Saturday,' I called after him. I don't know if he heard it, as he was already passing through the kitchen on the way to the front door. How extraordinary: Tonio was going to drop by for the third time in the space of a week. The previous day he had laid out his future plans, but it was like he had something *else* to tell us. I hadn't forgotten how proud of a new girlfriend I used to be. With the ongoing conquest still in full swing, I already wanted to show her off, not only to my friends but to my parents, too — even if only in words for the time being, and if at all possible with a picture as well.

9

After Tonio had left, Miriam called me to the kitchen. She stood at the open fridge. 'Check this out.'

The shelves, the vegetable drawer, the door compartments — every nook and cranny was jammed with cartons of ice tea and fruit juice in all possible flavours. There was a litre of Lipton Ice in the freezer, in case the young lady liked hers extra cold. Neither of us knew that Tonio had done all this shopping. It amounted to half a week's allowance spent on fruit juice and iced tea.

'Tonio knows how to look after his models,' I said.

'It won't be out of concern for lack of vitamins at his parents,' Miriam replied. 'I'll take them with me next week along with his clean washing.'

In the corner of the living room, next to the glass display case containing Tonio's rock collection, I saw two more styrofoam reflector sheets. A strong nicotine smell hung in the air. On the floor, a saucer with stubbed-out cigarette butts; I emptied it into the waste bin. So the girl — still nameless — was a smoker.

I came across the grainy white sheets elsewhere in the house. They gazed at me like monochrome paintings, telling me no more about the photo session than that they reflected sunlight or lamplight onto the model.

'What are we supposed to do with all that styrofoam?' Miriam asked.

'Leave it,' I said, 'he can clean it up himself on Sunday.'

10

Before dinner, I went up to my office on the third floor — not to work, but to raise the awning on the back balcony. It had rained a few nights ago, and the irregular *tick-tick* and drumming of the rain on the open canvas had kept me awake for hours.

The electric button, to the left of the French doors, seemed to falter — until I noticed that the awning was already up, neatly rolled into its aluminium frame.

Wait a sec. I knew for sure I hadn't raised it before we left for the Amsterdamse Bos — intentionally, to protect the parquet floor from the profuse sunlight that streamed in at that hour. I could have raised the awning and drawn the curtains, of course, but in order to air out the room I left the balcony doors wide open, and experience had taught me that the curtains would billow upwards, and on their way down sweep stuff from the nearby desk. The last time that happened, I had incited Miriam's ire by accusing her cats of being the cause of the destruction.

All these deliberations were still clear in my mind — even now, three days later, in the back seat of the police van. It was not a matter of forgetfulness. I had left the curtains open, lowered the awning, and fastened the doors by their hooks on the balcony wall. Now, upon returning, I found the curtains still open, but the doors were closed tight and the awning raised.

Tonio? We had a deal: he was free to use the entire house, except for the floor where my office was, because I was busy sorting through material, and there were stacks of handwritten, as-yet unnumbered sheets everywhere. I had a good look around. There was no evidence of them having taken photos here. No styrofoam sheets. No film roll wrappers in the wastebasket. No sign of the unwelcome rearranging to which photographers from newspapers and magazines so enjoyed subjecting one's home.

Was I hoping for signs of an amorous interlude? The book about Dutch police precincts, a reference aid for my novel that I kept stuck between the two seat cushions of the chaise longue, was still in place.

I opened the balcony doors. The slats and planks that used to be Tonio's old bunk bed lay precisely as our handyman René had left them, only a bit more grey-green after exposure to the snow and rain. To the right, an aluminium fire-escape ladder led up to the roof.

'Minchen, when we came back from the park … did you raise the awning in my office?'

'No, you must've done it yourself. I can't do everything.'

I was none the wiser. I decided to ring Tonio about it — tonight, or else tomorrow. Not to scold him for having invaded my workspace, but … well, maybe I'd find out some details of his love life. My God, what an old busybody I was becoming.

The phone call went by the wayside. Soon ... later, while he was recuperating, I'd ask. God knows how many hours we would have to spend at his bedside until he was himself again. There'd be enough time to talk. I would jabber him through it.

11

A critical condition: what *is* that, actually? Perhaps they were quick to call someone's condition 'critical' so that if it did turn out badly for the patient after all, they'd be safeguarded against the vengeful indignation of the survivors.

I was reminded of my cousin Willy van der Heijden Jr., who was declared clinically dead after a motorcycle accident. Illusionist-joker that he was, he rose from the dead, and six weeks later returned to business as usual, which in his case meant low- to medium-grade criminality. So it could swing that way, too.

No, bad example. Not even a year later, he was on the run, artificial knee joints and all, from the police, and crashed himself just as dead as before by smashing his car into a tree: no headlights on an unlit road. This time he skipped the 'clinically' phase.

I remember my mother calling me up with the news. 'A bad egg, that boy, but I had to let you know.'

While I was on the phone with her ,I looked at the eighteen-month-old Tonio as he crawled across the rug, drooling from the exertion. No such thing would ever happen to him, I would see to that. With the upbringing I was going to give him, he would never have to flee from the police, let alone with his headlights off.

'How's Uncle Willy taking it?

'He's a wreck, of course. He'd put all his hopes into that boy. The neighbours said he wandered the streets the whole night with his dog. Talking out loud. Yelling.'

'He might be dead already,' Miriam moaned.

'A critical condition,' I said, 'can mean anything. I'm sure they're doing their best.'

'He's being operated on,' the policeman said. 'They've been busy for hours.'

Goddamn. That did sound critical.

CHAPTER THREE

Wrong hospital

1

The police van took several successive curves, which our speed made seem sharper than they were. I either nearly slid away from Miriam along the slick upholstery, or was thrust up against her with a sudden force, which evoked a gagging sound from her.

'Sorry, baby.'

Three weeks shy of twenty-one years ago, we also embarked on a wild ride to a hospital, but in a much smaller vehicle: a Fiat Panda. Miriam had woken me at 4.00 a.m. with severe abdominal cramps.

'Are you sure it's your intestines?'

'I haven't been to the toilet all week.'

She held my hand. I could tell from her grip how much pain she was in, and how regularly the cramps came. She was trembling. We lay like this, in silence, for a good while.

That night, we had gone to bed arguing. Anticipating the increased washing needs, we had bought a washing machine a couple of days earlier. After the burly delivery men had left, their far-too-generous drink tip in hand, I noticed that the white casing was damaged. By the time I had got the manager of the appliance store on the line, my reserve of diplomacy was depleted: the jerks had screwed up, period. The same fellows returned later that day, now far less friendly, to exchange it. Only after they left did their revenge reveal itself. During the test run, the thing shuddered and stomped loose from the wall. Standing barefoot on the tile floor, I had no choice but to hop backwards away from the machine, lest its undoubtedly sharp bottom edge amputate my toes. While performing a life-saving jitterbug, I also had to find the off button in order to subdue the automatic monster.

Miriam was convinced that the delivery men had left the safety bolts in the drum on purpose. 'You always over-tip, that's why. Then they mess with you.'

It was approaching five-thirty. My hand was gradually becoming disjointed by Miriam's constant squeezing. Her beautiful, smooth forehead, which seldom perspired, was now beaded with sweat. 'This can't be just a stomach ache,' I said.

'I'll ring the midwife just to be on the safe side,' Miriam said. She wasn't due for another three-and-a-half weeks. The midwife had her explain in detail what exactly she felt. The call was brief. 'She's on her way. I might have to go to the hospital already.'

'Minchen, your overnight bag ... The folder says you have to have a bag packed and ready. We don't have one.'

'That's just like you,' she moaned, 'to start whinging about an overnight bag at a time like this. I've got other things on my mind, you know.'

The stabs worsened. The midwife arrived, her face still lined with sleep, just after six. She put a rubber glove on her right hand and asked me to wait outside. I suppose I could have packed a small travel bag in the meantime, but just stood there inert in the hallway.

'Now, honey,' I overheard, 'you're dilating already.'

So they were contractions after all, and they were getting stronger. I helped Miriam into her bathrobe. 'It's more painful than I expected,' she said.

The midwife's Fiat Panda was double-parked downstairs in front of the house. Heavily pregnant, Miriam looked too big for the compact car, but she just fitted. With the midwife at the wheel and us in back, the Panda was more than full.

'Help, my claustrophobia's playing up,' Miriam panted hotly in my ear.

The midwife turned left onto De Lairessestraat, where morning traffic, even this early, was already nervously picking up. The Fiat proceeded with little jerks — leaps, really — and Miriam whimpered.

'Just get me to the vu,' she whispered.

2

The van had a lot less traffic trouble now than the Fiat did back then. Morning rush-hour was usually not yet over at ten to ten, but this was Sunday. We drove past a tidily laid-out business park, out of which rose the terraced buildings of the Academic Medical Centre. Somewhere inside, amid the labyrinth of overlit corridors, masked surgeons were operating on Tonio.

If he was still alive.

Twenty-two years ago, just like now, Miriam sat to my left on the back seat of the Panda. Then, too, I hugged her tight, pressed her close to me, so that I felt every contraction pulse through my own body — well, on the surface, anyway, because I couldn't really *feel* the pain. Miriam occasionally gave my sleeve a tug to indicate that I should loosen my grip, which did not absorb the contractions.

Twice earlier, I had experienced similar mortal fear in a tiny Fiat. The first time occurred in the winter of '77, when Maria-Pia Canaponi, a young Florentine, drove me and a friend from the hilltop town of Fiesole down to Florence, hidden in the misty and shadowy depths of the Arno valley. As I recalled over the years, she didn't so much as drive as allow the car to simply fall downhill, even though the wheels did touch the ground here and there on a hairpin curve, but more like the soles of a mountaineer's boots graze the side of a cliff as he rappels down a rock face.

The other death-defying Fiat, also somewhere in the mid-seventies, bored its way through the hellish Parisian morning traffic. At the wheel was a local woman, her hat crumpled by the city's night life. She was trying to impress me (in back) and her girlfriend up front by ignoring red lights or, at the very least, by blindly changing lanes with her brim pulled down over her eyes. Arriving at her house in a suburb of Paris, sheer terror and heart palpitations made it impossible for me to perform up to snuff.

But now the claustrophobic tin can was jostling an unborn life. The midwife manoeuvred her car down the Cornelis Krusemanstraat towards the Harlemmercircuit — and that is where I must have lost track of where we were, distracted as I was by Miriam's birthing pains. I wasn't paying attention, and Miriam even less, so neither of us noticed that the midwife had turned right onto the Amstelveenseweg towards the Zeilstraat instead of taking the roundabout to the other leg of the Amstelveenseweg that led to the vu hospital.

Yes, I do recall my impatience at the open drawbridge over the Schinkel, raised like an unbreachable rampart, but it still did not occur to me that our rolling maternity bed was heading the wrong way. Miriam herself realised the mistake only when we reached the hospital. Once inside, the midwife and I helped her into a wheelchair. As we wheeled her through the foyer towards the lift, Miriam whimpered: 'This isn't the vu … I was supposed to deliver at the vu.'

'Oh, sorry, hon, sorry … sorry,' cried the midwife. 'My fault entirely. I must have looked at the wrong form this morning … Oh, how awful. Well, there's no turning back now.'

She had taken us to Slotervaart Hospital.

3

The two police officers turned us over to a small group of nurses in a reception area at the top of a short set of stairs. I can't remember which of the four or five of them handed me Tonio's wallet. The grey billfold with snap fastener lay heavily in my hand: its change pocket was laden with coins. I imagined that it still retained some of his body heat

— from his thigh, his buttocks, or his breast, wherever he had it at the moment of …

Stuck to the back of the wallet was a self-adhesive, computer-printed sticker bearing his name, a few series of digits and today's date (how new and nearby everything was). In our absence, they were already busy transforming him into a series of numbers.

The two officers took their leave with a handshake, and wished us 'sterkte' — courage, strength. I took the opportunity to study their uniforms one last time. Once this was all behind us and we knew how long Tonio's recovery would take, I could — no matter how shaken and depressed — return to my writing table and resume work on the police novel. I had pinned up a photo of a female police chief in standard uniform. Now I had been given extra information regarding how a rank-and-file policewoman looked in warm weather.

The policeman handed me a card from the Serious Traffic Accident Unit on the James Wattstraat, where I could request a more complete report on the collision. I had only to ask for the staff member whose name he'd written in with a ballpoint pen.

The officers raised a hand as they descended the stairs, heading towards the revolving door and their van, parked in the sun. Miriam and I followed the nurses to the Intensive Care Unit (Intensive Care, which was different than the Emergency Room. Ambulance, ER, ICU, OR: Tonio's body had made a speedy series of promotions.) On the way, one of them apologised for the fact that we had been informed so late.

'His wallet was full of cards, but we couldn't come up with an address right away for … for his parents. At moments like that, a life-threatening situation, we have other priorities. Saving a life always comes first.'

Life-threatening situation. A doctor was waiting for us at the junction of two corridors. We were told that Tonio had been on the operating table for 'hours' (it was approaching ten o'clock) and was still in a critical condition.

'The traumatologist will be out shortly to give you an update.'

I gathered we were now in the ICU. A young nurse, blonde and blue-eyed and as fresh as the morning, led us to a small waiting room and offered us coffee.

'Just some water,' said Miriam, who had already sidled against me on the three-seat sofa.

'Coffee for me, please,' I said.

The nurse left the room, leaving the door open. Above the doorway was a large kitchen clock: ten past ten.

'Ugh, no coffee,' Miriam said. 'It reminds me of when ...'

She reached for her forehead and cried, sputtering slightly. She didn't need to finish her sentence. I knew she was referring to that June morning in '88, when we mistakenly ended up at the Slotervaart maternity ward, and Miriam had gone into hysterics over my coffee breath.

I opened Tonio's wallet. The billfold section contained nothing but a five-euro note. The coins, all told, probably added up to a sizeable amount.

A year earlier, in August, after the premiere of *Het leven uit een dag*, I had studied his bar behaviour during the reception at De Kring. Tonio and Marianne had retired to a dark corner somewhere alongside the dance floor where the crew were swinging to the house music, and whenever he went to fetch drinks for himself or the girl, he paid with a banknote and jammed the change into the pocket of his wallet (the very one I was now holding in my hands). Those slight tendencies towards disorderliness: I lamented them all the more because I exhibited them myself at his age, and long thereafter, and still had not managed to overcome them all. Continually confronted, in matters both minor and significant, with our similarities, I was forced to imagine myself as a twenty-one-year-old. It worried me. Not for myself, but for him.

'If Tonio really is so much like me,' I said to my brother, who sat next to me at the bar in De Kring, 'then he's got an uphill battle ahead of him.'

Frans, who knew me in my early twenties and even lived with me for a while, sputtered out a feeble denial just to be polite.

There were plenty of cards and passes, complete with address, in the pockets of Tonio's wallet, so I suspected that there had indeed been more urgent matters than tracking down his parents.

'Here's an ID card from the Onze Lieve Vrouwe Gasthuis,' I said to Miriam. 'What would he have been doing there?'

'Jaw surgeon,' she said with a shrug of revulsion. 'Wisdom teeth.'

The nurse came in with a tray, and arranged the Thermos cans, cups and glasses on the table. 'The traumatologist will be in to see you shortly,' she said as she was leaving. 'If you need anything, just check the corridor, one of us will be there.'

4

Since being roused from bed, I had hardly spoken, except with Miriam, but every time I opened my mouth, first to the police officers and now to the nursing staff, I was painfully aware of the heavy odour of garlic on my breath. I didn't smell it myself, but seeing as we hadn't had breakfast yet I knew it rose straight from my gut. (This morning, when I went downstairs, the kitchen door on the first floor was open. Spread out on the bread board were four rolls, sliced and waiting to be buttered. Oranges alongside the juice squeezer. A still-life in the wake of bad tidings.)

What time had the policeman said Tonio's accident occurred that morning? Around 4:30? The flood of saliva brought about by the garlic overkill had woken me at about a quarter past four. No, don't go there: I wasn't about to start seeing premonitions and signs in everything. An upset stomach as a warning of Tonio's impending disaster? And what was I supposed to do with this cryptic message delivered by peptic Morse code?

Once again I couldn't help but notice the parallels with the circumstances of Tonio's birth. Then, too, stomach cramps that turned out to be contractions had taken us by such surprise that we skipped breakfast. The previous evening, we'd eaten Surinamese food from

69

Albina, a takeaway restaurant on the Albert Cuypstraat. I had ordered a portion of their dangerously spicy fashon sausage, which I only ate if I knew I had no social obligations for the next three days, because the dish transformed your mouth into an unwashed arsehole. And so I arrived at the Slotervaart maternity ward on the morning of 15 June 1988 with a contaminated mouth, augmented by an empty stomach. I dared not open my mouth for fear of endangering the delivery with my toxic fumes.

5

I don't know where the additional information came from, but meanwhile the exact time of the accident was established as 4.40 a.m. Four weeks before the longest day: was it already light by that time, or still dark, or midway? When daylight savings time kicked in, we set the clocks an hour ahead, which meant that for the next seven months the sun would rise an hour later. I seemed to remember that in the old days, before daylight savings time was introduced, it was already broad daylight when the Nijmegen nightclub Diogenes emptied out at four-thirty or five o'clock at this time of year. All right, we're talking about weekend hours. On weekdays Diogenes closed at 3.45, and in late May it was still pretty much dark.

I couldn't be totally sure. I decided to set the alarm clock for 4:30 the next day so I could check the sky at twenty to five.

But if it turned out to be still dark at that time, it would automatically raise the next question: did Tonio have lights on his bike, or at least those little clip-on lamps on his clothes?

I wasn't at my post this morning. No late-night revelry behind me, no hangover to sleep off, but I did just lie in bed, no denying that. Even waking up to a saliva flood and churning stomach presented me with no other thought than: once it's passed, try to get another hour of sleep … work to do …

I should have been *there*, on the Stadhouderskade, to restrain my recklessly cycling son, steer him out of harm's way. There was no one in the room to accuse me of anything, but I hardly needed a pointed finger to feel guilty, to *know* I was guilty. I sat next to Miriam shuddering and sweating with guilt for what I had carelessly let happen that morning.

My thoughts continued to hover around Tonio's birth — undoubtedly due to the congruence of the circumstances. The uncertain drive to the hospital … the torturously long wait … If I were guilty of allowing his accident, it's because I was accountable for his birth in the first place.

If, at that moment, someone had entered the room to tell me that back on 15 June 1988 I had intentionally let the midwife drive the wrong way in order to sabotage Tonio's birth, then I'd have believed it. From the moment that I wanted a child, I also *did not* want one. Ergo: my insidious ambivalence made Tonio a sitting duck from the word go. This morning was proof — perhaps irrevocable proof — of it.

6

Of course, there was a large clock in the delivery room, as conspicuous as at a train station: the time of birth had to be established unequivocally and on the spot. It was seven-thirty in the morning. Miriam lay in great pain on a bed, the midwife on her left side and a maternity nurse to her right. Normally not prone to being superstitious, that day I found myself wondering if being at the wrong hospital would bring bad luck.

They each held one of Miriam's hands while spurring her on. 'Breathe, honey! Breathe through the contractions!'

'Hey, don't bite!' shouted the delivery nurse when Miriam, reacting to a particularly strong contraction, sank her teeth into the nearest available limb. 'Pant! Don't bite!'

I looked on helplessly from a distance. My delicate little Minchen was not cut out for childbirth. I should never have saddled her with this.

When the contractions subsided for a moment, the redheaded maternity nurse who had met us at the lift went to fetch coffee. When she returned, she pressed a paper cup into my hand and whispered: 'I think your wife could use your help right now.'

So coffee in hand, I sat down on the stool next to Miriam's bed. I took a sip and bent over to whisper something encouraging, but before I could get a word out she cried: 'No, please! Not with that coffee breath! Ugh, it stinks … I'm so nauseous … I *can't* stand it …'

Never before had she looked at me (or through me) like that. Not only as though I were a complete stranger, but a hostile one at that. I noticed that even now, in the throes of labour, she emphasised the word can't — as a child she adopted this one quirk of her father's accent. 'I *can't* stand it.'

Her reaction made me recoil and nearly knock over the stool. So this was how ill giving birth could make you. I fled to the corridor, set the still-full coffee cup on a window sill on the way to the WC, rinsing my mouth a good five or six times, gargling with water until my throat went raw.

When the contractions resumed in full force, the women laid Miriam on the floor.

'Don't be alarmed, honey. You can push better this way.'

They put a pillow under her head, and there she lay, on the scuffed linoleum, with three women kneeling around her. The maternity nurse wiped up small amounts of faeces that came out with each push. The midwife put a stethoscope to Miriam's belly, offering the mother-to-be a listen, but Miriam shook her head vehemently as a sign that the hooks be removed from her ears: by now, everything was an intrusion. The midwife signalled me to come listen. I'd have rather not, but I didn't want to come across as an indifferent father. I knelt down next to Miriam, and with the stethoscope attached, I tried to hold my breath (it was the combination of Surinamese sausage and coffee on an empty stomach, of course, that had produced such a birthing-unfriendly stench). I listened to my imminent fatherhood. Eyes closed, I saw in my mind's eye a snippet of a documentary of a coral reef. The panicked gurgle of escaping gas bubbles. *Blurp, blurp.* An improbably fast, watery heartbeat. Acoustically, already a miscarriage.

I nodded and handed the stethoscope back to the obstetrician. I returned to my stool near the door. The women conferred quietly as to whether it wasn't time to break the membranes. A few moments later, I heard the metallic sound of fluids dripping, then gushing, then dripping again.

7

'Look, honey, this is the amniotic fluid.' The Fiat-midwife held the kidney-shaped bedpan up for Miriam to see. 'That red's just a bit of blood.'

It was one of those wards where nothing was done without the patient being informed. The heavily sagging body of my sweetheart rested on hands and knees on the floor like a pregnant animal ready to drag itself off to its den to deliver its cubs. The women crouched behind her continued their cries of encouragement. I thought the birthing process had begun. But no. Their exclamations were for the mother-to-be's excrement. 'Go on, girl, there's still more in there. Breathe through the contractions, give us a little push.'

Before unleashing a wonder, a woman first has to prove she is capable of abandoning all dignity.

Back when Miriam was still on the bed, the women whispered among themselves about the dilation, which with a crinkling rubber glove was established to be eight centimetres. 'At ten, we start pushing.'

Now, even more soft-spokenly, they measured eight-and-a-half, which apparently was enough to give the green light for pushing. There must be a reason for their haste. Miriam once again was lying on her back on the floor, her legs spread wide.

'You're going great, honey. We can already see a bit of its scalp … and some hair …'

I didn't like the looks of it. The women, Miriam excepted, carried on a continual consultation in a way that was meant to be inconspicuous but was betrayed by worried glances and hurried whispering. The only words I understood were: 'the other bed'.

8

'Don't be alarmed if a few people come in,' the obstetrician said to Miriam. 'Obstetrics interns. We'll be sure they keep to themselves.'

That took us by surprise. Of course I was too weak-kneed to protest. The room filled up with a few young women dressed in white nylon who couldn't have kept *less* to themselves. They crowded around Miriam. The doctor got up and instructed two of the obstetricians-in-training to wheel the bed out into the passage. Then a different, better-equipped one was brought in.

Maybe because the group of trainees had thinned out for the time being, I suddenly caught sight of a young man in a white coat, his back to me, sitting at a shelf unit attached to the wall. Judging from his posture, he was writing furiously. Miriam was lifted onto the new bed by six pairs of arms at once, and was commanded to resume pushing with redoubled pressure. From time to time, the white-coated man twirled around on his swivel stool to observe the birthing arena and continued penning his notes on the clipboard supported on his knee.

Perhaps it was lack of sleep that weakened (or obscured) my attention. The room was in the grip of the kind of panic that did not paralyse those present, but rather drove them to serious and purposeful action.

'Yea-a-a-ah … !' emerged from several throats simultaneously. All these years later, I harbour the tenacious recollection of how the unwashed infant was lobbed into my lap by the flick of a blood-covered wrist. I shall never forget the gooey splash with which the baby landed on my thigh. It was more like it had been flung, because the child appeared so lifeless and blue.

Nobody cried out that it was a boy. I had to determine this myself. The consternation continued. There were so many women crowded around the bed that I lost sight of Miriam.

The following observations are taken directly from my diary entry on 15 June 1988, because this is as close as I can come to Tonio's birth:

'With all those swollen, passively dangling limbs, the little sprog made me think of a bunch of carrots, or rather a string of pale blue sausages you saw hanging at the butcher's. For half a second, there was the panic: stillborn. But as she turned around, the midwife jabbed the little nipper in his side — a routine, almost malicious whap that got our son bawling. The piercing cries also brought on my own tears — finally. I prodded an index finger against the miniature fist. The fingers wound themselves viscidly around it. It was the little boy's very first grip on life.'

The baby was taken from me to be washed. I was finally allowed to give Miriam a kiss and to compliment her on the most beautiful delivery of all time. The interns now at a respectful distance, the doctor offered her apologies for the chaotic scene. Now she dared to confess that the last time she had listened with the stethoscope she could hardly pick up a heartbeat, so despite only partial dilation they had decided to get Miriam to start pushing. Since induced birth could not be ruled out, she had had the special bed brought in.

The way Miriam lay there, utterly exhausted, wan and looking like a wrung-out dishrag, I wondered if she'd ever really recover. Visions of the Kanadreuffe's mother in the novel *Karákter* — as a schoolboy I'd read the first few pages — who withered incurably in her childbed from one minute to the next, had forever plagued me: become a new father and see your wife age twenty years during delivery.

The afterbirth still had to be removed, but the umbilical cord came, twisted and gaudy, into view. The doctor handed me a pair of episiotomy scissors. 'It's a tradition here that the father cuts the umbilical cord. Things didn't go that smoothly today. We had to hurry.' She fastened two clamps next to each other on the cord. 'Can you do it like this?' Just clip it between the clamps … yes, that's right.'

It made a creepy, crunching sound.

'We'll give you a piece of the umbilical cord to take with you. Sealed in plastic. As a memento.'

I watched as the baby was washed, dried off (more like patted dry) and weighed. He was three-and-a-half weeks premature, and underweight. The scale's reading was given to the white-coated man, who was still writing everything down. Weight, length, the various times of the entire process. In the six months between high school and university, I had a job as 'timekeeper' at a machine factory in Eindhoven. Maybe that's what this man's job was called, too. He entered the time of birth as 10:16.

9

'Have a name for him yet?' asked the midwife.

'Ach, all those pretty girl's names …' I answered. 'Yesterday we were sure it would be a girl. Tonio. That's his name now. Not Esmée. Tonio. Hello, Tonio.'

His cries, as he was trussed into a nappy, were high-pitched and yet hoarse. Miriam's weakly beckoning voice nearly got drowned out. I went over to her.

'I've just unveiled the monument,' I said. 'Well done, babe … beautiful job.'

I kissed her wet cheek. The women removed the afterbirth. As though identifying a flower, the midwife began picking through it in front our very eyes, offering icily sober commentary about how the foetus lived in the uterus. I had rather preferred to preserve the myth of the afterbirth. An aunt who had worked as a maternity ward nurse once told me how some of her colleagues smuggled placentas home with them to feed to the dog (like they also stirred breast milk into their tea). For a moment, I was afraid the doctor would suggest we all munch down the afterbirth for lunch — which would perhaps have meant a return to the myth.

Miriam bravely endured being stitched up where she'd been torn during delivery. Later, she was taken by wheelchair, in which a sort of blotting paper had been laid, to the shower. The doctor took me aside.

'The baby's underweight, so we'd like to keep him for the time being …

in an incubator ... for observation. You can go have a look in a moment.'

10

The blonde nurse came to ask if we needed anything. No, there was enough water in the carafe, and I avoided the coffee after Miriam reminded me how the stuff could stink at inopportune moments.

'A tranquiliser, maybe?'

Yes, Miriam thought that was a good idea. A little while later the nurse returned, keyed up, with a handful of individually wrapped pills. 'The head of the trauma team will be here any minute.'

11

'As I understand it,' said Dr G., the traumatologist, 'the accident occurred on the Stadhouderskade just as it curves past the Vondelpark. It's a nasty spot. Notorious, I'm afraid: we see a relatively high proportion of accidents at that intersection.'

Dr G. was a tall, slender professor of surgery. He appeared self-assured by nature, but with us he had an slight air of diffidence. His expression betrayed sympathy for the parents: unlike us, he had seen Tonio's injuries, both the external and internal ones. He was in a position to assess the boy's chance of survival.

'I won't give you false hope,' he said without sitting down. 'He's still in a critical condition. I had to remove his spleen ... it was badly damaged. Half of it at first, and then the rest. The impact caused a serious trauma to the lungs. They've taken on a lot of blood. It's complicated by the fact that there was also substantial brain damage. We opened up his skull on the right side, because the brain has started to swell there. It desperately needs oxygen, which the lungs aren't producing ... The next few hours will be touch and go.'

As he spoke, his voice calm, Miriam sat next to me, shivering. A new and detailed map of the child she had given birth to was being unfolded in front of us.

'I'm going back to the OR,' said Dr G. 'You'll be kept informed of any developments, naturally. I'll stop by again before I go home.'

It was absurd that we had been brought here but couldn't see Tonio. An entire team of masked experts bent over his opened-up insides, and inserted tubes, tampons, scalpels, forceps, clamps. But maybe what he needed most was Miriam and me, simply to hold his hand.

Today, for the first time in a long while, I did not associate the AMC with champagne. From 2005 to 2007 I was administered my magic pill at the Endoscopy unit of the Stomach, Intestine, and Liver wing, under the watchful eye of Professor Lisbeth. As the study also included taking detailed notes of changes in the professional life of the guinea pigs, I had faithfully reported that my new novel was finished, and promised I would do my best to keep the alcoholic festivities to a minimum. At my next appointment, after being weighed and jabbed, I sat hooked to a blood pressure monitor when the door opened and in came Professor Lisbeth with a tray. Not with medical instruments, but a wine cooler holding a bottle of bubbly and three champagne flutes. It was the first time I ever heard the pop of a champagne cork in a hospital, followed by the effervescence of the wine and the clinking of glasses.

'To your new book!' Lisbeth was still wearing her white coat, but that only made it more festive. Her assistant, Ellen, had just tapped a quarter of a litre of my blood into a tube, so I could certainly use a pick-me-up. The impromptu reception was touching, and only there in the examination room did it hit home that the job was truly finished. The glistening eyes of the women told me that for them, too, this sort of thing only happened once in a blue moon.

Tonio's arrival put paid to a longstanding dilemma that procreation had finally undone, but my fear of losing the child was in no way diminished. My breathless efforts would now be dedicated to piloting my son safely through all the predicaments and perils of the world.

We got postnatal assistance far too late after the birth, and I had the impression that in order to make the girl feel not entirely unneeded, Miriam gave her little jobs that she could already handle herself. The aide continually came into my room to ask about my work. It was her way of flirting with men who she presumed had been shortchanged, physically speaking, during their wife's pregnancy. She took a broad view of her duties.

It was 26 June 1988. Now that the girl was in the house to assist Miriam and help look after the baby, I could nip out to the Dutch national football team's ticker-tape parade. They had just won the UEFA championship in a 2-0 victory over the Soviet Union.

The canal district, which had centrifugally grown from the Middle Ages till the Golden Age, had that day turned into a centripetal force. The orange or red-white-blue clad crowds hastened, as though riding a strong tailwind, in the direction of the city centre. So as not to feel like a complete football-crazed idiot, I let as many fans as possible pass, ambling with the air of a man out on an aimless stroll. I'd have liked to be wheeling Tonio triumphantly in front of me, but Miriam forbade it. She was already wary of pushy crowds. The thought of a trampled baby buggy was utterly intolerable.

An aunt of mine who had emigrated to Australia once spent two months back in Eindhoven in the late fifties, partly in order to take part in an old-fashioned Carnival celebration. She had dressed up like a Mexican, complete with an umbrella-sized sombrero, and tinted her face light brown with the wetted chicory-root coffee substitute that even fifteen years after the war my family of unfortunates still used as a taste enhancer. I don't know if the mocha-faced fans who passed me on all sides had adhered to this recipe of face painting, but the rasta wigs left no doubt as to the message: they were Ruud Gullit.

A somewhat whiter company, cloaked in smocks pieced together from the Dutch flag, carried a banner. The text, in tar-like block letters, mockingly referred to the 1981 anti-nuke protests and to the previous day's football victory over the Soviets: NO MORE RUSSIANS IN OUR BACKYARD, and in smaller letters: THEY'VE BEEN SENT TO SIBERIA.

I had followed most of the UEFA '88 matches with Tonio on my lap, enjoying a sense of wellbeing I had never experienced before. Now, I was walking toward the city centre nakedly empty-handed. When I was five or six, I used to carry our cat around for a good hour at a time. Once the beast had freed itself from my grip, his weight, fur and the rocking motion lingered in my arms, like a tingling, as though I was still tangibly carrying the invisible creature. I had the feeling it was the same thing now with the baby. I had carried Tonio through the room. I knelt down with him in my arms next to the speaker to listen to the oboe solo. Now, his imprint tingled in my empty arms — minus the warmth.

A twinge of treason: I had abandoned the nest. Mother and child had been left to the devices of an unreliable maternity aide.

At Museumplein, some 120,000 frenzied fans were waiting to hail the conquering heroes. How did they manage to get here from the canal bridges so quickly? Or had the crowd been standing here all this time, elbowing one another for the choice spots? Budging to the front, canalside, might cost the idolator a wet set of clothes, but here at Museumplein one was willing to lay one's life on the line to kiss the hem of the nation's garment. But the willingly parted lips were cracked by the sharp riot fences up front, near the stage.

It wasn't entirely clear whether the fire hoses were meant to keep the approaching throng at bay, or to offer some cooling relief to those who were in danger of getting squashed against the fence. Anyone who fainted was passed overhead like a crowd surfer to safer quarters.

Television images of Heizel Stadium a few years earlier flashed before

80

my eyes. Get me out of here. I had already left the nest unattended for too long. There, the Concertgebouw, beyond that and I was nearly home.

13

'Shouldn't we call Jim?' I asked Miriam. 'The poor kid won't have the faintest idea why Tonio didn't come home.'

We were sitting in the ICU courtyard in the sun.

'I don't know,' Miriam said. '*If* he sleeps, it's around now.'

'Sleeping disorder or no, Jim still has to hear what happened to Tonio.'

'I'll call his mother.'

Mobile phone in hand, Miriam walked to the middle of the small paved courtyard. A few moments later, I saw her hunched forward, talking into the phone. With her free hand, she continually wiped tears from her face. The Whit Sunday sun hung motionless and unmoved above the building complex, and dried her fingers.

'Jim's parents'll go to their flat to tell him in person. You know what, I'm going to call Hinde. See if she'll come here, with Frans.'

Miriam phoned her sister. I could not make out what she was saying as she walked along the concrete planters.

'She's getting a taxi now.'

'And she'll pick up Frans on the way?'

'He's in Spain. With Mariska and the baby. They'll fly back tomorrow.'

(After Hinde left her house on the Vondelpark, her appearance on the Overtoom, where she planned to hail a cab, caused a minor sensation among friends. Having quit smoking years earlier, she now stood early on Sunday morning with a long filter cigarette in her mouth, gesticulating like a nighthawk at passing taxis. Just then, our friend Nelleke drove by, on her way to deliver our mutual friends Allard and Annelie to Schiphol. There wasn't time to stop and enquire after Hinde's secret new life, as they were already late and the flight to Hong Kong was not going to wait.)

14

I was so delighted with Tonio's arrival that I did my utmost to include him in my good cheer right from the start. Music was part of that. I squatted with the two- or three-week-old infant in front of one of my stereo speakers, which screeched out Bach's oboe concerto. The volume was turned up high, but the little fellow didn't seem to mind. He had just been fed, and I shouldered him until a sourish burp erupted on my neck. If Bach's slow movements helped Chinese women during delivery, then they would also be good for a baby's digestion. Tonio wore a satisfied expression, a smile appeared to form on his relaxed little face.

The ritual of crouching together next to the speaker while gently rocking the baby accommodated a wide range of music. When my thigh muscles started to quiver, I would straighten up and dance across the room with him in my arms. At times, he almost floated in mid-air, the tiny body supported by and balancing on my fingertips alone. If the music (a menuet, for instance) suggested it, I would swing Tonio from side to side as wide as my arms would reach. And then up above my head ... back down, nice and low ... make a dip ... and then swoop back up ...

I danced as though under a spell (and I might have drunk some wine at dinner, too). I assumed the baby was just as content being flung about in my arms as he was resting on my thighs in front of the speaker. Until once, in my ecstasy, I did not close my eyes, and looked straight at Tonio's face. With every upward scoop, his expression was transformed into a chubby little mask of fear, complete with downward-curling mouth and wide-open eyes. God knows how often he'd worn that expression of terror without my noticing.

I immediately quit swinging and swaying and held the little boy gently against me. 'Oh, how stupid of me, my sweet Tonio, to fling you around like that ... Sorry, sorry.'

He did not cry, and his face had pretty much reverted to its relieved post-feeding look. It would be months before I dared dance with him again, and from then on I held him timorously tight. I would not soon shake the memory of that scrunched-up, agonised little head. I never told Miriam, and nearly brought it up now, in the courtyard of the ICU.

'Minchen, I just thought of something … a snippet from the past …'

'As long as it's not about Tonio,' she said. 'Not now, I can't handle it.'

'Yeah … never mind. Another time.'

It was difficult to hang onto that memory, because I suddenly saw Tonio's agonised *adult* face appear on the shady side of the courtyard. It had the same look as the infant in the summer of '88: the trembling around the eyes and mouth, the reddening cheeks, the expression of a boy in his death throes. Only this time he did not sail toward the ceiling in my arms, but was flung, together with his bike, over the front end of an unexpected oncoming vehicle and, further on, lurched across the roof of the car.

CHAPTER FOUR

The schoolhouse

1

'Let's go back to the waiting room,' I said to Miriam. 'Hinde will never find us here.'

The walled courtyard was making us more and more claustrophobic, but that cubby-hole, where the air was heavy with old coffee (forever associated with Tonio's birth) was no better. Hinde had not yet arrived. The clock above the door showed half past twelve.

2

During Tonio's first year, I did a good job of maintaining a stable day-to-day existence, dedicating life and work to my small family. Alarmingly, however, the managers of Huize Oldenhoeck, the brothers Warners (or, as we called them, The Warner Brothers of the Amsterdam School), contrary to their promise not to unload the apartment building designed by their uncle, had turned it over to a management company. From then on, every vacant flat was drastically renovated, stripped of every ornament that referred back to the original 1924 Amsterdam School interior, and then let to a new resident at three times the original price — preferably a member of the *corps diplomatique* stationed around Museumplein, because those folks paid no attention to the price and never stayed longer than a year, after which the rent could be hiked up once again for the next consul general or his right-hand man.

The high turnover rate in Huize Oldenhoeck meant there were always a couple of flats being renovated at any given time. In the lift or the stairwell (from which they hadn't yet ripped out the dark purple marble), I encountered, more often than not, a grey-dusted man dressed in a denim suit and cowboy hat: the project supervisor and, I found out later, one of the new managers.

'I'd never buy a second-hand car from him' is often used to describe an untrustworthy person. Well, I wouldn't take any car from this dungareed cowboy, not even if he paid me. Although younger than me, he had those deep grooves between his nostrils and the corners of his mouth that gave him the expression of a sad wolf; he could look at you as sympathetic and guilt-ridden as you please, his head cocked slightly to one side like a dog trying to figure out what his owner is saying. If I complained about the construction noise, explaining that I worked at home, he cringed with servility. The man had a guilty conscience, and took full advantage of it. He offered me fawning, hand-wringing apologies, promising to keep the inconvenience to a minimum. But, of course, nothing changed, except that the cowboy honed in on my Achilles heel. I imagine, in retrospect, how, as soon as I was out of sight he went from grovelling to gloating: he had figured out how to drive the Van der Heijdens from their flat, probably the most desirable in the entire building. Just step up the construction noise.

Yielding in turn to my own guilty conscience, I rented a room on the Kloveniersburgwal, a few doors down from where Miriam and I had been so happy in '84 and '85, so I could work in peace. I convinced myself (and Miriam) that this was a good a way to keep myself on track. Every morning I took tram 16 there, but the only thing I achieved was an overwhelming restlessness. Wielding scissors, glue and sheets of A3-sized construction paper, I fashioned a comprehensive montage of my notes for the new novel as they had accumulated over the last three years — including cardboard beer mats, which from the side gave the metre-and-a-half high document a decidedly wavy form. I kidded myself into believing that I could, on the basis of this rough but strictly ordered material, transfer a definitive version directly to the typewriter.

The higher the beer-mat draft, the more paralysing my ergasiophobia. Beyond that fussing with scissors and tape, my work amounted to nothing. Yes, I wrote erotic letters as a warm-up exercise for the 'real work'. (Admittedly, passages from those epistles did find their way, much later, into the novel.) I had more or less doubled our living expenses and halved my responsibilities as paterfamilias and breadwinner. At home, Miriam and the baby were at the mercy of the management cowboy. When I left the Kloveniersburgwal in the late afternoon, I did not always follow the 'responsible' route to the tram stop in front of the Bijenkorf. More and more often I cut hurriedly through the red-light district in the direction of the Spui and its cafés.

So the spring of '89 plodded along in a sort of padded emptiness. Restiveness reigned. Where had my choice for the 'everyday', unobtrusive life as husband and father gone wrong? Café visits hardly ever resulted in anything spectacular except for the liquor bill.

3

As hot as it was, Miriam trembled quietly and rhythmically — something in between a shiver and a shudder. As far as her shaking head would allow, she focused on a point on the floor in front of her, like you do when you're nauseous and the room is spinning and you're determined not to throw up.

'Minchen, I've just thought of something … That work space on the Kloveniers back in '89, that was a big mistake.'

Miriam did not look up, did not answer.

'I was so disillusioned. Huize Oldenhoeck, happily settling into that enormous apartment with you and Tonio, I had set my sights on it. Just like you did. And suddenly that goon with his Stetson and sledgehammer. Remember him?'

Miriam nodded, but it wasn't clear whether she was really listening.

'I understand my own disenchantment,' I continued, 'but that was no excuse to take refuge in bars, to miss out on so many evenings with Tonio ... that magical hour before he went to bed ... how he bonk-bonk-bonked over to me on his knees and elbows when I came into the hall. Always laughing.'

Miriam laid her hand on my thigh and gave it a weak squeeze. 'Don't torture yourself,' she said softly.

4

In mid-June 1989, I took a taxi to the Kloveniersburgwal. The lease was up as of 1 July. I had loaded my things into the boot, with the exception of the collage of notes, which I preferred to keep with me on the back seat. As I carried it down the stone steps, I only realised then how heavy all that glue made it.

I wanted the kind of vacation I imagined at the close of a working year: easy-going, without alcoholic bacchanals or daredevilry on motorboats and water skis. Tender togetherness with my little family, from sun to shade and back again. Occasional swimming or walking. Nothing more outlandish than a bottle of cold rosé at lunch under a parasol. Musing on the work that would resume after the summer ... finally, writing with fountain pen again instead of a glue stick ...

Agreeable visions, but it was Miriam who went in search of a house in France to rent for six weeks. She found a former *maison d'école* in the Dordogne, near the medieval town of Monpazier. The house, which belonged to the borough of Marsalès (all of its older residents had gone to school there), was not far from a campground popular with Dutch families. There was an artificial swimming pond with a sandy beach where Tonio could play. Couldn't get more low-key than this, and it was exactly what we had in mind. What *I* had in mind, at least.

We travelled by bus, which left from Stadionplein in Amsterdam in the early morning. At the back of the coach was a storage area for bicycles. Miriam had brought her bike, with child seat: this way we'd be more mobile with Tonio, who had just celebrated his first birthday and who had only now started experimenting with walking on his own.

I had negotiated a double-wide seat at the back of the bus with the tour leaders (that is, the two alternating drivers) so that I could stretch out on the folded-down seat backs with Tonio at night.

After an hour-and-a-half of sleep, Tonio sat straight up. The coach raced, far too fast for my liking, through the French night. His eyes wide open, dummy sucked tightly into his mouth, Tonio kept his gaze fixed on the front windscreen at the end of the aisle. Through it, the world came rushing toward us at full speed: dizzying shadow patterns, the headlights of oncoming traffic, the dotted lines of the street lamps bending every which way … his tiny body heaved and rolled with the shock absorbers. Leaning back and supporting myself on the palms of my hands, I wound my legs lightly around Tonio to prevent him from taking a tumble during unexpected curves. He gazed greedily, curiously, but cautiously as well and even a tiny bit frightened. Sometimes, he turned his head briefly and questioningly in my direction, as though asking me to explain this wildly careering bedroom full of strangers.

'Okay, little fella, now it's time to go to sleep.'

Every time I gently nudged him down, he bounced back up like a jack-in-the-box, his big eyes glued to the windscreen. He simply had to keep looking.

Perhaps I underestimated the fearfulness of a one-year-old. It prevented me from getting any shuteye myself. Of course bus accidents always happened to other people (who, according to the tour operators responsible, were 'at the wrong place at the wrong time'), but never to us. But the drivers also were putting in long hours, without a break, I'd sussed that out by now. Pit stops at a roadside restaurant consisted of the off-duty driver shunting the passengers to and from the toilets, while his colleague waited at the wheel of the purring and palpitating bus with its oversized tyres. This, in combination with the breakneck speed, did considerably cut down on travel time, while the drivers still earned their complete wage.

Tonio and I spent most of the night awake. I watched him, and he never once took his eyes off the teeming motorway. Gradually the dummy came into action; it had been clamped firmly in his jaw and I had to prise it out of his mouth in order to give him his bottle of water. His sucking meant he was relaxing. Tonio's eyelids started drooping just as it began to get light above the hills on the eastern horizon. By the time the sun was visible, Tonio was fast asleep. I laid him carefully between my legs. The jack-in-the-box mechanism had shut down. He slept until we arrived in Marsalès. Daybreak was apparently the sign to his small, frightened soul that the danger of night had subsided.

Damn it, Tonio, how I wish that early this morning, before daybreak on the Stadhouderskade, I could have mustered up the same vigilance as back then.

5

'What a horrible complex. Huge.' Hinde rushed into the room. 'I got totally lost.'

She was pale, her eyes wide with fear. 'To start with, the taxi driver set me off at the wrong entrance.'

She held a pack of cigarettes. 'Yeah, I just had to have smokes. Otherwise I'd never make it through the day.'

I suggested going back outside so she could light one up. But before we made a move to leave, the sisters fell tearfully into each other's arms.

The courtyard, an open terrace built atop a lower floor of the hospital, radiated the heat of the noonday sun. A perfect Whit Sunday. We sat on a bench between the planters, but before long we all felt that the sun was too strong. There were some outdoor chairs further up. We dragged them into the shade. The sun continued to reflect intensely from the light-grey paving stones, large windows and gravel-cement planters.

'Gotta do this today,' Hinde said, lighting a cigarette. Soon thereafter the young nurse hurried over to us. My heart clenched. I felt on my shoulder how Miriam stiffened, gasping for breath. That the nurse came charging at us like that, her blonde hair flapping in the sun, could only mean that there was news, bad news.

'Ma'am,' she said, panting slightly, 'you're not allowed to smoke here.'

'I don't normally,' said Hinde. 'It's just that my nerves ... this whole mess ...'

'I really do understand,' the young woman replied, 'but this is a no-smoking area, no matter what. So please ...'

'I'll put it out.'

Poor Hinde. She was forbidden even this one transgression in her new life. The nurse headed back — no longer running, but more like trotting — to the glass door, back to Tonio's sedated hell.

6

We were dropped off at the campground reception, which was run by the Dutch couple who rented us the *maison décole*. We'd be taken to the house later in a minivan once it was available, but for now we could wait at the campground's outdoor café. The bus drivers were already there. Instead of having a lie-down they went straight for large glasses of Heineken from the tap, while the departing campground guests dragged their luggage to the coach, which would leave in an hour's time for the Netherlands — with the same two drivers at the wheel.

Miriam and I were draped over our chairs with sleep deprivation, but the café itself was abuzz. Two girls of around ten, one a bit bigger than the other, descended with squeals of excitement upon Tonio, who couldn't really walk yet and tried to keep himself standing by grasping table legs and chair backs. No problem: the little ladies took turns lifting him from the ground and carrying him, happy as could be, hither and thither. A real-life baby doll, with a real-life full nappy, no less — their holiday enjoyment was sealed. Only a pity that there weren't two of these golden-locked cherubs.

Meanwhile, a distinguished-looking, white-haired older man appeared on the scene carrying a camera. I had already spotted him when we arrived: he had probably gone back to his tent to fetch his camera. He approached our table, almost quaking with emotion, and pathetically beseeched us if he could take a picture of Tonio.

'Honest to goodness,' he said hoarsely, 'I have never seen such a beautiful child. I simply *must* photograph him.'

'Go on then, just one,' I said.

The man commanded the little girl who had just lifted Tonio up over her head to put him on the ground. He clamped himself to her leg and smiled at the camera, just as he'd been taught. The photographer, in all his creakiness, threw himself to his knees in front of Tonio and took a close-up. He groaned, but I suspect it had nothing to do with his uncomfortable position, because he kept on clicking. He shifted his knees.

'Such a beautiful child,' he cried. 'I just can't get over it.'

Miriam and I glanced at each other. I got up, went over to the man and said, while laying a hand on his shoulder: 'That's probably enough, sir. Why don't we let the girls play with him now?'

I helped him up. He was teary-eyed. Another photo of Tonio, who was back in the arms of the other little girl.

'If you'll just give me your address,' the man said, 'I can send you a few prints. Here's a pen.'

I felt the sleepless night buzzing through my head. Was I seeing danger at every turn? Was the whole world out to threaten Tonio?

'Later,' I said. 'We've only just arrived.'

'That's just it,' said the man. 'I'm just about to go back to Amsterdam with the bus.'

'Then if I might give you a bit of advice,' I said, 'keep an eye out that the drivers take enough rests.'

Another Dutch campground guest rescued me, taking me for the Dutch writer and former chess champion Tim Krabbé. 'I've always wanted to play chess with you,' he said. 'Can I invite you for a game tonight? Here on the terrace. I've got everything with me. A timer, too.'

7

The girls were the Van Persie sisters from Rotterdam. Lily (nine) and Kiki (going on twelve). They were staying at the campground with their divorced mother and younger brother Robin, who was just about to turn six.* It was mostly Lily, with her broad mouth and uncombed curls, who took Tonio under her wing, and with a gusto I had seldom seen in a girl that age. As soon as she laid eyes on Tonio, she would insist he be removed from his pushchair. She agreed to stay within sight of us, his parents, as she carried the tyke to and fro, but refused to give him back. Tonio was too heavy for her girlish body; he kept sliding down her chest, and Lily would then shimmy him back up as far as he'd go. With any luck, Tonio would throw his arms around her neck, giving her a bit of extra grip.

Tonio loved all the attention and cuddling. With his head up close to Lily's, his laugh was broad and drooly, and he panted with flirtatiousness. And the important thing was: he and Lily were on the same wavelength. It was as though, their heads close together, they were continually in conversation.

Lily had the distinct misfortune that Tonio learned to walk during those first weeks of the holiday. As soon as he realised that his place was down there with both feet on the ground, he would thrash wildly in Lily's arms until she gingerly set him down — and not just in the hard grass, where he'd soon plop onto his rear, but near a large object, a table or chair, which he could hold onto as he walked around it. Best of all were the

---

* Robin van Persie would later become a well-known soccer player and a member of the Dutch national team, and is at present a star striker for Manchester United.

metal supports of his stroller, because they had wheels — he was mobile.

Kiki and Lily often showed up at the schoolhouse early in the morning, while we were still eating breakfast, to ooh and aah in admiration as Tonio's mother pushed dice of Laughing Cow soft cheese into his mouth. Soon enough the girls were allowed to unwrap the foil themselves and feed Tonio the bite-sized cheese cubes. His eyes sparkled, his drool became milky from the white cheese. All we had to do was watch out he didn't get overfed.

Sometimes the sisters brought their little brother Robin with them, who never spoke and always wore an angry little pout. After breakfast, Tonio resumed his walking lessons behind the stroller under the tutelage of Lily and Kiki. He was now between thirteen and fourteen months old.

In my recollection, I see Robin leaning up against the outside of the schoolhouse, one foot up against the wall. Surly and haughty, he watches the movements of the toddler, who enjoys his sisters' full attention. I sit at the picnic table under the apple tree, pretending to be absorbed in yesterday's already yellowed newspaper, but I cannot take my eyes off the scene before me. Tonio has the tendency to push a bit faster than the wheels can furrow through the rough grass, so that he leans back slightly and easily falls over. He's got the hand-grips firmly in his fists, above his head, so that as he topples over backwards he pulls the pushchair on top of himself.

'Oof.' The girls rush to prop him back up. At Tonio's eye level is a shopping net, strung onto the frame by an elastic cord, with tissues and extra Pampers. Every time he falls over backwards, the nylon netting falls over Tonio's face, like a loosely woven veil, and he doesn't like it much. Not much time for crying, though: practice makes perfect. His dismay is limited to a brief whine while his fingers tug at the butterfly net. Kiki and Lily leap to the rescue. Lily takes advantage of the situation by scooping Tonio up and nuzzling him. He tries to wriggle away: there's work to be done.

Robin's stance hovers between childish contempt (pff, he can't even walk) and an equally childish jealousy (my sisters don't give me the time of day, but they're all over that clumsy sprog). He, Robin, is not only good at walking, fast and slow, but he can creep, jump and climb, too. 'Robin's problem is,' says Kiki superciliously, imitating her mother, 'that he has no concept of danger.'

Tonio is back up on his feet, and screeches as he pushes the stroller. Again he's learned something new: he wrenches and jerks the stroller over a stubborn tuft of grass and walks on. The girls follow him with arms extended, prepared to catch him should he fall.

I am worried about the fearsomely large wasps here; they fly close to the ground, as though they're too heavy for their wispy wings. They look savage, and I imagine their stinger dripping with poison. I have already chopped one in half with a breakfast knife; it was pestering Tonio and I thought I was giving it a quick, painless death. Horrified, I saw how both halves stayed alive: the front half propped itself up on its wings, the back half — call it the weapon-wielding half — wobbled off, carrying the defeated stinger with the remaining legs.

'If you want, Robin,' I say in an attempt to include the boy in the adventure, 'you can keep an eye on those big wasps to see they don't fly near Tonio and your sisters. They're much scarier than the ones we've got back home.'

Robin doesn't answer. When I glance up from the paper a while later, Tonio and his entourage have already reached the other side of the yard. Robin is nowhere to be seen.

8

Four nurses filed from the corridor through the open glass doors into the courtyard. Two men and two women. They each carried a full cafeteria tray. Lunchtime. After blinking for a moment into the bright sunlight, they opt unanimously for a table in the sun.

'Life goes on, of course,' Hinde said. 'No matter *what's* happening inside.'

The nurses occupied a table some distance from us, but as it was otherwise so quiet in the courtyard I could clearly pick up snippets of their conversation. They spent some time quoting large sums in euros, the estimate ranging from two-and-a-half to three million.

'Say there's ten thousand staff, including partners,' said one of the men. 'That still comes out to 250 to 300 per person.'

'But for that amount you get Marco Borsato's cute bum,' one of the female nurses said.

'Don't forget Karin Bloemen's cute bum,' said the other man. 'And they call it a cold buffet.'

'*And* the Mart Visser catwalk,' said the second woman.

'I still think it's weird,' the first man continued. 'It's always cutbacks, cutbacks, cutbacks. And then they go and rent a whole convention centre for ten thousand of us.'

'Jesus, Jan, you really are a killjoy,' said the Marco Borsato's-bum woman. 'It's the AMC's twenty-fifth anniversary. Can't they throw a proper party for once? I've been here for twelve years and till now it's been a dry house.'

9

Twice since Tonio was very young (one and almost three years old), I have been pursued by obsessive visions concerning his safety.

Once, during that summer of '89, when we rented the schoolhouse in Marsalès, I took him out on the bicycle. I placed him in the child seat up front for what was perhaps the most wonderful and intimate day I had ever spent with him. Our destination was Biron Castle, but first we took a spin around the country roads, hardly bothered by any traffic. Tonio was getting on to 14 months, and his still-golden-blond curls fluttered right under my nose. I only had to tip my head down slightly in order to feel and smell his warm crown. Coasting downhill, a light breeze wafted through his hair. Only as noon approached did I put on his little white cap with the wavy edges, tying the lace under his chin, to keep him from getting sunstroke.

Earlier that summer, I had taught him the words 'cow' by pointing at the black-coated cattle, as always adorned with large yellow plastic earrings, on the grassy slopes. Until now, no cows had shown themselves along our route. We cycled through the fields, which were scattered with large rolled-up bales of hay, either as refuse or harvest by-product. Occasionally, Tonio would point a wet finger at one of the rolls, calling out with a thin voice, more sound than word: 'owww ... owww!'

Back in Amsterdam, I read a harrowing newspaper article about exactly the kind of child-seat we had used for Tonio in France. Designed for the flat Dutch landscape, it was attached to the handlebars by two U-shaped steel brackets, and was kept in place by its own weight. But on a steep downhill gradient, it had been shown, the seat could easily lurch out of place and hurl its infant passenger into the air. There was a particularly high rate of such accidents that summer in France, a traditional destination for Dutch cycling families.

To cycle from our schoolhouse in Marsalès to the lake, one had to go down quite a steep incline — Miriam, if she had Tonio with her, would always get off and walk, not because of the child's seat but because she didn't trust her own braking. That summer day, for our outing to the Château de Biron, I felt confident taking Tonio down that hill in his kiddie seat. I rode Miriam's bike. It was new, the rubber brake blocks were not yet worn. Still, as we whizzed down the hill, I felt a kind of tugging below that I didn't quite have under control. Tonio, confidently delivered into my care, was delighted with the speed and cooed ecstatically with outstretched arms.

I was relieved to reach the bottom, where the road levelled off along the lake. Nothing serious had happened, but after reading the article about the child seats I couldn't shake the image of Tonio being flung through the air. I played and replayed his fall, down to the minutest detail: how his body rolled alongside the bike, his golden locks smeared with blood and guts. The thought could creep up on me in the middle of the day, without any apparent reason, while I was working or telling a completely unrelated anecdote in the café. ('Well? And then? Now that it's finally getting interesting, the cat's got your tongue.') The obsessive visions had not ebbed in the ensuing twenty years. Since this morning it's been playing up continually, more intrusively than before, as though my irresponsibility back then ultimately contributed to Tonio's accident.

10

The blonde nurse returned, this time unhurriedly, greeting her colleagues as she passed them. They were busy collecting the remains of their lunch on the trays.

'Can I get you something to eat?' she asked, looking from me to Miriam and Hinde. 'They'll be busy with him for some time yet ...'

'Shall we share a cheese sandwich?' I suggested to Miriam. 'I don't think I can stomach much more than that.'

Miriam said nothing, only shook her head, looking down at the ground in front of her feet.

'I'll bring a little of everything,' the nurse said. 'How about some milk?'

I nodded. The week before I had read somewhere that a glass of milk takes the edge off garlic breath. On her way back to the corridor, the nurse stopped to exchange a word with her colleagues, before walking ahead of them toward the glass doors.

11

The other obsessive thought had to do with the Makelaarsbrug over the Oudezijds Voorburgwal in Amsterdam. It must have been springtime, perhaps closer to summer, because the ducks in the canal weren't constantly surrounded by their brood. The remaining ducklings were already partly grown. I had taken Tonio out of his stroller and walked with him onto the pedestrian footbridge. Brilliant sunlight from a sparklingly blue sky.

'Look, Tonio, the duckies.'

Just then, a mother duck swam with her young from under the bridge into the lacy shadows a tree cast over the water. I sat Tonio on the bridge railing. Under his weight a bit of air hissed from his fresh nappy. I held him tight, leaning him forward a bit to give him a good view of the ducks. He pointed, and babbled, and drooled.

'Big Italian eyes.'

A man's voice, suddenly close by. I got a fright, like when the sudden appearance of another person can startle you in the solitary intimacy of a room. It paralysed me just for a moment, but long enough for my knees to wobble and my arm to relax. I almost let Tonio's little body slip out of my grasp. I wrestled him from the railing and held him weakly against my body. Next to me, the smiling, long-time-no-see face of a colleague. The man touched Tonio's curls and said: 'Those eyes. He looks just like ...'

He mentioned the name of an actor from the movie *Moonstruck*, and continued on his way. I remember standing there rigidly for quite some time, with Tonio squirming in my arms. He wanted back on the railing. What could have happened flashed through my mind. You're startled, the child slips out of your arms. A splash among the ducklings. The father rushing down the stairs of the bridge ... jumping into the canal, desperately feeling around the place where the little boy went under ...

This obsessive image, too, stuck with me for the next twenty years. It could rear its head at any moment, not only at hazardous moments in Tonio's life. The vision, ironically enough, sometimes offered salvation in the partly inflated nappy, which, like Donald Duck's backside, bobbed up to the water's surface like a life vest.

CHAPTER FIVE

In love against

Krikkrak Locksmiths: 24-hour service, repair and replacement locks. Specialised in master keys, broken teeth, night bolts, key copy, etc. No call-out fee. Complimentary key ring.

From *Yellow Pages* 1992 (Amsterdam and vicinity)

1

I was still living in the Duivelseiland neighbourhood, but it appeared that my marriage's nosedive had come to a halt.

The madness of the annual Book Week was behind us. Now that I increasingly kept to myself in my work flat, still living out of my father's East Indies suitcase, it was Miriam who more often took the initiative. She would leave a message on my answering machine, only if to express her disgust at the crooning '*Hello, how are you ...?*' of the Electric Light Orchestra, which served as the intro to my own brief spoken instruction: 'After Mister Beep'. (A pun on a character from *A Room with a View*, a film Miriam and I had seen in better days — a reference I hoped would not elude her. Once pushed into a corner, one never passes up the chance to drop a hint, however subtle.)

Newsworthy matters aside: she occasionally invited me out for a drink in one of our former hangouts. She'd bring me a small gift, a CD or a bound writing book, and was so sweet to me that the onlookers — well aware of the extent of our crisis — prematurely concluded that we had made up. Once, with our glasses still as good as full, she tugged me away from the table: 'Come on.'

I could barely keep up with her, such was her tempo, over two bridges, left, right, until reaching Leidsegracht 22, where she seduced me on the living-room sofa (and not in bed). I was simply being forced to fulfil the marital duty from which I thought I'd been honourably discharged some weeks earlier. Afterwards, she was in a hurry to fetch Tonio from the crèche. I wasn't allowed to join her. Not a chance. I thought I savvied what was going on: now that she had so unexpectedly let herself go, she could at least use Tonio as leverage. I asked Miriam how things stood with us. 'You know ... between you and me.'

'I don't know,' she said. 'I'm still very much in love.'

We said our goodbyes at the edge of the canal.

'Say something nice to Tonio,' I said. 'Something sweet, for me. I don't want him to forget me.'

Left, right, over two bridges: I hurried back to the café, where in our haste we hadn't paid for the drinks. They were still there on the table — tepid, but drinkable. As I forced them down, something began to dawn on me. This infatuation of hers ... she was using it as a parry. Suddenly, in the costly clarity of post-coitus, I realised she wasn't so much in love *with* someone else as in love *against me*.

2

The next time she called, I answered. That is, the volume on the answering machine was turned up, the *'Hello, how are you ...'* sounded sickly and crackly, and after Mister Beep, Miriam's voice resonated through the room.

'Adri, just answer ... I know you're there. Adri?'

I removed the receiver and shut off the answering machine. 'You're in love against me,' I said.

'Oh?'

'Not with him — against me.'

'Does that exist?'

'You invented it.'

'Gosh, without even knowing.'

'There is another kind of *in love against*.'

'Nothing would surprise me anymore.'

'In love with each other, and together in love against the world.'

'Doesn't sound bad.'

'Shall we then?'

'I'll think about it.'

3

In love against. Now that I knew what I didn't know back then, and knew that Miriam knew what I didn't know back then, I can almost muster up some compassion for my rival. Our Man in Africa had served, even during his absence, primarily as a shield with which to deflect Miriam's weapon against me.

I left my Procrustean bed on Duivelseiland and moved back in with Miriam and Tonio on the Leidsegracht, even though for the time being I had to make do with the living-room sofa. I was not granted much sleep, for at the crack of dawn Tonio would come to claim his place. Sometimes I would awaken in response to his mere presence. I would open my eyes, and there the nearly four-year-old stood, eyeing me earnestly, stuffed animals and security blankets under his arm, a dummy between his lips that swung up and down in his mouth with the regularity and speed of an engine's piston. If his piercing gaze did not wake me, he would think of something, the corner of a teething rag or the fluffy tail of his monkey, with which to tickle me under my nose, until I got up, groaning, and relinquished half of the sofa to him. Together we would watch an episode of *The Big Mister Cactus Show* on video.

In fact, Our Man in Africa — also known as The Borderless

Correspondent — was, in the course of the whole unpleasant business, conspicuously absent — which did not lessen the imminence of his return.

'Adri, I want to close this book in style,' Miriam said one Thursday afternoon. 'If you go out tomorrow evening, do me a favour and for once don't go to one of your usual hangouts. During the hostilities I always *loved* bumping into you unexpectedly at Tartufo, Schiller, and De Favoriet. But not now. Okay?'

Upon further questioning, I learned that Our Man would be in the country very briefly, for just over a week, before flying back to the regions of Africa where the borders, to the chagrin (or delight) of the publishers of world atlases, could shift at any moment. Now that Miriam was no longer *in love against* her husband, the necessity of being *in love with* the correspondent was negated, and she wanted to relay this message 'in style', via a kind of farewell dinner.

Just to be sure — 'I'm not going to reserve anywhere' — she rattled off a whole list of cafés and eateries I would do best to avoid this Friday. 'It's painful enough as it is.'

Now that my rival had been vanquished, it did not require much self-sacrifice to grant him one last date with my wife. 'If need be, Minchen, I'll go to Haarlem for the evening. Or, if that's still too close for comfort, to Antwerp.'

4

I complied almost slavishly with Miriam's request (or command) not to show my face in the neighbourhood where she might rendezvous with her journalist. Accompanied by one of the 'regular girls' who had helped me through those lonely months, I did a pub crawl until the wee hours (Brouwersgracht quarter) where I would otherwise have never set foot. After all these years I can't remember who it was — Ilke or Adriënne or Bernadette — but I do recall her being offended by my extreme ebullience, because she could see it had nothing to do with her company. Even when

I looked into her eyes, I beheld the vision of a new future.

Damn, what a woman, that Miriam: how she, with chilling subtlety, managed to blackmail me into mending my ways with her deceptive strategy of being 'in love against' me. Far more effective than kicking me out of the house or charging at me with a blunt object.

By now it was two, half past two. I sat it out. After eating and Dropping the Bomb, they might have gone to Schiller to talk it out over drinks, but under these circumstances they'd never have made it to De Favoriet or another late-night pub. Miriam must be home by now.

I remember delivering Ilke or Adriënne or Bernadette to her front door, wherever that was. There is a vague recollection of the offer of a nightcap — no thanks, I'll be getting along now. I probably did not mention that my old life, now irreparably improved, was waiting for me at home. She had taken it away from me, but not for good, and in the meantime it had only appreciated in value.

5

It was three in the morning. I had a spring in my step, like a freed prisoner. Took the stone steps up to the front door in two, three bounds.

I assumed I had taken the wrong key from my pocket, the one to my flat in Duivelseiland, because it didn't fit. The teeth glanced off a shiny new cylinder lock that had taken the place of the old, dull one. The copper plate maliciously reflected my fingers holding the useless key. Around it, some of the canal-green paint had been chipped off, undoubtedly during the replacement, and these chips now lay at my feet among some wood splinters and two minuscule piles of sawdust. Apparently no one had walked through it yet. The new lock must just have been installed. I stood there, half paralysed, looking incredulously at the paint chips, the splinters and the sawdust. Once again, everything was turning out differently than I had been led to believe. So this was what being *in love against* could lead to. The fatal blow, right behind my ear.

I trudged down the steps and walked backwards as far as possible across the street, to the edge of the canal. I nearly had to pull my chin upward with my hand before I dared look. There was light in the sitting room, whose white curtains were drawn — which usually meant, at this late hour, that someone was home.

And there *was* someone at home. A Chinese shadow play was being projected against the white pleats, two wavy figures approaching each other. It was just like an old Hollywood film, with a private eye crouching behind a garbage can and the husband leaning against a streetlamp, nervously smoking and sprouting horns. The two figures stopped for a moment, and then wrinkled intimately through one another. My wife and the Borderless Correspondent, no doubt: I recognised Miriam by the terraced way she put up her hair, whose contours did not get lost in the shadow play.

Goddamn it, how could I have let myself be fobbed off to a distant neighbourhood, so that they could, undisturbed, carry out their plan to shut me out once and for all? Someone this naïve did not deserve any better.

And then: well well, a third silhouette appeared. Tall, masculine, with a large head cut off by the top of the window frame. An object was passed from one outstretched shadow-hand to another.

Ach, Minchen, Minchen, it didn't have to come to this. My Friday night bliss shot to hell, the bliss that wasn't to be mine. And Miriam? She had simply dragged in the happiness that hadn't just come naturally, and changed the locks behind her. No cutting corners.

But why such a roundabout charade? She could have just left me, which would have been bad enough. Why add insult to injury with such hard, durably executed symbols? Not to mention the after-hours surcharge. Slamming the door in someone's face was apparently not enough these days. If the poor sucker locked outside had the skin of an elephant and stayed waiting patiently for someone to open the door, then he could just see how a fine drill bit bored through the wood …

Meanwhile, damn it, I stood there in front of a locked door, which meant that I had underestimated the wiles of the other party after all.

Perhaps I had clung too much to the notion that Miriam was out of love with *me*, rather than *in love* with him, the other. The possibility that she was about to break off with Our Man in Africa did not mean I was automatically back in her good graces. It was my misjudgement to think that this whole 'in love against' thing was in itself something temporary. I no longer ruled out the prospect that she was so totally and fanatically *out of love* with me, and that, regardless of any other man, I was being unceremoniously dumped, right here on her front stoop.

6

I was reminded of a morning shortly after Tonio was born. Up early, I looked over at Miriam, my sleeping treasure, in the early morning daylight. Entirely unexpectedly, in a kind of wavelike slinking motion, her hand crept over the bottom sheet toward my head. A five-legged creature. Near my chin she scratched the light-blue fabric with her index finger, emphatically, as though she were trying to warn me of something, or wanted to gently wake me up to put an end to my snoring.

I wasn't snoring, nor was there any danger of it either, as far as I can recall. The hand, its fingers dirtied with an excess of pigment, pulled back, but quickly scampered back to resume its scratching.

'Minchen ...?'

I had to repeat her name a few times before she answered with a soft groan, from way down deep. She slept on. Except for her hand, which kept creeping toward my face, again and again, to resume the scratching. I did not know what it meant, but the gesture was strangely moving. Later, when she was feeding the baby, I imitated her manual drill, but she did not believe me.

Those funny things of hers I'd never see again. Not to mention all the wonderful things Tonio would do that would likewise be denied me from now on. Like just recently, when he raised a finger and called out:

'There come the knights!'

I went back up the steps of the stoop and rang the bell. In the still of the night you could always hear it ring upstairs. But not now. Of course, when we went out, Miriam would usually turn off the bell so as not to startle the cats, but now that she was apparently home, its off-ness could only mean yet another way for me to be shut out, shunned.

I wailed her name through the letter slot, perhaps more as a farewell than an attempt to elicit mercy. More or less at once, the upstairs door to the stairwell opened and I heard the downward cadence of footsteps.

In retrospect I have to conclude that those quick steps, Miriam's trotting downstairs, said it all: that we belonged together, and would stay together. That patter on the steps meant that my feelings were not to be hurt. She arrived, out of breath, to welcome me back. A fresh start, but this time a level higher.

She was almost there. I knelt at the door, my eyes level with the letter slot, my thumb holding the flap open.

'Adri, it's not what you think,' she called out.

It was not what I thought. The door swung open. (I don't know why, but I was reminded of the first time she opened a door for me. I stood on her front step with a bottle of Dimple whisky under my arm. 'I never drink whisky.' — 'Madam, I never eat muscatel grapes.')*

'First tell me what I *do* think.' (If it could be everything I *didn't* think, that would be enough to quieten the hell.)

'Come upstairs and I'll explain.' Her face was so overcome by embarrassment that I almost felt sorry for her. 'Don't just stand there.'

'I don't know what I'll find upstairs.'

'I'll explain everything.'

Her chagrin reversed the roles. At first, I was planning to play the injured party and skulk off, but in the end I followed her up the stairs, determined to make a scene.

---

* A line from *The Count of Monte Cristo* spoken by the hero, Dantès (the count of the title), claiming that he cannot eat any food in the house of his enemy.

I could hear men's firm voices through the open door to the flat. I held back on the landing to listen. I could have been mistaken, but it sounded like the discussion was about hinges and door furniture in medieval churches — not exactly a subject related to Africa.

The living room was vaguely changed, although I couldn't put my finger on it. When I entered the room, the conversation fell silent. My rival got up from the sofa, or better said: he leapt up, startled. When I extended my arm to shake hands, he jerked his head sideways, as though he expected a punch. Fortunately, he realised his mistake quickly enough that my well-meant gesture didn't fall completely flat.

The tall man, who until now I had only observed as a Chinese shadow puppet, knelt on the rug beside an open tool bag. He started digging around in the bag, maybe to avoid having to shake hands.

'Have the gentlemen been offered drinks?' I asked Miriam.

She pointed to the long-drink glasses on the coffee table.

'Who'll join me for a vodka?' I said.

The kneeling man, in overalls, declined. Our Man in Africa acquiesced with a sheepish nod.

Out of the corner of my eye, I could see how the first man fished two elongated objects out of his bag, and started screwing them together. That was the only thing missing in this farce. A silencer made sure that it produced no more noise than 'an arrow as it pierces a ripe piece of fruit', as I once read in an old detective novel. The ripe fruit: my head. Rotting and wormy. Full of rusty-brown flesh that oozed out through the holes that had been shot in the peel.

I realised that while killing time in the Brouwersgracht pubs I had become quite drunk.

I watched the tall man. He held an electric drill. He got up and walked over to the front door of the flat, and drilled several holes around the gap where the old cylinder lock had once been.

The scent of sawdust permeated the living room, but I smelled something else, something that had hit me the moment I walked in. Damp cardboard. I looked around the room. There were moving boxes all over, some with their flaps folded open. On each box, an orange cross in a black circle: the stylised pulley block of the ERKENDE VERHUIZERS logo. As long as I kept my eyes glued to that circled cross, my thoughts would organise themselves automatically. What on earth was going on here?

The bookcase behind the sofa on which the Borderless Correspondent sat seemed fuller than before. I might have had a lot to drink but I wasn't seeing double, certainly not double book spines anyway. Just to be sure, I squinted at the bookcase with one eye closed. Damn, there *were* more books, but from this distance I couldn't make out their titles.

Miriam came in with the vodka bottle.

'So,' I said, nodding at the boxes, 'today, treason smells like damp cardboard.'

She had invited me upstairs to augment my humiliation. I had to stand by and watch as the diplomat moved in with her, and colonised my bookcases.

'Don't be an idiot,' Miriam said. 'Those boxes have been up in the attic for the past year-and-a-half. Since 2 December 1990, to be exact, when we can back from Loenen, remember? You were so sick of all the moving that you decided these could stay put for the time being. Yeah? The rest of the books, they could wait. Well, today I finally got around to unpacking. *You* sure weren't going to do it for me.'

8

The locksmith had now installed the bolt to the flat. He tossed his tools into his black leather bag and handed Miriam a stocked key ring. He sat down to draw up the bill.

'Okay, my job here's done.' He handed Miriam the bill. 'No call-out fee.'

I drank another vodka with my rival. *Former* rival, it was now clear.

Miriam saw the locksmith out. Because I did not know what to say to Our Man, I went over to the window. The sky began to change colour. The locksmith put the black bag in the back of his van, which was emblazoned with the name KRIKKRAK in lightning lettering on the side, with a telephone number.

'You were going to explain,' I said to Miriam when she got back upstairs.

Miriam and her correspondent gave me an account, filling in each other's gaps, of their story. Before going to eat at Tartufo they had an aperitif at Café Zeppos on 't Gebed Zonder End. At a certain point Miriam discovered, maybe when she set out to light up her last crisis-cigarette, that her purse had been stolen. 'Just snatched from the back of the chair.' Not that there was much money in it, but worse than that: her house keys. Panicked that the thief would empty the entire building, they picked up the spare keys at Miriam's parents' (where Tonio was asleep in his guest cot) and sat waiting, the deadbolt securely fastened, for the arrival of the key guy. Plenty of 24-hour services in the Yellow Pages, but, when push came to shove, none of them really was open day and night. Finally they had found one: Krikkrak, for all your broken teeth. Miriam had telephoned a few friends to go find me. Of course they looked in the wrong cafés.

So much for the farewell dinner, without a single bite of food. 'As though it were meant to be.'

9

Miriam showed her Special Reporter out — for the last time, let's hope. I listened from the top of the stairs. A brief, inaudible exchange down on the front stoop. A burst of her cheerful, mocking laugh.

The door slammed shut. It could mean two things: that she had stepped over the threshold to follow the Borderless Reporter to the edge of the earth, or …

I was back amid the moving boxes, whose dank odour tickled my bronchial tubes, and listened intently. It was quiet, both in the stairwell and out on the street.

'So what're you standing there for, goofy?' Miriam was carrying her pumps. She must have crept upstairs in her stocking feet. 'Empty 'em, if they're bothering you.'

'So what's the verdict?'

'The verdict is that we're through. It was an impossible situation, tonight proved it all over again. I thought *we* had something, you and me …'

'That's news to me.'

'Well, come here then.'

We stood silently face to face. After a little while she said: 'I was afraid you'd be mad about the stolen purse … the keys … the locksmith … and all you do is moan about the moving boxes! Typical.'

'Learn to live with it.'

'I don't have much choice.'

10

For Miriam, the moving boxes were half empty. For me, half full. And that was the start of refinding our footing after our first major marital crisis.

Half empty: unload the rest of the books.

Half full: there's still room to load more in.

Was it the new locks, in combination with the sudden appearance of the moving boxes, that gave me the idea of roomier living quarters? I had to think long and hard about whether looking for a new house was the right way to reunite my family. De Pijp, the Kloov, Obrechtstraat, the Veluwe, the Pauwhof, Leidsegracht … all this moving had in fact only made us drift gradually apart.

In Huize Oldenhoeck, yes, there she was happy, until Tonio's first birthday. It was the environs of her earliest youth. She was born across the street, in the CIZ, the Centrale Israëlitische Ziekeninrichting — now a Jellinek rehab clinic for addicts. Her native soil. If I wanted to buy a house for her, it had to be here, and nowhere else.

11

'There come the knights.'

A friend had given me a CD of Shostakovich's *Symphony No. 11*. I played it that afternoon for the first time, while Tonio sat in the corner with his Lego. I had never seen a child so engrossed in play before. Off in his own world, as they say.

Somewhere in one of the inner movements the music falls nearly silent, followed by a *forte*, dry roll on the snare drum, and then another, even louder. Tonio leapt up, pulled the dummy out of his mouth and yelled, his arm outstretched: 'There come the knights!'

I have no idea what kind of fairy tale his concentrated Lego-play had criss-crossed, but he stood listening, his face enthralled and spittle hanging off his lower lip, until the snare drum was entirely drowned out by the rest of the orchestra. He planted the dummy back between his lips and dropped to his knees at the pile of Lego. I sat down next to him and asked: 'What was that, Tonio? What did you hear?'

He was completely engrossed in the plastic building bricks. 'Those were the knights,' he said quietly, absently. And as though in a kind of indifferent trance he kept on repeating, ever more softly: 'Those were the knights … the knights …'

12

Ten to five. The neurosurgeon came in first. She was still wearing her light-blue shower cap: the elastic had crept up to the point where it could, at any moment, lose its grip on her hair and flutter to the floor. The last of her two co-assistants closed the door, which had stood open all day, behind her — and then I knew. Tonio was lost.

The surgeon sat down on the short side of the table and looked at Miriam and me in turn. An almost bitter line around her mouth, undoubtedly due to the recent efforts in the OR. Her serious, unintentionally severe gaze eventually rested on me. She shook her head.

'It's not good,' she said hesitantly, followed immediately by: 'We couldn't save him.'

Miriam let out a stream of almost songlike cries. Her head slumped, wobbling, further and further downward, as though she wanted to literally lay it in her lap. With my arm around her shoulders, I pulled her close to me. Her trembling mixed with mine.

'The brain was badly traumatised,' the surgeon continued. 'It continued to swell. First on the right, then the left. Besides, his bodily functions started to fail. The blood pressure plummeted … terrible haemorrhaging … There was no saving him. We had to terminate treatment. He's being brought over to the ICU, so you can say your last goodbyes. He's still on life-support, but that will be stopped shortly.'

Terminal, but not yet dead.

'I want you to know,' I said with a tight voice, 'that we're grateful for all your efforts.'

Even now I was aware, although I didn't smell it myself, of my penetrating garlic breath. I am given the tidings of the imminent death of my son, they are about to unplug his ventilator, and my thoughts dwell on my own bad breath. *Aglio olio.*

The doctor stood up, shook our hands. 'My thoughts are with you.'

I blinked, and felt a cold wetness on my eyelashes and lids, as though old, forgotten tears had lingered there, cooled off long ago. The other women followed the neurosurgeon out of the room. The third doctor leant over to us and said: 'He might still be in the lift on the way here. A nurse will come get you when you can see him. You might want to say goodbye while he's still on the ventilator. Try not to be shocked by his upper body, it's quite swollen. From the internal bleeding.'

I had to play for time. Had to extend his life.

'You're terminating treatment,' I said, repeating the absent surgeon's words.

The woman nodded. 'To carry on would be futile … and irresponsible.'

I had to contain myself. I was in no position to resist this medical decision. (A decision that was already irrevocably determined by the force of the collision, by blindfolded Fate.) This was not a matter of euthanasia. I had to take care not to lose control, to demand that the treatment be prolonged. Those stories are well known. Family members, future next-of-kin, their fists clenched in the doctor's face, the bed in which their loved one lay protected by a human chain from the nurse whose task it was to disconnect the mechanical ventilator.

I nodded back. The doctor smiled sadly and left the room. I had to banish the vain thought of Tonio standing a fighting chance, and concentrate on Miriam, bolster her so she could go say farewell to her unsaveable son. She was still bent over, crying. Not full out — and that was exactly the heart-wrenching part: that there was something hushed and humble about her grief. Even now.

'Come, Minchen.' I took her by the upper arm. 'We have to prepare ourselves for this. To say goodbye. They'll come get us any time now.'

Miriam shook her head. 'I can't.'

'Think of that evening, two weeks ago, at the café on the Staalstraat,' I said. 'We had such a good time together. So intimate, the three of us. Think of that, as intensely as you can, when we go to him now. That evening, that was our farewell, without our knowing.'

13

It was probably not Tonio's idea, but his college classmates had decided to go out for drinks and dinner with their parents. A date had been set for the outing: 7 May, a Friday evening. Tonio had emailed the invitation to

Miriam with the message: 'I don't know if you two are into this, but …'

He knew that for the past year we had avoided socialising outside our home. 'But this is about Tonio,' Miriam said. 'We don't get much chance to show some interest in his studies.'

'All right, sign us up.'

May 7th was chilly. It was the day they found the man who had strangled Andrea Luten, that the dead pilots of the crashed Turkish Airways plane were found to have been negligent, and that the Dam screamer had apologised for the disturbance he'd caused at the recent Memorial Day ceremony. As though to underscore the week's incessant tumult, two helicopters hovered overhead the entire afternoon, one from the police and the other from the TV, in connection with the Giro d'Italia, which started here because Amsterdam had to live up to its reputation, cost what it may, as a 'gruesome party house', as the writer Gerard Reve put it. Distracted by the pulsating rhythm of the helicopters I decided not to count 7 May as a normal workday. Soon, a drink with Tonio. On the way to my shaving ritual in the bathroom I dove into bed to catch forty winks.

Meanwhile, a minor drama was taking place at our front door. My mother-in-law had impulsively — in an 'agitated state of mind', as the police reports called it — absconded from St. Vitus nursing home and taken a taxi to our house. She came to claim Miriam — the reason remained unclear, but this was obviously the last straw. I was aware of the regulations governing the mother-daughter relationship, in place for several months, but I tried to keep out of it as best I could.

Miriam woke me to inform me of the intrusion. Her ferocity was alarming: for the past year, more and more sewage had been seeping up from her youth. I could not quite put my finger on what it was exactly.

'What did you do with her?'

'Put her back in the taxi. I was livid. Just then Thomas showed up.' (She was referring to my editor.) 'What must he have thought! Me standing there screaming at my mother while shoving her into a cab. He brought this envelope for you.' And with a fake pout: 'And the flowers he had with him weren't even for me.'

She more or less insisted that, before we went off to meet up with Tonio, I have a drink with her to calm her nerves.

'Otherwise I can't face this evening.'

I shaved quickly, we tossed back a drink, and then it was time to call a taxi. The plan was to eat dinner in the Atrium at the Binnengasthuis, on the university campus. Congregate in the student pub down in the basement before moving next door to the restaurant. The taxi was not held up by the Giro preparations, so we were early (six-thirty) and took our place at the bar. Beer in plastic cups — well, why not.

Quarter to seven and still no Tonio. Miriam called his mobile number. Yeah, his bike was still at Central Station, so he'd taken the tram. He was almost halfway. See you in a bit. *Huuy*. (His goodbye alternated between 'huuy' and 'oi'.)

Suddenly there he was standing next to us, having slipped in just as unobtrusively as he always entered the living room. The shyish grin, combined with a nod of the upper body, by way of a greeting. He did not kiss his mother as a matter of course: it had to come from her. For me, a squeeze on the shoulder sufficed.

From the moment I thought that Tonio had reached adolescence I decided to minimise his embarrassment by refraining from embracing him in public. (Once, when I wanted to introduce him to an old friend we bumped into on the street, and brushed his bangs out of his eyes, he jerked himself loose and danced around me with clenched fists, using my belly as a punching bag.) But these things tend to go gradually. Sitting together on the sofa watching a TV game show, we both laughed at a candidate's flub and I playfully and teasingly pulled him close to me. I had expected a punch in return, but he stayed leaning against me just where I had tugged him. He wriggled a hand behind my back and squeezed himself even closer, as though relieved that this was still allowed in the 'cool' world he was creating for himself.

We hadn't seen Tonio in weeks. 'You're looking well,' I said, 'although I'm sure you don't appreciate hearing that.'

He dismissed my comment with a grin. Since his baby fat had dissolved, he'd regained the compact body he'd had at the beginning of high school. My gosh, twenty-two next month. Perhaps because just this once he wasn't wearing his long hair in a ponytail, I was struck by the resemblance to a photo of myself, taken in the summer of 1973, a few months before my own 22nd birthday. I'm standing on a rock in the middle of rushing stream, and, rightly or not, at that age I felt I could walk on water. Now that I had a good look at Tonio, I realised that since his high school graduation, four years ago, I hadn't treated him in line with his personal development. I had postponed getting to know him as an adult, and had bombarded him with the kind of advice you give an insecure adolescent. He in turn was too polite to correct me.

It was simple enough. Brittany 1973 and the subsequent years had not slipped out of my memory. If I wanted to avoid treating the 22-, 23-, 24-year-old Tonio as a child, I only had to think back on myself at that age.

The ease with which he put away one beer after another — there, in any case, he had taken a page out of his father's book, anno 1973. After chatting for half an hour, he started glancing nervously around the bar. 'I don't see too many of my classmates. And no parents at all.'

Tonio took a spin around the busy pub and had a peak in the adjacent Atrium, where the tables were already set. He returned to us and shrugged his shoulders.

'Maybe I missed something,' he said, 'that the date was changed or something.'

'Let's have another round,' I suggested, 'and wait it out.'

Another half-hour passed. Not one of his classmates, with or without parents, showed up. I felt bad for him as he did another round of the bar, this time less confident than before, and returned to us with a slightly worried grin. Poor kid. He had dragged his parents all the way here and there was apparently nothing to offer them. He groaned.

'I must have missed an email somewhere along the way.'

'So we'll go eat somewhere,' Miriam said.

Tonio had an idea. 'The Staaltraat,' he said. 'There's a pub there that serves food, where I go with my classmates sometimes. The steaks are pretty good, and they've got those thick-cut fries.'

Off to the Staalstraat. Amsterdam had the chills. Elsewhere in the city, some fifteen couples and their Media & Culture-studying children were assembled in a restaurant, waiting for Tonio and his parents. Meanwhile, we were installed at a small table in Eetcafé 't Staaltje, and had one of the nicest evenings in years. Thrilled to really be together. All three of us in good form. Tonio in particular was on a roll. I noticed how well-spoken he'd become recently. (I thought back on the meandering complete sentences he churned out, age seven or eight, in his melodious, high-pitched voice. My disappointment when later, his voice starting to break, he started talking in clipped phrases. As a surly teenager every word seemed be uttered with aversion.) Miriam and I tried to top his witticisms. The waiter who interrupted our laughing with a new round of drinks said: 'I wish all our customers were like you.'

We reminisced. Some of our memories caused us to fall silent, but not for long. We ironed out a few past misunderstandings. And the steak wasn't bad at all. The fries, too, had the expected Flemish knottiness.

After a longer silence, when melancholy got the upper hand, Miriam told Tonio that what she missed most since he'd left home was their Sunday shopping outings. Her eyes glistened. Tonio looked down at his plate. The upshot was that they agreed to go shopping, on a Sunday of course, for a watch he'd set his sights on, and whose price had already been approved at the time of his graduation.

Miriam: 'A week from Sunday?'

Tonio: 'Deal.'

Miriam: 'And afterwards, *patat* on the Voetboogstraat. Like the old days.'

Tonio: 'Deal.'

At around midnight we called a taxi. Tonio said he wanted to check back at the Atrium café. Who knows, maybe he would bump into one of his classmates, who could fill him in on what went wrong. The taxi driver came in to let us know he was parked on the corner. Tonio refused to be dropped off at the Binnengasthuis: 'Ridiculously close by.'

On the way to the taxi, I thought Tonio might need some extra cash for a the rest of the evening: he still had all night ahead of him, and would probably miss the last tram. I'd spring for a taxi. I turned toward him. He needed to go the same way we did, but strangely enough lingered a bit in the doorway of the pub. I let Miriam go on ahead and hurried back to him, a fifty-euro note folded between my fingers. Instead of giving it to him I let it loose in the pocket of my raincoat, and threw my arms around him.

I didn't quite understand this unexpected gesture myself. He and I, we only really hugged on his or my birthday, with Miriam as the sole onlooker. I gave him three big kisses on his stubbly cheeks, and said: 'I'm glad it worked out this way.'

In order to spare him any more of my emotions, I hurried off. Out of the corner of my eye I could see his shy grin in reaction to my embrace.

I slipped onto the back seat beside Miriam and the taxi headed down the Nieuwe Doelenstraat towards Muntplein. I stuck my hands in the pockets of my raincoat and felt the bill, folded into quarters. 'Oh, damn, I *still* forgot to slip him something extra.'

I looked back through the rear window, but Tonio was already out of sight.

'He'll manage,' Miriam said.

CHAPTER SIX

'Our little boy'

there's a puddle of blood to show the photographer
a typewriter ribbon to change, the house to shuck off
— Gerrit Kouwenaar, 'there are still'

1

Underneath the clock (five o'clock), the blonde woman appeared — the one who, during the course of the day, we had come to regard as our personal nurse.

'Your son has been brought from the OR to the ICU,' she said. 'I can bring you to him now, if you want to say your goodbyes.'

I pulled Miriam up by the arm. She took a few wobbly steps, as though drunk with sleep.

'Is it okay if I don't go with you?' Hinde asked. She stood up, too, with panic in her eyes. 'I can't face it.'

'All you have to do is wait for us here,' I said.

We followed the nurse into the corridor. Left turn. I held Miriam tight, my arm around her waist, so that we could only take small steps. *Goodbyes*. The day after our dinner at 't Staaltje, she and Tonio exchanged text messages: sure enough, he had missed an email informing them of a change of venue for the student-parent dinner. Miriam texted back that it was a lucky thing, that misunderstanding, because we had had a terrific evening together. That much was ours forever.

119

At the next junction in the corridor we took a right. It must have been busy in the ICU, because in a biggish niche there was a bed in which a woman lay motionless. Her jet-black hair was spread out loosely over the pillow, covering it almost entirely. An Indian (or, in any case, Hindustani: the women wore a dot on the forehead) family sat at the bedside. They sat stoically on stools, elbows on the bedcovers, never taking their eyes off the patient, who appeared to be in a coma.

What kind of impulse was it that made me hug Tonio so emphatically last Friday, right there on a street corner? I could now claim I was saying my goodbyes, then and there, to the *living* Tonio, but that would mean I had had some kind of premonition, like louche stock-exchange traders acted on foreknowledge of imminent market fluctuations.

The nurse walked with a calm tread, so that we, with our fused bodies, had no trouble keeping up with her. She turned to us as we walked, and said: 'We've had to improvise a bit with the space, but … well, you'll see him shortly. He's still on the ventilator.'

I pulled Miriam against me even harder, suddenly afraid that my common sense might fail me. I was worried that I'd grab the first doctor I saw and yell: 'You and your fancy machines … Don't stop now! Do whatever it takes! Keep him alive!'

That I'd demand the number of one or another medical ethics committee … call up the chairman of the Society for Intensive Care: 'He's still alive! Don't let them pull the plug!'

That primitive instincts would get the better of me, like the mother gnu on National Geographic. She kept returning to her dead calf to fend off the pack of hyenas lingering nearby …

The nurse stopped at a light-yellow nylon curtain strung between two pillars on opposite sides of the corridor. She pulled aside one of the flaps. 'Here we are.'

2

There, somewhere, I must have let go of Miriam — perhaps because the opening was too narrow for both of us. I took a step forward, and another. All at once I was standing in the middle of a sort of peakless tent, draped on three sides with the same nylon fabric, like the kind of shower curtain that always stuck to your body. On the fourth side, a few metres behind the hospital bed, was a large window. The bed was positioned with its head on the left.

It really was him. In that bed lay Tonio. Our son. So it had not been a misunderstanding when they came to tell us they were busy *with him* in the OR. Had I secretly hoped, deep down, that it would be a case of an identity mix-up amid the nighttime chaos? Forget it. This was Tonio. Our own, unmistakable Tonio.

I reached to the side, behind me, but my arm mowed through thin air. Miriam — where was Miriam? I looked back in the direction we came from. In the corner of the yellow tent, next to one of the pillars, Miriam sat on a low stool, supported by two nurses, as though they were forcing her down, to keep her from witnessing the terrible scene from close by. A dripping glass of water hung in the free hand of one of the nurses. Miriam, tears and trepidation in her eyes, made a move as if to stand up, to free herself from the grip of the caring hands. They let go.

We shuffled over to the bed. Miriam took my hand, squeezed it.

'Just look at him, our sweet Tonio,' she whispered, almost without crying. 'Such a sweet boy … Adri, this can't be happening.'

It had been years since I'd had this reaction. The sight of Tonio, as a child, banging into something, his head bashing against the corner of a table, always sent shivers over my scrotum. I never did look into whether this was a natural reaction, meant to protect the sperm for the eventuality of a replacement heir, but in any case the bottom of my scrotum scrunched up so that the testicles were tangibly pulled upwards. The last time this had happened was not when I'd witnessed Tonio injure himself, but afterward, upon seeing his wounds. A friend of ours on the

Apollolaan had seen Tonio's schoolbag, dangling from the handlebars, get caught in the spokes of the front wheel on his way home from school. Tonio had done a complete frontward somersault. I found him later that day in the living room, covered in scratches, scrapes, and bruises.

'Oh, Tonio … what happened to you?'

In '95 he considered his broken wrist a sign of machismo, but only because he had got it on the slick floor of the bumper-cars arena. Now, with the Apollolaan bike incident, he looked mostly abashed, as though he'd damaged something costly belonging to *me*. He related the accident, embarrassed and reluctantly, in as few words as possible. (Nor did it become a standard macho story in his repertoire later, when the wounds had long started to heal and itch. Perhaps he realised how vulnerable a cyclist could be in city traffic.)

The sight of Tonio in the hospital bed brought about the same reaction: a scrotum made of tanned gooseflesh, which had permanently lost its elasticity.

Of course, we had been warned about his swollen torso, the result of internal bleeding (they had given him one futile transfusion after the other). Nurses had draped the blanket loosely enough around his upper body so that the swollen trunk was less obvious, but once you knew, you saw it anyway.

They had snipped off his clothing, undoubtedly in the ambulance first thing this morning. His naked shoulders stuck out above the sheet. We shared the same body-hair type. Contrary to the fashion of the day, he did not go in for depilation. (He and his friends sometimes self-mockingly called themselves 'a bunch of old-fashioned hippies'.) I caressed his collarbone: the pattern of soft hair felt reassuringly familiar.

His beautiful face was more or less unscathed. We had to make do with the right side — didn't get to walking around to the other side of the bed. The proud profile. Strong nose and chin. The full lips, which were so good at combining a grin with a smirk. The eyebrows that tended to meet in the middle. The closed eyes, which would never again open and reveal their gold-flecked brown irises.

How often had I stood watching Tonio as he slept … But this was different. It wasn't fake-sleep. He wasn't sleeping, nor had he woken from the dream that was life.

The mouthpiece of the ventilator device was an innocent light-blue, like a piece of a child's toy. The regular murmur of the artificial breath, with a hint of a slurping sound, had something comforting about it, like someone in a peaceful slumber. It also reminded me of how he lay sucking on his bottle of watered-down chocolate milk, as in a trance, taking deep breaths through his nose, the inward-looking expression serene and tranquil — just like now.

Judging from his stubble, Tonio hadn't shaved since Thursday, when he photographed that girl. A double black-red dotted line of dried blood traced a path straight through the whiskers; it climbed from the neck up over the chin, crossed the mouth, and ended on the upper lip — as meticulously parallel as the stylised rail tracks on a road map. The wound stripe looked rather gentle, in fact, like a benign scratch a daredevil gets when he takes a spill. Oops. Slip-up.

When he was at that age when children still garble many words, he'd mix up 'scheren' (shave) with 'schreeuwen' (scream). I often gave Tonio a raspy stubble-kiss just before shaving. He would rub his offended cheek, vexed, and retort, quasi-angry: 'You have to *schreeuw*, y'know … you have to *schreeuw*.'

Because the homo duplex now pulled out multiple stops at once, I was reminded of a line of poetry by Gerrit Kouwenaar: '*men moet zijn winter nog sneeuwen*' ('there is still a winter to snow'). Nearly twenty years ago, Tonio handed me a parallel line.

Men moet zijn kaken nog schreeuwen. There is still a chin to scream.

Yes, my son, I still had to scream. It was a wonder that I did not stand here bellowing at the top of my lungs. I leant over to his face and gave him a manly stubble-kiss. The scream, that would come later.

Had I expected — feared — that Miriam would scream out in agony? Sniffling softly, she kept repeating: 'Tonio, that sweet boy … just look at him, Adri.'

Miriam also kissed his cheek. She pulled her head back, and shook it, No. 'He doesn't smell like himself. There's this intense medicinal odour about him ... do you smell it?'

I had already smelled it.

'When I'd bring around his clean laundry,' she said, 'and he had just got up, he had that delicious boy-sweat smell about him.' She caressed his face with the back of her hand. 'That's gone now.'

As a young mother, Miriam claimed to be able to smell when Tonio was coming down with something. 'Take the dummy out of your mouth ... and now breathe out hard.' She'd sniff his breath. 'You see? Acetone-breath. I hope you're not coming down with flu.'

Then the little fellow would run excitedly to his father and repeat the operation, giving me a blast of his damp breath in my face. 'I've got acetone-breath,' he'd announce proudly. 'I might get sick'.

I never smelled anything other the scent of fresh apples. Soon thereafter he'd be poised theatrically in bed on his knees, his bum up in the air ready to accept the thermometer.

'They've shaved him,' I said.

To mask the incisions, they had draped a small towel loosely over his head, like a sheik's headdress but without the diadem. I only now realised they had shaved his head. If he were to wake up, it would have grown perhaps a millimetre or so. I would greet him with: 'Been to the barber?' followed immediately by: 'So now you call an ambulance to take you to your exams ...'

To which he would reply: 'Jeez. Good day at the typewriter, I see', which was his standard retort (once coined by his mother) to my bad jokes.

A small red plastic tower, a kind of chess piece, stuck out of his forehead (or a bit higher; the lack of a hairline made it hard to tell): the drain that had been screwed into his skull to tap fluid from the swollen brain. It made me think of his wrecked brain, which wouldn't even be able to take in the blandest joke, should he even come out of his coma.

A youth of sound body and mind. Before he went off to live on his own, Tonio was examined from head to toe: entirely healthy, not the least medical smudge. In the last twenty-four hours of his life, he couldn't have been more handicapped, both physically and mentally. He could no longer even breathe on his own. Both sides of his brain were irreparably damaged. In God's name, what had been the point and the purpose of Miriam and me having had such a beautiful boy in our midst for a good twenty-one years, a child whose lust for life kept us in good health and spirits, only to now have to say goodbye to the most critically handicapped creature imaginable, with a life expectancy of nil and whose mental capacity had been reduced to nil?

All those years of being proud of that handsome and clever individual we two had brought into the world ... In the end, it was this terminal wreck I had sired and she had borne for us.

Time to go. It hit me hard, the thought of having to take this image of Tonio, the way he lay there, with me for the rest of my life. Does one's final impression make an exclusive claim to legitimacy? I had to fight, on behalf of both Miriam and Tonio, to give the unspoiled version of my son its credibility back.

I looked around me. Aside from the three of us, there was no one in the yellow tent, but beyond the nylon I could feel the presence of the staff. 'Minchen, we should go. They're going to turn off the ventilator.'

I was shocked by the irreversibility in my words. Turn off meant: until death arrived. Put it off. *Now.* My brother Frans, Tonio's only uncle, was still in Spain. He couldn't get a flight back to Amsterdam any sooner than tomorrow morning. I remember having heard that, in exceptional cases, like when a close relative had to travel far in order to say farewell, they would extend the life-support for an additional twenty-four hours. Longer than that was irresponsible and inhumane. Frans did not require more than that amount of time for a night's sleep (or sleeplessness), the flight to Schiphol, and a taxi to the AMC. Meanwhile, Tonio would have the chance to ... to what? Snap out of his coma and return to the land of the living?

'Our sweet Tonio,' Miriam said, weeping gently. 'He was always so nice to everyone.'

She planted another kiss on his ashen cheek, which only dented under her lips, its elasticity having ebbed away. With one last kiss, on his forehead, her chin grazed the drain.

It was as though I were now in a hurry. I took Miriam by the shoulders from behind and pushed her gently toward the opening in the curtain, back into the corridor.

3

Clutching onto Miriam and weak at the knees, I drifted through the corridors of the ICU. It felt as though I had just quarrelled with someone, had lashed out at him, and now, leaving the place of the argument, my knees wobbled as I walked off, in the creeping realisation that I was wrong and might just as well have gotten a clobbering myself.

We passed the niche with the Hindustani family surrounding the comatose patient, where it appeared that not an elbow had been moved, not a lock of hair shifted. Instead of going to the left we kept on walking, losing our way. It was as though I was pushing that last image of Tonio out in front with my forehead. At the next junction, where I thought we had to turn left, I froze. I dug my fingers into Miriam's upper arm.

'Minchen, when they turn off the life support ... that's really when we should be at his side. We can't let him die alone ... it feels like betrayal ...'

I spoke agitatedly. We hurried back, past the Hindustani niche, all the way down the hall, and finally found the yellow curtain. Tonio was still connected to the ventilator. At the foot of the bed, monitoring the apparatus, was a nurse. She did not look up when we approached. She was focused on the blue digital lights on the instrument panel, which registered Tonio's vital functions — as yet still in order. She may have been the one instructed to turn off the ventilator, and our return had taken her by surprise.

Miriam, not about to be put off by Tonio's chemical smell, resumed her caressing and kissing his face, whispering things I could not make out.

I directed my attention to Tonio's right hand, which lay inert on the edge of the bed, the fingers curled indifferently between straightened and bent — just a thing that had been put there. The nails were nicked, and with a dark outline of dirt.

When I first knew Miriam, I used to tease her about her 'filthy fingers' — a matter of pigmentation, whereby her fingers got darker as they approached the tips. Only now did I see that Tonio had inherited his mother's natural colouring, but on closer inspection it was simply that his fingertips were just plain dirty. I pointed it out to Miriam.

'Look, the dirt under his nails. He obviously skidded across the asphalt.'

'His nails were always dirty. How many times did I tell him …'

She said it almost straightforwardly, like a belated remark on child-rearing. The nurse was still standing at the foot of the bed, without looking up at us, as though she hadn't even noticed our presence. She carried out vague procedures on or around the blinking apparatus, but out of the corner of my eye I couldn't make out *exactly* what she was doing.

I took Tonio's hand, which felt limp and heavy. The fingers were swollen, reminding me of his limbs when he was hurled, fresh from his mother's womb, like a bundle of sausages onto my lap. He was still unwashed. There was not much life yet in the puffy, purply arms and legs. All the available nursing hands were needed to combat the perceived complications with the mother, which turned out to be less urgent than all that, but meanwhile there I sat with that sticky creature glued to my jeans. (I wore them for several weeks longer, without washing out the dried placard of blood and slime, like a proud Indian with bear blood on his vest.) Bawling, that it did, but without the body joining in. To check whether it was alive I poked my finger against the tiny hand. Immediately the minuscule fingers closed around it. Mission accomplished.

I laid Tonio's hand down and put my thumb underneath it, lightly stroking the palm of his hand. There was no movement; the skin felt lukewarm. Normally you'd say: his hand felt pleasantly dry and cool.

Now, I knew this was a temperature between life and death.

I continued rubbing my thumb against his palm in a regular rhythm — until the machine at the foot of the bed suddenly began beeping impatiently, and, startled, I jerked my hand back. The sound, in its electronic chilliness, had something agitated about it, like a mother bird's alarm calls when her nest is under threat (in our backyard ivy). Miriam got a fright and started trembling. Nothing had visibly changed in Tonio's inert state. I looked over at the nurse, who kept her eyes glued to the monitor, and did not seem fazed.

'Does this mean it's happened?' I asked.

'Oh, no,' she said airily, without taking her eyes off the small monitor screen. 'It even just seemed to pick up slightly.'

'Pick up ... meaning ...?'

'Well, just that ... I'm seeing some improvement.'

I don't believe her words actually elicited any real hope in me, but they did throw me for a loop. (Later it appeared that Miriam fortunately did not register what she had said.) The alarm beeps had stopped. Did this mean that what the nurse had taken to be an improvement had already fallen by the wayside?

Suddenly I was no longer so sure she had been given the task of turning off the ventilator. Perhaps it was her job only to monitor the machine's signals, hence her unbiased observation that there was 'some improvement'.

4

This time, we reached the waiting room without getting lost. The fear in Hinde's eyes could not have been linked to Tonio's fate, because she already knew that. It had to do with us: how we were bearing up, how she had to succour us. I understood. I was never so afraid of anything as someone else's unquenchable heartache.

Before we could sit down, another wave of panic came over me.

'Minchen, they're taking him off the ventilator *now*. We can't abandon him *now*.'

We hastened back to the yellow curtain even quicker than the previous time. Tonio in his bed. If the light-blue mouthpiece had lain on the sheet in front of him, there would have been room for the thought that it had been poorly attached and had fallen out of his mouth, or that in his deep slumber he had spat it out — but the thing was just gone. They had removed it, and put it away, so that some desperate family member would not get it into his head to restart the ventilator.

Tonio was no longer breathing. How long ago had they cut off his breath? We hadn't been gone for more than two minutes. It had probably just happened … no more than 30 seconds ago … We couldn't ask the nurse, because she was gone.

Had they intentionally wanted to shield us from that obscene moment when his life would be irrevocably brought to a halt by a human hand? Or had we indicated by walking off that we had chosen not to witness it?

'It's really happening now, love,' I said to Miriam. 'He's dying. You can see the colour draining from his face.'

Dying. I tried to believe it myself, otherwise I'd never be able to pinpoint the moment. There was the homo duplex again. Alongside all the unfathomable grief into which I sank, there was still room for other emotions. Like pride. I was proud of him, the way he lay there dying, serene and sovereign. He could do it, he did it, he died. It was more than anyone could say for me until that point. I was still childishly consumed by my own mortal fear. As dying went, Tonio was head and shoulders above me.

He was brain-dead, of course, from the moment we first saw him here in the yellow tent. The real dying he did on the operation table. In stages, one failing bodily function after the other. 'He's dying,' I'd said to Miriam. I left it at that.

That the colour drained from his face was accurate insofar that he now became even more ashen than at first. He would have already lost his light olive complexion early that morning, on the Stadhouderskade.

Now his face had even lost all hint of a sheen. The slackening skin pulled the pores open.

If in the past I succumbed to fearful daydreams, losing control of my thoughts and visions, I would occasionally arrive at the image of a newly dead Tonio. I'd get so angry at myself that I would jump up from the chaise longue and wring the obscene thoughts out of my head with both hands. Balls of my hands pushing into my eye sockets, rubbing as hard as possible, until nothing was left of the image except the exploding sparks of light on my abetting retina.

Well, here he lay, Tonio. Dead. All along I had been taking a visionary advance on what, unimaginably, still turned out to be possible. Where was my anger now?

5

All of a sudden, she was back, the nurse who had observed a slight improvement in Tonio's readings the last time we were there. No, it wasn't her after all — it was another one. She fiddled with a few of the buttons on the machine, which as far as I could see was already switched off. I also noticed that, with the exception of the ventilator, all the tubes and wires were still attached.

'Only the mouthpiece has been taken away,' I said. 'The rest is still there.'

Without looking at me, the young woman replied: 'Everything has to be left in place as much as possible until the forensic photographer has been here. Pictures of the external injuries are always taken with the equipment attached. I don't know why, but those are the rules.'

I didn't want to ask if, for the sake of the photo shoot, she shouldn't reattach the ventilator, just to complete the picture. It would be no easy task. Since removing the mouthpiece, Tonio's lips had started to part, and the tongue began, ever so slowly, to stick outward, thick and lazy, like a sleepy Down's patient. I nearly asked her to stop what she was doing and call her colleagues, a doctor if necessary — anything to stop that obscene swelling of the tongue. But just then she walked away from the bed, the yellow curtain rustled, and she was gone.

We had never known him like this. Tonio was already transforming into unrecognisableness.

Miriam focused on another disturbing detail. With her thumb she tried to push Tonio's left eyelid, which was creeping open, back into place. Elastic as it apparently still was, it kept shooting halfway open. In the old days, they put coins on the eyes of the deceased to keep them from opening. The homo duplex reminded me of a book, by Dickens perhaps, that I'd read as a boy, in which some poor bloke tried to steal the coins from the face of a body laid out for viewing. The thief found himself being stared at wide-eyed and accusingly by the deceased.

We had better leave before Tonio, who had at first lain there so peacefully, would take his leave of us with an unfathomable gaze and stupidly extended tongue. We both kissed him once more on the cheek and forehead, Miriam murmuring: 'My poor darling ... my sweet Tonio.'

On the morning of 15 June 1988, I had seen him, aided by the gloved hands of a midwife, emerge from his mother. He tore her open in order to gain entry to the world. She gave him, with a drawn-out scream of surrender, permission to rip her perineum in order to push his way through. Nearly twenty-two years later, I witnessed how he disappeared back into his mother — not in the guise of a dead person, but in the form of a dark cloud of grief that would be indissolubly stored in her.

I took a step backwards. While Miriam bade farewell to our son with a few last whispers and caresses, I looked at him for as long as possible — not only his face, but his entire body, from head to toe and back again.

Because he was so small, they had put him straight into an incubator after his first washing. For observation. While Miriam was being stitched a maternity nurse brought me to the ward where he lay in his glass cradle, with its white rosettes in the side walls, through which ministering arms could be stuck. He wore an oversized nappy and was fastened to all manner of wires and tubes. His cry was thinner and higher-pitched than

I'd ever heard before from a newborn. His knees were tucked way up, perhaps because he'd gotten used to the position during all those months. But, damn it, this was my son, no two ways about it.

'It's a tradition here on the ward,' the nurse said, 'to take a photo of every newborn baby. The first one is on the house, we always say.'

'With pleasure.'

She aimed the Polaroid at the side of the incubator. Just as she was busy adjusting the camera, Tonio stopped crying. While at first the puggish face had been facing upward, it now turned in our direction. The nurse took the photo. I imagined that the flash penetrated his still-blind eye membrane and set him off crying again. The camera hummed in the woman's hands and Tonio's very first portrait glided out, still hidden in a black square.

'That's what I call photogenic,' she said, flapping the shiny card. 'Stops crying at just the right moment. Half a second, couldn't have been more than that, but it was enough.'

She blew against the dark surface, as though her breath would bring the image to life. And it did. Her unique method of photo developing succeeded: the contours of the cocooned Tonio gradually came into focus.

We still cherished that now-faded first Polaroid. Soon, almost twenty-two years later, Tonio would once again, tubed and wired, be photographed in a hospital — this time on his deathbed, and very likely for the last time. Human existence didn't make any sense at all, but the circles were always neatly complete, and that was exactly what was wrong with it.

That my own life-circle could contain Tonio's would make a jinxed geometric figure of it for the rest of mathematical eternity.

Miriam and I knew that this goodbye was definite and everlasting. I obstinately want to recall that we stepped backwards until we were behind the yellow curtain and in the hallway. More likely is that we kept turning around, in order to imprint, more sharply and deeply, that last image of him.

6

Shock. There was no other word for it. I had seen the phenomenon in others before. Then it was active shock, which did not only manifest itself via the facial muscles, but it seemed as though the entire body desired to participate, without, however, offering any semblance of solace. Hands grasped the chest, fingers clawed in the mouth, breath imitated a wheezing bellows.

'No ... *no.*'

My shock was a silent, cold shock. Blood, tears, other bodily fluid — it all seemed to be drawn away from the surface and led into my chilled insides, and to freeze there.

7

Another memory of Tonio in his incubator. His willy (the wrinkled little gumdrop I first checked to determine the sex of my child) was taped downward, toward his feet, apparently to prevent the little fellow peeing all over his not-yet-healed navel. You can't start too early teaching boys to aim.

What had they done with his genitals during that endless operation? In a documentary about John Lennon's murder they interviewed a doctor from the hospital where the wounded musician had been brought. 'There lay the hero of my youth, naked, with his penis taped to his thigh.'

Now that I'd recalled that bit of the documentary I couldn't get the image out of my head: a naked John Lennon with his member taped down to facilitate the autopsy. Ach, Tonio ... that fine instrument of yours: you still had so much to accomplish with it. You had only just started.

8

We ran into our blonde nurse in the hallway, who, even after an entire day's work in this transit station, had not lost any of her freshness. Was she waiting for us, or did our paths just coincidentally cross? She walked with us, a small stack of manila folders pressed against her bosom.

'Are you doing okay?' she asked. And right away: 'Of course you're not. What am I saying.' The upbeat expression vanished from her face for the first time all day. 'Oh, sorry, sorry.'

Her apology sounded sincere, even a bit desperate, which did not suit her. Maybe she was still an intern.

'Don't apologise.' I heard the woodenness in my own voice. 'You've been a terrific help today.'

At the corner near our waiting room she said goodbye, her face plaintive. Her shift was over.

'I'm terribly sorry for your loss.'

She had one of those slender hands where you could feel the bones glide supply over one another.

A female doctor sat on the two-seater, with a clipboard of papers that needed signing. Not a single word of her explanation got through to me. While the Rotenstreich sisters tearfully consoled each other, I put my signature next to the 'X' the required number of times. I could only think of the joint autograph sessions with Tonio in a variety of bookshops in the mid-nineties. He so wanted to sign his own name under my autograph on the half-title page, but had agreed to the condition that the customer specifically request Tonio's contribution. Tickled pink, he would give a shy smile when the buyer asked: 'May I also have your son's autograph?'

Now I was signing papers on his behalf.

9

Scheltema Books, Koningsplein, Saturday 22 June 1996. For more than two-and-a-half hours, Tonio perseveres in signing his name under mine, after which he claps the book shut and hands it to the customer. He is enjoying himself, but his smile has something ironic to it, as though he knows he's taking them for a ride, which he enjoys in equal measure.

'Did Master Tonio also contribute to the book?' an older man asks.

'No,' replies Tonio, his voice cracking into a high-pitched laugh. 'I don't even know what it's about.'

There is a lady from the radio. She holds a microphone in the air to register the ambient noise, and briefly questions a few people in the queue. Suddenly I've lost track of Tonio. As I sit there signing, I see him out of the corner of my eye standing next to the radio presenter. If I concentrate, I can hear him cheerfully and uninhibitedly answering her questions, at length and in more or less complete sentences.

'Of course I'm allowed to autograph, too. He's my father, and he sat upstairs for *sooooo* long, and I had to wait *sooooo* long for him to finish … Here it is —' (he takes a book from the stack, opens it) 'look: "For Minchen and Totò and their infinite patience" … that's mama and me. Because we never complained … only sometimes, just a little.'

And so on and so forth. When he returns to the table and unscrews the cap of his fountain pen, he sighs: 'Heh, finally, my first interview.'

'So, Tonio, schmoozing about me again, eh?'

'Oh, it was nothing, just Yes and No questions.'

When, three weeks later, I am to repeat the exercise at Athenaeum Booksellers, Tonio passes. 'Two autograph sessions a year — kind of boring.'

10

The doctor collected the signed forms, refastened them under the clip, and got up. I couldn't just let her go.

'What happens to my son's body now?' I asked. 'I've been told ... the injury, it's to be documented any time now by a police photographer ... a forensic photographer ... but after that?'

'Then he'll be brought by lift to the mortuary.' Something in her tone of voice told me that she had already, maybe a few minutes ago, explained all this. 'Down in the basement. He'll remain there until whichever undertaker you choose comes to collect the body.'

What stuck with me most of all was that she used *he* and the *body* in the same sentence.

11

Before we got into the lift, Miriam accosted an ICU nurse. 'Have you got any tranquilisers for us? We won't make it through the night otherwise.'

The woman was not aware of our case, so we explained our need for some Valium. She grudgingly pressed a few measly strips into Miriam's hand.

'Can't I have more than this?' she said. 'I'm really not planning to go peddle them on a street corner.'

Shortly thereafter I got into the lift with a fistful of Valium. The sharp corners of the foil strips jabbed into my flesh. In my other hand I held Tonio's wallet. Miriam carried the plastic bag with his mobile phone.

Down in the main hall, Hinde requested a taxi at the reception desk. I looked at Miriam. She was pale, but did not cry. She just kept gently shaking her head. Yes, here we were. Recovering from a gruesome experience. Legs trembling. But soon we would leave the horror behind us. The colour would return to our faces, and everything would get back to normal.

That's how it felt.

'Twenty minutes,' said the concierge. 'It's busy.'

We went outside to sit in the late-afternoon sun, settling down on a low cart, perhaps for transporting laundry. Hinde went off to smoke a cigarette at a safe distance from the revolving door. I was drained, and did not know what to say. Miriam, too, was silent. Even the sunlight made a tired impression, having shone so fiercely on our misery all day.

Just ten minutes later, the taxi arrived; maybe it wasn't even ours. But since the driver made no moves to enquire at the reception, we quickly got in: Miriam and I in back, Hinde up front. 'Oud-Zuid, please ... Johannes Verhulststraat.'

The last time I had been in a taxi was some two weeks before, after that unexpectedly intimate goodbye with Tonio on the Staalstraat. The fifty-euro note I'd forgotten to slip into his breast pocket. Just like then, I looked back out of the rear window as we drove off, and now there was just as little sign of him as then.

I tried to imagine Tonio as we had left him to his immobile fate in Intensive Care, lying on a temporary bed that in a short timespan had been transformed from a deathbed to a bier. (At least, I always thought a deathbed was the bed a person dies on, not the bed on which a dead body lies. A dead body lies on a bier.) At the request of the forensic photographer, the nurse will have pulled the sheet back to the foot end while he attached his camera to the tripod. First, he documents Tonio's roughly stitched open side, where the car had hit him full on. The man ensures that the bruises and discoloration are properly lit. Then he takes pictures of the other incisions in the torso, and of the drain and saw lines on the skull.

Ecce homo, or what's left of him. Three days after photographing that pretty girl at our house, Tonio undergoes his final photo session — with himself as the model.

Due to the parallel-tracked bruise stretching from the neck, over the chin, and to the nose, the photographer would take a close-up of Tonio's face. I resented the fact that the last portrait of his good-looking kisser would be so unflattering, with that obscenely swollen tongue sticking out between the lips. As though his last message to the world was an extended tongue, like in the old days when a convict thumbed his nose at his executioner on the scaffold.

The taxi got onto the motorway toward Amsterdam Zuid. The radio (or maybe it was a CD player) blared hip, whining Arabic pop music — electrified bouzoukis, with the vocals alternating with unadulterated rap.

'Could you please turn down the radio?' Hinde asked.

The driver reacted with less empathy than you'd expect, considering the building where he had just picked us up was a hospital, and his passengers were clearly distressed, if not outright distraught.

'We've just had some very bad news back at the hospital,' she said in a renewed attempt.

'Okay, okay,' the man grumbled. He turned down the volume the tiniest fraction. Who were we, after all, to disrupt to his 'labour vitamins'?* Arabic rap — something new, at least. At that very moment, we heard the ringtone of a mobile phone, but muted, like when a woman's phone goes off in the bottom of her handbag. It wasn't mine. I would have recognised Miriam's. But Hinde did not react, nor did the driver.

Suddenly it hit me that it had to be Tonio's mobile ringing in the plastic bag they had given us. It was lying on Miriam's lap. The bag hadn't been sealed, but was tied shut with one of those plastic zip ties you needed to cut with scissors. Miriam and I stared, paralysed, at the plastic-wrapped mobile phone. (Perhaps she had felt it vibrate on her thigh.) The caller had to be someone who wasn't in the know. So it could be anybody — except for Jim, and even he hadn't heard the latest, definitive news yet.

The phone stopped ringing just as Miriam was about to dig her nails into the plastic bag and tear it open. We waited for the voicemail signal, but there was none: apparently the caller chose not to leave a message.

'Something just occurred to me,' I whispered to Miriam. 'They gave us his mobile and his wallet, but not his watch.'

'The collision ...' Her voice sounded flat, exhausted. 'Maybe it flew off his wrist. The band was getting loose.'

'Then the police would have found it. They cordon off the whole

---

* 'Arbeidsvitaminen' is a long-running (since 1946) popular-music radio show in the Netherlands.

area after an accident like this. Yellow paint outlines all over the road …
you remember what the policeman said this morning. They reconstruct
everything, comb the place for clues. Maybe they've kept Tonio's watch
as evidence.'

I was reminded of the photos of wristwatches from a museum in
Hiroshima. Melted and deformed, their hands immortalising the precise
time the atomic bomb exploded. 'It might have stopped at the moment
of impact.'

'*If* he was wearing it.'

The taxi took the exit ramp, a three-quarter curve, so that Miriam, too
listless to resist, got squashed up against me. The warm, soft body that
had made Tonio possible and in which he, in turn, had left his mark.

'Last Sunday,' I said. 'You two were supposed to go into town … to
buy him a new watch. I never heard any more about it.'

'Tonio emailed that morning to say he was "beat". Always that word,
"beat". Could mean anything. From a hangover to the flu. Because of his
beatness, we put off the watch-shopping until next Sunday.'

'Not today?'

'It's a public holiday — we weren't sure if the shops would be open.'

'Minchen, in the Staalstraat that night, in the pub … do you remember
if he was wearing his watch then? He was so keen to get a new one, that
maybe …'

Awful, this conversation. As if we were desperately in search of
anything of Tonio's that was still ticking. At the mention of the Staalstraat,
Miriam began to whimper. She was so proud of him that evening — his
wisecracks, his keen remarks. He had become his own person.

'I wasn't paying attention,' she wept.

'It was one of those oversized monsters,' I said. 'He nearly always
wore it. I always noticed if he *wasn't* wearing it.'

'Well, then he *must* have been,' Miriam said, turning her head the
other way. I knew it was time to drop the subject.

12

Leidsegracht, 1992. When I got home I saw Miriam, shower cap on her head to keep out the dust, bent over a cardboard moving-box. She clapped two books together, releasing the dust that had managed to gather despite the closed box.

'Put them back, Minchen. I've found us a house.'

'In the Veluwe, I hope?'

'On your native soil. Your old neighbourhood.'

'May I see it first?'

'Right now, if you like.'

The manager of the pension fund, who (like the Veluwe landlord Roldanus) had given us a three-year lease, was not in the least bothered (unlike Roldanus) by our request to vacate at the halfway mark, provided we could find a new, creditworthy tenant. But before we could do so, the pension man had found one himself: a concert pianist. The top two floors were perfect for his two grand pianos. I wondered privately if the small spaces had much to offer acoustically, but maybe the pianist only played modern music on a piano packed in a down duvet, tapping the keys through a rubber mat while a tin woodpecker chipped away at the legs. I was far too relieved to have been let out of our lease and able to move ASAP to the new house on the Johannes Verhulststraat to worry any further.

(The ad agency's pension funds did not exactly strike gold with the new tenant. After transferring the two months' deposit, the payments dried up. By the time he was in arrears for an entire year, and the summons-servers had come and gone, the pianist, whose name no one had ever seen on a concert poster, had absconded. One day I received a phone call from Cristofori, the piano-rental company situated on the Prinsengracht, a stone's throw from the house. A woman asked if I could provide her with the forwarding address of my friend, the man who had taken over the flat on the Leidsegracht.

'You see, he rented two top-of-the-line grands from Cristofori …
defaulted on his financial obligations … and now it appears that the pianos
have been moved to his new residence. So we thought that perhaps you
could …'

I explained to her that the concert pianist was no friend of mine; I had
never laid eyes on him, not even on stage. The Cristofori lady also told
me, with a sigh of indignation, that the man had the audacity to lower
both grand pianos, enlisting the help of some construction workers, who
were busy renovating the basement on orders from the agency, out of the
house.

'The guy's got a lot of nerve,' I said.

'*And* two of our best pianos,' she added.

I told this all to Tonio that evening while tucking him in, on the upper
bunk of his new bunk bed. I jazzed up the story with the image of a man
who, two wing-shaped grand pianos attached to his shoulders, flew off
one night into the wild blue yonder.

'There's no such thing as a wild blue yonder at night,' he insisted. 'At
night the sky is nearly dark, depending on how far under the horizon the
sun has set.'

A man flapping off with two grand pianos as wings, he didn't seem
to have much problem with. He made me repeat the story over and over,
and had a good belly-laugh at the prank we'd pulled on our landlord by
leaving that piano-playing mythical creature behind.)

The formalities surrounding the purchase of the house were
completed. We could be summoned to the solicitor's at any moment. At
least once a day I would take tram 2 down Leidsestraat to Zuid. In Café
Bar-B-Q, at the corner of the Banstraat and the Johannes Verhulst, across
from the new house, I'd sit at the window gazing across at the yellow-
brick façade. It was the left half of a twin house. Our front exterior had
recently been sandblasted, while that of the right-hand house looked as
though it had never been cleaned, and had collected all the soot and dirt
of the past century. A lung specialist had his practice in the grimy right
half of the yellow twins. The owner of the Bar-B-Q told me that the

doctor's standard reply to comments by his patients on the filthy state of his façade, was: 'That is simply to illustrate the point of your visit, to show you what your lungs look like after forty years of smoking.'

There wasn't much more to see of our house. Faded curtains hung in the windows, the sills lined with withered plants, a silent anti-squat brigade. I just sat there and looked, repeating to myself that we were about to start a new life. Tonio, who had just turned four, would grow up there, leave home after graduating high school, and years later, once it had become truly ours, would return with his own family while Miriam and I would downsize. For the next decade-and-a-half we would be secure there, the three of us. I turned to the bartender and asked if there was much burglary in the neighbourhood.

'Only if they know there's something to be had,' he replied. 'People with art or a stamp collection.'

I didn't collect postage stamps, and until now our art collection consisted of a few of Tonio's framed drawings, like his brilliant portrait of the cat Cypri.

13

The taxi exited the A10 and descended into Buitenveldert.

'A critical condition,' I said. 'I've been wrestling with that term all day. With what it means ... especially its elasticity. That "critical" had something comforting about it. As though, with a little extra effort, the doctors would be able to fix it ... Now I know a critical condition can also turn out, well, critical.'

'Then for me it has a whole different gist,' Miriam said. 'When the police rang the bell this morning, I knew right away something was really wrong. Even before they opened their mouths. When I heard "critical", I knew he'd die. Or was dead already.'

'He was still alive.'

'All day I thought it would turn out badly. Of course, you never know for sure. Tonio could live without his spleen. Like people manage with just one kidney. But when I heard about his brain trauma … both halves starting to swell … I just prayed he wouldn't come out of it as a vegetable.'

'By the afternoon,' I said, 'my nightmare was a Tonio emerging from a coma. Severely brain-damaged, just enough left to be able to comprehend his condition. Oh, my God, what have I done? Look what my recklessness has caused. I think I'd have died from *his* regret, *his* shame … compounded by my own.'

Then it was quiet for a few moments, aside from the Arabic music and Miriam's sobs. We drove past the old Olympic Stadium, approached the Harlemmermeer roundabout, near where my father-in-law Natan lived. Hinde turned to her sister and said: 'Papa and Mama … how are you going to tell them?'

'Not over the phone,' said Miriam.

They decided to discuss it at our place and then cycle around to their parents' homes, one at a time — in which order was still up in the air. I was surprised to have been so routinely excluded from such a painful mission, but I did not protest.

14

We got out of the taxi. I looked up, along the yellow-brick façade. Electric light shone through the half-opened curtain of Tonio's old room — Miriam had probably left the light on when she got dressed there early this morning, trembling with trepidation.

I remembered a time, August '98, when we returned home from holiday to find a six-member family standing on the front stoop. They were looking up on cue from an old man, who seemed to be the group's guide. They spoke American English. When one of them saw us head for the front door, our suitcases in tow, the old man approached us. He introduced himself in Dutch and told us that he had lived here until the age of sixteen, shortly before the war broke out. He had been able to flee to America via Switzerland — to New York, where he still lived. Now he had been joined by his wife, daughter, son-in-law, and two grandchildren for the couple's fiftieth-anniversary trip to his home town, including a visit to the house where he had spent his youth.

We gladly invited them inside. Tonio ran ahead; he saw it as his duty to show the visitors what he considered the highlights of the house: the basement full of Lego, and his own room with its K'Nex Ferris wheel. The old man's father had been a wine merchant, and the basement had been the storeroom. While Tonio's laugh echoed throughout the house, the whole family was in tears. The wife and the daughter were particularly hard hit. The father had told them so much about the house of his youth, and now … now here they were, actually walking around in it! Renovations had transformed much of the place over the past sixty years, but once in a while the man got choked up when he recognised certain things from the 1930s. The stained glass in the balcony doors, the ceiling ornaments, the maid's room up on the third floor.

When we retired to the living room for coffee, he pointed to a cupboard door. 'There's a secret hiding place in there. My father had a small safe built in.'

Miriam opened the cupboard door. The bottom was covered with a piece of linoleum, which, sure enough, covered a small hatch. We had never noticed it. The cache was empty (but it set the wheels of Miriam's imagination spinning, resulting in a thriller-like novel a few years later). It was an emotional moment for the man, and his whole family, to be able to point out something tangible that had been his father's.

I let my gaze climb the yellow façade, behind which Tonio had grown up — never to return, not today and not in his old age. Thinking of that old man made me feel a wave of sorrow for Natan, Tonio's 97-year-old grandfather, who would soon hear from his daughters that his grandson was no longer alive.

15

Miriam and Hinde were probably on their way from their father's house on the Lomanstraat to the St. Vitus retirement home in the Jordaan, where their mother lived. How do you tell your parents that their only grandchild has been killed in a traffic accident — right now I could not imagine it. I just wanted them to get back home as soon as possible. I was scared.

In the course of the day, I had visited the toilet far more often than usual, for ever-shorter spurts of colourless urine, like after you've been sitting in rain-drenched clothes in a draughty train station waiting room. Now, too, the urge arose, like a chill on the bladder, despite the warmth of the summery Whitsun that penetrated the house. I sat on the edge of the sofa for a good fifteen minutes, my fists screwed into the seat cushions next to me, ready to hoist myself up and go to the bathroom. When I could finally bring myself to get up and leave the room, I lingered indecisively on the landing. My hands lay on the balustrade connecting the handrail of the staircase leading upstairs and downstairs. There I stood, looking down the stairs to the front hall, my back safely to the wall of photos.

The WC was to my left, next to the spare kitchenette. Opposite its door, Miriam had covered a mangled bit of wall where the fuse box used to be, with portraits of Tonio. They dated from various ages.

Tonio as a toddler, with an obligatory smile that doesn't quite mask the put-out earnestness.

Tonio with bravado, butch-ish cap on his head, broadly grinning in between the giggly sisters Merel and Iris. (Judging from the bared teeth, still pre-braces.)

Dressed up as the Dutch cabaret artist Dorus, complete with moustache, bowler hat, and dust coat, from when he had to sing (or lip-synch) the song 'Two Moths' at a talent show at the Cornelis Vrijschool.

As an eight-year-old, autographing books at Scheltema with his father. (In the photo, taken by Klaas Koppe, he hands a freshly signed book to a customer.)

With his friend Jim in Antwerp for the presentation of the Golden Owl 2004 (not to me), each with a large mug of Jupiler beer in hand, doubled over laughing. Tonio's mouth wide open with hilarity, showing off the sparkling braces he's still got at age fifteen.

Tonio's self-portrait as Oscar Wilde, the result of a group project at the Amsterdam Photo Academy, fall 2006.

There was no avoiding this portrait gallery when you left the WC. I don't remember exactly how it got started — it had been years earlier — but from a certain, indefinable moment, I could not look at these photos with the usual tenderness. I wondered if it was because of the panda that had hung there between two small portraits of Tonio ever since his graduation in 2006.

16

As I am about to step from the landing onto the top tread, I hear Tonio and Merel's voices coming from the bathroom. The door is ajar. Involuntarily I stop and listen. The silence is broken by the tinkle of a child's pee.

'When I'm done,' says Tonio, 'then it's your turn. I'm not going to flush first, 'cause that's bad for the environment. We have to think of the environment. Now you, Merel.'

The seat is lowered with a thwap. Again the sound of child's pee, augmented with that special gurgle which is the sole domain of girls.

'Two pees without flushing,' says Tonio, 'is better for the environment. When you're finished, you can go ahead and flush. Then it's still good for the environment. Right, Merel?'

A little embarrassed, I continue downstairs. I have the impression that environmental concern is not the basis for Tonio and Merel being together in the bathroom, although it does certainly benefit from it.

It must be around the same time, early spring, that Tonio presents his mother with a curious maths problem. Merel stands next to him, giggling.

'Okay, Mum, if I got Merel pregnant, how long exactly would it take for the baby to come?'

Miriam believes her sexual education has fallen short, and starts explaining: 'Well, you have to consider roughly ...'

'No, we want to know *exactly*,' Tonio interrupts impatiently, 'because we want the baby to be born *exactly* on New Year's Eve. Right, Merel?'

Whenever Merel is bashful, and doesn't dare laugh out loud, her cheeks puff up like a hamster's. Her lips, already full, jut out even more, and she hooks her pinkies, as though to test their opposing strength. She nods vehemently. 'Yes,' she says, almost inaudibly and, for the occasion, with a low, boyish voice, 'that's what we'd like to know.'

17

We celebrated Tonio's eighteenth birthday on 15 June 2006. By late afternoon — it was a sunny day — the guests started trickling in, one by one or in small groups. One of these days, maybe tomorrow, the Ignatius final exam results would be announced, but the party mood forced the butterflies about the test results to the background. Tonio no longer a minor ... unbelievable. Each time he left the room, and Miriam called him back to open the next present, I fully expected to see the child I knew so much better than the adult he now was. His late baby fat hadn't entirely disappeared yet, and although he still had that gawky posture he didn't attack the gift-wrapping, like an excited puppy, the way he used to. Everything he now carefully unwrapped and held in his hands was greeted with a satisfied grin.

The phone rang for the umpteenth time. Miriam answered.

'Tonio, for you.'

He put down the latest gift (a light meter, a notch up from his present one) with the rest of the presents on the mantelpiece and took the receiver. The company chatted away, but I kept one ear tuned in to Tonio's call.

'Oh, thanks,' he said. 'How did you know it was my birthday?' And a moment later: 'Oh, that. Of course. I guess that slipped my mind today.'

Something in his voice, a shrill exclamation, maybe, made the room fall silent. 'Yes, thanks.' He hung up and turned around. 'My form teacher,' he said with a shrug. 'I thought he called to wish me a happy birthday. But … uh … it looks like I've passed my exams.'

For the next half hour, the three of us forgot our guests entirely — no, they simply did not exist. Tonio and I sat on the sofa, arms around each other's shoulders. Miriam knelt in front, her bosom resting on our knees, and her hands nearly reaching our backs.

'We've done it,' she kept saying, in tears. 'We've done it, the three of us. How great, how great, oh how great. This, this moment, we have to hang onto it. Forever.'

And I, wanker that I am, let it happen. I just sat there with a throat like a wrung-out dishrag, and let Miriam do all the talking. Tonio wavered, his face taut, between keeping a distance and giving in. Fighting back the tears, as they say. The way he looked at Miriam, awkwardly trying to read our feelings, he reminded me of the five-year-old kid who stood in front of me at the cremation of his grandfather, speechlessly observing the tears and uncontrolled twitches on my face, not sure whether he should try to comfort his father or cry, too.

Forget it, today was his eighteenth birthday. The guests could all look the other way in courteous silence — but *they* wouldn't see him snivel, no fucking way.

Just as Tonio was exercising an old Dutch tradition by hanging his schoolbag on the flagpole out on the balcony, adorned with a kite-tail made from used notebooks, his old sweetheart Merel came cycling by. I couldn't see her from the sofa, but recognised her voice.

'Congratulations!' she called out.

'Yeah, thanks … thanks!' he shouted back.

That was all. He came back inside.

'Who was that?' asked Miriam.

'Oh … just Merel.'

'Couldn't you have asked her in?'

Tonio shrugged his shoulders. Something in his expression, the corners

148

of his eyes and mouth, betrayed a certain insecurity: yes, maybe he should have done. 'Merel also did her final exams,' he said evasively.

God, Tonio, the love of your life all those years. Cruel children: cruel to each other, cruel to themselves.

18

If he played in my workroom, Tonio would often come stand behind me and peer over my shoulder, reading what I was writing or had just written. He sometimes asked what it all meant, but, as I explained it, his thoughts usually drifted back downstairs to his Warhammer armies and half-built K'Nex towers. Once he recognised his name, and his parents', in a freshly written paragraph.

'Is it about us?'

I explained that it was a diary entry. (In those days, I kept a typed diary on loose sheets of paper.) He thought it was pretty weird. Later that day, I took him aside. 'When you turn eighteen, Tonio, I'll give you a book with the notes I made throughout your life. About your birth and all sorts of things you've forgotten, or never knew, or will remember once you've read them ... I'll make a really cracking book out of it.'

Tonio looked at me briefly, not unobligingly, and said: 'Oh, great.' And off he ran.

On his eighteenth birthday, the day that coincided with his exam results, I did not have the promised folder, or book, ready to give him. Nor did he ask for it. Of course he didn't: his life did not need to be written down; it had to be *lived*. Certainly from that moment on.

'*Oh, great.*' Writing out the original, telegram-style scribbles in longhand gives me the feeling that I'm making good on an old promise, not so long after his eighteenth birthday. The hideous part is that it's not enough to provide a record of his birth and the ensuing childhood years. I cannot avoid an account of his last day. What I had wanted to give him was a book with an open end. Now, it runs the danger of becoming over-complete.

19

The graduation ceremony was, thanks to the summery weather, held outdoors. The abundant sunlight made the glassy sand particles in the schoolyard's paving stones glisten.

The Ignatius. Unlike Miriam, I had not come here often. All those PTA evenings — what right did I have, actually, to leave them to her? Yes, that one time with the combustion engine, I was there then. Perhaps it was the presence of his father that made Tonio, initially paralysed with nerves, grow in his role so quickly. In his determination to explain *everything*, he came across as a bit pedantic, but endearingly so.

I thought of William Faulkner, hammering away at a typewriter in his study, *Rhapsody in Blue* on the record player, whisky within reach, and his daughter in the doorway, begging her father to come to the school's PTA family evening. No, honey, out of the question. Daddy has to catch up with Shakespeare, and he's got a long way to go yet. Another time, sweetheart.

I was so damned chuffed, there in that schoolyard, that Tonio had graduated from the gymnasium. It was not the shadow of my own body that lay at my feet — no, it was pure pride, sharply outlined against the grey paving stones. I was too high from the whole thing to consider whether I really deserved that pride.

Each graduate was called forward and got a personal word of congratulations from his mentor. It went in alphabetical order. Although Tonio wasn't at the end of the alphabet, he became restless. At first he had laughed out loud at the various form teachers' wisecracks, but now even his smile had started to fade. Finally it was his turn to be handed his diploma. Miriam and I pushed our way up front.

Tonio's mentor (his biology teacher) had, in his speeches, assigned an animal to each of his charges. He handed Tonio a framed photo collage that included a portrait of Tonio in 2000, his first year in the class (short hair and glasses); a portrait of him in 2006, shortly before his exams (long hair, no glasses); and in between them, a photo of a giant panda.

'... Tonio, ladies and gentlemen, has the good-naturedness and cuddle factor of a panda. Inversely, he also shares the panda's defencelessness and vulnerability, making him a bit of a pushover ...'

Fortunately, I will never forget it, because with the sun's help it was burned into my memory: how Tonio, slightly dizzy, meandered toward us through the tightly packed crowd, his diploma and the panda under his arm. We embraced him again, this time more ceremoniously. He pulled a face that seemed to say: *Was that everything?* It was already behind him. I recalled my own post-graduation lustrelessness of 1 June 1969.

Miriam asked him how he liked the speech. Tonio wiggled his hands: so-so. Pushing it. He didn't fancy being branded as good-natured and defenceless — no way, that wasn't him at all.

'Cuddle factor, okay,' he said with a grimace. 'You can always shake it off.'

His eyes wandered restlessly toward a couple of ex-classmates, who beckoned him. He handed us the diploma and panda collage for safekeeping. 'I was going to hit a few parties with the guys.'

'Been invited?'

'Don't have to be.'

'D'you remember when you gave that party three years ago, you and your friends kicked out a few party crashers? There was a police car at the door when Miriam and I got home.'

'And we didn't even need them by then,' he said. 'Who says I'm defenceless?'*

---

* Author's note: After having written this paragraph yesterday, this morning's paper (25 August 2010) sported two front-page photos of a newborn giant panda. The first photo, taken from a CCTV image, showed mother Yang Yang with the cub in her mouth. It is so tiny that at first glance you think of a premature foetus. The second picture shows Yang Yang, with her front paw, cradling the resting minuscule creature. Caption: 'Giant pandas are seldom born in captivity in Europe.' The mother, her sad eyes sunk in pools of runny mascara, looks up at the camera.

20

So as not to rub Tonio the wrong way, Miriam did not add 'the three pandas' to the portrait gallery right away, but from the very first day the collage did hang on the landing, months later, it seemed (to me, at least) that the biology teacher's 'defenceless' pronouncement has started to seep onto the adjacent photos. It wasn't like I wanted to admonish Tonio not to 'let them walk all over you' every time I left the toilet. It went deeper than that. What I saw in passing, or thought I saw, even out of the corner of my eye, was a glimpse of a vulnerable life.

I also had this with snapshots of murdered children, like those shown in missing-person programmes on TV. Rowena Rickers, the Nulde girl who had been chopped in pieces ... The sisters from Zoetermeer, whose father smothered them with a pillow ... Despite the trust with which they looked into the camera, I believed I read a premonition of the inevitable, their gruesome deaths, in their laughing eyes. Of course, you could label it as 20/20 hindsight. But maybe a projection, like a magnifying glass or an X-ray, makes visible something that has previously gone unnoticed.

So what was it about that unmistakable vulnerability I observed — over so many different periods! — on Tonio's face? I noticed it as much under the impudent brim of the cap between Merel and Iris as behind the nerdy Dorus glasses. How could my original fondness for those photos have been transformed into permanent anxiety?

Late last year, I caught myself opting more and more for the upstairs toilet, in the bathroom, rather than the small downstairs WC. The alternative route was also lined with photos, but less unnerving ones (even though the one of Sailor Vos* in Café Zwart, preparing to fly at a friend of mine from Berlin, was certainly not exactly comforting). The odd time I did use the downstairs WC, I always found an excuse to allow my gaze to glide over the photos without really looking at them.

Now. As I stood looking over the balustrade, I forced myself to turn

---

* A pet name of a local celebrity.

with a jerk and face the wall of photographs. What had I expected? Now that Tonio had today shown his most vulnerable side, the spine-chilling defencelessness was still fully visible in his photographed face, no longer as a premonition or potential danger, but as a *confirmation* — and that changed in one fell swoop the aspect of the entire portrait gallery. He was dead.

21

Tonio was four when we moved. In the fall he'd start school at the Schreuder Institute. Holding back time (or, for me, the contrived attempts at it) was a thing of the past. We had now found the ideal fortress from which we could give Tonio the freedom, little by little, to educate himself for future — a fortress we could drag him back into at any given moment.

The movers had left. Horsehair blankets still covered the furniture, and everywhere low walls had been erected out of moving boxes: almost a familiar sight, considering that some of them had remained unpacked during the two Leidsegracht years.

I was dead beat, as was Miriam. She had managed to improvise a bed for Tonio in the corner of what was to be his room. (It was due for renovation, as the parquet floor had been stomped to splinters by the destructive children of the former owner, H.P. Lolkema, nicknamed Mr Horsepower.) I went in to check on him. He had lain half uncovered, surrounded by his various security blankets arranged in top-secret order, and in the middle of it all swam a rubber ducky. The dummy had tumbled out of his mouth, and lay on the pillowcase, still stuck to his lower lip.

I had done a decent job of steering him through stormy waters to this bastion of security. He was safe, and apparently was not visited by nightmares. Once things were unpacked and more or less in place, we would tackle Tonio's room. Order a bunk bed next week, for starters, for the slumber parties he was so looking forward to organising.

'Night, kiddo,' I whispered. 'Don't let the alien walls give you a fright in the morning.'

I went back to the balcony at the rear of the same storey. Miriam was flopped in a folding chair, with Cypri on her lap, who, after an initial reconnaissance of the house, also had to give in to fatigue.

'He's asleep,' I said. 'So peaceful.'

22

Mr Horsepower hadn't bequeathed us just any old 'ding-dong' doorbell. It was a complete carillon, with tubes of various lengths that sent its message soaring up to the furthest reaches of the house. The violence of the chimes hadn't been so noticeable before, but now, in the stillness of the move, we jumped out of our skin. Someone must be holding his finger on the button, because it sounded like the Munt Tower on the hour, only without a melody. We both sprang to our feet.

'We're getting rid of that doorbell,' Miriam said. 'It gives Tonio the "fries of his life", as he puts it.'

When the chiming subsided, we both pricked up our ears to hear if Tonio had woken up. No, not a peep. To prevent another round of bells, I ran to the intercom. 'Hello?' It was Mr Rat, whose crackly voice announced that he'd come 'to consecrate the new house'.

Trouble already.

My patience with people had already started to wane before we went to live in the Veluwe. In retrospect, I was surprised by how, ten years before, I'd blindly trusted pretty much everyone. If that trust got breached, I'd take it from there. I kept an open house, but I learned the hard way. Time and again, I would allow dubious characters to come nosing about, and then knead their findings into the kind of story they felt worth relaying to others. I was naïve enough to be flabbergasted by the versions that eventually reached my own ears.

I had bought the house on the Johannes Verhulststraat from a retired porn boss. The basement was his warehouse; the shelves left behind by the wine wholesaler Leuchtmann came in handy. The neighbours sighed with relief to see the end of the delivery vans with tinted windows. Once the papers had been signed, I set off for my regular café, where the news had already been making the rounds that 'Adri had taken over a chic brothel in Zuid'. I kind of liked this sort of grotesque gossip, as opposed to the systematic bad-mouthing that had no other aim than to injure the subject.

The moving boxes weren't even unpacked yet, but Mr Rat, accompanied by his fiancée, a Miss Piggy lookalike, were of the opinion that any further delay in sniffing out the new premises would be irresponsible. Maybe they had picked up some of that 'chic brothel' chitchat.

'We've come to inaugurate the house,' he said, handing Miriam a bottle of white wine, which had been thoughtfully wrapped in aluminium foil to keep it cold. 'God, Adri, you look beat.'

Well, yes, I hadn't got much shuteye the previous night, as so much still needed to be packed. But my hospitality got the better of my sleepiness. We sat out on the balcony, and I opened the bottle.

Whether it was the summer evening chill or the white wine, Mr Rat kept excusing himself to go to the toilet. Every storey had one, but with each absence I heard a different flush. And each interval lasted a little longer. Mr Rat was having a good sniff around the place.

'Now I know why your face looks so worn out,' he announced after the umpteenth inspection. 'You're medicated up to the gills.'

'Beg pardon?' Miriam and I looked at one another.

'Yeah, the door to your study was open, and there were all these boxes of sleeping tablets. Zero-3. They say it's heavy-duty stuff. Enough to floor a horse.'

After that remark, I should have floored him, and with a less innocent means than Zero-3.

'Those are weight-loss tablets, Rat. Three days a week — Monday, Wednesday, Friday — you starve yourself. Instead of eating, you swallow a couple of Zero-3 capsules every two hours. They expand in your stomach, so you think you're full. I can hardly recommend it.'

A shadow of irritation glided over Mr Rat's face. Considering his own addictive tendencies, to yet a different menu of substances, he was not about to be denied this discovery. He shook his head. 'It's a well-known fact that Zero-3 is a potent sleeping pill. My regular doorman on the Reguliersdwarsstraat sells them, too. No need to be secretive about it.'

'Next time you need to pee,' I said, 'open one of the boxes and read the leaflet.'

Mr Rat somehow didn't need to pee after that. Seen enough, mission accomplished. As I was tied up for the next few weeks with readying the house, it was a full month before I heard, along the grapevine, of my addiction to downers.

'Well, what do you expect,' I replied. 'I live in a brothel. I'd never sleep a wink otherwise.'

So this was how I began the new, sheltered life of my small family: by naïvely letting in a mole from the old, unsheltered life.

23

I took advantage of Miriam and Hinde's absence to make a couple of telephone calls. Not to my father-in-law, no, not just yet: I had to be certain his daughters had already told him the news. It wasn't a subject to be conveyed via crossed lines.

For the past twenty-five years, my sister's landline had been permanently connected to the answering machine, so I was not surprised to get her voicemail when I for once called her new mobile number. To soften the blow somewhat, I began by saying 'something serious' had happened to her nephew, and asked her to phone me back.

And then my brother, who was still in Spain. When I had spoken to him that afternoon, eons ago, Tonio was still alive. I had told him bluntly that it was not good, but somewhere in the scintillating silence between Holland and Spain there was still hope. Now I had to tell him the bare truth. I don't know anymore how I put it, but a week later Frans recalled in his funeral speech that I had said: 'The poor kid didn't pull through.'

Two ageing, choked-up brothers on the telephone, falteringly asking questions and giving answers about the most horrible conceivable scenario — no, an *inconceivably* horrible scenario that had nevertheless occurred. We had been raised by a mother who, whenever her children wanted to go out, hysterically summed up all manner of imaginary dangers, and then insisted her brood stay home, if need be under lock and key. Now that a suchlike imagined hazard had finally become reality, we didn't know which way to turn. This was *not* part of our upbringing.

'It's so awful,' Frans kept repeating with a strangled sob. 'This is so terrible.'

There wasn't more than that to say. It said it all. He would fly back to Amsterdam the next day with Mariska and the baby, and come to us as soon as possible.

24

I heard tell that Uncle Willy, when he learned of his son's death, went wandering with his dog through the neighbourhood. He took such big strides that the animal felt compelled to run, tugging so forcefully at the leash that my uncle had to lean backwards to counter it. Neighbours who met him, or saw him pass by yet again, said he talked non-stop, loudly, to no one in particular — not even to the dog.

Not two hours ago I had watched my son die. Did I feel the need, like Uncle Willy, to roam the streets, orating or not, pulled along, if necessary, by an imaginary dog? I just sat there on the sofa, ostensibly calm, waiting for the Rotenstreich sisters to return from their hellish mission.

I thought back to the telephone conversation with my mother, a good twenty years before, about Willy Jr's fatal accident. She and my father were now both dead, but I still had to imagine how I would break the news to her. No, not over the phone, that was too cruel. I'd take a taxi to Eindhoven. In my mind's eye she still lived, alone, in that house in the 'Achtse Barrier' neighbourhood, where Tonio had spent many an overnight visit in the early '90s. Her shadow behind the matte-glass door.

'You here, what a surprise. You should have rung, then —'

'Mama, it's Tonio.'

I push her gently inside. She tries, stiffly, to look over her shoulder. 'Nothing serious?'

We're in the living room. 'He's had an accident.'

She sits down on the edge of the easy chair, hand covering her mouth, yellowy pale. The hand shakes — Parkinson's — so it's like she's giving herself tiny slaps on the cheek. 'Tell me it's not true.'

'I wish I could.'

'Oh ... is it bad?'

'The worst.'

Sniffing, she begins to cry. The hand flaps, out of control, in front of her face. 'Dead?'

'Tonio's dead, Mama. He's gone.'

'Even his back beamed.'

Those words, spoken by my mother, echoed endlessly through my head. At Eastertime 1990, Tonio, then nearly two, spent a week at my parents' in Eindhoven. When we went to fetch him, getting out of the taxi we decided not to ring the bell, but to surprise them by sneaking through the backyard and kitchen.

The living-room curtains were drawn to keep out the sun, but a narrow window at the side was uncovered and open. My father sat at the table demonstrating something (a tow truck, crane, or fire truck) to Tonio, who stood next to him and paid close attention.

'There's a little peg here, you see? If you pull it out ...'

My mother leant over the table, entirely taken in by Tonio's greedy attention. She had so thoroughly brushed his still-blond toddler's hair that it wafted about his head and shoulders like a cloud. We crowded up to the narrow window, our heads pressed together, and felt it was almost a pity to disrupt this scene of happy domesticity. We stood there and watched in silence.

All at once, aroused by some kind of instinctive blood-call, Tonio turned his gaze over my father's busy fingers and toward the window. He saw us. Out of his throat, out of his tiny body, came a protracted primeval scream like we'd never heard from him before. There was something frightening about it, like an animal in danger, but the undertone was one of triumph. He ran in circles, completely berserk, too excited to find his way through the kitchen, so instead we hurried inside.

As small as he was, Tonio must have possessed an amazing lung capacity, because he brought forth a steady stream of noise, without appearing to stop for a breath that combined joy, wonder, and indignation. (Indignation, too, of course: his way of wordlessly conveying his consternation at our extended absence.) The stomping of his little legs at least brought some cadence to the monotonous, high-pitched wail. He clamped one arm around Miriam's leg, the other around mine, apparently determined to hold on forever. I looked from my father to my mother. Their faces, hesitating between surprise and resignation, betrayed their thoughts: we're out of the picture now.

Later, my mother told me that Tonio, halfway through the week, had regularly expressed his doubts as to whether we would ever come pick him up. She said he tended to do so with a brief show of melancholy. He would heave a deep sigh and then resume his interrupted playtime.

Tonio was so relieved that we hadn't forgotten him, and that we'd come to take him home, that on the way to the taxi, each of us holding one hand, he did not even look back at his grandparents standing in the doorway. My mother later said to my sister: 'Boy oh boy, it really was something ... so sweet ... even his back beamed.'

At home, Tonio demonstrated the tow truck, crane, or fire truck and said to me: 'There's a little peg here, you see?'

25

Half past seven. The time Tonio was to come around to eat chow mein. Or should I say, he always promised to be here between six-thirty and seven, and it became seven-thirty. Except when he dropped by unannounced, in which case it was usually earlier, between six and half past. All the above-mentioned times had now been exceeded, including the seven-thirty mark.

Dear Tonio, you should have long been here already. Where are you now? Already on the stainless-steel autopsy table in the basement of the AMC, or still on your deathbed in the yellow nylon tent in Intensive Care? If they haven't carted you downstairs in the freight lift yet, the forensic photographer, who showed up a bit late, might finally be packing up his equipment. The nurse has laid the sheet back over your naked, wrecked body, and is waiting for a colleague to come and help her wheel away your gurney: she has already kicked the wheel brakes loose with her foot.

Okay, that's how it stands with your dead body. But how about *you*? Where are you? We don't have to talk about your soul, and whether it flapped awkwardly around your bed, this being its first foray outside the nest, or flew off in a straight line. No metaphysical ornithology right now. What I mean is pure mechanics. The always-flexible line in which you moved and lived and breathed. An elusive zigzagging line cannot be erased from the world, just like that.

I only have to close my eyes to see you walk into the living room. On the way to the kitchen to pour myself a drink, I walk past the door just as it gently opens. Even though I'm expecting you, I get a fright, because I didn't hear you on the stairs.

'Tonio, dearest ... don't we knock anymore?'

Last Thursday you shaved for that girl ... come on, what's her name ... and a five o'clock shadow once again accentuates your grin. I greet you with a hand on your shoulder, it's warm from cycling, as it should be. You're panting slightly from running up the stairs, so that I feel your breath on my face from close by.

'Where's Mama?'

I can't very well tell you she's gone with Hinde to Grandpa Natan and then to Grandma Wies to tell them what happened early this morning to their grandson …

'Gone to the Suri. You wanted chow-chow, right?'

'It's *chow mein*. A chow-chow is a Chinese dog. Jeez.'

Your staccato laugh, always with a hint of melancholy in its undertones (a matter of intelligence: only fools laugh outright cheerfully). As usual, you stink of cigarettes. Your clothes, which Miriam regularly washes, are saturated with the stench of rotten nicotine. Of course, your roommate has been a hardcore smoker since he was fourteen, and smokes pot besides. You guys are like farmers when it comes to airing out the place: never open the windows, lest the smell of manure get in. Last time I visited, I asked you point-blank: 'You smoke, too, don't you?'

'Ah, sometimes I have one in a bar,' you replied. 'You know, to go along with the guys.'

Your answer put my mind at ease. But now I think you were skirting the issue. I'm going to ask you again tonight, and then I want a straight answer. Come on, Tonio, you're going to be twenty-two in a few weeks. No more hide-and-seek. 'Something to drink?'

'I'll wait for Miriam.'

It's not just that no one mixes a meaner screwdriver than your mother — you don't want to give the impression of being a glutton. Although I suspect you can put it away as well as the next guy. I noticed it, by the by, after the premiere of the film *Het leven uit een dag*. (I hope you didn't cause that Marianne, your date, too much trouble.)

Tygo has followed you upstairs. He's at your feet, waiting to be petted. You scoop the big tomcat from the carpet with both hands at once, and flop backwards onto the corner sofa: your regular spot. While you stroke him with great swipes, Tygo twists himself on his back over your thighs. Let me have a good look at you, Tonio. You are unarguably handsome, shaven or not. Too bad about that 1.73m — a few centimetres shorter than I. You'll have to settle for it, I'm afraid, you're full-grown now.

You've got short parents and short grandparents. Miriam and I were never preoccupied with genetic details like height when planning a family. A person only feels small when he's reminded of his stature by a taller person. It's usually a dumb hulk, whose tallness only makes him dumber and hulkier, and which emboldens him to profess: 'The tall always have a head start.'

A recent study even showed that tall men earn on average more than relatively shorter ones. See? — the tall guy's intimidating appearance is going to be legitimised by job-search committees and accounting offices. Hell with 'em. Remember that nearly all geniuses were short. The brain can communicate quicker with the hand, it's as simple as that. The argument that it's some kind of subconscious sublimation of a physical handicap is just plain bullshit.

'How far apart are we sitting now? A good four metres. I can still smell your smoky clothes. Tonio, there's something I want to ask you … something that's been eating me the past few days. Before that, too, but this week it cropped up again. Since the photo shoot with that girl, last Thursday, to be exact. You don't have to answer me. I'm only asking because it bugged me way back when, too. From the time I was seventeen until I turned twenty. You take after me in so many things, and your life now, as a student, has so many parallels with mine at your age … so … if you're embarrassed by this, then let's just forget it. Tonio, are you still a virgin?'

26

At the annual Amsterdam cultural fair 'Uitmarkt' in 2003, fifteen and thus already too old to co-sign books with his father, Tonio hung around with me at Querido's stall. As I chatted with passers-by who enquired about future, as-yet unpublished works, I was amused to listen in while Tonio joshed sheepishly with Isolde, my editor's daughter. They were just two months apart in age, and had shared a playpen as babies. Later they attended each other's birthday parties. They had played together at Arti. But instead of taking advantage of the longstanding familiarity, he kept the pretty thing at arm's length with ribbing and raillery. She in turn, not to be outdone by Tonio's repartee, gave as good as she got. You could say they dallied in tender derision.

Later, he returned the bag I had given him for safekeeping. 'She and I are going to a do a round of the Uitmarkt,' he shrugged, grinning almost apologetically. I watched the two of them as they walked off. He exhibited the same tick I had at his age when I walked alongside a girl: drawing his shoulders up unnecessarily high, giving yourself a sort of hunchback.

27

Tonio sat, in my imagination at least, across from me in his regular spot these past years, and I occupied the sagging sofa that by rights was once his. Even in my vision, I was unable to seduce an answer out of him.

Like he was fond of the morning intimacies with his mother …

Early one morning, shortly after the summer of the move, I awoke to someone tugging at my arm. It was Tonio. I lay on the living-room sofa, where I had passed out after a nighttime glass. Laughing and blurting out indignant yells, he hung on my arm. I could feel in his toddler's body the force with which he tried to drag me to the floor. That sofa was his morning domain and was at this moment being desecrated by my massive dozing presence. I gave in and slid to the carpet, and rolled around a bit for good measure. He shrieked in triumph. But the victory was not yet complete: I was chased out of the room. I saw Miriam come out of the kitchen with a feeding bottle of watered-down chocolate milk. Before he took it from her he checked it, as he did every morning.

'To the brim, and not too hot?'

'Full as full can be, and not too warm. Feel for yourself.'

A bit later I peeked around the doorway. Tonio was sprawled on the sofa, leaning against his mother, sucking lazily on the bottle and blinking as he watched a video of his favourite cartoon duck, Alfred Jodocus Quack. He swung a swatch of polka-dotted fabric left and right, as though swatting at flies. Every now and then he removed the nipple from his mouth, held the bottle up to the light to check on his drinking progress, and to judge how much longer this paradisal interlude between sleep and school would last. It was his timepiece, his liquid hourglass.

28

Tonio had been dead for hours now, and I had not committed suicide yet. I had often pondered issues like cowardice, lack of solidarity, frozen feelings. If he had been kidnapped, or otherwise had gone missing, I would be out scouring the most unlikely places, out of breath, in search of him. But for his death, I had no answer.

As a boy, I entertained obsessive, morbid thoughts. Say I had to bring my mother the news that my little brother or sister had been killed in an accident. I placed my parents' grief above my own. What's more, I was dead scared of their grief. Better to kill myself than to be confronted with their despair. Dilemma: even though I didn't have to be there to witness it, my suicide would augment their grief by 100 per cent.

Once I became a father myself, I was not relieved of these obsessional fantasies. If I were to lose my child, could I then go on living, or would I forfend the pain by doing myself in as quickly as possible? And then there was Miriam, to whom I also had a responsibility. I could suggest a double suicide as a kind of painkiller.

I made a little moral deal with myself, which in itself was no less obsessive. Thinking back on the Makelaarsbrug and on the risky child's bike seat, I came to the decision that I would commit suicide if I had in any way *caused* my child's death.

Tonight's dilemma was that I could not feel any *less* guilty of Tonio's death. It didn't take a dodgy bike seat to point to my guilt. I could not prevent his death, which was damning enough. On the other hand, I did not want Miriam to have to deal with two corpses in one day. I could not give the disburdening of my guilt priority over the comforting and care she needed.

The longer I thought about it as I waited for Miriam, the more futile the question of suicide became. Tonio was dead, and my self-destruction would be a joke by comparison.

29

It was to be expected that, now that our marital crisis was resolved, various people would do their best to keep the recent conflict alive for a while longer.

'Did you hear? They've made up.'

No, what kind of pub talk was that. They craved drama, and if that was in short supply they would just be creative about it.

Months after my homecoming and our move to the new house, my mother-in-law, herself about to leave her husband, told me that 'at the neighbourhood club' it was a foregone conclusion that we, her daughter and son-in-law, 'had split up'. She was at our place for a visit; we sat in the living room having tea. Tonio was playing on the floor.

'What do *you* think, Mum?' Miriam asked, with that special incisiveness in her voice that she reserved for her mother.

Wies had the habit of quickly running her thumb and index finger over her nose before she struck. 'Yes, well, you *know* ... people don't just say this kind of thing for no reason.'

I looked at Tonio in his play corner ... On his immobile little back I could see he'd suspended play. His grandmother's words had alarmed him. A cluster of Legos clutched in each hand, he sat and listened intently. Tonio had just heard the incomprehensible news that his grandparents (she nearly seventy, he eighty) would soon be separating. Now Grandma Wies dropped in to announce that she had it on good authority 'at the club' that the same thing was about to happen to his father and mother.

Split up.

'No, they don't, do they,' said Miriam, even sharper now. 'People don't just say this kind of thing for no reason. Gossip doesn't just materialise from thin air. Right? Always an element of truth to it. Maybe the *whole* truth. Where there's smoke, there's fire. But tell me, *Mum*, what's *your* conclusion, sitting here on the sofa in our new house? Does it look to you like we're about to split up?'

'You *know*, Miriam ... I'm only repeating what I've heard at the club. That's all.' And, after considering for a moment: 'People don't just say this kind of thing for no reason.'

Tonio had not gone back to his Legos. He turned his head, and looked at the tea-drinking company with big, serious eyes.

'Wies, aside from everything you hear and believe at face value,' I said, 'do you really think it's a good idea to come unload it all in front of your grandson? A child of four has ears, and more importantly, feelings, too. You could have at least asked Miriam or me beforehand if there was anything to your clubhouse cackle.'

She shrugged her shoulders and looked down at the tips of her shoes. 'I only said that people don't just say this kind of thing for no reason.' Her lowered voice was perhaps a concession to Tonio's feelings.

Maybe it was also to spare his feelings that I did not boot granny out of the house then and there.

30

The Rotenstreich sisters were back — shattered by the news they bore, and the reaction it had elicited from the old folks. They didn't say anything, and I didn't ask.

'Minchen,' I said, 'we haven't touched a drop the past two weeks, no problem. But I won't survive tonight without an anaesthetic.'

Miriam and I each took one of the pills we'd been given at the hospital and washed it down with some vodka. Hinde passed. She made a sandwich with one of the rolls Miriam had already sliced when the doorbell rang this morning. They weren't entirely stale, despite the summery warmth that had carried on all day.

'Okay, so tell me,' I said flatly (I still had to get acquainted with my own reaction), 'how did your parents react?'

'My father took it pretty quietly,' Hinde said. 'Didn't say much. He's always been one to bottle it up, but all the more so now. Shocked, of course, but with him you have to read between the lines.'

'My mother just started screaming,' Miriam said. 'She kept repeating how awful it was for me. She was being honest, that I'll have to give her.'

Pill + vodka: I remember little of what we talked about that evening. Each of us sat trapped under our own bell-jar of bewilderment. Intermittently, Miriam burst into fits of tears.

'This can't be … it *can't* be.'

Yes, I did speak on the phone with my father-in-law, but I can't recall who rang who. 'I turned off the television,' he said with his still-beautiful Polish accent, 'and just sat for a while talking to myself. Why, I kept asking myself, why a boy of not even twenty-two? And why do I, an old man of ninety-seven, have to go on living? Why?'

31

'Are we being punished,' asked Miriam a while later, 'for having been so happy, the three of us? For being such an ideal threesome?'

For the first time today, her anguish had an undertone of anger. She eyed me fiercely through her tears.

'Minchen, as far as we know,' I answered weakly, 'this was just a matter of blind fate … and blind fate doesn't hand out specific punishments.'

'So why does it *feel* like that? It feels like retribution. For our arrogance, that we dared to be so happy together.'

32

'If you two think you'll be all right on your own,' Hinde said, 'I think I'll go home now. It's not going to be much of a night, for me either, but ... I think I'm better off in my own bed. And there's Dixie.'

'If you can't face it at home,' Miriam said, 'just come back here. You've got the key.'

Hinde promised. Dixie was her cat.

'I'll leave some bed things on that couch.' Miriam pointed to the chaise longue across from the TV. We hugged Hinde goodbye and thanked her for her help and for sticking with us all day.

'Don't mention it,' she said.

Miriam walked her sister downstairs. They stayed in the front hall, talking and crying, for a while longer. After the door clicked closed, I heard Miriam climb the stairs. She walked past the living room and slowly continued up to the bedroom level. As the most dreadful night of my life was unfolding, she left me alone.

I sat stock-still, listening. Cupboard doors clattered upstairs. Heels on parquet. I didn't hear her come back down: suddenly she was there in the living room, a pillow under one arm, and folded sheets and blankets under the other. She laid the bedding on the chaise longue and sat down next to me on the sofa.

We did not speak. Too exhausted, too numb to console each other. The valium and the vodka did their work, and we gladly encouraged the torpor with new portions of alcohol. The only point of thinking was if there was the chance of finding a solution. I couldn't even think: here we are, two people with a problem. There was no problem, because there was no possible solution, ever. Death itself could loosely be considered a problem: how do we deal with that stinking, irrevocable fact? A dead person, however, was too dead to constitute a problem.

Miriam took a sip, set her glass on the end table, and shoved it as far from her as she could. The booze did not agree with her. She laid her head on my shoulder; it slid, as though of its own accord, down to my chest, and then further, onto my lap. She cried almost inaudibly, with a quiet, rustling sound, like water singing in a kettle. The only thing she said fitted into a drawn-out, tremulous sigh.

'Our little boy.'

INTERMEZZO

15 September 2010

Rough winds do shake the darling buds of May,
And summer's lease hath all too short a date.
—William Shakespeare, *Sonnet 18*

1

The blind wall is back.

In fact, the house is ours thanks to the back garden's minimalist dimensions. During the years of its vacancy, from '89 to '92, it attracted numerous couples in duplicate, with the intention of splitting the large brownstone into a duplex. Their enthusiasm, according to the estate agent, invariably plummeted at the sight of the garden: no more than a postage-stamp courtyard enclosed by two high exterior walls, a fence, and the side of a warehouse. The subsided, moss-covered paving stones gave under your feet, turning every step into a cakewalk. The only growth, aside from the slick moss, was the cautious sprout of a golden rain. And two families' worth of children were supposed to play out here?

For me, the restricted space was a blessing — saved me all those gardening Saturdays. Right away, Miriam figured out which corner Tonio's lidded sandbox could fit into, leaving enough space for us to have dinner now and again with friends. An artist/landscape-architect acquaintance promised to transform the little courtyard into a 'garden room' (whatever that may be) one day, but never got around to it.

I had more trouble with the blind wall onto which our rear windows looked out. It was the side wall of a block of houses on the Banstraat, wedged between Johannes Verhulst and De Lairessestraat. It wasn't, incidentally, totally 'blind'. In addition to a few ventilation grills, there was, to the left and more toward the front of the house, a small bathroom window, half hidden by a wisp of withered ivy. You hardly ever saw light behind the matte glass.

This made for a rather dreary view, like facing out onto railroad tracks, and in fact almost derailed the purchase altogether. But in the end, nature solved the problem. At the bottom of the wall, fresh shoots had sprouted from the clipped ivy, and had begun a careful climb upward. Over the years the unsightly wall became covered in a glistening green carpet of leaves, where a passing breeze could bring out all the various tints of green, shimmering like a mosaic.

In the eighteen years that we lived here, from the summer of 1992 to the summer of 2010, the ever-thickening blanket of ivy, at some places a metre thick, had never been trimmed. Birds nested in it. In the spring of 2007, while I was working temporarily in South Limburg, Miriam decided to surprise me upon my return by giving the grubby courtyard a makeover. Italian stucco and new tiles. Everything antique-pink and terracotta. She had a veranda installed a metre and-a-half above ground level, with French doors leading to the library, and an awning above it.

The puny golden rain, too, had reached maturity in the course of nearly two decades, and spread its broad crown out over the little garden. In good weather we spent many fine hours out there, sheltered by the high adjacent walls as the evenings cooled off. Gardener friends, though, started to raise their concern about the density of the growth.

'D'you have any idea how much weight is hanging on those shoots?' a friend asked. 'If that all comes crashing down, it could take the whole exterior wall with it. Then you'll be staring straight at your neighbour reading the paper in his armchair.'

That would be the good man Max Nord, who, if all was well, lived behind that side wall, and I did not want that on my conscience. Earlier this year, I resolved to have the ivy trimmed in early summer — and then suddenly it was Black Whitsun, which put paid to that promise. The thick, green wall-hanging and the golden rain, as it passed its prime, were from then on the decor for our daily sessions of despair. Here, on the wooden love seat under the compact arbour, Tonio had sat, three days before his death, with the girl from the photo session. Everything around it had to remain intact as much and for as long as possible.

But since we also had to consider the neighbours, who were now living in fear of their wall, we arranged with our regular handymen to resume maintenance the following February.

2

Last night, when I went to bed just before midnight, it hadn't happened yet. As was my habit, I stepped out onto the bedroom balcony to take in a few lungfuls of air, which otherwise were now permanently deprived of fresh oxygen. I decided to ask Miriam if she'd drive me to far-off woods and beaches this fall, so I could stroll without having to share my story with passing acquaintances.

The ivy leaves glinted in the light of the moon, which would only set after 1.00 a.m. If anything had been amiss then, I would have noticed it. The night was clear and tranquil, insofar as a city can be tranquil at that hour. I could never hear another ambulance or police siren without imagining they were headed for the Stadhouderskade.

This morning, 15 September, it was as though autumn was suddenly upon us. Even before I opened the bedroom curtains, I could hear the rain and the wind. It had something enduringly familiar about it, that bare, blank wall across from my window. It brought me back to the early nineties, when the ivy was still only a thin covering on the lowest few metres of the wall.

I slid my feet into a pair of slippers, opened the balcony doors, and stepped outside. Our little back garden was a disaster area. The thick ivy had, perhaps in a hard gust of wind, pulled itself loose from the wall, and like a huge, heavy curtain it buckled as it sank. Thanks to the restricted space between the wall and our veranda, the wall covering had rolled itself up neatly during its free fall, and now lay like a gigantic coconut mat ready to be beaten by a carpet beater the size of a telephone pole. The green Goblin tapestry, which we had always looked upon with such pleasure, had now shown us its back: a gnarled pattern of climbing stems and aerial roots, beautiful and mysteriously intricate as the underside of a Persian rug.

The avalanche of leaves had simply pushed aside the still-slender oak, with its supple trunk, but the golden rain appeared to have been devoured, crown and all, by the huge roll of ivy, like a body rolled up in a hearth rug. At closer inspection I could see the very top of the tree sticking out above the ivy mat, far from the place where I assumed its roots to be. The golden rain, which had grown and matured side by side with Tonio over the last eighteen years, and which he had seen in full bloom just before his death, was no more.

So the blind wall was back. Off to the left hung a ragged, dense lock of ivy that half-covered the bathroom window. And down below, nearly at the paving stones, there was a bit of growth left, like a kind of fig leaf for the wall.

It was eight in the morning. The ivy must have come loose between midnight and a quarter of an hour ago. How could I not have heard the snapping branches, the noise of the avalanche?

Miriam had left for the fitness centre at half past six. If she had noticed the devastation she would certainly have woken me up. I rang her mobile, and left a message on her voicemail: that she mustn't be alarmed when she got home and opened the living-room curtains. Alarmed and well, she phoned right back.

'The cats ...' Her agitated voice. 'Have you checked to see that they're inside?' From the unmistakable sound of grating pedals I could hear she was on her bike. 'For all we know they're buried under the ivy ... squashed.'

Tygo, more than Tasha, had a tendency to climb up the golden rain in search of prey, a sort of play-hunting, quacking as cats do at an unreachable nest.

'Hang on,' I said. Now I was uneasy, too, and went down the stairs, phone in hand, to the pantry, calling the cats' names all the way. They were curled up as usual in their basket. 'Safe and sound. Both of them inside.'

'Oh, thank God.' Miriam wept with relief. 'I was sure we'd lost them. Nothing would surprise me now. I got right on my bike.'

We would never know if the cats were out back when the whole thing came tumbling down, and had managed to reach the safety of the cat flap in the nick of time.

Miriam and Tonio had gone to Lanzarote for New Year's 2002–2003. I stayed at home, because of course something required urgent completion. Miriam had admonished me to bring the cats inside on New Year's Eve before the fireworks started, and lock the cat-flap so that Cypri would not panic and run into the garden, where the noise of the explosions ricocheted even more against the walls.

It was one of those flaps with a variety of settings, and I misjudged the procedure: the cat could get out but not back in again. When I returned early that morning she was nowhere to be found indoors. I rang Miriam in Lanzarote, who was already having breakfast with Tonio at the hotel. In her forgiving voice, she piloted me along all of Cypri's possible hiding places. The cat was fifteen-and-a-half, and had diabetes. I wondered out loud if she hadn't crept under the half-rotting wooden fence to die. Her voice choked, Miriam kept urging me on from the other side of the world, with Tonio occasionally chirping in his encouragement.

'Just keep calling her name.'

Had we ever told Tonio the role Cypri had played in the run-up to his conception? Maybe not, but he had always regarded her as his personal pet, from the moment that he, still a baby, lunged at the cat, who was curled up next to him on the sofa, in order to pet her. He lost his balance and fell on top of her, and paid dearly for it: a blood-drawing swipe, complete with a throaty hiss. Neither of them took umbrage; it was as though the incident served as mutual hazing, because from then on they were inseparable.

'Cypri ... Cypri ...'

Finally an answer, thin and plaintive. The cat had got her head stuck between two bars of the basement grating. Finding her flap locked, she had tried to get into the house this way, ignorant of her diabetic swollenness. I still had the mobile phone on, so Lanzarote could follow every step of my rescue mission. Only once it was successfully completed did I get read the riot act for my irresponsibility and negligence. Tonio also joined in mocking my stupidity, giggling with relief.

'So Adri, got any New Year's resolutions for 2003?'

3

The sad part about having dogs and cats is that they only last, on average, a decade-and-a-half. Those who cannot live without a house pet are confronted with this fact four or five times in their life. Pets are far more loyal than people. We don't lose them to unfaithfulness, but rather to their life expectancy.

If I look at the lives of my contemporaries, it seems as though their existence more or less corresponds in relationships or marriages to the number of house pets. A human love affair has, on average, about the same longevity as your typical dog or cat — except that now, the relationship with the pet ends with its death, and the end of a marriage with the death of love.

Cypri died a year-and-a-half later, just shy of seventeen, as a result of her illness. I was working in Houthem-St. Gerlach, Limburg that spring, so that this time I was the one to follow, by mobile phone, an event taking place in our backyard: Cypri's burial.

Shortly before that (it was May 2004), Tonio had phoned me excitedly with the news that 'finally, something actually happened in boring old Amsterdam Zuid'. On the way home from school, he noticed on the Apollolaan a small crowd gathered near red-and-white police cordons, behind which men from the forensic team could be seen combing the area.

'A liquidation! They've bumped off Willem Endstra. You know, the underworld banker. Just like that, in front of my school!'

And then he informed me, less wound-up, of the death of his cat. They had taken Cypri to the vet, where she'd been put to sleep. Before they took her body back home, Miriam and Tonio went in search of a suitable coffin. At De Gouden Ton, Miriam asked for two bottles of Bordeaux, 'in a box, it's a present.' Since she could not keep the real aim of the packaging a secret, the salesman took the two bottles back out and gave her the box, complete with wood shavings, for nothing. 'You can always come back for a good Bordeaux sometime, ma'am.'

Cypri had leaked profusely during her last days, so the vet advised them to line the wine box with a plastic garbage bag.

'We're going to bury Cypri next to Runner,' Tonio said. Runner, his Russian dwarf hamster, for whom he, years earlier, had composed the brief 'Requiem for Runner' together with his guitar teacher.

So I witnessed the funeral by telephone from South Limburg. Miriam and Tonio took turns relaying the proceedings.

Tonio: 'She'd been letting everything go the last few days ... and now she's lying on the garbage bag, and now it's all dry.'

They slid the wooden lid onto the box, which, said Miriam, fitted the cat to a T. I listened to the hushed discussion between mother and son. 'D'you think the hole's deep enough? So the crows can't get at her?'

4

The two Norwegian forest cats, Tygo and Tasha, were Tonio's only heirs … and that was it. They were his choice, as tiny kittens. Tygo and his sister Tasha …

After Cypri died, Miriam was against getting another cat for the time being, but once Tonio had seen pictures of Norwegian forest cats online there was no stopping him. He scoured the internet until finding a cattery in Veghel, North Brabant, that specialised in this particular breed. In the summer of 2005, a year after Cypri's death, he put on his sweetest, most seductive face and managed to convince his mother to drive him to Veghel, where according to the website a litter had just been born. With their second visit, shortly thereafter, a silver-grey cat and a rust-coloured tomcat, brother and sister, caught his eye as they rolled and tussled with each other. Tonio's choice was already made, but they had to stay with their mother awhile longer. He kept in contact with the cattery via internet, monitoring the growth, week by week, of his little Norwegians.

The day he could fetch them approached. Now he only had to con his old man out of 425 euros per cat, and the adoption would be complete.

So on a Sunday in November, Tonio, with an ironic kind of pride, carried a cardboard box full of fluffy joy in from the car. Tygo and Tasha (they'd been named weeks earlier) stretched out on the kitchen table after the journey, only to curl up in a bread basket, where they fitted perfectly. Tonio photographed them from above. They lay there harmoniously, head to tail, melted like a yin and yang sign into the contour of the basket. It is framed and hangs on the wall, alongside a recent portrait of Tonio that Miriam has turned, for the time being, to face the wall.

5

Before Miriam hung up to continue biking home, she exhorted me to lock the cat flap. I left it open. The ivy had rolled itself neatly up as it slumped to the ground, so there was no danger of it slipping any further. Nor was the golden rain a hazard anymore.

Back in June, I had caught Miriam up on the library ladder at six in the morning. She had propped it up against the tree in order to rescue Tygo, who was too scared to climb down, from a fork in the branches. A proper library ladder has a hinged mounting bracket which grasps the upper bookshelves perfectly for no-tip climbing. That bracket was now draped loosely over the rounded branch, and the ladder wiggled with it, ready to fling Miriam, her outstretched arm just about to grab the cat, to the ground. Alarmed by her cooing and calling, I got out of bed and went to the balcony, from where I looked down on her rescue efforts. I didn't dare yell to her to come down this instant, for fear she'd get a fright and crash off anyway.

The ladder made a nearly 180-degree twist, but Miriam managed to scoop the hefty tomcat off the branch and bring the two of them to safety.

'Minchen, *never* do that again, will you? That's not what a library ladder's for. I really can't handle any more accidents. Let the damn cat sit up there for a couple of days and then call the fire brigade. You let your cat mania go too far sometimes.'

This incident proved once again that such a thing as a domestic quarrel was no longer possible. A petulant remark, the slightest raising of the voice, a sharp look — it all felt like a snub to Tonio.

6

I went back upstairs and out onto the bedroom balcony. On the roll of ivy, and among the undulating pleats of the remaining tapestry, skittered a dozen or more jays. I'm not an avid birdwatcher, but I do recognise a jay when I see one: his beige plumage, his black-and-white tail, the edge of his wings speckled like a Palestinian *kaffiya*. A few more sat on the fence between us and our neighbour Kluun.

I had read about it in the paper. Tens of thousands of Eurasian jays emigrated from Eastern Europe, where they had thrived, and settled in the Ardennes, only to spread their wings further to the Netherlands in search of acorns. The onslaught has only just begun: in the coming weeks, they expect a hundred thousand at least. Those few in our tumbledown backyard were perhaps just the reconnaissance team. I saw them yesterday for the first time. They skipped about, as though surprised and disoriented, over the ivy's aerial roots, possibly wondering what had happened to the previous night's lodgings. Jays have the reputation of being quite muddled, and are thus apt to forget where they have hidden their stash of beechnuts. This was the impression they gave me now: surely they're here somewhere … there you go, we've covered them too meticulously again …

Tygo and Tasha emerged from their cat flap, and with their Norwegian gusto put paid to that Eurasian fumbling and fussing. The birds took flight over the backyards, and the cats in turn gazed confusedly into their newly formed wilderness. With cautious pawsteps, Tygo mounted the oversized roll, while Tasha sniffed around the splintered trunk of the golden rain.

'See, Tasha?' I said quietly, 'You no longer need that tree to get to the birds.' At once she turned her silver-white head in my direction and opened her jaw a few times in a soundless meow. Then she joined her brother on top of the hillock of ivy.

'For God's sake, let's not get wound up over the ivy, too.' Miriam's voice behind me in the bedroom, panting from the stairs. Female heels clattering over the parquet. She stopped next to me and looked down into the abyss. 'Yeah, I know … it's a huge mess, but there's nothing to be done. Worse things have happened.'

'That's just it, Minchen … we sat for nearly four months on those few square metres grieving over those worse things.'

I pointed to the wrought-iron skeleton of the small arched alcove, which had been bent completely out of shape by the force of the falling ivy. The white loveseat was half buried.

'Tonio sat there with his model. Three days before he died. He photographed her there … If we hadn't had that spot to cry our eyes out we'd never have survived the summer.'

The cats now sat side by side, looking up at us with their white chests puffed out.

'Then that's the how it was meant to be,' Miriam said. 'Summer's passed ...'

'Um-hm. The season is finished. Night after night the same show, and now the sets are being dismantled, rolled up, taken away. For the continuation of the heartache, ladies and gentlemen, we offer you the living room.'

Miriam persisted in not caving in at the sight of what did, after all, amount to the destruction of her backyard, but in the end we both hung over the balcony railing in tears. That golden rain ... when we moved in back in July '92, Tonio was four, the slightest puff of breeze blew pale flakes off the little tree, but we didn't realise these were withered blossoms. The following May, the golden rain brought forth small yellow cobs, no bigger than baby corn.

'I'll have them plant a new golden rain if you want,' I said. 'But what matters to me is that Tonio grew up with *this* one, and that he got to see it in bloom just before he died. That mess down there makes me feel like from now on, *everything* of ours is going to get dragged down ... everything we thought we'd achieved, built up ... everything that still bonds us with Tonio.'

'Don't think like that.'

'I can't help it. Murphy's law, with its never-ending chain of discomforts, has something comical to it. I have the sensation that for the past few months we've been living under a law that's only brought a never-ending chain of *disasters*. The one seems to bring about the next, without a logical connection. And the end is nowhere in sight.'

The cats now lay on their side atop the roll of ivy, paws intertwined — play-fighting, but only half-heartedly, giving one another the occasional random lick.

'So now you understand,' Miriam said, 'why I freaked out this morning about Tygo and Tasha.'

181

BOOK TWO

The Golden Rain

CHAPTER ONE

The White Elephant

there is shopping to be done before darkness
asks the way, black candles for the basement
— Gerrit Kouwenaar, 'there are still'

1

Whit Monday. In a daze, I ascended the stairs to my workroom: the seventeen treads that only yesterday morning separated me from my novel, and which the ringing of the doorbell rendered untakeable. On what I referred to as my sorting table lay the unfinished manuscript, and next to it a new work schedule. Today was to be the first day. Just look, there it was, in black and white: 'Monday 24 May 2010/Day 1'. I looked around the workroom with something approaching curiosity. The maps spread out on the long table. The desks with three identical electric IBMs. The folders containing newspaper clippings about the murder.

Here is where it should have happened today.

Were it not for …

I went to the back balcony and opened the doors. Whit Monday promised to be just as fine a pre-summer day as the day before. The unperturbed hard blue sky. Early yesterday morning, Tonio might have seen, at most, a hint of colour fade into the sky. This was all the summer he would see this year, this life.

Once again I was taken aback by the awning above the balcony doors, which I had found retracted last Thursday after the photo shoot, knowing for sure I had left it open. I could no longer question Tonio about it. The girl on the Polaroid snaps, maybe she could clear it up. Where was she now? The capable young photographer who had immortalised her on film had, after this tour de force, set off permanently for a different place.

The loose slats from what used to be Tonio's bunk bed were still lying on the wooden floor of the balcony, against the railing. René, the handyman, had stacked them here, maybe two years ago now, presumably planning to bring them back down to the basement. He had used them to strut the scaffolding when the gutters on the street side had to be replaced. Before the scaffolding was taken down, René had carried the narrow planks over the roof to the back of the house and via the fire ladder down to my balcony. Perhaps I was working and he didn't want to disturb me. When he left them there, they were still bright yellow and shiny with varnish. Over the past two years, the elements had turned the wood a greenish-grey, matching the colours of the balcony itself.

Suddenly, out of those faded, mossy slats rose the image of the intact bunk bed Tonio was allowed to pick out when we moved into this house. He was so proud of it, especially because it meant the prospect of sleepovers with friends. One evening, when the eight-year-old Tonio had his steady girlfriend Merel over for the night, I went to check on them a couple of times. Merel was on the bottom bunk, Tonio on the top. Across the room, on an improvised bed, slept Merel's elder sister Iris, who was always present as supervisor of all daytime games and activities.

The second time I peeked in, I found two little heads lying on the top-bunk pillow. An hour later, the equilibrium had been restored, with Merel back on the bottom bunk.

'It's fine with me if you and Merel want to sleep together,' I said the next morning, 'but why'd you kick her out again so soon?'

Tonio, indignant: 'Yeah, well Merel lay there farting the whole time. It was gross.'

'Oh kid, those marital inconveniences … you may as well get used to them.'

I leant over the balcony railing and looked down into the garden. The domed canopy of the golden rain nearly covered the entire courtyard. Unlike a few days ago, the blossom panicles shone bright yellow through the green of the leaves. To the left, against the terracotta-stuccoed wall, was the two-seat bench under a small alcove (not much more than a wrought-iron arched frame). Here, too, judging from the test snapshots, Tonio had photographed the unknown girl. They were to go to an 'Italian blockbuster night' together in Paradiso on Saturday. According to the police, no one was with him at the time of the accident. Had he said goodnight to her just before, back at Paradiso? Was she even aware of his fate?

We didn't have her name. Perhaps we could find a number or a message from her on Tonio's mobile phone, which was still sealed in plastic. We still did not dare listen to it.

Wandering aimlessly through the house, I kept coming across, in the strangest places, those snow-white sheets of styrofoam that Tonio had used as reflector screens. It still bothered me that he brought them up from the basement without bothering to put them back. Being irritated with him, for as long as it lasted, kept him temporarily alive.

The tripod was still in his old room — without a camera, but rather with an umbrella-shaped reflector screwed onto it. Tonio was undoubtedly planning to clear everything up the next time he came around. First things first: the photos had to be developed and printed. Everything pointed to his determination to be of service, down to the smallest details, to the nameless girl.

One of the thicker white sheets was lined with parallel lengths of black tape, giving it the effect of a striped awning. I turned a desk lamp toward it in an attempt to recreate the lighting effect Tonio might have had in mind, but I couldn't quite work it out.

2

Tonio's birth on 15 June 1988 brought with it certain consequences. I was bound to protect, to warm, to clothe, to feed, and to educate the boy until at least adulthood. As far as my love for him went, my commitment would extend until long after adulthood — until my own death, and then some.

He did not survive me. The world has been thrown out of balance, but I am still accountable for the consequences of my 'baby fever' back in 1987. Now that things have taken this awful turn, I cannot in retrospect renounce the choice, make him, for example, Death's 'poor relation'. To regret my decision of July 1987 would be an act of cowardice, and would sully his memory. Unthinkable.

Even in his deceased state, I am bound to accept him — and care for him — unconditionally. I *knew* that the child I had set my sights on would be mortal, no matter how able-bodied he came into the world. Back then I accepted, albeit with a knot in my stomach, that mortality as a calculated risk. I had even prepared myself to accept, however slim the chance, the risk of his *premature* death.

So grit your teeth, chattering if need be. Bow your head, but then raise it again. By bringing Tonio into the world, an untimely death was one of the unwelcome risks I saddled him with. I had gambled with his life, and lost.

Miriam is still undiminished H&NE, the only woman I ever wanted a child with. Now that her son is dead, I must care undiminished for her, just as for him.

3

Or was there a viler implication behind the disaster that had befallen us? Even though it was thirty years ago that, before Miriam became H&NE, I doubted how suitable I was for fatherhood (or, better put, how suitable fatherhood was for me) — it could be that I was now being punished for my initial presumptuousness, and was forced to return to the original plan: write and *do not* start a family.

Yes, perhaps that was the message ... that any man who dared a half-hearted attempt at fatherhood might be robbed of it at any moment.

4

In aeroplanes I always paid close attention to the rumble and hum of the engines. A steady sound meant everything would be fine. And as far as turbulence went ... a *little* bounce was a good sign: in this way the aeroplane was buying off my composure.

Today I was not sitting in a Boeing, but was still trying to follow all its noises, vibrations, and movements by proxy. As long as I just thought of Frans and Mariska and their one-year-old son Daniel on their flight from Spain to Amsterdam, it had a calming effect. They would no longer see Tonio alive, but they felt the full impact of this loss. Being a father himself made Frans a more full-fledged brother. But then again, now that I myself no longer had a son to contribute ...

5

Life is all about economy. Supply and demand. Work and pay. Give and take. Barter. Market forces.

A sharp line separates the world of economy from the realm of fate. There is no point in standing on the economic side of the line, shouting: 'Tonio is dead! What did I do to deserve this? I invested so much in him ... from a warm nest to corn flakes!'

Each side of the line is governed by entirely different laws. Today, on Whit Monday, it is all about economy. What happened on the other side of the line, in fate's wasteland, is for now of no consequence, except that a dead body has been transported from that side to this one. The body must be washed, retouched, clothed, boxed, carried, and buried. There is a price list, complete with colour photos.

The funeral home sent an elegantly dressed woman, in no way your gloomy female mortician. She appeared to be touched by a grief we did not even exhibit openly. We sat down with her in the library, the French windows open, awning unfurled. No, not a cremation — a burial.

'I need a place where I can go occasionally,' said Miriam. 'Cremation is so absolute.'

The woman asked what kind of funeral we had in mind.

'As intimate as possible,' I said. 'A crowded affair with music and speakers, we couldn't handle that now. And there's something else …'

I related my last conversation with Tonio, last Thursday, when I had complained of the number of funerals that week that I thought I shouldn't miss.

'*So who's the third?*'

Same old mistake: counting myself into the total. As the eldest of three children, I used to keep an eye on my brother and sister at busy carnival fairgrounds so they didn't wander off. I would count … one, two … one, two. Sooner or later, panic would set in. Weren't there three of us? Where was the third? Oh yes, of course, that was me.

Tonio and I had a good laugh about it last Thursday, over that third mourner. Now, just a few days later, the memory of that blithe conversation was instrumental in the decision to limit the funeral list to immediate family and his two best friends.

The woman was entirely amenable. She made no effort to talk us into other, more luxurious, options. Miriam had set her sights on a red-brown coffin, a colour she felt suited Tonio. But aside from that, our order was minimal. Book the usual number of pallbearers. No memorial cards. We would write up and send the obituary to the newspapers ourselves. Everyone can organise their own transportation to the cemetery and back to our house, where we would arrange for coffee and sandwiches.

Miriam had searched the Internet for a small, quiet cemetery, and came up with Begraafplaats Buitenveldert. The woman would inquire into available plots, and would let us know as soon as possible. She didn't think it would be a problem.

'We'd appreciate it,' I said, 'if the location could be kept quiet for now. The obituaries will only appear after the funeral. I might not be quite as big a celebrity as some, but you never know, there might well be a few paparazzi who come up with the idea of shooting a few grief pics.'

The woman swore secrecy. Considering our sober choices thus far, it was with a certain hesitance that she handed us a photo brochure with the flower arrangements. Miriam chose a Biedermeier composition, if only not to have the coffin entirely bare.

'Maybe some evergreen?' she asked. 'People are often taken aback by that gaping hole the coffin has to go in. The pine branches are laid out so that when the coffin is lowered, they bend with it and tend to make the hole less cavernous …'

Coincidentally or not, I had recently reread Harry Mulisch's account of the first funeral he attended, from 'Anecdotes on Death', which for some forty years I'd considered one of his best pieces of writing. The author was eleven, and was made to wear his Cub Scout uniform to the ceremony, to give it some panache. Mulisch describes how the brother of the dead boy (an accidental death), after the coffin had been lowered, steps too far forward with his handful of sand and sinks through the pine branches into the grave. Crack goes the coffin. The branches spring back. The boy's father then steps into the grave. He helps his son back out.

6

It was just like sitting here with the accountant, discussing our financial situation — perhaps the only difference being that the accountant usually looked more worried than this undertaker. What on earth were we doing? With every provision we agreed to, with every one of her notes, we bought more and more into the slapdash suggestion that Tonio might actually be dead. The show of thoughtfully picking out a cemetery plot, a coffin, six pallbearers, a flower arrangement — we were betraying Tonio at every turn. A duplicity that started the minute we let her in the door. I suddenly had the feeling Tonio was standing behind me, shaking his head — smiling, as though he didn't know what to make of this deadly serious piece of chamber theatre. We had to put a stop to this, quit embarrassing him. The joke with the long faces had gone far enough.

We couldn't allow the woman to leave. Once the door closed behind her, she would set the whole machinery of her company in motion. With each turn of a cog, Tonio's death would inch closer, and eventually, if we didn't watch out, would even be a fact.

7

'Evergreen around the grave,' I said, 'is only going to make me think of that Mulisch anecdote. The thought that he would be the next one, in his cub scout uniform, to step into that hole … No, no springy pine branches, thanks.'

'Understood.' The woman smiled. 'And will you want to make use of the chapel … for music, a eulogy?'

'I'm planning to say a brief word at the grave,' I answered. 'That's all. We want to keep it short and sober. Maybe that's most in keeping with the spirit of the deceased. Even though we never really talked about it. Whenever we discussed his future, it looked a whole lot different.'

'Then we should talk about the viewing,' the woman said. 'At the moment, Tonio is at the AMC mortuary. You're now authorising us to bring him to one of our funeral homes, where he'll be available for viewing. Probably the one in Amsterdam-Oost, I'll have to check. Do you want to see him there?'

'We've already decided,' Miriam said, 'that we prefer to remember Tonio as we saw him just after he died. He still looked just like the Tonio we knew … and loved so much. We don't want any other images to overshadow that.'

'But do you want a viewing?' the woman asked. 'I mean, for other visitors.'

'Yes, but he has to look good,' I said. 'There'll be a few friends who want to see him.'

The woman asked what clothes we wanted Tonio to be dressed in. Miriam went upstairs to get his going-out jacket, which he had worn to the Book Ball and to the premiere of *Het leven uit een dag*. When she got back, Tonio's favourite shirt was draped over her arm, the one he had on just before the photo shoot last Thursday. These were not 'work clothes': he wanted to look good for the girl. Just like having shaved. After the photo session, his model departed, Tonio pulled on a T-shirt, leaving the dress shirt behind — not knowing it would come in handy for the coffin.

Miriam also had a pair of his jeans. 'I'll wash and iron them today.'

'Fine,' said the woman. 'When can we pick them up?'

'This evening, if you like.'

'I should mention,' I added, 'that his torso swelled up considerably from the internal bleeding. I'm not sure the shirt will still fit …'

'Don't worry,' she said, getting up. 'We have experience with this kind of thing.'

I didn't ask any further, but suspected that Tonio's proud dress shirt, meant to impress the photo model, would have to be snipped open at the back to make room.

The undertaker's visit concluded with a recap of Tonio's interment scenario. Once she was gone, we flopped, suddenly exhausted, on the terrace, awaiting my brother. Frans and Mariska must have landed at Schiphol by now. Maybe they were giving instructions to her parents, who would babysit Daniel, or else they were on their way to our place, either by tram or taxi.

In *A Sorrow Beyond Dreams*, Peter Handke tells of the scene in his mother's family home after her brothers (it was 1942) were killed: they 'dared not look at one another, not knowing what state they were in.'

That's how Miriam and I looked away from one another that afternoon, 'not knowing what state we were in'. It was as though we were ashamed of ourselves, because just now, in a process of horse-trading, we had willingly turned Tonio over to a corpse-processing factory.

8

People are always said, somewhat reproachfully, to be 'so ill-prepared for death'. I can confirm that this is true, and that it also applied to us. What we were also poorly prepared for: condolence calls. If an etiquette guide to this existed, I had never seen it.

For years, our friends Josie and Arie had visited us with their little daughter, Lola. The first thing Lola would do was ask for Tonio, who was usually holed up with friends in his room, whose door sported a large poster: GENIUS AT WORK. She was always welcome. Tonio had the courtesy to come downstairs and fetch her, and when she got bored among the 'big boys', bring her back.

Lola grew in spurts — by now she was already eleven, nearly twelve — and her absence was awkward, the sole advantage being that I couldn't make the mistake of reminding her that Tonio lived on his own now. ('Lola, I'll make sure he comes around next time you visit.')

I went out onto the veranda with Arie, where my brother and his wife had already installed themselves. Josie busied herself deeper in the house with an uncontrollably weeping Miriam. There was, in fact, nothing in the house except the wet, snorting grief of Tonio's mother. We sat there a bit clumsily amid the anguish, and did not know 'what state we were in'.

'Nice, the golden rain,' Frans said. 'But I'd get that ivy trimmed if I were you. Look there, it's like a metre thick in some places. Great for the birds, but imagine how much weight is clinging to that wall.'

'It's not my main priority right now,' I said. 'Here, under the ivy and the golden rain, Tonio did a photo shoot last Thursday with a girl ... we don't even know her name ... I'm not trimming away any memories for the time being.'

'Adri,' said Frans, 'if it's too painful to talk about, then don't, but ... what exactly happened yesterday morning?'

'I don't know much more than the police told us. They're keeping mum until their investigation's been rounded off. The driver who hit Tonio was being questioned at the same time they came around here. That girl from the photo shoot, the one I just mentioned ... Tonio told me a few days ago she'd invited him to Paradiso on Saturday night ... for an Italian night, eighties blockbusters, whatever. I assume Tonio left Paradiso at about four-thirty. He crossed Max Euweplein on his bike, and probably took that footbridge next to the casino, the one that slopes down to the Stadhouderskade. I guess he was going to cut through the Vondelpark on his way home. To De Baarsjes. I don't know if he went cruising across the road at full speed ... it's a pretty steep slope ... anyway, it was there, just near the traffic lights, that the car hit him. The traffic lights were turned off, or flashing, the police weren't really sure.'

Having to tell all this to my younger brother was humiliating. His son, his only child, born when he was fifty-three, had just had his first birthday two months ago. All those years that Tonio was here, Frans had hesitated to start a family. I'd always let him know what a blessing a son was for me. And yet he still had his reservations. Now I had to explain, in so many words, how vulnerable a child could be, even when it was past the age of twenty. I gave him a full account of my defeat.

'And the driver ... do they know if he was speeding?'

'No, I only heard that it wasn't a hit-and-run, he reported it right away.'

It struck me that the two women present sensed exactly when they had to follow Miriam into the kitchen — and not to help her refill the glasses. 'I just can't believe he's gone for good,' you could hear through the open window.

I had the impression that I, more than anyone, was polluting the almost summery spring evening with banal chitchat. Sure, it was mostly about Tonio and the past two days, but I did not manage to get through to the crux of what had really happened. I even caught myself making a few bitter comments having nothing whatsoever to do with the accident. They just came blurting out, as though wanting to prove, entirely on their own, that even without Tonio, life, in all its facets, no matter how vulgar, simply goes on.

9

It's just how these things go: you see your visitors out, and before each one goes on his way, you stand there on the front steps confirming each other's remarks — about the waste of a life, about the incomprehensibility of loss.

'That something like this can just *happen*,' Josie repeats, her eyes glistening in the light of the streetlamps. 'Run over like that on the street ...'

Once everyone has gone I take a few steps out onto the sidewalk. I look up: whether the sky is as aloofly clear as it was the night that Tonio ... The sodium-vapour light of the streetlamps obscures my view of the stars.

I realise that, for as long as I can remember, I regarded it as something sacred, something *mysterious*, rather than as a major stroke of ill fortune: a parent who loses a child, and has to go on living with it. A neighbour of ours lost her beautiful daughter to leukaemia. Well-mannered lad that I was, I was expected to go into the living room, where the girl was laid out for viewing. She was no longer pretty. Her cheeks lay sagged and blubbery, either from the medication or from the illness itself, on the pillow. Her mother, smiling, led me to the bier, but suddenly was overcome with grief. She threw her arms up in the air and cried, in a cramped sob, 'Just open your wee eyes *one* more time.'

It has stuck in my memory in dialect, whose pronunciation of 'wee eyes' — '*eugskes*' — made it sound all the more heart-rending.

What the child was asked to do in return for all that grief was minimal, but she still did not comply. The *eugskes* remained shut.

My sister once had a friend with light-blonde hair and chubby, pale legs. Antoinette. They called her The White Elephant, but at the same time she was treated with a certain respect, because her older brother had been killed in a motorbike crash when he was seventeen. The story went that the boy's father 'still, every night', before going to bed, would take a few steps out the front door to the edge of the sidewalk and peer up and down the street, as though his son might come home any minute.

For me, *that* has been the image, for the past forty years, of a father who has lost his son: a man who leaves the front door ajar, and under the light of the streetlamp pricks up his ears for the putt-putt of a motorbike.

I am now that man.

10

While Miriam and Josie were at Buitenveldert Cemetery picking out a plot for Tonio, I sat in my workroom trying to compose a memorial note. We had told the funeral home I would write it myself, and that we would not have it typeset, but just duplicate it on my own home photocopy machine. Being computerless, this was my customary procedure with all my writing. No, they didn't have to post them for us either: I wanted to add a personal, handwritten note to each copy and enclose a photo of Tonio.

During his first (and only) year at the Amsterdam Photo Academy, Tonio had participated in a group project: a realistic remake of a portrait of Oscar Wilde. Part of the assignment was that they had to track down an original themselves. One afternoon he burst into my workroom, out of breath from running up the stairs.

'Adri, d'you know anything about Oscar Wilde?'

'Are you finally going to read a book?'

'It's like this ... we've got an assignment to recreate a portrait of Oscar Wilde. But we haven't been able to come up with a good photo of him. Only some vague junk online.'

'You could have saved yourself the climb: down in the library I've got a few books about him, with photos.'

We went downstairs and I showed him some of the better portraits of the writer. He had to laugh: all I had to do was reach onto a bookshelf, and he was saved. With his usual eagle eye, he paged straight to the photo of a young Oscar Wilde that would eventually become the model for their project.

'There are a few others of a somewhat riper Wilde.'

I paged through the book until landing at the familiar picture of a massive Oscar, bowler hat in hand, the fragile Bosie at his side, and also managed to find the remake of Gerrit Komrij as Oscar Wilde and Charles Hofman as Bosie. 'See, here's how you should tackle it.'

'I think the first one's better, with the walking stick. He's much younger there. See, one of us has to pose. None of us is over twenty.'

At the Waterlooplein flea market they found a cheap, threadbare fur coat, which, with the right lighting, could be made to look suitably chic. They neglected, however, to check the coat for living creatures — and as a result, after the photo session not only Tonio (who was still living at home) but Miriam and I both, thanks to the clumsy exchange of pillows, all ended up infested with nits. In a throwback to Tonio's primary school days, we got out the pediculicide and flea comb.

Tonio, having the right hairstyle and having not entirely shed his baby fat, was the most likely candidate for the role of Oscar Wilde. The group got perfect marks for their work. Miriam and I decided to include this photo with each memorial note, because it shows him at the focus of his greatest passion, photography — as both portraiteur and subject. Miriam and I had, for starters, 200 A5-size prints made at the photo shop.

11

Amsterdam, 25 May 2010

In the early morning of Sunday 23 May, our son Tonio
(born on 15 June 1988) was hit by a car while riding his bicycle.
The accident occurred on the corner of the Hobbemastraat and the
Stadhouderskade. From four-thirty in the morning until four-thirty
in the afternoon, surgeons at the AMC fought, together with Tonio,
for his life. He did not pull through. Tonio died shortly after leaving
the operating room, with us at his side. He was our only child.
As a student of Media & Culture, he had actively and ambitiously
taken life by the horns. He had recently informed us of his intention
of pursuing a Master's degree in Media Technology. It was not to be.
His passing leaves us devastated.
We hope you will appreciate that Tonio's burial
will be kept intimate,
and that for the time being we are not able
to receive visitors at home.

Miriam and Adri

Enclosed: Self-portrait of Tonio as Oscar Wilde (2006), taken
during his studies at the Amsterdam Photo Academy.

12

I feel him sitting next to me. I feel him standing before me. I feel the
warmth of his breath in my neck — in short puffs, caused by his chuckling,
for he is reading, half out loud, over my shoulder, like that time when I
wrote to a publisher who had mistreated me. '"Dear bookmonger" …
good one!'

But mostly I feel him *in* me, as though I were a pregnant woman. I feel a hard kick in my gut, then a few lighter kicks for good measure. It feels like he's struggling to turn over.

In the spring of '94, he and Miriam came down to Angoulême, where I had gone a few weeks earlier to work on a story. Tonio was five, nearly six. The doors of the TGV opened, and he hurled himself straight from the top step into my arms. Without so much as grazing the platform tiles with the toe of his shoe, he suddenly dangled from my shoulders, laughing, kissing. I can call to mind, any time of the day or night, the affectionate force of his grip. I shall feel Tonio in my flesh for as long as I have living nerves.

Five years later, in Marsalès, I fetch him from a table-tennis tournament at the campground. I watch for a little while from the sidelines how he wields the paddle as twilight falls. He has taped little plastic tubes filled with yellow luminescent liquid to the back of his hands. Their purpose is to confuse and distract his opponent. A flick of the wrist, and the light stick traces a sort of Chinese character in the air. His ruse does not work. Tonio loses time and again. After the last set, I push him playfully in front as we walk home across the low dike that traverses the swimming hole. I press my fingertips into the sides of his nape, just under the ears. His skin is flushed and moist.

'Hot neck you've got there.'

'*Do-hon't.*' He makes the automatic defensive gesture with his elbows that goes with his age (eleven), but does not really try to shake loose from my hand. 'Jeez, I didn't even win a single set. Those light sticks are worthless.'

My thumb glides upward, caressing the sweaty hairline on the back of his neck. The damp warmth will never evaporate from the heel of my hand.

In all phases of his life, Tonio left imprints of himself in me — from the time he literally fell into my lap, straight from the womb, until that last hug on the Staalstraat, when in my emotional absentmindedness I forgot to give him that last fifty.

13

Miriam came home in an artificial kind of high spirits, and with the almost cheery announcement that she and Josie had found 'a pleasant, quiet spot for Tonio'. The papers made a note of the plot number: 1-376-B.

'When you see it, you'll like it, too.'

'I believe you. I'll see it Friday.'

Before I could become irritated with her cheerfulness, I reminded myself that it could, at any moment, make way for bottomless grief.

There was a postage-stamp-sized notice in that afternoon's *Het Parool*:

Cyclist killed in collision on Stadhouderskade

Amsterdam Zuid — A 21-year-old cyclist died Sunday afternoon in hospital from injuries sustained in a traffic accident on the Stadhouderskade. Early Sunday morning he collided with an automobile. The 23-year-old driver was given a breathalyser test, but had not been drinking.

'There you have it,' I said to Miriam. 'The story of our wonderful boy in a couple of lines. There are Dutch literary critics who think I might take an example from this kind of brevity.'

In the same column of *faits divers* was another postage stamp containing more upbeat news: the cost of a new driver's license in Amsterdam was to be lowered by a tenner, from 46 to 36 euros.

14

Jim sat dejectedly in the curve of the corner sofa, even paler than we'd gotten used to seeing him these last few years. The whiteness of his face, wreathed by hair as dark as Tonio's. Jim made erratic motions, as though he wanted to say something but couldn't find the words. His mother sat beside him, and continually rubbed her hand over his back — a firmer action than caressing or stroking. He allowed her to do it.

Tonio's bosom buddy. They had known each other since nursery school, and were like brothers. There was a brief estrangement at the time they each went off to a different school (Jim had a learning disability, possibly dyslexia). Once during that period, I bumped into his mother on the Van Baerlestraat, on the viaduct over the Vondelpark. We exchanged slightly awkward greetings as we passed: our sons, after all, weren't hanging out together anymore. When we were already several dozen metres apart, Jim's mother turned abruptly and shouted something along the lines of: 'It'll work out between them, you'll see. They're made for each other.'

'I'm sure it will,' I called back. 'It's just a phase.'

And sure enough, not much later they rediscovered each other, the bosom buddies. Thereafter the friendship continued uninterrupted, but not without its hurdles. If Tonio came round on a Sunday evening and we'd inquire into Jim's chronic insomnia, he would shake his head dispiritedly, eyes cast downward, no matter how cheerful he was when he came in. Tonio didn't say it in so many words, but you could tell he saw the situation as fairly hopeless. Since we didn't like seeing Tonio go all glum, that hour or so that we had him all to ourselves, we didn't press it, and eventually stopped asking altogether. He did hint that once their lease on the Nepveustraat ran out, he would think about living on his own, or in a student flat.

I sat on the sofa next to Jim's father. As a staff member of a medical team, it seemed, he had been indirectly involved with the case of the murdered policewoman I would have been writing about now, were it not … I listened to him with more than the usual interest: notwithstanding his attempts at discretion, I was picking up plenty of nearly first-hand details, despite it being for a novel I was forced by circumstances to set aside and would probably never return to.

And yet my attention was distracted by Jim, who was talking to Miriam about Tonio. About how Tonio had made such a self-confident and go-getting impression recently, and had consequently seemed so content.

'… yeah, he'd worked it all out himself,' I overheard. Jim was referring to the channels through which Tonio had hoped to get his master's degree in Media Technology — the plan he had filled us in on the previous week. Jim underscored his statements with a lot of silent nodding, and I could see on his taut features that he was fighting back the tears.

Even when I tried to resume the conversation with his father, I still kept more than half an ear attuned to Jim. Perhaps my waning attention became evident, for the father suddenly raised his voice a little to call over to Jim: '… then maybe he was taking a detour to pick up some cigarettes.'

I didn't hear Jim's answer clearly, but I assumed it was all about the mystery of why Tonio was at that intersection in the first place. Someone else in the living room said: 'Wrong place, wrong time.'

Cigarettes. I purposely did not get involved in the discussion, because it might mean I'd hear that Tonio smoked — not just 'once in a while with the guys', to be cool, as he'd once told me himself, but systematically enough to find himself without in the middle of the night and go out of his way to buy a fresh pack.

Of course, Jim might have phoned him to ask if he'd pick up some smokes for him on the way. I didn't ask, because I did not want to know the truth.

So as to get off the subject one way or another I asked Jim about the Polaroid girl. Yes, he'd heard Tonio mention a photo shoot, but he didn't know any details. He couldn't even help us out with a name. He had never seen her.

'Did you have the impression that Tonio talked about a particular girl … I mean, without mentioning her name?'

'Well, he was pretty preoccupied with girls recently,' Jim said evasively. 'He talked about it a lot — whether he was going about certain things the right way, and so on.'

15

'... and he cursed his fate.' As a boy I had read this in countless books. There was something cosy about curling up next to the coal stove and reading about the hero who, defeated by dark and evil powers, clenched his fist and cursed his fate.

Now that I know myself how it feels to curse one's fate, all that cosiness is gone. I lament Tonio's fate. I curse mine.

CHAPTER TWO

The betrayal

there's a grave that needs digging for a butterfly
exchanging the moment for your father's old watch —
— Gerrit Kouwenaar, 'there are still'

1

Miriam carried Tonio's mobile phone with her everywhere. It became something of an obsession. If she happened to leave the phone in the bathroom, for instance, she'd run back in a panic to fetch it.

'He's really not going to ring,' I said, when her fussing over the mobile started to get on my nerves.

'It's that girl,' Miriam said. 'I've got the feeling she's still in the dark. Nobody in Tonio's circle of friends knew her.'

'Maybe we should have run the obituary right away then.'

'No, oh no.'

When Miriam went off to shower, she left the mobile lying on the bed, and although she had turned up the volume she still missed the call. In any case, she was too late, because the voicemail had already been activated. It was a call from an unidentified number, given on the display as: 'no caller ID'. I found Miriam sitting on the edge of the bed, listening anxiously to the voicemail message.

'She didn't leave her name.' Miriam handed me the phone. 'But it's got to be her. Listen.'

'... tried Facebook, but your page is quiet. I was wondering how the photos turned out. If they're no good, I'm sorrier for you than for me. You're the one who did all the work. It was a nice afternoon anyway. Okay, hope to hear from you soon. Bye.'

I thought I heard a trace of a British or an American accent. I handed Tonio's mobile back. 'The voice matches her Polaroid, anyway,' I said.

2

This kind of loss, it just happens to you. The longing follows of its own accord, just like the heartache.

But the loss does not necessarily make you feeble, nor does it present you with a measure of grief that simply has to be accepted without you being allowed to give it some kind of form. As absurd as it was in the given situation, there were always choices to be made. Should we give in to the pain, or resist it? We incessantly asked each other these kind of questions.

'Would Tonio have wanted his demise to destroy us?' (Me to Miriam.)

'We can't ask him anymore.'

'Say we did ask him when he was alive ... just to be on the safe side.'

'Knowing him ...' said Miriam, 'no, I don't think he'd want to see us go under. He'd have preferred that by staying alive ourselves, we kept his memory alive.'

'But how about *us* ... what do *we* want? To sink into ruination because of his downfall? Make no mistake, there's something comforting in that. Now that he's gone, we can just let ourselves go to pot. Him kaput, us kaput. Maybe we owe it to him.'

'If I really put myself in his shoes, Adri ... no, he wouldn't have wanted it. We have to go on. Because of him. For him.'

'Let's first give him a proper burial. Then we'll see ... or not.'

If we were to map out Tonio's last hours and days in detail, we were certain to bump into that girl from the photo shoot sooner or later. Even without a phone number or address, not even a name, there'd have to be a sign of her somewhere. She did exist, after all.

But … did we really want to? If we did track her down, we might discover a budding romance — which could have led to something more.

'The funeral is Friday,' Miriam said on Wednesday, 'and we still haven't contacted that photo girl. I wish she'd ring again.'

'Let's just let it run its course,' I said. 'If there was something between them, then she's bound to make herself known again.'

'I'm so afraid she still doesn't know what happened. She could be sitting there waiting for Tonio to call … or for a reply from him on Facebook … she just won't get it.'

'We've tried calling all the available numbers,' I said. 'None of his friends know her. At most, they vaguely know about a photo shoot. No one can come up with a date. Not even a name. Y'know, Tonio and photo sessions … he did so many of them. No, we're just going to have to wait this one out.'

While I thought: we should make a beeline to the Netherlands Forensic Institute, to have that call — 'no caller ID' — investigated.

And then there was that excruciating doubt. Did *I* have to go looking for her? What was the point of reconstructing Tonio's final days? He had irretrievably vanished from the existence that offered itself for reconstruction.

No, I could better devote my time to the memorial letters. I had laid the photos I was planning to enclose (Tonio as Oscar Wilde) in a small stack, face down, on my writing table. This way I could slide a photo into the envelope without looking him in the eye, for each and every letter compounded the betrayal I was carrying out.

Despite this precautionary measure, Tonio was inevitably present in my workroom, in varying and ever-changing life phases. 'Adri, if I pass the photos to you, it'll go faster.' 'You keep writing the same thing, but with different names ... why's that?' 'Adri, it would be so much more efficient if you had a computer with an address spreadsheet. One click of the mouse and a string of self-adhesive stickers rolls out of the printer. You really are from the Dark Ages, aren't you?'

They were fine, early summer days, all of which blindingly reflected Whit Sunday. I sat at the desk closest to the open balcony doors, shaded from the sun by the awning.

Occasionally, Miriam came in to cry at my side. No, we didn't need to know yet more suffocating details: she was grief-stricken enough already, why add insult to injury. We would bury him on Friday morning, and the obituaries would appear in the evening papers that afternoon. After a day like that, our job was to deal with our grief, together, in the safe haven of our house.

4

The day of his funeral was as divine a summery day as the day he died.

'Today I must bury my son.' I formulated that sentence over and over in my head while performing a series of everyday actions: brushing teeth, showering, shaving.

I tried out a number of variations: 'Today I am going to bury my son.' As many as necessary, until I had the ideal choice of words in my head. This was 'terra cognita': many a morning it went like this, before I ascended the stairs to my work room, to write down the first words of a new chapter.

'Today, I bury my son.'

It was, for now, still just an observation, hardly more than that. No sickening emotions went with it. I was calm even *before* taking the pill Miriam offered that was supposed to calm me down. My hands did not shake for even a moment while shaving.

While getting dressed, I silently rehearsed the brief speech I had planned to hold at the grave. All week I had almost obsessively hurled the facts concerning the accident as I knew them onto paper, plus what I recalled from Tonio's last two visits to our home. I wanted to record everything that might come in handy in reconstructing — I still did not know why — the finale of his life. But I could not bring myself to compose a eulogy. My brother would give a longer speech, which put my mind at ease. I'd been engaged in restless, anxious conversation with Tonio all week, and it had exhausted me.

Since our premature return from Lugano last May, I had hardly been out of the house. I'd spent all those months at home, rarely dressed in anything but grotty jogging pants and a baggy lumberjack shirt. All right, I'd bought a dark velvet sport jacket for the premiere of *Het leven uit een dag*, which since that event was still on the very same hanger on the very same closet door, the tie that went with it draped over the hook.

Tonio was at the premiere, too, dressed in style. He had invited Marianne, an elegant girl he knew from the Amsterdam Photo Academy, a little older than he. They never (much to my regret) really had an affair, but Tonio always invited her to more official events like the Book Ball, if we were able to get our hands on an extra pair of tickets.

That evening at the film premiere in The Hague, I noticed how much more mature and self-assured he had become. The tux jacket looked great on him. He was outgoing, jovial, witty. After the film, he and Marianne joined the musicians of the pop group Novastar, which had provided some of the film score. They had a bang-up time. Later they rode with us in the taxi-van that took the whole bunch of us back to Amsterdam for the afterparty at De Kring.

Now that I was to bury him, it had to be in that last jacket he saw his father wear, corresponding necktie and all.

While my brother and I stood at the bar, burning through the generously allotted drink vouchers, Tonio and Marianne sat in their own corner, drinking and chatting. It appeared to be a lively conversation. The film crew took over the dance floor, and the director came by every so often to dole out a new round of vouchers.

Marianne, I knew, lived with her parents in Noordwijk, and would be sleeping over at a girlfriend's place in Amsterdam. The night wore on. As closing time approached it was decided that she would sleep on Tonio's sofa. They would take the night bus to his neighbourhood, or else walk, it wasn't really clear.

When they came to say goodnight, I suddenly felt sorry for Tonio. When he was tipsy he would always sway a bit on the balls of his feet, almost unnoticeably, back and forth. He was looking pallid, the corners of his mouth were turned up in a slightly stupid grin. As supple as he had been all night, he was now rigid and wooden, his shoulders hunched. Marianne was just as casually cheerful as she'd been all afternoon and evening, accommodating to Tonio. How he resembled me. My eloquence all too often also had to come out of a glass. When I was Tonio's age, I recognised myself in the words of Boudewijn de Groot's 'Testament': 'out pubbing / I drank too much, hoping to wow her / and got the drubbing I deserved'.

I slipped him some cash so they could take a taxi. And, with that, he vanished out of my life again for weeks.

5

The burial was scheduled for ten o'clock. Laughable mundanity: at quarter past nine I leant with my elbows on the balcony railing on the second floor, clipping my fingernails. Through the opening between the houses, I caught a glimpse of our friend Ronald Sales as he walked down the street. Back in 2001, he had made a portrait of Tonio, then thirteen, for my fiftieth birthday. We hung it in the dining room, which we called the *Salon de Sales*. The memory of the mischievous smile on Tonio's face on 15 October when he brought me the framed and wrapped portrait was enough to make me jump from the balcony here and now. Only the psyche-numbing pill kept me from doing it.

Ronald walked bent slightly forward, so it looked like he was fighting his way against the dusty early-morning sunlight, as though into a hard gust of wind. Of course he was one of the few invitees, and was making his way to the line 16 tram stop on De Lairessestraat. There was something so easy-going about the scene that I might well have called his name, waved, and shouted: 'See you at the cemetery!'

I took my time cutting my overgrown nails, which had been a nuisance all week at the electric typewriter. In my haste to set my notes about Tonio on paper, my two index fingers so often missed their mark that the cuticles had become raw. The image of Tonio's inert hand on the edge of his deathbed pierced my consciousness for the umpteenth time this week. The grimy fingers. The nails: not too long, but with crescents of dirt under them. No, I am not going to equate his hand with the dark-edged envelope of a death announcement — must put that behind me now.

And yes, plenty of associations. I knew that a dead person's fingernails and toenails kept on growing, just as one's hair did. The coffin of the poet Jacques Perk, who had died prematurely, was opened in front of his father before being reburied. The man turned away in anguish: 'That beard … that beard!'

Some time after the liberation of Eindhoven, my father came upon the body, deep in the Sonse Bergen woods, of a parachutist dangling from a treetop. The first thing that struck him were his non-regulation fingernails — no paratrooper would ever get his chute open with those.

All week, every time the doorbell rang I saw those two young police officers before me. *A critical condition.* But when it rang now, just before nine-thirty, I didn't flinch: I knew it was Hinde, who would ride with us to the cemetery. Even that demonic bell was tamed by my inner calm, forced into submission by Miriam's evil little pill.

First via the Lomanstraat to pick up my father-in-law. The double row of trees darkens the street, all year round. Natan had already turned off the living-room lamp he usually left on. He appeared out of the shadows at the front window. From what I could see of his upper body above the half-curtains, it was clear he had shrunk even more. Ninety-seven. He waved to say he was ready. Hinde got out to go fetch her father.

This was the house where Tonio spent countless weekends in the days when Miriam and I went out a lot. Never a peep of discontent. The Wednesday before Whitsun he had dropped in on his grandfather, as he often did, at irregular intervals. Bit of a chat, and the extra pocket money (accepted under protest) was of course welcome. He never let on how he felt about his grandparents' divorce, back in '93.

Natan pulled the front door closed, and paused to check the doorknob. He let his elder daughter lead him across the street, shuffling, looking at the ground. Once they reached the car, he looked up, and, upon seeing Miriam and me, a smile came over his pale, sad face, but his wet eyes did not join in the expression. I got out and helped him onto the back seat.

'So,' he said, once he'd sat down.

On the way there, my thoughts were with my interrupted work schedule. Today, Friday 28 May, was supposed to be 'Day 5'. It was more than just an indicator — something akin to a particular day's own name. It was more like saying *Tonight, One Twentieth In The Can*. If the first five days of the schedule had yielded twenty-five new pages, the minimum, I wouldn't have been dissatisfied, but perhaps just a bit disappointed.

Sometimes a numbered date got, later on, a nickname as well if it had distinguished itself in one way or another. (The Crash. The Acquittal. The Dirty Blank Line.) The first five days of this schedule would never get a nickname, nor the notation of the number of pages each day yielded, just as the days that followed would not.

6

Much more than older Amsterdam-Zuid, the Olympic Stadium neighbourhood and Buitenveldert seemed to consist of light patches meant to reflect the bountiful sunlight. Turning onto the street where the cemetery was located, I looked over my shoulder to my father-in-law and said: 'Don't worry, Natan, I'll stick with you.'

He nodded in gratitude. Miriam pulled into the car park. Some of the mourners were already standing against the pink brick wall next to the gate. We got out and approached them, slowing our pace to accommodate Natan. Whether it was the pill, I couldn't rightly say, but even now there were no overwhelming emotions churning around inside me. We had a painful job to do. Just get through it. We hadn't ordered a big convocation. It did not have to last long. *Afterwards* I would think about what this all meant.

The woman from the funeral home came over to us. We went through the details of the sober ceremony. I would say a few words, then invite my brother to deliver his speech. I excused myself: 'Just have to greet a few people.'

All at once, I stood face to face with my tearful mother-in-law. She was being supported by two nurses from St. Vitus.

'That sweet Tonio,' she sobbed, 'he'd never hurt a fly. Why? ... Why?'

I kissed her. 'We'll talk later.'

I spoke briefly with my brother and his wife. With my sister, who wore a wig because of the chemo and radiation. Tonio's two best friends, Jim and Jonas. Jim's younger brother and parents joined him; Jonas had brought his mother. Friends: Josie and Arie, Dick and Nelleke. I told Ronald I'd seen him walk down the Banstraat toward the tram stop. 'As though you were struggling against the driving sunlight,' I said, but he didn't get my drift, and I felt like a fool.

A light-grey hearse drove, almost noiselessly, up to the gate. Six young men, all dressed in light-grey tailcoats and light-grey top hats, slid the red-brown casket containing Tonio's body out of the hearse and placed it on their shoulders. In perfect unison, they went into motion. I slipped my hand under Natan's arm and led him slowly behind the pallbearers. They were all equally slim, and their youth was undoubtedly meant to tally with the age of the deceased entrusted to them.

I wondered if it had been wise to take that pill. Hardly gave it a second thought when I'd placed it under my tongue to marinate. It would, I figured, take the edge off the situation. What I now experienced was not so much indifference, but rather an emptiness — in myself, and in the coffin. Two congruent voids.

Natan's shuffling must have made us fall behind: suddenly we were overtaken by Miriam, Hinde, and their mother, still supported by the two sturdy nurses. Other members of the group passed us on both sides.

The sun shone over the well-kept cemetery. The modest procession snaked between the meticulously trimmed hedges. My brain, chilled from the medication, had room for thoughts like: *A graveyard like a labyrinth, and make just enough about-turns with the casket in the dead-end passages until, in the heart of the maze, one hits upon the open pit and the evil spirits have been sidetracked.* I wondered how the ghastly pain of the past few days could have quitted me now, of all moments, when the object of my loss was being borne ahead of me, about to vanish into the earth forever.

7

I saw two rabbits sitting on the path. It touched me, how they sat there motionlessly, watching the approaching cortège, and then darted into the hedge. Buitenveldert Cemetery was famous for its rabbits, which nibbled on the plants and flowers on the graves. None of the deceased's relatives protested — it was all part of the package.

I tried to imagine (perhaps to recapture some semblance of feeling) how I would have pointed out that pair of bunnies to a seven-year-old Tonio, and how he would have said 'awww ... cute', but instead I saw him in the child's seat on the handlebars of my bike, age one, his finger pointing at the rolls of hay against the sloping French meadow, and squealing: 'owww ... owww!'

It wasn't far to the grave. The immaculately grey young men placed the coffin on the electric lift above the grave, nodded in respect, and marched, light as feathers, off behind the hedges. They appeared to be executing a thoroughly planned choreography that would have done quite good service as a ballet — only the six dancers would have been wearing grey tights under their tailcoats instead of trousers.

Once everyone had assembled in a semi-circle around the grave, I took a step forward, right up to the coffin. I did not manage to stand upright on both legs. My restless left foot found its way to a wooden beam (an old railroad tie, maybe?) that bordered the edge of the pit.

'I'll say a few brief words,' I began, 'and then I'll turn it over to my brother Frans.'

The woman from the funeral home and the cemetery caretaker stood at a polite distance, in the opening between two hedges, keeping a discreet eye on the proceedings.

'Dear friends … Tonio had many talents, but that did not include a talent for arguing. Differences of opinion, yes, disagreements aplenty, but I never once, in his entire youth, succeeded in getting into an all-out row with him. Worrying. Okay, once. A real quarrel. Well, almost. After two abandoned studies, it didn't look like there was much direction to his life. I summoned Tonio to our house, and took him to task for his lack of ambition. But even then you couldn't call it a proper row. Tonio forestalled escalation by insisting he was veritably *exploding* with ambition, and he'd prove it. For starters, he would get a part-time job while laying the groundwork for a definitive course of study, so he wouldn't have to rely entirely on his parents for financial support. He was so convincing about it, and so damn charming, too, that once again I didn't manage to turn a little squabble into a full-fledged father-son clash.'

On the coffin lay the Biedermeier flower arrangement out of the funeral home's brochure. Every time my eye fell upon it, I felt as though I was addressing Tonio directly, and I did not want that. My gaze drifted up to the blue sky. My foot fidgeted and shifted incessantly over the beam.

'Tonio kept his promise. He got a job, and last September started in earnest on a Media & Culture major. Last Wednesday he dropped by our place. He gave us a preview of the future he had planned out for himself. After his bachelor's degree, he planned to get a master's in Media

Technology, which meant commuting regularly between Amsterdam, The Hague, and Leiden. He had his act together.'

8

He dropped out of the Amsterdam Photo Academy after a year. The Royal Academy in The Hague was his goal. Part of the admission process was to create a photo series with the theme 'club life' in any chosen context, and to approach it as originally as possible.

The summer of 2007, and with it the admissions deadline for the coming academic year, approached. I had gone to Château St Gerlach to be able to work in peace, but of course Tonio managed to find me. That assignment from the academy … he wasn't really getting anywhere with it, he told me over the phone from Amsterdam.

'I'm not really the club type,' he said.

'Well, then let that show through in your project,' I said. 'It's not like they're making you go play klabberjass every Tuesday night.'

'Play *what?*'

I told him the story of my father, his Grandpa Piet, who wasn't the club type either, but all the more a pub type, which in turn my mother objected to. In order to get at least a weekly dispensation to go the pub, he joined a klabberjass club. One evening he won, quite by accident, a tin of butter cookies donated by the local baker: one of those large square tins with a net weight of five or six kilos. To celebrate his victory, he drank himself totally and shamelessly blotto, and then had to make his way home with that tin of biscuits. Being the first one up the next morning, I found the tin, battered and beaten, on the kitchen table. It was half empty, and what was still left inside had been pretty much reduced to crumbs. When my mother sent me off the baker to fetch bread before school, I espied, at irregular intervals, small heaps of crumbs along the sidewalk: the exact spots Grandpa Piet had fallen flat, booty in hand. The café where he had celebrated his triumph was right near the bakery where I had to buy the bread.

216

'If I had to do a photo essay about a club, Tonio, I'd make it about a klabberjass club. You start with the card game in the pub. There, on a separate table, is the trophy: the tin of butter cookies, say. The winner in his finest hour … and then, on his way home with his trophy under his arm, you photograph his demise, heap by little heap. The winnings, crumbled step by step.'

Poor Tonio, my advice was of little use to him. 'The fifties, Adri … I can't show up in The Hague with an historical documentary.'

Then he grudgingly mentioned an earlier, rejected idea. 'Grandpa Natan, doesn't he go out to eat four times a week at a Jewish community centre? It's always the same people … a sort of dinner club?'

We worked this idea out over the phone. In the end, Tonio produced a wonderful, intimate, and melancholy-steeped series of photos focusing on the regular diners in the Beth Shalom canteen. His grandfather was the pivotal figure in the series. He photographed him at home, as he waited for the shuttle bus, and then as he left Beth Shalom when Miriam came to pick him up.

It wasn't really an appropriate subject for an eighteen-year-old budding photographer who was out to mercilessly document the new face of the world. But, oh, what an intimate *Weltschmertz* he captured in those photos. And with such tenderness and compassion … The festive pennants emblazoned with the Star of David, strung across the ceiling like festoons (they hung there year-round). The red plastic water jugs on the tables (the magical red reflection on the tabletop). The solitary woman, a napkin tucked behind her heavy necklace. Grandpa Natan, head uncovered and in his shirtsleeves, at a table full of men in sport jackets and yarmulkes …

Tonio kept in touch with me between sessions. He asked if I thought it would be disrespectful to photograph a spastic man whose food had the tendency to fly every which way. I happened to have volume 6, odds and ends of the author's own choosing, of Gerard Reve's *Collected Works* with me. I read Tonio an excerpt, by way of inspiration, from the story 'Three Words.'

It is 1940. The still-quite-young author is with fellow writer Jan de

217

Hartog in a soup kitchen on the Spuistraat.

'Here it comes, Tonio. Do with it what you will.'

Two women dressed in white, uniformish smocks, who apparently ruled the roost here, were busy installing an old, decrepit man at one of the tables, dragging and lifting him into his place. When he was more or less seated, one of the women knotted an enormous, grey-and-blue checked, ragged standard-issue towel around his neck. The other woman brought a small zinc washtub and placed it on the table in front of him. Was he going to be washed and shaved? No: the first woman deposited a dish of food in the tub, and the man, growling softly, began to eat. Much of what he brought to his mouth with the spoon — for a fork would have been utterly futile — fell back into the dish, or next to it, but always within the confines of the tub, from which the man could simply fish it out again.

We were still standing at the door. Jan de Hartog observed the tableau motionlessly, whereby a strange, sculpted serenity came over his face, and his eyes took on a visionary expression, as though he were witnessing more than just this particular scene, and discerning in eternity something imperceptible that had unexpectedly become visible.

'That is God,' he mumbled.

Tonio thought the excerpt was 'pretty amusing', but doubted whether he could put it to use in his photo essay. 'Me and Dutch literature,' he said. 'We don't click. And whether that spastic man at Beth Shalom is God … I dunno … that's for other people to decide.'

9

I told of the student-parent mix-up two weeks before his death. The unexpected intimacy in a café on the Staalstraat. How naturally he took the lead in the conversation, and in what good form he was. How, in saying goodbye, having nearly got into the taxi, I went back to slip Tonio some extra pocket money. How I, emotional from the evening, hugged him, gave him three kisses, and how he grinned back sheepishly. And how, later, in the taxi, I realised I'd forgotten to give him the cash.

'In retrospect, we can say — but it remains in retrospect — that that awkward accolade was in fact a farewell ... now no longer possible. It was good. Bye, sweet boy.'

I nodded to Frans that it was his turn. I sat down next to Miriam, ran my hand briefly over her hair. People might have expected us to fall into each other's arms, weeping loudly, but we didn't, and *not* because we were too well-mannered for that. Later, I found out that Miriam felt the same way. The grief kept itself to itself — but with every fibre tensed, to be sure, ready to burst.

10

'... It sounds ironic, but only in the past week, since his accident, has an important aspect of Tonio come to life for me. Of course, I knew he'd been taking photographs for some years; we had even asked him to take pictures at our wedding. But in fact I'd never really seen more than that remarkable self-portrait as Oscar Wilde.

'This week I found my way to a website with a selection of his photos, and they struck me in my head and my heart. The old folks eating at Beth Shalom, the penetrating portrait of Miriam, the young junkie lying on a bed in the shadows, the silent girl at the window, the un-Luganic street scenes from Lugano, candids of partiers at festivals or the Book Ball — he always seemed to want to study and lay bare a situation from the "back" or from the "inside out". And he succeeds, often with abrasive sharpness.

'This kid's got talent.'

'Hey Tonio: what are you up to now? It wouldn't surprise me if you're studying the back side of life. And mumbling out loud: "How's that work, actually? What makes it tick?"

'In any case, you'll always occupy our thoughts, now and for the rest of our lives. Or, to paraphrase a writer very well known to both of us: *You are not dead.*'

11

With a vehemence that made her ugly, my mother relentlessly hammered the dangers of traffic into us kids. All through primary school, we were only allowed to cycle within a certain area. No crossing busy roads. Don't bike along the canal.

'You want me to have to deliver you to the graveyard?' she would shout with her face right up close to ours, spraying saliva and banging her fist against her forehead.

Ever since she let a friend convince her to slide into the 1.20m end at the local swimming pool, where she 'felt the water tugging at her', the pool was off-limits as well. 'It sucks you under. You'll drown. I'm not letting you go.'

Of course, we biked along the canal, sometimes so close to the edge that the reeds crackled under our tyres. We crossed the busy Mierloseweg without reporting it back to her. And you could get into the pool with a borrowed season pass.

None of us had to be delivered to the graveyard — well, except my father, almost, after he — drunk as a doornail — drove his scooter into a ditch, and was pronounced dead on the scene by the ambulance personnel.

The outcome of my mother's nightmares skipped a generation. I had to deliver her *grandson* to the graveyard. Because I wasn't hysterical enough in hammering home the hazards of road traffic? Had the worried-to-death bitch finally been proved right, here at Buitenveldert Cemetery?

12

A few lines of Ben Jonson's poem 'On My First Son', which the poet Menno Wigman had sent me the previous day as a gesture of comfort, played through my head:

Farewell, thou child of my right hand, and joy;
My sin was too much hope of thee, loved boy,
Seven years thou wert lent to me, and I thee pay,
Exacted by thy fate, on the just day.

Seven years — in Tonio's case it would be trebled, but otherwise Jonson, four centuries earlier, expressed my loss with exquisite precision:

O, could I lose all father, now …

Dispiriting, mood-deadening pill or no, there was that sudden cramp in my chest. Had Miriam and I opted too blindly for such a no-frills funeral? Had we really acted in Tonio's spirit? Were we not selling him short?

Even a person of twenty-one has, in the occasional doldrums, visions of his own funeral. Who did Tonio envisage standing at his grave? At least the few friends present here today. Girls? Around me I saw, excluding my aged mother-in-law, only middle-aged women. There had been girls in his life. He knew what it was like to be in love. Thinking back on the Tonio of last week, I can't rule out that he'd been falling in love again. That girl from the photo shoot — we didn't know her name, but … shouldn't we have done more to try to track her down?

'So who's the third?'

In our preparations, constricted by panic and grief, we had denied Tonio a weeping beloved at his graveside. We should have stood here, the three of us: me, Miriam, and the model, who would no longer be nameless.

Even if this wrong couldn't be righted, I had to find her, to question her, find out if she had meant something to him ... he to her ... If need be, we would come here again and grieve with her, at a grave by that time filled in, grassed over ... well, then, what the hell, so be it.

13

And then there were a couple more lines from Ben Jonson's 'On My First Son':

Rest in soft peace, and, asked, say here doth lie
Ben Jonson his best piece of poetry.

If I wasn't mistaken, a ray of irony twinkled through the heartrending lines. 'Here lies my best piece of prose ...' Would I ever be able to say that about Tonio in all seriousness? No, but I could try to keep him alive *in* prose. Not so that people would say 'his best prose' ... But that I would, in whatever style, offer them a Tonio of flesh and blood.

I hugged Frans, almost jealous of the sob I felt (or heard) shudder out of him.

A cemetery worker operated the handle of the machine that set the device into motion. Slowly, with the reassuringly sober hum of a household appliance, the coffin containing my son's body sank into the precisely dug grave. I wanted to force myself to think an appropriate thought, but came up with nothing of use, only self-evident observations, translated into words, such as: 'Tonio's remains are being entrusted to the earth.' Entirely in the style of the captions under the illustrations in my old volumes of Jules Verne: 'The foundering ship sank vertically.'

I did not hold Miriam tightly, nor did she hold me. We both did think something along the lines of: *I'll find him/her by and by.*

'I would like to say something.' The weepy voice of my mother-in-law interrupted the metallically humming silence. She took a step toward the grave, which took some doing, as the two burly nurses from St. Vitus were clasping either arm. 'Darling Tonio, I hope I'll be joining you soon. I'm done living. I'll be with you soon.'

The winch with the coffin had reached its lowest point. The humming stopped. Now the only thing we heard was my mother-in-law's crying, dotted with stammering, by now unintelligible, snippets of text. The woman from the funeral home stepped forward and indicated that, if we so desired, we could scatter sand into the grave with a long-handled shovel.

Instead of heading for the exit, I went along the handful of mourners. I stroked Jim's younger brother, Kaz, who was crying, along the scruff of his neck. To do the same with Tonio's friend Jonas I'd have had to reach higher than I was able — he'd grown so tall since their school days. I gave his upper arm a heartening squeeze. Jonas stayed over nearly every Friday night during their last year of high school. They became proficient at smuggling in beer, above the rations we allowed. They thought it was fun, or cool, to get sick from it. They chatted endlessly, watched films together. Sometimes I hovered on the landing to eavesdrop on their excited voices, the exuberant laughter, and tried not to think that one day it would end, that after their exams each would go his own way.

As the shovel was passed from hand to hand, I went over to my mother-in-law, who had stayed put where she was, wedged tightly between her two chaperones. 'Adri, that dear Tonio ...' She began crying all over again. 'I don't need to live anymore. I want to die. I'm going to Tonio.'

One of the nurses reassured me with closed eyes and slightly pursed lips, as though to say: *Not anytime soon, she isn't.* I looked around me. After taking their turn with the shovel and sand, the company moved toward the exit in small groups. Again I wondered if I hadn't let Tonio down by offering him such a brief, modest funeral. If I had *any* feeling since this morning, despite that wretched pill, it was a vague fear: that I had let him down in life, and now I'd let him down in death.

Thomas Mann had been a god to me. I couldn't read another word of his after learning, from a biography, that after his son Klaus's suicide, he did not go to Cannes for the funeral. He chose not to break off a speaking tour of Scandinavia.

I had just buried my son. But was I really *there*?

A writer, not Thomas Mann, once described the feeling of betrayal that took hold of you after burying a loved one — after you literally turned your back on the open grave, leaving the deceased, in his new solitude, to his fate. (Pff, 'fate'. Not much more 'fate' than what damp and maggots had in store for him.) I asked myself if I felt this kind of betrayal now that, accompanied by my friend Ronald, I removed myself from the grave. Tonio in his new solitude. If I were honest, I'd have to admit to myself that I was not aware of any more betrayal than I *tried* to feel, under the influence of the idea at hand. Never again would I quash my pain with some vulgar pill.

Chatting with Ronald about a celebrity buried here somewhere, the betrayal issue kept nagging me. I felt I had betrayed the Tonio who cycled on his own through the Whitsun night. That I wasn't standing on the Stadhouderskade to steer fate the other way — *that* felt like betrayal. And if I couldn't have prevented the crash, I could have at least been kneeling at my beloved son's side as he lay there, blacked out and bleeding on the asphalt.

August 2002. Miriam felt like a *poulet de Bresse*, preferably pre-cooked, and thus we came to be in Bresse on a warm, rainy summer morning. Bresse: why not have a look at the cathedral, too, while we're here? The three of us strolled through the city centre — and all of a sudden, sooner than we'd expected, it towered above us at the end of an ancient lane: huge, dark, massive. Looking up in fascination, I walked slowly toward it — and all at once was splayed out on the cobblestones. Tripped over one of those cement barriers that the authorities had snuck among the medieval cobbles to discourage parking in the alley. A loud cry of pain: my shin was grazed by the octagonal cement.

Almost in tears himself, Tonio tugged at me, trying to help me get up. Hearing me let out such a shout, he thought I'd broken something (like, earlier that year, my shoulder and foot). Paleness showing through his suntan, he kept hold of my arm, caring and kindly, for quite some time. In order to justify this to himself, he saw to it that his tenderness turned into bristly annoyance.

'They're out of their minds,' he said, regaining some of his colour. 'They *know* people are going to be gawking at the church.'

14

In the course of my life, I developed a problematic attitude to death. I kept it at a distance.

For years it was death itself that kept its distance. My paternal grandparents had died before I was born; my mother's parents were still young and not yet mortally unhealthy. My parents each survived a severe stomach operation at around age thirty. My siblings did not die in a traffic accident, nor did any of my friends.

Death manifested itself solely at a distance. The Indonesian neighbour. The other neighbour's young daughter. A friend of a friend.

And when death came closer, I evaded it. My father and my mother both suffered long illnesses, and I was not often at their side. When Tonio, ten years old, said he did not want to see Granny Toos for the last time, and not dead either, I was happy to keep him company while the rest of the family went to look at her in her coffin before it was shut. I sat on a bench outside the viewing room at the crematorium. Tonio stood between my spread knees, and I gathered him close. He pried my chin upward to see if I was crying, and if so, how badly. Not so bad. Watery eyes. He made a point of crying as restrainedly as I did. When I noticed him regulating his tears, employing whatever kind of internal clinch, I clamped him even tighter. 'Adri, not so *ha-a-a-a-rd.*'

At funerals and cremations, I always yearned for the reception, preferably in a café, where the taste of death could be openly rinsed away.

15

With the exception of Jim's little brother (who had to go to school) and Jonas's mother, everyone came over to our house. Miriam had ordered wine and sandwiches from Pasteuning, the local deli and caterer, that would be delivered on call.

As we'd done on the way there, Miriam and I took Natan and Hinde with us in the car. Our return home after the funeral couldn't have been less of a happening, and that was exactly our aim.

What at the cemetery appeared to be a modest handful of people now managed to fill an entire living room. Pasteuning brought the order so quickly that it was as though they had been waiting in the delivery van at the curb.

I slid into my regular, sagging corner of the sofa, where I felt safest. All the same, my mother-in-law sat down on the nearby chaise longue, and assumed her special conversation position.

'Adri, it's not *that* big a deal, but *why* a Catholic cemetery?' As always when she, tendentiously or not, raised an issue that was vexing her, she first rubbed her nose vigorously with thumb and index finger. 'I don't understand.'

I knew I'd best avoid bringing up my own Catholic background, because I'd renounced it (in her presence, too) more often and more thoroughly than a dribble of holy water, a First Communion, and the grand total of, yes, one (1) confession required. Tonio had a Jewish mother and, through her, two Jewish grandparents, so, yes, a Jewish funeral might have been plausible. The Catholics not only worshipped a false Redeemer, but they also blamed the Jews for nailing that Redeemer to the cross. *Not that big a deal.*

Back at the cemetery, where she yelled to Tonio that she'd be joining him soon, I felt briefly sorry for her. Now she was spoiling it all, by sticking her manually polished nose into it. I had no desire whatsoever to explain to her — again — that our choice of Buitenveldert Cemetery had nothing to do with religion, but everything to do with the happenstance that it was a small, out-of-the-way graveyard, where we could be sure no

226

paparazzi would be perched in the trees.

'Wies,' I said, laughing, but I meant it, 'it's been ages since I've heard you stick up for Judaism.'

I could say what I wanted, but *listen*: that was something she seldom, if ever, did. She rubbed her nose again for the next confrontational question. Her chaperones stood with their sandwiches in the dining room, which was bathed in full sunlight. Everyone else had found a spot in the front room. They ate, drank, and talked.

'What worries me is …' said my mother-in-law, her voice breaking, 'what about your writing?' Followed by, less as a question than as an observation: 'How *are* you going to keep on working … !'

God, no, not today, don't let this happen on the day I buried my son: that the woman who, all those years ago, openly doubted my ability to put food on the table, and with every minor success wailed pathetically: 'As long as he can keep it up', that she was now going to go into convulsions about the progress of my literary labours. One of the nurses came to my rescue with a reminder that it was time to be getting back to St. Vitus. The two chaperones still had work to do there.

'Wies, maybe you should start saying goodbye to people,' said the woman, who had introduced herself earlier as Brigitte.

'Well!' she huffed, reaching for her nose but not polishing it as usual, 'I'm *certainly* not saying goodbye to Natan. What do you people take me for?'

Her face took a crude expression unsuited to the occasion.

'Brigitte meant in a more general way,' I said. 'You can just skip Natan.'

So there you had it: two people who had lost their family, in part (Wies) or entirely (Natan) in the war, and then, at the funeral of their only grandson, bitterly refused to even shake the other's hand. I was sorely in need of a drink. On the way to the kitchen, I thanked Brigitte and Margreet for their support. I made a mental note to send them each flowers at a later date.

I hung around in the kitchen until I could be sure the St. Vitus delegation had left. Back in the living room, I checked to see that the remaining guests had been seen to. Dick, who I never saw drink (but did see, on occasion, sniff nostalgically at a hip-flask of whisky, as a remembrance of alcoholic days of yore), had allowed Miriam to set him in front of a full bottle of vermouth. I expressed my surprise.

'I won't get through this sad day otherwise,' Dick said. 'The only problem is … *if* I drink, I always drink the vilest, nastiest possible … sweet vermouth … which has a built-in limit. But Miriam gave me a whole bottle of Noilly Prat. And, unfortunately, I really like it.'

16

Always a wondrous experience, the animated conversation and drinking during a post-funeral reception. I tried to participate, but as relaxed, almost indifferent, as I was at the funeral, I was now uptight. Perhaps the pill was wearing off. I tried to combat the stiffness with ice-cold vodkas, but my speech remained under lock and key.

Tonio's best friends, Jim and Jonas, chatted, both drinking beer. There was nothing that afternoon which could evoke Tonio's presence more vividly than those two faces. When they were about fifteen or sixteen, we took them to Lanzarote for the Christmas holiday. A girl of about their age, Tania, also went along — I'd not only never met her before, but never even heard of her. It was unclear who she was 'with' — all three equally, was my impression after the first few days.

Tania was not about to let herself be intimidated by the boy-dominance. As soon as we arrived, they attacked the bedrooms: mattresses were pulled from beds and dragged to the largest room. They were going to sleep together, the four of them — no ifs, ands, or buts.

What followed was a week of delirious fun, during which Miriam and I seemed to have become completely invisible to them. As soon as we appeared, their expressions, in all their exuberance, went all glassy, and we simply dissolved. At the seaside restaurant where we ate dinner, they had their own table, which danced around the place so furiously as a result of their animated discussions that the restaurant staff had to ask them to get up, so it could be brought, pizzas and all, back to its original spot. We did exist, if only for a moment, when it came time to pay the bill, insofar as they were able to point us out as the folks with the cash.

It was almost a privilege to witness, close up, four young people who enjoyed one another's company so intensely, Tania no less than her three roommates. On New Year's Eve, Tonio asked if they could drink vodka and Coke to usher in the new year. I said they'd better not dare put away even a millimetre more than half of the bottle.

'You're minors. Miriam and I are responsible.'

'Yoo-hoo, guys,' Tonio cried, 'we can have half.'

When I want to fetch some mineral water from the fridge later that evening, Jonas was filling the empty vodka bottle with water.

'Jonas, did you really think I wouldn't notice?'

The kid gazed stupidly back. He was completely blotto. The next morning, I saw *another* empty bottle the four of them had snuck in, bobbing in the swimming pool among the clumps of grass they'd beaten into it with a golf club.

I was never able to ascertain the position and role of Tania in this constellation. When they said goodbye back at Schiphol, where she was met by her mother, Tania gave each of her companions an equally sisterly hug. Only Tonio made a fleeting, tender gesture (running the back of his hand along her jawline, or maybe he tucked a lock of hair behind her ear), and looked at her intently, without suspending his smile. That was all. After that, we never heard another word from or about Tania. Months, perhaps a year later, I raised the question with Tonio.

'Hey, that Tania ... from Lanzarote last Christmas ... have you seen her at all?'

'No,' he replied, in a tone that said: *Why should I?*

'And Jim ... and Jonas ... do they have any contact with her?'

'Nope.'

'Did something happen on Lanzarote ... that might have made her angry?'

'No, how come?'

'No reason. Just wondering.'

17

I'm never keen to recognise omens. Maybe that's why I only really see them when the damage is already done and they've lost their prophesying function. Omens that no longer contain a forewarning lose their dangerous sheen: they dry up.

I once kept a list of calamities I came across in novels that later, exactly, or nearly so, befell the author. Omens that the writer himself set to paper, cloaked in fiction. If I were to take heed of all the dire portents in my own novels, I would soon have to stop writing altogether.

Since Black Whitsun, the foretokens predating that day keep rearing their head. The air around me swirls with them. Wherever they hid (a nasty habit of omens) prior to 23 May, they have been resounding — now that it's too late to be alarmed — for weeks on end. They visit me in my sleep, and do not give me a moment's peace. They're like annoying insects, and they seem to multiply relentlessly, keeping pace with my increasingly guilty conscience.

At the time, I did not even notice the majority of these omens. Those that were too obviously a warning disguised as a symbol, I cast to the wind. Others, I manufactured myself, choosing not to regard them as forebodings.

I had written a number of 'requiems': two for childhood friends, for my father, for my mother, for a colleague, even (the shortest of them all) for a cat who'd been bitten to death. It never occurred to me that one day I'd have to write a requiem for my own son. Now it's as though the first five were premonitory studies for what, as a matter of survival, I am now forced to execute.

Weerborstels, about the cousin who had smashed into a tree while on the run from the cops, was in fact a requiem, too. It was a novella about a problematic father-son relationship, which ended fatally for the son. My creative thinking did not, apparently, allow me to imagine that Tonio, another vulnerable-boy-in-the-making, could meet the same fate as my cousin; otherwise, I'd have certainly abandoned the project.

At the end of his speech, my brother quoted the last line of *Weerborstels*: 'He is not dead.' Later that day, Frans reminded me that I had dedicated the novella to Tonio. 'I remember noticing it,' he said, 'because in those days you always dedicated your books to Miriam *and* Tonio.'

I checked it at once. *'For my son, Tonio.'* He was right.

'It's so plainly the story of a father and his son,' I said. 'I guess I wanted to make that clear in the dedication.'

It was disgusting. I had related a draft version of *Weerborstels*, then still entitled *Met gedoofde lichten*, in a long letter to my brother in the summer of 1989, when Miriam, Tonio, and I were staying at the schoolhouse in Marsalès. Tonio's first birthday was just behind us. The main character Robby was based on my cousin Willy, who the previous year had met his end (in more or less the same fashion: 'met gedoofde lichten' — with his lights off). At the beginning of the novella, I had given the young Robby similar traits to the six-year-old Robin van Persie, who occasionally joined his sisters in our schoolhouse yard. A kind of bashful brazenness … timid audacity.

I had been given a couple of boxes with extra copies of *Weerborstels*, the annual Book Week freebie. Tonio later sold them at the Vondelpark market on Queen's Day. I insisted he not ask for more than a guilder per copy. At his request, I autographed the books. He would proudly show his customers that he was the dedicatee. 'For my son, Tonio.' He was prepared to add his own signature, for a price.

When he showed me his takings at the end of the day — nearly three hundred guilders! — I asked him how many copies he'd sold. Well, he still had some left over, for next year. This morning, he'd started out at two-and-a-half guilders apiece, but when he saw that they sold like hotcakes he upped it to five guilders, and later yet to seven-fifty. 'Nobody seemed to mind.'

'But I do. Damn it, Tonio, I said it had to be for the fun of it. I could die of embarrassment.'

'Adri, come on, a guilder … you're selling yourself short.'

'Selling your winnings short, you mean.'

18

Dick had polished off his bottle of Noilly Prat, and now sat nursing a foul glass of very ordinary vermouth with evident distaste, compensating the sickly-sweetness with the occasional sniff on his hip flask of whisky (not too long, though, because then too much would evaporate, and it had to go a long way).

As the delivery time of the afternoon newspapers neared, I paced with increasing anxiety over to the landing, peering down the stairs to check whether they were already lying on the mat under the letter slot. What did I expect to find? The truth, in the form of an obituary? Did a *suspicion* need to be confirmed on the 'family announcements' page of the evening paper?

'What with all that modern communication stuff,' I said, back in the living room, 'all those mobile phones … email addresses … the internet, God knows what else … Facebook, Hyves, you name it. Twitter … you'd think *somebody* should be able to trace that girl.'

'She mentioned Facebook on Tonio's voicemail,' Miriam said. 'They must have chatted with each other there.'

'You've got Polaroids of her,' Jonas said. 'Why don't we put one of them on Facebook, circulate them among Tonio's friends … Maybe she'll turn up that way.'

'Except that Tonio pulled a fast one on us,' I said. 'He took those snapshots with him, maybe threw them away, because they were just test shots.'

Jim offered to look through Tonio's room for the prints. Meanwhile, Jonas would try to track down the girl via a Facebook message: 'Seeking the roughly 20-year-old girl, name unknown, who Tonio van der Heijden photographed on Thursday, 20 May.'

Miriam reminded me of my initial reservations. 'You've had a drink now,' she said, 'but yesterday you wanted to just let it be. We wondered whether we really wanted it, you know, her identity and all. Say we find out they had something together ... or could have ... Do we want to torture ourselves for the rest of our lives with ... yeah, with what? A love affair for Tonio? Maybe our future daughter-in-law? The mother of our grandchildren? ... I don't know if I want to have those kind of thoughts. I never used to have them when I saw Tonio with a girl. It doesn't get us anywhere. Yeah, where *all* roads lead. To Tonio's grave.'

The remaining guests sat motionless, silent.

'Miriam,' I said, 'we also have to think of Tonio. I remember how proud he was when he showed me those snapshots ... his grin, when I commented what a good looker she was. He said she'd invited him to Paradiso. That's not something he'd tell me otherwise, don't you think? There was obviously something there. *Of course* he wanted us to meet her. I'll bet he was disappointed she was already gone when we got back from the Bos. Minchen, we owe it to Tonio to find her. If he can't introduce us to her anymore, then we have to track her down ourselves.'

'I think,' said Miriam, 'it's only going to cause us more pain.'

'And what if *I* think we shouldn't steer clear of that pain?'

19

Whenever Miriam enters the room, I'm pleased to see the familiar presence. Still, after all these years, I feel that pleasant, mild shock: there she is. Since Whit Sunday it's as though I'm seeing double. It is my wife who steps through the doorway, and at the same time, like a not-quite-lined-up superimposed image, it is a mother who has been robbed of her child. The second figure refuses to stay within the outline of the first one, no matter how much I blink.

Saturday morning. More than the queasiness of the hangover, it was the stomach-turning realisation: *Yesterday I buried my son.* The previous day, I had watched the coffin containing the body of my son being lowered into a hole in the ground, and I did not cry, and after that I drank myself into a common stupor. I couldn't even remember how the afternoon ended, let alone the evening.

Right after I had pulled open the curtain, swearing at the bright sunlight, the double vision of Miriam entered the room: the mother of my child, and the now-childless mother. Closing one eye to blot out the double vision did not help. Her expression was one of heartache, fear, insecurity. I went over to her, placed my hands on her shoulders. 'What is it?'

'You exploded at me last night.'

'I can't remember a thing.' That's what you get with vodka, a drink that not only prevented a headache, but, just to be on the safe side, also disengaged one's short-term memory, perhaps to erase recollections that might bring on a headache after all. 'What was it about?'

'Everyone was gone, and I wanted to go to bed. You didn't. You wanted to talk. I didn't. I was all talked out. And then you started in … angry … that I only thought of myself.'

'Oh, Minchen.' I pulled her close to me. 'I was angry, but not at you. At what happened. At everything this dirty trick has brought us.'

This appeared to reassure her. 'You were already angry in the afternoon,' she said, 'when the papers were delivered. Having to see Tonio's name in bold letters on the obituary page … you were fuming. You hurled the papers through the living room.'

Miriam made breakfast. She returned to the bedroom with the tray, the newspaper, and a large stack of condolence letters. More bereavement ads, but this time Tonio's boldface-printed name did not elicit anger; the various messages surrounding it were too implausible for that, too absurd — although there was nothing to laugh about either.

Side by side in bed, propped up against the pillows, reading all those shocked condolence letters together … It was a bad piece of theatre. A cheesy sequel to *Who's Afraid of Virginia Woolf?*, with George and Martha in the marital bed, passing messages of sympathy back and forth after the fatal accident of their made-up twenty-year-old son.

I had asked Miriam for toast with jam, but couldn't even manage that. Weak coffee with lots of milk was all my stomach would tolerate. The only organs where the terrible truth could permeate were my intestines. The diarrhoea that began on Whit Sunday had gone on for a week.

20

What feeds the gut-wrenchingness of Tonio's death the most is the razor-sharp recollection of all our senseless bickering in his presence. Lead-in, build-up, climax, cool-off, reconciliation — it's all forgotten, leaked away into the folds of time. At the moment itself, our disagreement and each one's highly personal sense of rightness were a matter of life or death — for the innocent bystander, Tonio, as well, at age three, five, eight, eleven, thirteen. With the exception of certain recurring arguments and their variants (the 'classics'), none of it has stuck — and as far as Tonio is concerned, it's anybody's guess what effect it all had on him.

The idiotic quarrelling that's supposedly inherent to every marriage, not even the bad ones. The contorted arguments. Being right just for the sake of being right, like a sort of *l'art pour l'art*. The raised voices, with or without sprays of spittle. The 'did-so-did-not' level of the school playground.

(Diary entry, Tuesday 8 April 1997)
08:00 woken by familiar sounds coming from bathroom. Intimate murmuring between mother and son. Sleep draws me back down, deep into the old, fragile mattress (which really needs replacing), but I decide to regard the time of awakening as a sign: the recently implemented eating regimen requires me to have breakfast between eight and nine.

I open the bathroom door: M. is sitting on the closed toilet-seat lid

235

combing Tonio's hair. He looks up at me, startled but smiling. ('You've broken your own record,' he said recently, the last time I got up that early.)

I say: 'Keep your snappy comments about broken records to yourself today, okay?'

He pulls a puckered lemon-face, as though he feels he's been put firmly in his place, but his bright, brown eyes sparkle with mockery. Downstairs I pick up the morning paper from the doormat and take it with me back to bed. A work crew, armed with an electric apparatus, has begun sanding the living-room floor. (In May they will attack my office.) The entire house is gradually covered in a thin layer of snot-green powder, a mixture of old paint and the underlying wood.

Before M. takes Tonio to school, I am given a sober breakfast of wholegrain bread and sugar-free jam (no butter), plus the recommended ration of cappuccino. When M. returns, I give her the tips I'd promised for the 'ur-book' issue of *Maatstaf* (Mallarmé, Proust, Genet, Mulisch, Reve, etc.)*

Home renovation has its benefits. I spend half my days in espresso bars throughout the city, reading and scribbling to my heart's content.

[…]

15:30 tram 24 back to Zuid. Alight Beethovenstraat, walk home via Apollo, Hilton, Christie's. At our front door I bump into Ronald Sales, who is delivering the portrait he did of me some years ago. We bring it inside, and decide to celebrate my purchase in the Vondelpark. Tonio asks if he can go with us, and straps on his new roller skates (which he wheedled out of me with the Golden Owl prize money.** Until now, I have neglected to pen here a report of the award ceremony, which I

---

* *Maatstaf* was a Dutch literary magazine (1953–1999). The December 1997 issue was devoted to 'ur-books' by twelve well-known Dutch authors (including Van Der Heijden): excerpts from early or unpublished manuscripts that would form a first, or 'ur', version of later writings. Miriam Rotenstreich was one of the magazine's five editors at the time.

** Belgian prize for Dutch-language fiction. Van der Heijden won the fiction category in 1997 for *Het Hof van Barmhartigheid* and *Onder het Plaveisel het Moeras*.

simply watched on television at home. Tonio went berserk: how was it possible, his father being awarded a prize on TV while he sat there next to him on the couch.? When it came time to answer questions posed by the presenter over the phone, I could barely understand her over Tonio's whooping and hollering as he bolted jubilantly through the room. 'This is the best night of our lives … !')

He skates ahead of us, the wheels grating against the asphalt, via Corn. Schuytstraat and Willemsparkweg toward the park, every so often looking over his shoulder to make sure we lag appropriately behind. Forbidden beer at the Film Museum's outdoor café. Tonio nearly runs over publisher and restaurant tycoon Bas L. […]

18:00 back home. Tonio is pleased that I'm eating in tonight — which, let's just say because of the renovation chaos, has gone by the board of late. When I confess to M., who is in the kitchen preparing dinner, that I've been hitting the beer with R., her mood nosedives. 'What about your diet? Not to mention that this diet of yours is the reason you didn't want to go out with me Friday night.'

She's right, of course, but that doesn't stop me from going on the defensive. The quarrel, which branches off into endless hair-splitting, makes the delicious chicken dish lose some, if not all, of its taste. I notice that Tonio is put off by our squabbling and wrangling. When M. starts to cry, his lower lip quivers in unison with her sobs.

'May I please be excused?' (I still don't know where he picked up that snippet of etiquette.)

'To do what?'

'Ask Camiel if he can come out to play.'

He leaves his chicken untouched, and charges down the stairs to his friend, two houses further on. You always read that an athlete's brain produces a chemical that enhances their performance and stamina, allowing them to push themselves beyond the normal limits. I'll bet a similar kind of chemical, of a slightly different compound, is also produced in the brain of bickering people: they wear each other out with fallacious arguments and just keep on going, far beyond the boundaries of dignity.

237

When Tonio returns, we are having coffee — in the bedroom, where the television is temporarily housed for the duration of the renovations. He looks seriously at his parents' faces. When he's got something earnest to say, he drops his voice an octave. Like now.

'So did you guys call a truce?'

21

When Tonio was still small, two conflicting thoughts sometimes hit me simultaneously: the awareness of my parental negligence, juxtaposed against realising how bravely, and unreproachfully, he faced every situation that spotlighted his father's shortcomings.

This clash of concepts could leave me completely paralysed. Like a naughty schoolchild, I would drag myself off to a corner of my workroom, where I would intensely whisper the words 'my brave little boy' a few times.

That helped — until the next exhibition of my inadequacy, which Tonio once again ungrudgingly withstood.

Now that I had failed to prevent a fatal accident, and for once he *didn't* manage to salvage himself, my private profession of love, which was never meant for him to hear, poured forth without end. 'My darling, brave boy. My little hero.'

'When I think back on it,' I said, 'Tonio never upbraided us. To our face, at least. Maybe he swore at us later, out of earshot. But really read us the riot act, you or me … no. Never.'

'I was always careful,' Miriam said, 'no matter how cross I was, never to bad-mouth you to Tonio. I didn't want him to ever be able to use it against you. And I know you did the same thing. When I hear from Rietje the kind of vitriol Bram dares to hurl at her … the most unbelievable vulgarity … of course, he picked it up from his father.'

'It's not thanks to us,' I said. 'It's all Tonio's own doing. Whenever I looked at that honest face of his, it never occurred to me to complain to him about you. Even if I had to hold back ... I'll be truthful about that. He stayed neutral until he was actually forced to stick up for one or the other of us. Remember that time the three of us were crammed into that one hotel room in Jarnac? I was there to write a piece. The people who gave me the commission had promised the best hotel in the area. Well, if *that* wasn't a wet blanket. I lay there on that too-small bed, bitching about how uncomfortable it was. You had made the arrangements by phone. Tonio listened intently to our discussion. Once he realised the organisers had shafted us from a safe distance, he cried out with all the indignation he had in him: "But Adri, there's nothing *Mama* can do about it!" He was five, almost six. It was in a restaurant there ... a few days later, I think ... where Tonio made that double portrait of us.' I pointed behind me with my thumb toward the wall above the head of the bed. 'Little red hearts circling around our heads ... Lovey-dovey parents. He so wanted it to be okay between us.'

'Without being sappy about it,' said Miriam, 'it's pretty safe to say he was more of an example to us than we were to him.'

22

Miriam and Tonio were witnesses to the fact that I've always tried to protect them. Of course, I failed now and again, more than I'd have liked,.

What I still bitterly regret, now more than ever, is the reckless hospitality I cultivated in the second half of the 1980s. Everyone was welcome — my open-door policy was indiscriminate. Once, when I was a newcomer in the Dutch literary world (a terrain that, in those days, still seemed rather clearly delineated), I walked into the art-society club Arti with a small group of acquaintances I'd bumped into along the way. I happened upon an older colleague, who nodded condescendingly at my table and asked: 'Are *those* your friends?'

He answered his own question with a scrunch of the nose. The fellow knew exactly which illustrious, important, and influential people he should surround himself with. At that age, though, someone like that hasn't any friends left, only an assortment of 'big cheeses' gone mouldy.

Having the *right* friends — nothing could be further from my goal. I took 'em as they came. As a result, all and sundry wafted in and out, not all of them with good intentions. The one sniffed around my marriage, the other my business affairs, yet another my work in progress. You never knew, of course, what information could come in handy, or when. And indeed, nearly twenty years after I started to keep my distance from people, certain colleagues from back then still find it necessary in interviews to comment on what went on at my parties, or that more than once I had to be helped (heaven forbid), drunk, into a taxi.

I grant everyone his contribution to the *petite histoire* of Dutch literature, even though it still won't protect it from extinction, but they do have to keep their mitts off my family. There is a passage in *Advocaat van de hanen* informing the reader that the main character Quispel is in the habit of giving his wife a wallop — one of his many flaws. *Aha!* thought one of the sniffers who was posing as a friend. *Gotcha!, he's as much as admitted it himself.* The rest was simply a matter of perseverance in spreading it around, complete with authentic-sounding details, because you didn't hang around at this kind of pig's house for nothing.

This feat of mine has wafted my way numerous times over the years, sometimes in the form of a question, but usually as a statement of fact. It wasn't Quispel who hit his wife; no, it was *me*. The pushiest interviewers even opened with the declaration: 'People say you beat your wife ... tell me about that.'

My first reaction was to throw the bum out. (A colleague who I discussed the matter with later, said the interviewer had missed a golden opportunity. 'He should have asked: "Do you *still* beat your wife?" Try getting out of *that* one.') But on second thoughts it seemed to me a good chance to set the record straight: how a rumour like this, its origins in literary fiction, can make its way into the world, and the kind of damage it can cause its subjects. The interviewer listened patiently, as did my voice recorder, but in the printed version of the interview I could find no trace of my argument. What did I expect? The public wants drama, scandal. They want to watch a marriage disintegrate, and are hungry for all the gory details.

Friends — the real ones — have often asked why I take this kind of gossip to heart. But only *these* friends — the rest just go with the flow. I have a wonderful relationship with Miriam, and I want people to know that, and not have them think just the opposite — that is my childishly naïve wish.

The worst thing about the scuttlebutt was that made its rounds while Tonio was still in school, and I was worried he'd get flak about it. He never mentioned it, but he was the kind of child to keep this kind of business to himself in order to spare his parents. He knew enough children from broken homes, but was never afraid that his own parents would get divorced.

Miriam and I have been together for thirty-one years, twenty-three of them as a married couple. We skipped the first 'seven-year itch', but thereafter we had our share of crises, like the Leidsegracht one. And yes, we've lost our temper plenty of times, and there have been blows, from both sides. (Never in front of Tonio.) Back in the Loenen days, I once had to stay indoors for two weeks after Miriam (that sweet Minchen) had given my face such a thorough makeover with her nails that it resembled a currant bun with those bits of red dried peel. And I deserved it, too.

More importantly, we never just sank into silent lethargy, like those couples you see in the breakfast room in Parisian hotels with nothing to say to each other. Miriam and I have always kept the communication channels open — strongly worded, if necessary. I consider myself lucky that Tonio knew his parents like this: talking, bickering if need be, but seldom in icy silence.

'So did you guys call a truce?'

It wouldn't have been terribly surprising if Tonio's crushing death had put the lid on our communication once and for all. Fortunately, we manage, even in pain, to continue our never-ending conversation, even if we have to freely admit now and again that for certain ancillary horrors, there are no words.

I love you, Minchen.

23

Miriam brought the second round of coffee into the bedroom. Another novelty of the past week: she bangs against everything with the tray, even against cupboard doors that do not stand directly in her path. In addition to her memory, it seems that the nerve centre of her motor skills has taken a knock.

'If you don't concentrate on it ...' she said. 'I mean, if it only simmers at the back of your mind, then it's as though it's only temporary. Awful but passing. And then ... it just happened to me down there in the kitchen ... then it hits you, all of a sudden, just like that ... that it's permanent. *He*, Tonio, was temporary. And now he's gone for good.'

Miriam sat down on the edge of the bed. Maybe her hand was feeling for mine, but because she wasn't really looking, her gaze on the open balcony doors and beyond, her fist landed with a sharp crackle on the newspaper laying across my lap.

'Yeah, temporary,' I said. 'That's the dirty trick your dozing subconscious plays with you. All of a sudden you bolt awake, pricked by the stinger of ... remember those monster wasps in the Dordogne? We were so afraid our little Tonio would get stung. If you chopped one in half, the two halves just kept on going.

'The stinger of the truth, you mean ...'

'Something like that.'

'I think the subconscious dozes most of the time,' Miriam said. 'Out of self-preservation. More than the occasional jolt of the truth ... of this kind of truth, anyway ... no one can take that, surely?'

I took her hand from the dent it had made in the newspaper.

'Sooner or later,' I said, 'we're going to have to put a stone on his grave.'

'I'd rather not think about it. Not now.'

'Just this, then I'll drop the subject. Maybe it's a good opportunity to … hmm, never mind. Another time.'

24

It's been a week now. I wade through a murky anguish, from which I'm not sure I'll ever emerge, but the fact that I managed to endure Tonio's death last Sunday without dropping dead on the spot myself, and without hurling myself from God knows what floor of the AMC, still amazes me, or, better put: amazes me every day a bit more.

How did I get through that day at all, in fact, with the piling up of ever-more-dreaded news? Me, who tends to leave envelopes unopened that just *might* contain unpleasant tidings.

The announcement that morning that Tonio was 'in a critical condition', and at that very moment was lying on the operating table, resulted in an unprecedented shock, but for the duration of the afternoon there was still room for the 'no longer life-threatening' sign. Once we'd been crammed into that sauna next to the ICU, a dialectic unfolded (between hope and fear, life and death, Miriam and me, the surgeon and us) that prepared us, step by step, in a pitching motion not unlike a ship, for what is called The Inevitable. There was a kind of numbing logic to the whole process — a logic that kept one step ahead of lunacy, and made the result only just bearable.

The appearance of the neurosurgeon, straight from the OR and still wearing her blue shower cap, did not immediately signify a pitch-black antithesis for our last hopeful expectations, but a consistent synthesis of the undulation between hope and fear, just as we had experienced it the entire day. She shook her head, making the plastic cap creep higher up on her head. Tonio had not yet died, but had no chance of survival. He drifted, as they say, between life and death.

After the unfathomableness of what had taken place deep in the previous night, by daylight the subsequent steps seemed almost *too* logical, without the hospital at all striving for such logic. Be that as it may, calm dialectic and unemphatic logic made it possible for us to survive Tonio's deathbed in that improvised tent in the ICU.

It did not prevent each of us, in our own way, once we left the hospital, from being drawn into a chaotic vortex of conflicting feelings that were not only unassuagable but intolerant of any form of logical collating.

You would think that since last week I'd be able to open every letter without trepidation, and that bad news or overdrafts wouldn't even make me bat an eye. Surely the worst possible news — Tonio's death — should have immunised me?

Nothing is further from the truth.

For a good part of the day I undergo internal nervous trembling, as though it wants to tell me: the worst is yet to come. As if Tonio's death was only a prelude to that 'worst'. This notion is destined to become the refrain of this requiem.

I do not want to know the Very Worst. That letter, I leave unopened. The nervous quivering goes on unabated. But what in God's name could be worse than Tonio's death?

This: the reality of his death. That it, one of these days, will *really* dawn on us. My nerves are steeling themselves for that moment, for me, but also on Miriam's behalf.

We had to figure out where the best survival plan was lurking: resisting the pain, or surrendering to it.

We had a bit of leeway in our options, but the most essential freedom of choice had been relinquished: Tonio was irrevocably dead, and now irrevocably buried, too. Whatever we did with those doses of pain, this fact remained incontrovertible. We could neither deny nor avoid it. We were in its grip.

25

With the funeral reception winding up, my brother had gone downstairs to Miriam's workroom to call a taxi, and in the process had spilled a glass of red wine over her keyboard — the first in a chain of computer incidents in which we believed we saw the hand of Tonio at work. He had always been on call whenever we had a computer problem; now it seemed that he was bent on sabotage.

After ringing for the taxi, Frans left his wallet lying next to the phone, which resulted in him giving the driver his watch as collateral when he ran inside to borrow some cash from his wife, who had gone home earlier to relieve the babysitter. He, Mariska, and the baby came by for an hour on Sunday, giving him the chance to not only pick up his wallet but chip some dried wine from between the keys on Miriam's computer. (The mouse, too, had been drowned in the accident.)

I had not seen Daniel, the only child to whom I could claim unclehood, since 7 March, his first birthday. He'd grown, of course, his little face taking on the look of an individual. With his wispy, white-blond baby hair, he resembled Tonio at that age, as I remember him from Marsalès, although Tonio had more sumptuous curls. I also recognised Daniel's attempts at walking, the recalcitrant coordination. While Tonio used his stroller as a support (regularly pulling it over on top of him), Daniel navigated our living room without any ambulatory aids, accepting in return a few more falls to the bum, his nappy letting out a puff of air with each fall.

When I got upstairs, I found him sitting on the rug. Maybe because I had snuck up from behind and suddenly crouched down beside him, he started wailing at full volume. Nothing out of the ordinary, but for me it was just that, once again, I had the feeling that as the father of a newly buried son, I gave off a hearty scent of death, which fresh-faced toddlers would have nothing to do with.

His bout of tears was brief, and once I was seated on the sofa, Daniel made an attempt at rapprochement. He kept sliding his half-full drinking cup toward me over the end table, which I was then expected to take. Later, he repeatedly did his best to get my foot, resting firmly on the rug, to budge. He screeched with drooly delight when the shoe snapped back to its original position, the toes still wiggling themselves to rest.

What would have been more natural than to feel envy? My brother had a son, and I no longer did. No, I wasn't envious — not even a tad. I had been as pleased with Frans's belated fatherhood as he himself was. It was just that … in Daniel I was reliving Tonio's efforts and progress. Growing from your birth to first birthday, then learning to walk and talk — that was hard work, a full-time job, a hundred-hour workweek. And thus had Tonio, growing and learning, completed twenty-one years of his life, without being able to cash in on all that hard work.

In the euphoria surrounding his birth, I had appointed myself Daniel's mentor. I looked into his blue eyes, so full of self-evident confidence in a bright future. I silently gave him my best wishes. He was back on the rug, irreparably breaking my foot. Danny, I wish you a life five times longer than your unfortunate cousin. For the time being, kiddo, we've got statistics on our side.

Frans mentioned that he'd come across an online obituary of Tonio, written by Serge van Duijnhoven, complete with a variety of portraits. The feeling that these past few days were an absurd parody suddenly reared its head again. We'd been friends with Serge since before Tonio was born, as a 16-year-old gymnasium student and doomed poet, who sometimes dropped by with his bosom buddy Joris Abeling (killed in a car accident in '98). They wanted to hear from me how they could conquer the world from their provincial hometown of Oss. They had already stood at Boudewijn Büch's Keizersgracht doorstep, but he chased them off. (Büch didn't even have to open the door; he came up from behind on his way back from the bakery, holding half a loaf of brown bread, sliced: for the two barnstormers, a fatal detail.) Incidentally, Serge wasn't so doomed after all, for he paid a visit shortly after Tonio was born to bring him an inscribed silver spoon. And now he had written Tonio's obituary … proof that nothing in the world made sense anymore.

26

Later that evening, long back at home, my brother rang.

'That website, the one with Tonio's obit … a woman left a message … wait a sec, I've just clicked it off by mistake … a French-sounding surname. Tell Miriam to have a look. She wrote a short message in English, seems Tonio recently photographed her daughter. Let's see if …' (I heard the tap of his nails on the keys.) 'No, she doesn't mention the daughter's name. The mother's called Françoise Boulanger. Doesn't give her daughter's surname either. Might be something else, keep that in mind.'

The mother did not leave an email address. Miriam phoned Tonio's friend Jonas to see if he could find something out. Jonas would get right on to it.

27

Last night I was up at 3.00 a.m., and didn't get back to sleep. I had a drink of water, which sent my guts into paroxysms. Gurgles, little eruptions, snaps like bursting bubble-gum. It reminded me of what I heard when I laid one ear on Miriam's pregnant belly (the other ear plugged up with my pinkie) in early 1988. This was Tonio inside me. Gargling, buzzing, snoring. Maybe, in the shadowy depths of his switched-off consciousness, he could hear his own guts going mad while the surgeons worked on him.

At about half past eight I open the bedroom curtains. At the sight of the light-blue sky, my stomach contracts even more violently, from bilious revulsion. My son is dead, and will never return. Once again, I experience the terrible loneliness of his end. Rotating blue lights sweep like splatters of disco lights over his motionless body on the asphalt. (Please tell me he's not groaning in pain.)

The defeat of having lost him. We'll see if I survive my all-consuming sympathy for Miriam. The fear of losing control — over her life, and over mine. The fear of the fury that is still fighting to get out, which until now has more or less kept its cool.

And so begins a fine spring day in early June 2010, the month when Tonio would turn 22. It would take some getting used to, exchanging the active 'birthday' for the passive 'birth date'.

Miriam joins me a quarter of an hour later. A pattern is emerging: she's less miserable in the morning. The truly paralysing dejection sets in around late afternoon. Then she takes (like I did the day of the funeral) a valium-like pill, which isn't strong enough to hold back the sudden fits of tears. She doesn't want it to, because 'when I cry I'm closer to Tonio'.

We eat side-by-side in bed. For me, a crust of bread just to have something in my stomach, and espresso with hot soy milk. My recipe was always: two shots of espresso, watered down slightly. Since Whit Sunday, my stomach will only tolerate a single. Evening liquor does not pose a problem, but maybe it leaches the lining of my stomach to the point that by morning I'm yearning for warm milk.

'I've got to go pick up the reprints,' Miriam says.

'How many did you order? Fifty?'

'A hundred.'

'Don't forget envelopes. The cardboard ones.'

Every day, staring in shock into the emptiness anew. This kind of irrevocable loss makes you obdurate. Every time, that same disbelief. Can it *really* be true, is he really gone, for good?

28

Thursday: I last saw him alive (not counting his artificially life-supported, brain-dead presence in the AMC) two weeks ago. In *De Volkskrant* a bereavement notice from his old school, the St. Ignatius Gymnasium, where he studied from 2000 to 2006. He was firm in his decision to enrol there, having attended orientation evenings at various Amsterdam high schools. Ignatius and nowhere else. I was so proud of him. Now, four years after his graduation, I read in the newspaper a stanza of Auden that

Tonio's former teachers picked out.

The stars are not wanted now
put out every one,
Pack up the moon and
dismantle the sun

Among the messages of condolence posted to our house are heart-rending letters, which in tone and wording far exceed the requisite courtesy. Apparently, the seriousness of this abides little pretence. And yet, everyone turns inevitably and swiftly to business as usual. 'Life goes on,' the adage goes, and so it does. Tonio's classmates are in the middle of their exams; soon, summer vacation will be upon them.

A few friends remain on call, without being pushy. Others keep a welcome distance. The form letter we sent out on May 25 explicitly stated that 'for the time being we are not able to receive visitors at home'. So in fact, we were avoiding them, rather than they us. Loss and grief damage a person. It's as though it's contagious: you could infect others with it, and you don't want to be the source of it all. At least Miriam still has her shopping rounds, now and then with a neighbour's helping hand, but I act like a leper swinging his rattle as he avoids healthy folk.

So I see almost no one, but if someone should happen to ask: 'What does something like this do to you?', I waver between 'My life is ruined' and 'My life is over.'

My life is just as ruined as Tonio's body, as it was wrenched open by the surgeons at the AMC.

My life is over, and serves solely as an enclosure for his amputated existence.

Café or restaurant: I can't bear the thought of it, with the exception of the café at the Amsterdamse Bos goat farm, where I am inclined to go drink coffee because I'm fairly certain no one I know goes there. We go by car, via Buitenveldert, a route that almost passes the cemetery.

Yesterday, yellow traffic signs indicated that the Bosbaan, the rowing

249

lake, was closed due to sculling competitions. This meant we had to take a significant detour through a nondescript bit of Amstelveen, cutting through the southern end of the park. Being a regular competition venue, we had, through the years, been sent this way often enough; but despite the adequate signposting, Miriam kept taking wrong turns.

'I'm telling you, my mind's shot,' she said, stopping the car. 'Since May 23, my memory's like a sieve. Even the simplest names … I just draw a blank.'

During the first week after Tonio's accident, entire days just vaporised. She often finds herself standing in a shop and not for the life of her able to remember what she is there for. Moreover, she expresses herself badly, at times groping awkwardly for words. If she says anything directly related to the death of her son, she tends to interrupt herself with: 'There it is again. As if I hear myself reciting a line from a script. As if I'm in a play.'

'Don't forget,' I said, 'that your brain's taken quite a drubbing. You've been walloped with the worst imaginable news: Tonio in a critical condition, Tonio dead … your mind has never had to tackle something like this. It's not equipped for it. Remember that driver who had rammed into a tram? He sat there at the wheel, dead as a doornail, but without a scratch, without a drop of blood. Turns out he died from his internal injuries. I imagine the brain going through something like that, being knocked senseless by the whack of bad news. Your noggin's black and blue, and your brain's underneath.'

'Well, what about you?' We were driving again. 'I never hear you fumbling for a name.'

'Somewhere else in me has taken the beating. Think of what we're doing right now. I only dare to go to the goat farm, because I'm terrified of bumping into someone I know.'

We drove into the park. Splashes of light danced through the car's interior.

'Are you embarrassed?'

'Yes, I'm ashamed of having lost my son. I'm ashamed, in front of you and the whole world, that I couldn't prevent his death. I've failed.

I'm ashamed of my defeat.'

Over the past twenty-plus years, my goal of piloting Tonio unharmed through life had taken a few knocks in the form of misgivings and cock-ups. But even those, we eventually got over, conquered.

And yet, each year we were forced to release him more and more into the world. Walking to school on his own, sleepovers with friends, camping with friends' families ... school trips, his first time alone in the tram, with buddies to the squatters' den 'Vrankrijk' ... the occasional puff on a joint with the guys on Museumplein ... to the Photo Academy after graduating high school ... the pop festival in Budapest ... his move to De Baarsjes ... that nocturnal holiday on Ibiza ...

And then, in the middle of the night on Whit Sunday: the Paradiso nightclub.

How much right did I have to my pride at having brought up my boy so diligently, having prepared him so thoroughly and turned him over to the world? Didn't his accident negate all that, underscore my failure as a father? Not only at the end, but in complete retrospect as well?

Miriam tried to reassure me, but was unable to undo that overwhelming perception of guilt, shame, and defeat.

29

A diminished consciousness: Miriam is not the only one to suffer from it since the accident. If my thoughts start to go all murky, I catch myself harbouring only negative notions about Tonio's imaginary future. Smoking, drinking, which both get out of hand. Poor grades: in the end, no college diploma. Women trouble. Loneliness. Letting himself go to pot. Aches and pains. Premature ageing. Oblivion. An ugly death.

Only a confused mind can worry about a future that's never going to happen. But why such *black* thoughts? If I really want to daydream about an impossible future, then why not wish Tonio a rich, successful and triumphant one?

I try to imagine him the day before Whit Sunday. Saturday 22 May 2010. He's in love, or on the way. He won't repeat past mistakes. He stands at the mirror, looks himself in the eye, and lisps the slogan he's seen so often on T-shirts, posters, and beach towels:

TODAY IS THE FIRST DAY OF THE REST OF YOUR LIFE

His future would begin today. Well, his future, 'the rest of his life', got off to a pretty sorry start. The deed was *so* self-destructive that it even colours my notion of his non-existence black.

So many things whose effect on his life I'll never know. I'd even be curious what the less attractive aspects of my character eventually did to him. The knowledge of his possible rejection of me, because of events I'd long forgotten, would now be something sacred for me, because then he'd at least have had a future.

30

As we walk along a narrow wooded path from the car park to the goat farm, we bump into the girlfriend of a colleague. She is visibly startled, and passes us with a stammered, embarrassed greeting. Much too late, I realise I should have gone after her — to say I understand completely that we haven't heard anything from her, because there are no words for it, and that the embarrassment is entirely mine.

'See? That's what I mean,' I say to Miriam.

The early-summer weather, which kicked in a few days before Tonio's death, pursues us relentlessly with 'what could have been'. In the shade, it's still matutinally cool. Shadows, streaks of light … Tonio is everywhere. His absence has nestled itself in all that one sees. Everything is occupied by our loss.

All is still quiet at the goat farm. The children are at school. Miriam orders sandwiches inside. When she returns, I dump the plastic bag of condolence letters onto the table. Using a jam knife, I slit open envelope upon envelope. I read the letter or card, and then pass it to Miriam. It strikes me that she skims the words more and more fleetingly, and then folds the paper shut. Her face retains its impassive, resigned expression, and does not appear to react to the message or the person who wrote it. After God knows how many letters, she shoves the pile away from her.

'You read them. I can't take it anymore.'

It really is absurd: a couple sitting in the divine spring sunshine, reading condolences for their recently deceased son. Here, amid the smell of goat manure, where as a child he would dart to and fro with a dripping ice-cream cone. I sweep the letters back into the plastic bag. When I look up, Miriam's face glistens in the sun — from snot and tears.

I ring my father-in-law. He spends as much time as he can watching tennis on a special sports channel in the semi-darkness of his downstairs flat. 'I try to let that ballet distract me,' he says. 'And otherwise I've got all the time in the world to babble to myself, about Tonio.'

31

Miriam points to two couples with children. The one man is demonstrating an iPad-like apparatus to the other.

'Ugh,' she says. 'Those men with their toys. No hint of a conversation with their wives, just this one-upmanship with their latest gadgets. Why don't they just go and have a peeing contest over at the creek?'

We don't talk much today either, but that's because we're both sitting here thinking of our son, who would not reach his twenty-second birthday. Which is in itself a kind of conversation. A goat stands on one end of the seesaw in the small playground; a boy of about six on the other. The animal is completely unfazed by being lifted up into the air and then being let back down again.

'You know what's exhausting?' Miriam says suddenly 'That every day the pain takes on a different guise. Yesterday I fretted about our future, yours and mine ... how we're supposed to move on ... and today it's the fact that Tonio wasn't able to round off his life that eats me up. Tomorrow ...'

'And so goddamn unfair,' I add, 'that while he was alive he had no inkling as to his premature end.'

'Well ... maybe better that way.'

'I don't know, Minchen. Yes and no. If he'd seen it coming, he wouldn't have been so jolly those last days. On the other hand ... Kellendonk, for instance, knew he'd die young.' He took measures. If he'd lived out a full life, I don't think he'd have clenched his entire body of thought into that one book."

Now there's a goat on each end of the seesaw. The two animals must weigh about the same, because the plank, now free from the ground, balances in mid-air, until one of the goats jumps off, and the other end of the seesaw lands with a slap on the half-buried car tyre.

'The past week you've talked a lot about shame,' Miriam says. 'Being ashamed of what happened to Tonio. Well, if Tonio knew he'd die young, like from some illness ... I don't think I'd get over my *own* shame. I'd have interpreted every word, every glance of his, as a reproach. Even if he didn't mean it that way.'

32

While Miriam goes to pick up the photos, I proceed with the detailed, telegram-style reconstruction of the days since 23 May. I am shocked, though, by the blow that Tonio's death has dealt Miriam's memory. As far as I know, I remember everything about the accident clearly, in living colour, but I cannot guarantee that it will remain so. One of these days, my own memories might crumble and sink into a black hole behind closed eyes. And then Miriam won't be able to be my recall crutch.

Why this obsessive notation of everyday facts having to do with

---

* Frans Kellendonk (1951–1990) was a Dutch novelist. He died of AIDS just after his 39th birthday.

** *Mystiek lichaam* ('Mystical body', 1986), for which he won the Bordewijk Prize the following year.

Tonio's death, funeral, and the aftermath? I don't know. I only know that I cannot let a single detail fall into oblivion.

Outside, the fierce early-summer day rages, while here I sit up on the third floor doing a sort of bookkeeping, recording the events that have killingly trundled on since Tonio's vanishing. Just after noon, Miriam comes upstairs with the hundred reprints of Tonio as Oscar Wilde, and the heavy-duty envelopes.

'Look, a classmate of his emailed this …'

It was an address list of Tonio's fellow students. I set my diary notes aside to send his Media & Culture classmates a copy of our form letter, with a few handwritten personal lines, and include the portrait. I've laid the photos face down on the table, so as not to have to continually look Tonio in the eye.

And then, while I pick up these pages again and begin to put them in order, I see Tonio all of a sudden, nearly two years old, standing in the springtime sun. My father and mother had been visiting, and left behind a two-piece outfit for him: light-grey, shiny, part silk. The top has a decorative hood.

I freeze, the papers clamped between my fingers. He's wearing his new clothes for the first time. Miriam has just dressed him and, smothering him with kisses, enthuses about how wonderful he looks. 'A little silk-clad prince.'

Seated motionlessly at my work table, as though the image might evaporate with the least movement, I watch as the little boy takes careful, demure steps across the yard in Loenen, until he stops in the sunny part of the garden. He's not entirely comfortable in his new clothes, but, at the same time, Miriam's compliments make him aware of the specialness of his appearance. Not one to avoid the spectacular, he deliberately chooses the sunlight, which shimmers as it falls upon his curly blond locks.

Just then, Mrs Roldanus appears from the hedge of her garden, on her way to the garage. Tonio takes a few steps toward her, while his hands feel their way over his belly.

'Look,' he says, with that thin, high-pitched voice. 'Look.'

He shows the woman something that dangles from a string tied around his waist. It is a little heart made of silver-grey silk, maybe intended as a mini-purse, or maybe just for decoration. 'Lo-o-ok,' he sings.

'Ohhh, Tonio, how pretty!' the woman says, crouching next to him.

She looks genuinely touched — how couldn't she be — but then again, that creature would, a few weeks later, prove to be an accessory to the disruption of our Veluwian idyll. A self-proclaimed interior designer, she had, naturally, already been privy to the covert plans for the coach house, on our property. Her attempts at appeasement consisted of self-adhesive birds, which she stuck all over the windows and doors of our quarters, including, of course, the glass windbreak, so that no wayward sparrow would crash into the windowpanes.

It's as though that little silk heart, even more than Tonio's golden curls, attracts all of that moment's sunlight. For years, that image had lain unobserved in the depths of my memory. And to rediscover it anew: I don't know if I should be glad or miserable. It doesn't matter. The pain is just as profound either way.

33

Would that Tonio's death were just a problem that, after his abrupt disappearance, we could tackle, solve, bring to a satisfactory conclusion …

There was no solution, so perhaps his death was not, strictly speaking, a problem at all.

So as not to fall to pieces ourselves after the initial shock, we found a parallel problem that might stand a chance of being solved. It was hardly original: a loved one dies unexpectedly, and the survivors want to get to the bottom of what exactly happened, as though the knowledge can somehow bring them a bit closer to the departed. The more mysterious or violent the circumstances of a loved one's death, the more the thirst for details seems to become.

For us, even without any sign of violence, that need could not have been greater.

34

We sit on the veranda, attempting to defer the first glass of the evening. A pitch-black sombreness puts a clamp on my mouth. I suggest that for God's sake we go inside and turn on the eight o'clock news. Maybe there's some news about Joran van der Sloot in Peru — as if that interests me.* We're too late for the headline news, but we *are* treated to the despair of a prominent Dutch football player over a torn hamstring. A report on the upcoming elections gets filtered out of my consciousness entirely.

Of course, we should have stayed outside, in the shelter of the enclosed terrace. Miriam wants to watch an episode of *Cold Case*.

'Minchen, I'm not going to spend the rest of my life watching that crappy American TV show with you.'

She begins to whimper. 'Just to sit half-knocked-out on the couch in front of the tube, so as not to have to think, that's all I ask.'

The TV gets switched off. After a smattering of peevishness from my end, we settle down in the gradually darkening living room, conciliatory and shamelessly grief-stricken. Miriam cries more than on previous evenings.

'So awful … *so awful* that I'll never see him again.' Her words rustle almost inaudibly along with her breath. 'That I'll never be able to hold him again. All those normal, everyday things … gone, gone, gone. Pick up his washing, and that he just crawled out of bed, smelling of that delicious boy-sweat … I miss him so much.'

We solemnly promise each other that we'll pick up our lives, and move on: with work, and with trying to stay fit, because Tonio would

---

* Van der Sloot, a young Dutchman who lived in Aruba, became notorious for his involvement in the mysterious disappearance of an American tourist there in 2005. In 2010 he confessed to another murder in Peru, where he is presently serving a 28-year sentence. Both cases attracted widespread international media attention.

have wanted it that way. From now on, Tonio would be the bottom line, so that we never forget him.

'We'll also stop drinking,' Miriam says. 'You know what? I don't even like the taste anymore.'

I don't much either tonight, but it doesn't stop me from going at it full force. With each glass, I feel more clear-headed. After Miriam goes upstairs, I stay on the sofa, brooding, staring into the black hole that was once Tonio.

35

Sometimes I catch myself morosely thinking of a horrible imaginary accident that has overcome someone I know. A good friend. In my thoughts, I comfort them, but the catastrophe is too huge and too irrevocable for me to be of any real help. I give them my tears of impotence; more than that, I can't do.

And then, as I emerge from the daydream, it hits me that it is *us*, Miriam and me, to whom the irreparable has happened.

I tell this to Miriam.

'Might be an emotional detour,' she says, 'so that you can allow yourself a little bit of pity.'

CHAPTER THREE

Chime bars

1

After his move to De Baarsjes, I sometimes didn't think about Tonio for days. Not explicitly, at least — subconsciously, of course, he was still always puttering around somewhere. His normal life carried on outside my field of vision.

Since his death, there isn't a moment when he is not in my thoughts. Even when you can barely call it thinking, I feel the presence, the blackness, the gravity of his death.

With a Sophist sleight of hand, I could make a plausible argument that he is more important to me dead than alive.

Nothing doing. But ... dead, he leans on me more than alive. As a young man in full swing, he possessed the means to escape my attention for brief or more extended periods of time. But the dead Tonio rests unavoidably heavily and immobile in the groaning hammock of my attention.

If Tonio paid one of his usually unannounced visits, he would silently open the front door with his own key. He'd take the stairs up to the first floor without so much as a creak of a tread, abetted somewhat by the thick runner and his supple gait. He only had to give the living-room door, which did not close properly, the tiniest of shoves with his fingertip.

And all of a sudden there he'd be, in the middle of the room. His broad smile told us it was intended as a surprise. Apparently, it never occurred to him that he might catch his parents in a compromising situation. At that hour, after all, we were usually on the sofa, glass in hand. He was always the mischievous kid playing hide and seek ('Anyone seen Totò recently?' 'No, I guess he's run away …') and then, weak from giggling, he'd stagger out from his hiding place.

The Norwegian forest cats, too, knew that the door was warped and didn't stay closed. If they wanted to get in from the landing, they would stretch out full-length and pat it open with their big front paws. It made its own special click. Once I called out, crouched at the newspaper bin: 'Tygo, shut the door behind you. It's draughty in here.'

That snicker. It was Tonio, followed by Tasha. His half-apologetic smile said: *Fooled you, didn't I?*

He would flop onto the sofa, Tasha cradled in his arms. She relished and revelled in the attention her stepdaddy lavished on her; but, unlike her brother, she had to be held down with a firm hand, otherwise out of pure flirtatiousness she would leap from his lap.

'Fancy a drink?'

'Yeah, a beer would be great.'

Since Whitsun, I have often heard and seen the living-room door spring open under the light touch of Tonio's fingers. The click does something to my heart. I see no hand appear in the crack, no arm following it. It is, in fact, one of the cats. Or a draught.

'Minchen, for God's sake … close the door all the way from now on, will you. I have a heart attack every time it swings open, 'cause I think it's … Just push hard until it clicks shut.'

It didn't really help. Whenever she gave the door that extra shove, the tears welled up in (or poured out of) her eyes. It gave her the feeling, she said, that she was being forced to shut out even the memory of Tonio's visits.

The new situation is ever-present, palpable even at those brief moments when you are granted a respite from it. This is for good. From now until the end of my days, Tonio's death will never *not* be there. I saw him die in the hospital, and at that moment it nestled itself in me, divided equally between my head and my guts. My brain endlessly replays images from his life. It sits uncomfortably on my heart, squeezes the appetite out of my stomach, and causes burning cramps in my intestines.

His brake shoes engulf my feet. He slows down everything.

I am in no position to accuse Tonio of recklessness.

An all-round aptitude test given at Eindhoven high schools in 1964 indicated my suitability for gymnasium studies. It was a foregone conclusion that I would attend Augustinianum. My mother was pleased with the result, not because of the high-level education it would afford me (she had only a vague notion of what it entailed), but because Augustinianum was located on the 'safe' side of the Eindhovenseweg, so that I, with my morning absent-mindedness, wouldn't have to turn left across a dangerous junction, as did my former schoolmates on their way to St. Joris College on the Elzentlaan. But I was determined to join my old pals, and even a thousand motherly admonitions wouldn't stop me — including the argument that the St. Joris teaching system was about to be abandoned and was about to embark on a five-year rearguard struggle.

So from September '64 onwards I rode to Eindhoven every morning with my Geldrop townsmen, Wil and Hans. As we approached the city limits, we passed Augustinianum on the right, and a bit further up swerved left across the busy road toward St. Joris: all in all, the permanent decor of my mother's nightmare.

She was right, insofar as, particularly at that hour, I was a sluggish sleepyhead, lost in thought on my bike behind my animated friends. Maybe it would have been more effective if she had actually *discouraged* me from going to Augustinianum, for instance because of the demanding courses or work load. My stubbornness ushered in a lifetime of regret for having chosen the wrong school. The most unpopular goody-two-shoes of my old school was safely out of sight at the gymnasium, but then all of my old schoolmates vanished from St. Joris after the very first Christmas break, only to resurface at the less-demanding Geldrop middle school, leaving me completely on my own.

It happened during the first week of school — almost. I lagged behind Wil and Hans, as usual. They had just taken the dodgy turnoff, standing high on their pedals. In my haste to catch up with them, I didn't bother to look back over my shoulder as I turned.

More than the screeching tyres, I felt the whoosh of air as the car passed me. It had grazed me, no more than that. I'd nearly been hit by a convertible sports car. It stopped. The driver lifted himself halfway out of his seat and turned around. There I stood, trembling, bike between my legs. It was not the first time an enormous shock affected my sense of perception; even now. I only have to close my eyes to see the man, a guy of about twenty-five, wearing light-brown leather gloves and green-tinted sunglasses.

'Hey kid, you got a death wish or something?'

He shouted it with a kind of arrogant swagger, but not unkindly.

'No-oo,' I replied sullenly, maybe a little whiny, as though I was obliged to answer. 'Course not.'

The man slid back behind the wheel. Without looking back. he stuck an arm in the air as a sort of farewell. The stench of burning rubber wafted off the asphalt. The skid marks from where he'd braked were short, angry smears. I waited to cross until all the cars had passed, walking my bike, weaving and trembling on jointless legs. My friends greeted me with jeers. As I cycled further — this time keeping up with them — I noticed that my front wheel had been bent out of kilter. The driver of the sports car hadn't even got out to see if his finish had been scratched.

No, I do not walk around the livelong day chastising Tonio for his recklessness. I do torment myself with questions like: why was I granted that split-second advantage back in 1964, that Tonio, forty-five years later, was not? Without that elbow room, it would have been my own parents who had been immersed in grief, and no Tonio would ever have existed, no life and thus no death.

Through what Miriam and I have gone through, I can almost tangibly imagine my parents as they might have grieved for me. I can hear their voices.

'Just a boy, not even thirteen. He'd just started his new school. Terrible waste.'

'Sports car. A speed demon, of course. One of those damn spoiled rich kids … No condolence card, no flowers, nothing.'

My mother could not much have enjoyed having been proved right: I should have chosen Augustinianum after all. She would be more prone to curse *all* schools. Institutes whose only purpose was to pump knowledge into innocent young lives, at their peril.

I torment myself further with that split-second. The question, born of desperation, takes on grotesque proportions. Such as: why was my split-second of good fortune not anchored firmly enough in my genes so that a half-century later, Tonio might profit from it?

4

It's starting to look a lot like an obsessive-compulsive disorder. I continually scan the course of Tonio's life in search of individual moments that, without turning his existence into a topsy-turvy mess, might be stretched or shortened just enough so that years later, on Whit Sunday 2010, Tonio's bike and the unknown vehicle would have just *grazed* each other.

I find plenty of such moments, but their recollection alone does not suffice. You need the sensation of a time machine: I have to have the visionary perception that I am truly *back* in a certain episode in Tonio's past. I tinker with that fraction of time (at most a couple of seconds) so subtly and vigilantly that nothing in his life noticeably changes. His subsequent, known existence is in no way affected or thrown out of balance.

I am back in the incessant 'Why?' stage. Eventually, the 'why?' rolls off Tonio's child-tongue so automatically, about everything and nothing, that it takes on a blasé tone. 'But why … how come? Why?'

If it's already inquisitiveness, it is not yet urgent enough for it to interrupt his playing. 'Why, Adri, why?' He asks this while focusing all his attention on separating two Lego blocks with his pliable fingernails. His facial muscles quiver from the effort. By clamping his jaw tight, and curling out his lower lip, the pacifier shoots loose and dangles on the plastic chain against his chest. What did I say to provoke that 'Why?'

'Mama needs to cut your nails.'

'But why? … why?'

Because otherwise you'll tear them on your Lego — but I don't say this, having been driven up the wall enough today from explaining things. Tonio prises the Lego pieces apart, and tries to repair a damaged nail with his baby teeth. He spits a sliver out, a white splinter, and then repeats his question: 'Why?'

Plenty of spare moments passed between those last two whys. So it's here that I tie a small knot in his lifeline. Two, three seconds, and even then I've held a good margin over. Tonio doesn't notice a thing: I've only shortened my own silence, simultaneous with his, by a couple of seconds.

'Have a look at your torn fingernail,' I say, 'and then you'll know why.'

A few seconds before real time allows, he runs to the bathroom to get the small nail-clipper out of the top drawer, which he can just reach, and bring it to his mother in the kitchen. From now on, everything in his life will take place an imperceptible fraction of time sooner.

Maybe one day, long past middle age, he will discover the ruse. I might still be alive as the elderly grandfather of Tonio's children. Scientific progress will allow him to recalibrate the amputated moments of his life, just as measurements taken from an atomic clock in an aeroplane high

264

above the earth have to add a second to normal ground-time, otherwise the calendar will fall behind.

All right then, make my illegally activated leap-seconds public — they will have saved Tonio's life.

5

And so it went. In my memories of Tonio, I kept looking for situations tangible enough to picture myself, in time and space, back to where they occurred. Sometimes I would delete a few seconds from the timeline; another time, I would add three or four. It was a game — obsessive, but it remained a game. In the end, it did not accomplish anything, except that the neurosis only strengthened its grip on me. I would do better to return to what actually happened in the early hours of Whit Sunday, without the facts taking any notice of my cut-and-paste in Tonio's life.

6

Before Tonio's fatal accident, I had always been surprised that people who, once visited by Fate, insisted on questioning it over and over. Instead of accepting the irrevocable, they became, in my eyes, whining children who kept asking the questions that had already been answered. Or for which there *was* no answer. 'How in God's name could this happen?'

'In God's name, why? Why? *Why?*'

'Tell me again what that third witness said.'

'If he had first … instead of just … then …'

Now I understood. I wanted to know *everything* about the accident. And not only that. I needed to know every detail of his last days and hours — everything since I had last seen and spoken to him.

There was no getting around bad news. But I always gave the *details* of bad news a wide berth. I did not want to hear them. It was painful enough if someone ended our friendship, but the inevitable letter spelling out the reasons, I left unopened.

Now I longed with frantic eagerness for every detail of what had happened to Tonio between his departure from our house on Thursday afternoon and his departure from … life … three days later. The only one we had sounded out until now was Jim, but he wasn't there that Saturday night. Jim said Tonio had mentioned a girl. Something about a photo shoot for a modelling portfolio; but more than that, Jim didn't know. He had not met her, did not even know her name. All he could tell us was that Tonio had gone out that Saturday evening. And, oh yes, that Tonio had promised to be home by four, so that Jim had someone to chat with. Maybe they'd watch a film together.

What role had that model played in Tonio's last days? That was the question that came roaring back at me, ad nauseum.

About two years ago, I recall, Tonio worried about girls. With all my might, I had wished him a steady girlfriend, or a whole slew of casual ones, as long as he was happy. Now one appeared to have presented herself. I knew nothing of their relationship aside from that it must have been pretty fresh, and yet I felt, as it were with my whole fatherly heart, that something special had been brewing between them.

'We've always been solution people,' Miriam had said a few days after the accident. It had become almost a mantra for her (and me). 'Now we've been saddled with a problem which by definition has no solution. That frightens me. We have a whole insoluble future ahead of us.'

Perhaps that is why we set out to reconstruct, as exhaustively as possible, Tonio's last days: we were looking for a parallel solution. By laying out all the facts, right down to the last piece of the puzzle, it was as though Tonio might be recouped — even if not alive and well. Maybe tidying up all the open-ended questions would give us a sense of solace. Another reason could be that we felt obliged to round off the story of his brief life. I could rebuild his nearly twenty-two years from photographs, impressions, and memories, but the final stage — not yet.

7

'You've got an email address now,' I said to Miriam. 'You could write and ask for her mobile-phone number. Include your own number, so she has the choice: call you or let you call her.'

'I'd suggest — now don't get angry — that we first figure out how serious it was. Right now, I can't bear the thought of yet another dashed illusion. I want to know if that photo session was purely professional. And I want to find out just what went on with those two on Saturday night.'

'Go on.'

'Jim thought Tonio was out with Dennis on Saturday. A mutual friend.'

'Do we know him?'

'He's been here before. Nice boy. Tall, compared to Tonio. I'll ring Dennis first. Maybe he went to Paradiso with Tonio and that photo girl. Dennis might be able to tell us more about her.'

The best thing was not to force anything, and first try to come up with a solution here at home, even though we called it a 'parallel' solution — which was just a word anyway. We decided to invite the friends who had been with Tonio in his last days to come around. Jim had been here already. The Paradiso girl, if we could track her down, could wait until we'd found the photos. According to Jim, Tonio had definitely gone out with Dennis that last night. So Dennis could tell us if that girl had joined them — and if not, why not.

Jim gave us email addresses of some of Tonio's friends, and in a few cases their home address and mobile-phone number. Dennis and his sister's particulars were there, too: they lived with their father in a house on the Govert Flinckstraat.

8

What all this digging around in Tonio's last week might unearth remained to be seen, but in the process we discovered that actively searching for a way to come to grips with the loss only exacerbated the pain. To passively endure the loss and drag ourselves as stoically as possible from one day to the next seemed the best medicine for now. We awaited Dennis's visit, and meanwhile I answered the condolence letters. Miriam took care of the administrative side of Tonio's death — cancelling his college courses, his subscriptions, his bank accounts. To put it bluntly: deconstructing his identity. The details of his extensive operation, even though it had not led to his recovery, had to be processed with the health-insurance company. The unused portion of his insurance premium was reimbursed: yet another piece of hard evidence of Tonio's demise.

Excising a person from the world is no easy task. Certain administrations simply would not let him go.

Miriam re-examined the dental check-up card we had found in his wallet. She glanced at her watch: today, an hour from now, he had an appointment. Miriam rang the dentist, who was ours as well. She had missed the death announcement, and was just wondering, she admitted, if this time Tonio would actually show up for his appointment.

'He was such a sweet boy,' she said. 'Someone you could never get angry with. Well, just once. He'd done a sloppy brushing job, and I gave him hell. The next time, two months later, he came back with a spic-and-span set of teeth.'

That evening, we combated the pain passively with alcohol.

9

At four o'clock, the exact time of his now-cancelled dentist's appointment, the doorbell rang — that blood-curdling screech that for the past two weeks had been the memorial melody of the absent Tonio. We still hadn't gotten around to having the electricians install a friendlier doorbell. A ding-dong, for instance. Miriam reminded me that we had moved in here eighteen years ago to an electronic chime, totally in keeping with the taste of the former owner, porn baron H.P. ('Horsepower') Roukema, who, according to the estate agent, marketed 'plastic products with a specific function', the profits from which were used to fill his house with kitsch. The chiming doorbell consisted of brass tubes of varying lengths and pitches. The painters had removed it in order to replaster the entrance hallway, irreparably damaging the bell's mechanics. The doorbell people had installed an electric bell that could be heard all the way up in the former maid's quarters in the attic, but that also, for eighteen long years, had grated on our nerves and tormented two generations of housecats.

'How about a chime,' Miriam suggested. 'You know, like when we moved in?'

I almost went along with her, but then remembered a scene from the film *Who's Afraid of Virginia Woolf?* just in time. When George comes home, you hear exactly the same chime that Horsepower Roukema had saddled us with. George associates it with church bells, because he's going to bring the news to his wife Martha that their son, on the way from boarding school to his twenty-first birthday party, has died in a car that crashed while swerving to avoid a hedgehog. The boy turns out to be a private invention of the childless couple. George feels he has the right to kill the son off because Martha, against their hard-and-fast rules, has discussed the boy with others. While Martha ('You didn't have the right, George') is comforted by late-night guests, George mumbles (in Latin) a requiem mass at their living-room bar.

Thus a chime would remind me even more of Tonio than that ear-splitting chainsaw of a bell that was sounded by a policeman on Whit Sunday. And this was not the end of the *Who's Afraid ...* associations. Tonio was, like other youngsters who had flown the nest, a creation of his parents, of their powers of imagination. In our conversations, his life was settled up in our presence, while physically he was elsewhere.

The big difference being that, in this game, there were no pre-agreed rules giving me any say about his life and his death.

10

Miriam enquired through the intercom who it was. (You never can be too careful: imagine a half-drunken idiot from the bar down the street, double Holland Gin-and-cola, intended as a token of comfort, under his jacket, like the priest who used to come around with a holy wafer for a sick person, in a powder box hidden between two buttons of his cassock.)

'Dennis.'

'I'll buzz you in,' Miriam said. 'Shut the door tight behind you, okay?'

From where I was sitting, in my regular, sagging corner of the living-room sofa, I could hear the buzz of the front door. The visitor must have long legs, I thought, because he took the stairs three at a time. It was indeed a young man of considerable height; he entered, panting in a healthy way. Seventeenth-century blond curls danced on his shoulders, but his three-quarter-length cycling shorts and a pierced eyebrow bearing a silver ornament brought him straight back to the twenty-first century.

I vaguely recognised him, and suddenly recalled being introduced to him once, a few years ago, on the dimly lit landing in front of Tonio's old room. Tonio was proud and awkward in equal measure. Dennis must have shot up since then, because I didn't remember him being so tall. You could hardly imagine a greater contrast to Tonio, with his dark, straight hair and modest (1.73-metre) height. The way they moved, too. Tonio was hurried and jerky in his movement, his neck slightly bent; Dennis, on the other hand, was aware that, even in syrupy slowness, those stilts of his would get him from A to B fast enough.

Miriam, looking awfully small behind our visitor, offered him something to drink. I hoped he'd ask for something alcoholic, so I could join him. Dennis asked for tea. Miriam went off to the kitchen, and I offered Dennis Tonio's usual place on the corner sofa. He looked at me with his large, open, friendly face. Light, thickly lashed eyes. Dennis was one of Tonio's three best friends. The other two were Jonas and Jim.

Faced with this beanpole, I wondered if Tonio had ever suffered from his modest stature. He had never blamed us, his none-too-tall parents, for passing on our shortness genes — although, of course, I don't know what he said out of earshot of his father and mother. For three years, I cycled to school with a tall classmate who never failed to remind me that I, at 1.76m, was 'way too small' for my age. The boy suggested that one's height had everything to do with attractiveness, especially in regard to 'the women'. Compared to me, he was, in his own words, 'sitting pretty'. If I looked over at him, at how he planted his heels on the pedals, feet pointing outward, I could hardly call him a shining example of manly elegance. He considered himself athletic, but was basically a brutish dunce who used to crib from my homework. The athlete graduated by the skin of his teeth, went to the Academy for Physical Fitness, and became a gym teacher. Over the years, I bumped into him now and again. I still couldn't offer much more than my (by now) 1.77m, while he had only become even more well-proportioned, glowing with vigour and virility. He was married, but there were no children, no way — because, you see, they were both obsessive travellers, which in turn had everything to do with their status as nature-lovers. During school holidays, they jetted to corners of globe where they could be closer to the rough country, where animals could still be observed in the wild. (They had, for instance, once spent a night in the Amazon on a wooden platform high up in a rain tree, where they were woken the next morning by a real-life monkey who had pissed on their sleeping bags — well, okay, a few drops anyway.) He belonged, in short, to that brand of man who calls himself a naturalist because he doesn't miss a single documentary about wildlife reserves, and spends his summers picking blackberries along railway lines.

Despite his yearning for the jungle, the gym teacher still lived in our hometown. Once, in the mid-nineties, having been sent there with an interviewer and photographer to make a mini-documentary about the depressing domain of my youth, I happened to bump into him. He was on a bike, dressed in a peacock-blue jogging suit, and had just come from the school where he taught children to do a bird's nest on the rings. The interviewer, who smelled a juicy anecdote 'about the old days', invited him out for a drink. In the café, my old classmate grabbed his chance to show those Amsterdam journalists that even here in the provinces you had your share of drama, and that temptation slithered like a snake in the grass. How often hadn't it happened to him at school … the love notes stuffed into his coat pockets … 'Goddammit, man, fifteen-, sixteen-year-old girls. It's no picnic.'

So I admit that the six-foot-two-eyes-of-blue was still reaping its benefits, despite the fading six-pack. Later, after reading the draft text, it took some serious doing to get certain of the gym teacher's inanities scrapped from the article — in his favour.

I noticed I was getting wound up again. Nobody — *nobody*, d'you hear — would denigrate Tonio on account of his appearance. There you had it again. Nothing attested more bluntly to the inconceivableness of his death than my anger over lesser creatures who *might* hurt him with their condescending remarks. But looking at Dennis made my indignation fade. I had to be on my guard, but not with the soft-spoken lad with the open face. Dennis spread his arms and said: 'I still don't have words for it. Tonio was …'

'Are you still studying?'

'I'm still at … studying audio technology. I do the sound mixing for some pop groups.'

'Weren't you a drummer, too?'

'Not in a regular band anymore.'

11

I took advantage of Miriam's absence to ask Dennis if he had gone to Tonio's viewing at the funeral home last week. (What a question! — and I just … asked it.)

'Yeah, sure I did.' He nodded with his entire upper body. 'There were four or five of us. We biked over. There was a girl, too. She didn't want to join us at first, but then she did. Cool.'

'Not that girl he'd been photographing?'

'No, not her,' Dennis answered. 'She wasn't part of our group of friends. At least, I never met her.'

'I'll be up front,' I said. 'Miriam and I didn't go see him. When we said our goodbyes at the AMC ... just after they unplugged the life support, and he was in fact already dead ... he still had his own face. The face we always knew. Just before that, it had been alive. That's how we want to remember him. We were afraid he'd look totally different once they'd laid him out for viewing.'

'It was still totally him,' Dennis reassured me. 'Totally Tonio. Just like we knew him.'

I knew he wasn't criticising our decision, but still a pang of guilt ripped through my heart. If what Dennis said was true, then we had let Tonio's body, entirely recognisable as his own, lie in that open coffin for days on end, alone and unseen. Only four or five friends had had the courage to cast one last glance on him. Maybe the betrayal I'd felt the whole week *wasn't* unjustified after all. Maybe I should have held a constant vigil, right up until the last moment, coping with his gradually drooping face — that sweet, beautiful face that was now shut off to the world by lid and earth, and could only be pieced together from photo-album snippets.

'Dennis, tell me' — I tried to make my voice sound as natural as possible — 'was Tonio wearing a red-and-white striped shirt in the coffin?'

'Sure was,' he smiled, as though he were happy to please me. 'His favourite shirt. His macho shirt. He was wearing it.'

'Oh, so it fitted after all,' Miriam said as she came into the room with a tray. 'We were wondering, because ... he was so swollen from the internal bleeding.'

I considered — but kept it to myself — that they might have had to cut the shirt open at the back to get it to fit. I recall the woman from the funeral home asking if we wanted Tonio shaved. Yes, he should be clean-shaven, we'd said.

'Should we have had them shave off his stubble, actually?' I asked, primarily to bring the discussion of the open coffin to a close. 'I mean, it was his style.'

'In the coffin, he had a heck of a five o'clock shadow,' Dennis insisted. 'Like always.'

'Maybe it was too difficult,' Miriam suggested, 'because of the wound … they might not have wanted to tear it open.'

I closed my eyes, and saw the double-dotted line of clotted blood — almost geometrically parallel — that ran from his neck up over his chin and upper lip.

'I didn't see any wound,' said Dennis. 'His face was flawless.'

'Touched up, of course,' I said. 'Dennis, how *was* Tonio recently?'

12

According to Dennis, Tonio had been really at home with himself the past few months.

'You could really *see* him grow. When I met him, about five years ago, he was a chubby teenager. He'd slimmed down recently. Everybody thought he was a handsome guy. It was like he grew in life, too. Tonio was just a great guy. He made friends more easily all the time. It was cool to be with him in a café or the disco. He'd talk to anybody and everybody. People gravitated toward him, just 'cause he gave off this air of: that guy, there's where it's at. Especially when he was taking pictures. He took pictures everywhere.'

Dennis paused to collect his thoughts, as though he was weighing up whether to tell us something or not. 'He was happy.' Dennis nodded. 'Tonio told me he was so happy these last weeks.' He nodded again, harder this time. 'And you could tell.'

I wanted to ask him to describe his last night with Tonio, but I didn't know if Miriam could bear it. I cast a sidelong glance in her direction. She sat smiling agreeably at Dennis. She liked hearing that her son had been happy. It hadn't sunk in yet that this made the tragedy all the greater.

'Dennis, we gathered from Jim that you and Tonio went out last Saturday night,' I started. 'Paradiso, wasn't it?'

Dennis looked at me, startled. 'Paradiso? Nah. We were in club Trouw, that new disco on the Wibautstraat. You know, what used to be the printing presses for *Trouw* and *de Volkskrant*. I heard that from my dad — he works in newspaper layout.'

'The previous Thursday, he told me he'd be going to Paradiso on Saturday night. Some Italian theme, with oldie hits by Eros Ramazzotti and some others. A girl had invited him.'

'Not Goscha?'

'I can't remember him mentioning her name. I've seen Polaroid snaps of her. She was the one Tonio was photographing that Thursday afternoon. Here in the house.'

'Oh, *that* girl ... what was her name again ... from the photo session, yeah, that's it. Tonio talked about her constantly, and now I can't come up with her name.' Dennis thought for a moment, and then shook his head. 'That Italian show ... wasn't it Friday night? Anyway, it fell through. Don't know why. Tonio and I spent all of Friday evening at Café Terzijde. Kerkstraat. He tried to contact that girl on Saturday, to ask her to go to Trouw with us. It was already pretty late, so it didn't work out.'

'And you never saw her?' asked Miriam.

Dennis shook his head. 'Tonio'd only just met her, I think. He was always asking me for advice. How he should handle things, you know, with her.' He smiled, amused. 'D'you know what I really admired about Tonio? He listened. He could take criticism. If you explained that he was going about something the wrong way, like with a girl, he'd take it seriously. Not like irritation or anything. He wanted to get it right.'

'Okay,' I said, 'so Tonio didn't go to Paradiso with the photo girl, nor was she at Trouw. You were. We'd like to know how the last night of his life went.'

'We arranged to meet in the Vondelpark at the end of the afternoon,' Dennis began. 'There was a party at Vertigo, the Filmmuseum café. We both thought it was no good, so we left pretty soon. Had a snack somewhere, then we biked out to De Baarsjes. We dropped by Goscha's place. She's a girl we met at Trouw at the beginning of April. She lives near Jim and Tonio. So we had a few beers at Goscha's, and that's when we decided to paint the town red, the three of us. We got to Trouw at about midnight.'

It was busy. And because the rumour had spread that Roxy legend DJ Dimitri would appear as a mystery guest on Whitsun Eve, tickets were hard, if not impossible, to come by. To mollify the crowd at the door, the club had reserved a few tickets 'for the regulars'. Dimitri had actually quit the late-night house circuit some years earlier and had holed himself up on an organic farm where he worked with handicapped children. Word went around that he was back in the saddle, DJ-ing at parties left and right, but incognito and under an assumed name.

Whether the three of them fell under the category of 'regulars' or not, Dennis couldn't recall, but in any case they had wangled themselves three tickets. The music was disappointing. Techno, yes, but who on earth still danced to Kenny Larkin? And whether the pot-bellied DJ, who wore his headphones like a dog collar around his neck, was the famous Dimitri in disguise — who could say? He didn't play classics, which was Dimitri's trademark, but maybe it was all part of the camouflage. The hours-long solo set, though, was a nod in the direction of Dimitri.

'How was the atmosphere?' Miriam asked. 'I mean, aside from the music. Did you enjoy yourselves?'

'It was fantastic,' Dennis replied. 'Tonio used to like watching the dancing from higher up. Sometimes he'd take pictures, but that night he didn't have his camera with him. I had to keep going up there with him. He couldn't get enough of it. Big smile, you know what I mean. It did something to him, that churning mass of people. It meant something to him. I don't know what. He was such a unique dude. He was just growing.'

'Didn't he dance, too?' Miriam asked.

'Sure,' said Dennis, 'but not so often. He preferred to watch. Now that you mention it ... we danced together that night. We dipped.'

'Wait a sec,' I said. 'There are different kinds of "dip". You used to call someone a "dipsomaniac", referring to his mental state. But "dipping" on a dance floor?'

'Here, look,' said Dennis, elaborating with the appropriate gestures. 'You grab your partner upside-down by the legs and then let him slowly sink head-first to the floor. Like you're dipping a carrot stick in dip sauce.'

The sight of Tonio's gruesome hand with the dirty nails shot before my eyes, as it lay — already dead — on the edge of his hospital bed. How many times had he walked on his hands away from Dennis during that dipping, to get such filthy fingernails? I now had to ask the question whose answer I was far from keen to hear.

'Did you guys drink a lot?'

'Lots of beer, yeah,' Dennis said with a smirk.

13

That dream, the other night. I spent the night in Paradiso, where a huge party was to start early the next morning, at dawn. It was my job, as a kind of doorman, to open up for the first guests who rang the bell. I had my CPAP machine with me, and slept with the ventilator mask on in a bare, high-ceilinged room — until the bell rang. I went to open the door, groping my way through the pitch-dark hallway. I unlocked the door: no one there. I peered down the street, both ways. But it wasn't a street, it was a square: Paradiso stood, for this occasion, where the Stadsschouwburg theatre should be. The city was dead-still. The sun had not risen yet; but above the skyline, dawn was breaking in television-blue. On the Leidseplein was an abandoned carnival, the attractions and rides shut down, with canvas covers and metal rolling-shutters. I closed the door and tried to go back to sleep on the floor, the mask back in place.

The next time I awoke, there was a small group of guests in the main hall. A man and a woman sang 'Mexico' by the Zangeres Zonder Naam, but with the pathos of an opera duet.' Without having heard the bell, I opened the tall, heavy door. The sun, while still not visible from where I stood, must have come up by then, because above the houses and treetops the sky was a soft copper-red. There was still no one outside. The door wobbled back shut.

I was waiting, I knew, for Tonio.

14

'Anything stronger than that?' Miriam asked.

'Only that one shot of tequila Tonio had,' said Dennis. 'Between beers.'

'And after closing time?'

'We rode off at about four. Before that, we sat on a bench outside the club. Just to chill.'

I realised that, in his account of the evening, Dennis had hardly mentioned the girl Goscha.

'Not for long, though,' he continued. 'We biked back into town, cut through one of those side streets to the Weesperzijde. Blasiusstraat, maybe. Over the bridge to the Ceintuurbaan. We stopped to chat at the corner of Sarphatipark.'

'Why there?' asked Miriam.

'I live in the neighbourhood, Govert Flinkstraat — the bit between de Van der Helst and Ferdinand Bol. It's my dad's house; my sister and I live there with him. I invited Tonio and Goscha to come to my room to chill. At first, Tonio wanted to, but he'd promised Jim he would be back home by four. They'd watch a film together or something. Jim, with his chronic insomnia … Tonio wanted to at least keep him company for a bit. In the

---

* The 'Zangeres Zonder Naam' (Singer without a Name) was the stage name for Mary Servaes, a popular Dutch torch-song performer, active from the mid-1950s until her retirement in 1987. Her legendary performance of 'Mexico' in Paradiso in 1986, recorded live, brought her a new generation of fans.

end, only Goscha came with me. No big deal — she fell asleep pretty much right away.'

'Did you see Tonio ride off?' I asked. 'I assume he continued down the Ceintuurbaan. Did he have trouble biking? Was he weaving around?'

'I wasn't really paying attention,' Dennis said, 'but if he'd been weaving all over the place I would definitely have noticed. No, now that you mention it, he just rode off as usual.'

'Did you ever ride with him to his place in De Baarsjes?'

'Sure, lots.'

'What was his regular route?'

'Ceintuur, Van Baerle, Eerste Huygens, and then left on the Overtoom. And then the rest.'

'Tonio was hit on the corner of the Hobbemastraat and the Stadhouderskade. That intersection's not on his route.'

'No idea how he got there.'

'Dennis, do you think he might have wanted to check back at Paradiso … if that girl was still there?'

'What time was the accident? Quarter to five, right?'

'Four-forty.'

'Then Paradiso would already have been closed. Not much chance of meeting up with someone then.'

'And you, Dennis,' Miriam asked, her eyes wet, 'how did you hear about the accident?'

'It was the next day. I was sitting in the park when I got the phone call.' Dennis shook his head for a long time. 'I just *couldn't* believe it.'

15

Tonio's friends told us that he had 'loosened up' recently and made friends more and more easily. In that, too, he resembled me. It meant that years of timidity, insecurity, and loneliness preceded it. The downside of the pride that you are part of your son's genes.

When he had just started studying at the Amsterdam Photo Academy, we treated Tonio to a trip to Paris, where he wanted do some photography. He was eighteen. I imagined him wandering through Paris on his own, snapping pictures everywhere, but at the same time hungry for adventure. I had hung around Paris in the early seventies, too, visiting museums and buildings, unflinchingly hoping for the unexpected.

His dates betray that he belonged to a certain generation, one that is perhaps waiting for a suitable designation in the wake of Generation X and Generation Nix. But I will never be able to say: 'Tonio is typical of his generation.' He had too little time to become what would be called typical of his generation. If he was a promise of something, then he's now a promise in a state of decay.

There's a good chance that I will curse his generation's subsequent achievements, because he was deprived of taking part in them.

From the age of eighteen, he travelled to Budapest, Paris, Ibiza, Berlin. In desperate daydreams, I conjure up erotic adventures for him … passionate affairs with girls, recklessly executed, so that there's no way to rule out that one day, via one or another *Lost Family* type of TV programme, a son or daughter of his might turn up. We cherish his DNA. (Miriam suddenly stood there recently, in tears, with Tonio's hairbrush in her hand: the hairs, still curling out every which way, moved in the sunlight.)

16

After a brief silence, Dennis told us that, earlier this afternoon, before coming here, he went over to Jim and Tonio's apartment in De Baarsjes. They had gotten rid of the worst junk on Tonio's desk, perhaps with a visit from the survivors in mind. 'No, really, it was a huge mess … all those sticky Coke cans, to start with. Dozens of 'em.'

I thought with regret that his desk should have been photographed before the clean-up: it would have produced a far different scan of Tonio's brain than the one made on Whit Sunday at the AMC.

Dennis and Jim had scrolled through Tonio's computer files as well. 'That dude had taken pictures! ... and some were really good, too ... would be a shame to let it go to waste. He's worth remembering as a photographer.'

So the two had planned to make a rough selection of Tonio's pictures in the next two weeks, and then run them by us for approval. We were free to veto any of them, and the rest would be put together for a small exhibition. 'We'll find a space somewhere,' Dennis said. 'Maybe we can make a book of them. My dad works in layout. I mean, yeah, Tonio was such a damn-good photographer ... you just *have* to do something with his stuff.'

Miriam and I glanced at each other, touched. Two sweet friends had decided that Tonio's photos mustn't go to waste.

'Whatever it costs,' I said, 'we'll take care of.'

'Maybe the Jewish Historical Museum can spare an exhibition room,' Miriam suggested. She used to give guided tours there. 'I'll sound them out.'

Of course, we were also curious as to what else lurked in Tonio's computer (and not just pictures), but we promised to leave his computer in the Nepveustraat until Jim and Dennis had made their selection.

'Did you come across any pictures of that Paradiso girl on his computer?' I asked. 'Tonio had her pose here' — I pointed to the glass cabinet with his rock collection — 'and up in his old room, you've been there before.'

Dennis shook his head decisively. 'No, a series of the same girl, here in your house ... I'd have noticed it for sure. It's strange, though. When we were cleaning up Tonio's room this afternoon, we didn't come across a single camera.'

Before he left, Dennis made me promise I would open the exhibition with a speech.

17

Last night, just before going to bed, I saw, very clearly, Tonio's body as they had washed, dressed, and laid it out. Strangers' hands, with no discernible face to go with them, arranged his unresisting hands. Other hands, just as unfamiliar, washed his lower torso, with complete meticulousness and professionalism.

And cutting through this image, I see Tonio as a thirteen-month-old baby on the shoulder of a French country road. A sycamore cast its shadow over him, complete with bright flecks of light where the sun bored its way through the treetop. It was that afternoon in the summer of '89 that I had taken him to Biron Castle on the bike. His nappy was full and heavy, but he didn't utter a peep. My own nose told me that he needed changing. And so I laid him on the grass alongside the road. There was no living being in sight who might take umbrage.

I took my time changing him. There was, after half a day in the child's seat, plenty of cleaning to do. He lay there so contentedly in the dry grass, gurgling in a singsong way, grasping this way and that with his pink little hands, already tanned a bit mocha-coloured on the back. I found a rusty oil drum, swarming with flies, where I could deposit the dirty diaper, and washed my hands in an almost, but not yet, dried-up brooklet.

I sat there with Tonio on my lap for some time before pulling a fresh pair of pants over his clean nappy and lifting him into the child's bike seat. He smiled so gaily at me, as though to express his gratitude for this divine day, which we had managed to contrive just for ourselves in the midst of an increasingly complicated world. We cycled further, and Tonio kept greeting the bales of hay on the hillside with 'owww … owww!'

But once I saw Marsalès signposted, my heart sank with the thought of my gradually worsening relationship with Miriam. Maybe, if she saw us return like this, father and son, high from an adventurous day … relaxed, tanned … then …

Miriam and I wanted to remember Tonio as we'd left him, still warm, in the Intensive Care of the AMC, and not deformed by the rigor mortis that would soon take hold of his facial muscles. After we'd left, his body had been photographed for legal purposes and then brought to the mortuary in the basement. There, it was claimed by the undertakers of our choice, to be laid out for viewing at a funeral home. In the days between his death and his burial, we had not set eyes on him. Nor could I form an impression of how he lay there in his open coffin.

Last night, after what Dennis said about his visit to the funeral home, I had a powerful vision of how it must have been: the strange arms that picked him up and moved him. After lowering him into the coffin, his head wobbled a bit from side to side, with a faint smile. God, he had beautiful, full lips, a sharply drawn mouth.

We had given strange hands permission to wash, shave, dress, and make him up in our absence. We did not witness any of this ritual, one that always struck me as sacred. As unbearable as it was, I *had* to imagine how those unfamiliar hands had to bend and force his stiff leg to get it into the leg of his jeans.

Later, after the viewing, the owners of those hands would peel off their latex gloves and throw them into a garbage can with a sky-blue bin liner, like a whore in her brothel disposes of used condoms. Next customer. New latex.

Had we turned his body to strange hands too soon, that Black Whitsun?

18

Thanks to the digital efforts of Jonas, the Paradiso girl suddenly had a name — Jenny — and an email address. And so she took her place on our list — as yet unseen. Tonio could no longer introduce her to his parents. Now *we* would have to make contact with her, invite her around, and, on behalf of Tonio, hand her the photos he had promised her.

One stumbling block was that the SD cards and film rolls from that session still hadn't turned up. Jim and Dennis had promised that in the course of putting together a selection of pictures taken by their dead friend, they would check around the flat.

A few days after Dennis's visit, Miriam shoved me from the landing into Tonio's old room. A white reflector screen still leaned against the wall. She pointed to a large plastic supermarket bag.

'I thought our old video cassettes were in there,' she said. 'Have a look.'

In the bag were seven cameras, mostly digital ones. His Hasselblad was there, too.

'Maybe he was planning to bring them back home that Sunday,' I suggested, 'if he'd eaten here as planned.'

'I'm more tempted to think,' she said, 'that he was counting on me bringing them in the car when I returned his clean washing after the weekend.'

'But what's strange is that the film rolls and SD cards from the pictures he took of that girl … of Jenny … would have sat here all weekend. That's not like him.'

'Maybe he took them out.'

'But Dennis didn't find them among Tonio's stuff. Could be that he brought it all to the photo place to have it developed.'

'Open up one of the cameras then.'

I didn't dare, layman that I was, for fear that I'd expose the film and ruin the whole lot.

'Okay,' Miriam said, 'then we'll ask Jim. He's bound to know how to open those things.'

19

I cry very little on the outside. Rarely do I emit tears and sobs and the gestures that go with them. I suffer from a sort of internal keening. *It cries in me.* I can lie motionless on my back in bed, and listen to *something* wailing uncontrollably inside me. I do not have the inclination to comfort that something, or to try to bring it under control. I prefer to encourage it: go on, let it all out, it's never enough.

20

A random day, a few weeks after Tonio's accident. Woke up much too early. The previous evening, I hadn't even bothered putting on the breathing mask — by not doing so, depriving myself of the artificial sleep of the righteous. All that's left is the alcoholic sleep of the besotted, cruelly interrupted by regular bouts of respiratory arrest.

Eight o'clock, curtains open: again, another perfect summer day in the making. The blue sky, the mild morning temperature, they all gang up to make the loss tangible, hand-wringingly kneadable. Miriam, already up, appears with breakfast.

'It's like my days are chopped in two,' she says. 'In the morning, I can usually face it. But by afternoon ... after two it gets difficult. And only gets harder after that. Evenings are still the worst. If I didn't have that pill ...'

'And at night? Do you still sleep okay?'

'Yes, thanks to that pill.'

By half past ten we are already fleeing to the Amsterdamse Bos. Everything is Tonio — the car, too, where he sat in back during all those trips to the Dordogne, for hours on end, amusing himself with a gameboy, a headset, a stack of old *Donald Duck* comics. Weeks before we left, I was continually nauseous with anxiety: about what could happen to us on the freeway, especially the little boy on the back seat, whose life depended on our vigilance. The minute I stepped into the car on departure day, all the anxiety and nausea disappeared. It was mostly thanks to Tonio himself, who radiated such sincere faith in his parents that I was transformed into an immortal child myself, who would come to no harm as long as father and mother were close by. Golden boy: he enchanted the world's worrisome side, and lightened it, in both senses of the word.

21

Of course, I've thought about it a lot over the years: what it means to be alive, to breathe, to move. About the consciousness that was planted in me, *me* of all people. About the miracle of inspiration.

But that same incorrigible ruminator as a rule regards life as something to be taken for granted. You can't mull over every breath you take, for otherwise you will choke.

Since Tonio's death, I miss taking my life functions for granted. Not continuously, but if I 'catch' myself experiencing the kind of wellbeing associated with an hour without grief, I have the tendency to recall the pain as quickly as possible. I give myself a telling-off: I have, after all, forfeited the right to a normally functioning existence.

What else is your child but an external enclave of your own flesh and blood? Through my own recklessness (others might speak of 'fate' here), I allowed that enclave to be forsaken. A part of me has been amputated, so how will I ever be able to say I feel at home with my body?

The road to the Bosbaan is closed yet again because of a rowing competition. To get to the goat farm, we have to follow the signposts marked with a '1', weaving through the monotonous offshoots of Amstelveen.

The streets are bathed in brilliant sunlight, which doesn't give a damn about the boy it will never again be able to warm. Miriam speaks (for those familiar with the undertone) rather excitedly. I am more reticent, resentful of the summer day that the sun-worshipper Tonio has been denied.

'It's weird,' she says, rounding off a monologue I've only half followed. 'Every once in a while, it's like I almost feel satisfied.'

'I know what you mean,' I said. 'It's really fragile. Then, all of a sudden, there's the fear, or a pang of guilt again … anxiety or intense bitterness … What sneaks up on me most of all is that impotent rage. I'm angry on Tonio's behalf. Because he won't be able to complete his life. Because his short time here was taken up with school and studies that will never come to fruition. All that top-notch groundwork ... cut short.'

'Do you also dare to just be angry ... you know, for yourself?' Miriam asked. 'I mean, simply because you don't have a son anymore?'

'Very occasionally, I permit myself a tiny bit of self-pity. A pathetic little voice in my head starts whining. Look at me ... I've been at it for nearly sixty years, not building my own future, but Tonio's. I took a course, too ... in fatherhood. And just to be sure, grandfatherhood. All for nothing. Waste of time and effort. Everything told me Tonio wanted to show me what he was worth. But I also wanted to show *him* what *I* was worth. "Up to your ten pages a day yet?" he asked a few days before the accident. Kind of teasingly, of course, he had every right, but there was always something sincere and attentive in his curiosity. I wanted to buy him an apartment, so I could say: "Here you are, Tonio: those ten pages a day." If a writer can have his own son as a muse, then I've simply lost my muse. When I mentioned that to Mensje recently, she remembered that once, in a bar, I said I was in love with Tonio. He was knee-high to a grasshopper.'

22

At the goat farm, we find a table in the sun. Under the round overhang, a sort of miniature bandstand, a children's party is underway. Miriam goes to fetch coffee and water.

Suddenly, there's tumult. A young man, a foreigner, is yelling something in more or less unintelligible English at an older man, who, taking refuge under the brim of a too-youthful skipper's cap, is seated at the next table. He ignores the shouting, even when the young man advances in his ire. When the manager comes to intervene, we realise at once what the problem is. The man with the cap had seen the foreigner's two-year-old son run after a chicken: the kid was probably trying to nab the animal. I must have been somewhere else with my thoughts, because I didn't see the older man get up to scold the boy, and in doing so grab the child and (claims the father) poke him in the eye.

Major hubbub.

Meanwhile, the wife of the man in the cap has returned from the toilet. She sits down next to him. Surrounding their table are the manager, the parents of the little boy, who is shrieking and whose one eye is clearly redder than the other, and a few bystanders who have come forth as witnesses to the drama. A guy with a beard calls the older man a 'trouble-maker'. From under the brim of his cap, which shields his eyes, he defends his behaviour in superlatively arrogant terms. I feel an uncontrollable anger well up in me, and shout at the man that he's an arsehole. I raise my voice, rubbing his nose in his arseholeness, even though I did not witness the incident directly. Miriam and the manager tell me to calm down, but I am unable to halt my tirade. A seething anger has to get out. The man with the cap, in his made-up dignity, gets up, collects the dogs from under his table, and stalks off the terrace with his wife on his arm. Only then do I manage to pull myself together, albeit with choked-back sniffs of disgruntlement and indignation.

The father of the little boy comes over to thank me — for my solidarity, I guess. He tries to offer me a reconstruction of the incident, but because of his poor English most of his testimony eludes me. I do not tell him that my solidarity was false and that I was only using the unfriendly man in the cap as an excuse to vent an anger that came from an entirely different source.

23

Miriam comes out of the goat shed with a taut face. 'I can't go in there anymore without thinking of Tonio, how he used to be ... He was so crazy about the animals, could squat there forever next to the piglets. He thought they were so sweet.'

'There's something defenceless about them,' I say. 'That'll be it. Now we know what he recognised in them.'

'Seems like there are fewer goats than there used to be,' Miriam says, 'so I asked the attendant. And I was right. They've cut back on the goats. They've had fewer visitors. Because of Q fever.'

'People are complete idiots,' I say, still trembling with residual anger. 'Always afraid of the wrong things. They just have to see one spray-painted goat on the news, and they're convinced they've seen the devil.'

We head back to the parking lot. Out of habit, we make a left turn toward the Bosbaan. Two racing bikes ride ostentatiously in front of us without making any effort to let us pass. Then Miriam remembers that the Bosbaan is closed, a golden opportunity for cyclists on this bit of road. It is no trouble, a pleasure in fact, to turn around and drive back through the sun-pricked treetops — until the revulsion returns, because this light-green speckled budding of the woods simply goes on without Tonio.

We drive through Amstelveen. I say: 'I can't believe I chose this nondescript polder-padding as the scene for a novel.'

'I was going to drive you around a few key spots, wasn't I,' Miriam says. 'The police station ... the neighbourhood where the murder took place ... Café 1890.'

'No need to now. That novel's been scrapped. I'm writing a book about Tonio, and that'll be that.'

24

Buitenveldert under rainy skies: it lends the neighbourhood an acceptable degree of sombreness. Buitenveldert glimmering in brilliant sunlight: a hell of melancholy. We cross Fred. Roeskestraat, where the cemetery with Tonio's grave is. I haven't been back since the funeral. No matter how much I try to avoid the thought, I am forced to imagine his body in the red-brown coffin. Its protracted decomposition in the cool earth, the uppermost clumps of which are hard and dried out from the warm sun of the past days. The rabbits, who by now have gobbled up the Biedermeier bouquet, dart across the bare plot, where, soon, a stone slab will be placed, surrounded by stone borders. His self-portrait as Oscar Wilde, the one I have sent to dozens of people these last few days, is there, in a waterproof frame. We want to have the photo incorporated, one way or another, into the headstone (maybe as an old-fashioned enamel medallion).

'Oh yeah,' Miriam says, who seems to have read my thoughts, 'my father wants to chip in fifteen hundred for the headstone.'

'That reminds me … How would you feel about inscribing it with the name Rotenstreich? I still owe it to Tonio. Ever since June 16, 1988. And to your father. Last chance, you might say. What do you think?'

She does not answer. I glance sideways. The corners of her mouth struggle to hold back a burst of tears. Last week, too, we had to pull off to the side of the road because Miriam's vision went blurry.

25

The Filipino brother and sister who clean our house every Saturday have placed a large stack of condolence post on the cabinet in the hall. I take it out to the veranda, armed with a letter opener. There is a card from Tonio's old teachers at the gymnasium, with a verse by Auden, the same one Ignatius had used in its newspaper condolence announcement. That nice couple, Gert and Marie-Jes from Maastricht, who write me three times a week, have included twenty euros 'for roses'. ('… cherish the golden moments with Tonio …' wrote Gert in his last letter. The moment I read that phrase, back here on the terrace, an unexpected gust of wind blew through the spent golden rain. A cloud of faded yellow petals wafted over the neighbour's backyard.) There are touching letters from an old friend from Geldrop, from my former editor, from some of Tonio's ex-schoolmates. Dozens. I will answer each and every one, if need be with a few personal lines at the bottom of the mimeographed letter. They will all get the photo.

Should someone encounter me here on the veranda, he would see a man wielding a slender knife to open one letter after the other, smiling as he reads the contents, and then setting the letter aside. On the face of it, the man sits like a king in the shadow of the golden rain's crown, which scatters yet more sere petals with each puff of wind. The Norwegian forest cats, silent witnesses to the most terrible summons of his life, weave between his calves, their plume tails upright.

Miriam, outwardly calm, comes to announce that she is heading over to the garden centre. 'Pick out some plants. It'll give me something to do.'

I hand her Marie-Jes and Gert's twenty euros. 'For roses. Why don't you buy a creeper? That arch where Tonio's model posed … it could use some filling up. Our Maastricht friends would approve.'

Once Miriam is gone, the feeling of extreme tension and anxiety returns. It concentrates around my stomach, robbing it of all appetite. It wrings out my intestines, which still regularly spew a yellow poison: the form my disgust with life has assumed.

If I don't think about it directly, that spastic anxiety almost seems more like a precursor to something than a reaction to the fatal incident. As though a yet greater calamity is on its way. Yes, that's it: everything in and around me is sending me warnings. That Tonio was mowed down on the street like a dog is nothing by comparison. Just wait, the worst is yet to come.

26

When people are showered with attention for an anniversary or a death, it is usually the vast quantity that they call 'heart-warming'. I have, however, never been able to regard the truckloads of letters that have reached us as having an added-value effect.

There were intensely affectionate letters, in which the writer confessed a powerlessness to express himself or herself, after which even the feeblest of words came across as comforting. Most correspondents appeared to be of one mind that 'the loss of a child is the worst thing that can happen to you … your worst nightmare come true'. A relatively large number of parents to whom this had happened, many of them complete strangers, wrote to us.

There were pre-printed cards with an appropriately subdued motif, the words 'WITH CONDOLENCES' and only a signature underneath. On one of the cards, the printed word MOTHER was crossed out with ballpoint pen and replaced with the handwritten SON. Also okay.

I had to admit that pathos, as it pertained to our situation, never sounded insincere. The same went for our own words. When I wrote to someone that Miriam and I had gone 'through an ice-cold hell of loss and heartache', it simply *was* so.

Of course there was also a small minority of thrill-seekers, snuffling around the anguish. Free melodrama, served up by reality: irresistible. But here, too, the sensation was short-lived, except for those directly involved.

After these past weeks, my fingers still tremble too much from the jolt to be able to pen a handwritten answer. Sometimes I write a few lines by hand, and I barely recognise my own handwriting, it's that shaky. Pouring strong liquor on a practically empty stomach every evening can't help much, of course. I can't manage without my 80-proof painkiller. Bombay Sapphire helps me face night-time. The next morning, the pain is back, mixed with disgust, which for the time being refuses all painkillers.

Among all the notes of affection, the first poison-pen sentiments also reach us, relayed by sympathetic friends in a tone or with a look of 'oh brother …'

'Now he knows what it is,' was one firmly worded message. 'Why doesn't he write a book about *that*. Something real for a change.'

Hard to believe, but true: even an unfathomable loss is capable of eliciting ill will. So now we've crossed that line, too. Chosen ones who gild their lives with the death of their child.

The Netherlands has been a Christian democracy for many years now. The slogan is 'family as the cornerstone of society'.

When, in 2005, I was invited for lunch at the Trêveszaal, the baroque ministerial conference room, a number of Christian Democrats greeted me the most warmly. The prime minister introduced me to a German guest (the speaker of the German senate) as 'one of the Netherlands' most respectable … eh … respected authors'. Even if they never actually read a book, at least they know who you are. They needed to drum up a smattering of representatives of Dutch culture to impress the foreign delegation. They always *ask* things of you, and never give you anything in return. I haven't heard a word of sympathy from those cornerstone-preachers now that *my* cornerstone has been yanked out of place.

The hypocrisy of politics does not end with the death of a child. The 'cornerstone of society' lie is followed by the lie of 'coming to terms' with the loss. As essential as procreation was once preached to us, the new essence, when that progeny passes away, is the process of 'coming to terms'. Psychologists, psychiatrists, victim assistance, self-help books, medicine, priests, and psychics are there to help us through it. We are surrounded by well-meaning advisors who promise us that the pain of the loss will recede with time, and in the long run it can be turned into 'something positive'. We, Miriam and I, still have *each other*, which can only speed up the process. (The well-meant advice does not take into account that an uncontrollable and secret chemistry takes place between our individual senses of loss, which almost doubles the pain.)

Instead of maintaining an embarrassed silence, because the counsel as to the necessity of the family has been proven wrong, people just go on glossing over the rough spots. 'Come on, you two, chin up, grit your teeth and grieve, chip away at it. Been down that road before. Two, three years, and you'll see, it'll wear off. You'll be able to think back on the good times with a wistful smile.'

My prognosis is different. The pain of the loss will not wear off. Not with Miriam, not with me. As the years go by, until the day we die, the pain will only increase, following a fickle law that now, just a few weeks after Tonio's death, has already made itself known.

27

Many of the condolence letters expressed the hope that Miriam and I would be able to support *one another* in this process; this was occasionally joined by the warning that everyone deals with loss in their own way: 'It doesn't always tally.'

They were right. Miriam and I gave each other daily briefings on our confused sensations and conflicting feelings. Already at breakfast (how I handled the loss during the night), but especially in the evening, when the aluminium caps to the gin and vodka bottles got unscrewed. And in between as well, while I answer the condolence post and she comes up to my workroom to let the tears flow freely. Miriam could cry. In response, I would feel my eyes prickle and well up, sometimes as far as wetting my lashes, but with me the grief mostly leaked inward, as I constantly, embarrassedly, assured her. With her, the pain got worse as the afternoon wore into evening. Mine surprised me at unexpected moments, in stabs.

If I had a defiant day, then she might be taking a first, cautious step in formulating a kind of resignation. The next day, it would be me who saw an opening, not her.

Indeed, it did not tally. But what we were lucky not to have, right from the start, were the mutual reproaches. We did not accuse each other of having failed, directly or indirectly, of preventing the accident. (She was a lousy bike-riding teacher. Going off into traffic after drinking, he got that from his father. Etcetera. None of it.)

My father had kept contact, even after 1949, with an old army buddy from the police actions in the Dutch East Indies. They had both started a family, so sometimes years went by without them seeing each other. Once, when their eldest children were already adults, the couples bumped into one another on the street. How're things? My father enjoyed bragging about the school or university progress of his brood. After some hesitation, his friend admitted that his eldest son was no longer alive.

'His own choice,' said the wife. The boy had jumped from a high building. 'It nearly meant the end of our marriage.'

After their son's suicide, the pair hurled the most awful accusations back and forth. In the one's eyes, the other was entirely at fault, and vice versa. The man (according to the woman) had poisoned their son with his old traumas from the Indies. The divorce proceedings had begun. They saved their marriage by the skin of their teeth. Their lives were ruined for good.

Miriam and I see no reason to blame one another for anything, and while a torrent of accusations to and fro might channel some of the grief, we are not going to give in to it. (The self-reproach is a different story altogether.) We have our hands full on plugging another hole. For years, we were satisfied with our love for each other. The ripening of that love resulted in Tonio. And thus a sworn triumvirate was born. It could take a knock or two, perhaps because we always managed to patch things up in time.

Now that blind fate has evicted Tonio from that rock-solid triumvirate, Miriam and I are fastened only to each other. We stagger around on wobbly knees, groping about, crazed with fear. After a long, marvellous journey through Tonio's developing life (that playfully rocking labyrinth), we are back together: thrown back to our own devices. Where are we to go now? Tonio's absence is a *fremdkörper* in between us.

It appears that, in our desperate attempts every evening to recall everything about him and hold it tight, we are reliving the journey of his life, complete with this requiem as a chronicle. But it is no more than a voyage through time with no foothold, a sentimental journey, a reconstruction, an empty rerun.

28

Miriam arranges the potted plants and flowers from the garden centre on the veranda, and waters them with the hose. 'Wonder if they'll make it this time,' she says. 'I don't know what colour my thumb is, but it's sure not green.'

'Ice-blue,' I say, 'from mixing long drinks.'

A while later we sit down to a perilous mix of Campari, vodka, and mineral water, with a lemon wedge and lots of ice. 'We've got to quit drinking,' Miriam says. 'I don't even like the taste anymore, you know that?

'Bitter,' I concur. 'It's medicine. That powdered aspirin we used to dissolve in water tasted just like this.'

Nevertheless, the alcohol finds its way in, glass after glass. I tell Miriam about the intense anxiety that preys on me most of the day. 'As though a SWAT team might appear at any moment to haul me in.'

We drink. Ice cubes tinkle as they slide to the bottom of the empty glass. The Campari, under the golden rain, makes geishas of us: red-painted lips and a white face.

'There's another side to it,' I say. 'The anxiety I was just talking about … it's not unlike being desperately in love.'

'Gosh,' says Miriam, 'you've got that feeling pretty much at your fingertips.'

'You'd almost think that there's an unwelcome kinship between them … I mean, between grieving a loss and unrequited love.'

'A really distant kinship then,' Miriam says, who is put off by the subject. 'Love can go unanswered as cruelly as you like, but you always get over it. Don't you? We've got nothing to get over. There's no getting over Tonio.'

29

Monday, 14 June 2010. I sit at the open balcony doors in my workroom, and return to the task of answering as many condolence letters as possible. In shaky handwriting, I express my thanks for the comforting words, and it becomes an activity that in some way or another offers a kind of self-soothing — and it even works if I kid myself into believing in it.

From time to time, I prick up my ears, as I think I hear the shouting or honking (vuvuzelas) in the run-up to this afternoon's Netherlands-

Denmark match. I am mistaken: it is nothing but city noise.

Later, Miriam comes into my workroom, beside herself. She had gone into town to pick up another batch of Tonio's Wilde portraits, but felt so threatened by the traffic which roared by from all directions that she hurried home before the match began. She describes the violence of it, and I believe her, but lament the skittish vulnerability that she — a first — has experienced in busy traffic.

It's like — even though I hate the term — a kind of occupational therapy. As long as I keep diligently answering the condolence post, I'm able, if only just, to contain the despair. Cutting corners is not an option — leaving, for instance, a standard condolence card with only a name and address unanswered — because Tonio is always looking over my shoulder. I have to do this on his behalf. It is my duty.

Most people have sufficient imagination to see what happened to us on Whitsun as 'an absolute nightmare'. They understand that such a stifling, oppressive dream is impossible to just shake off, but it seems to be the intention that the horrible atmosphere gradually wears off ... that you have to take the sting out of it yourself, somehow ...

The reality of the situation, however, is that on 23 May a seed was planted for a nightmare that would sprout in the ensuing weeks. The nightmare unfolds, unrolls, unpredictably, and will certainly do its best to devour or destroy us. The monster grows like a weed, and spreads its rootstalks randomly.

While all these well-meaning people think we'll have gradually defused the nightmare by now, the struggle against a continually burgeoning adversary is still in full swing. The outcome is uncertain: either we bite the dust, or the struggle will continue to rage until our dying day.

30

At about five o'clock, I give Miriam the stack of reinforced envelopes containing the answers and photos to post. When it was warm out (and when wasn't it), I'd go out to the veranda with the afternoon papers, and she would join me later on. Every day, the same ritual. We would browse the various sections, hardly interested in the news, anticipating the moment when one of us would open the conversation. Curious, despite the certainty of the subject: Tonio, the loss, the pain.

First, Miriam went inside to fix the drinks. For me, a Bombay Sapphire with Royal Club tonic; for her, a herb vodka with mineral water on the side.

Our initially passive approach to the loss had done little except augment the pain. To sit around waiting to see what the grief would do to us — that was not Miriam's and my style. Answering the condolence post started to get on my nerves. Too often, I read that 'the feeling of loss will lessen over time'.

'I don't want to avoid the pain,' I exclaimed one evening. 'I claim it for myself. We're not the types to sit back and act pathetic. I hear myself, way too often, blubbering about the blindness of fate … as though we're supposed to just accept it and shut up. That fact that we'll never get Tonio back shouldn't mean we can't fight back against a fate that's got shit for eyes. I want to know exactly how fate, blind as it was, got his cruel hands on our Tonio.'

31

Today, 15 June 2010, Tonio would have turned twenty-two. He has now even been robbed of his birthday. From now on, we'll only be able to talk about his 'birth date', and honour it every year. Strange to think that that date, 15 June 1988, will tumble ever further into the past, together with a Tonio who will never get any older. His life froze on 23 May 2010. Even his death-date, which henceforth will travel faithfully with the passing years, has more life to it than Tonio himself.

He is so irretrievably petrified in his death that, even with all our trained creative ingenuity, we cannot make a single impression of what his life post-Whitsun 2010 would be like. It's better to keep looking back at his life as we knew it, and fish out all the half-forgotten and unreclaimed moments. For starters, we have twenty-one birthdays to look back on and relive.

So long as Tonio lived, my own actual age did not exert any terrifying effect on me. *He* had youth, and I borrowed from it. As long as I could exchange thoughts with him as to the goings-on in the world, I felt self-evidently young, or rather: ageless.

When I revealed this thought to an interviewer two or three years ago, and she kept asking exactly how old I *did* feel then, at fifty-six, I answered quite truthfully: 'Oh, about thirty-two.'

That raised some hackles. Who did I think I was! Late one afternoon, in my regular café, I was having a conversation with a friend, and up walked a certain Laurens. The guy had already dumped on me before. He glowered at me and said: 'Thirty-two, huh?' He nodded gloatingly, and repeated, before disappearing behind the draught curtains: 'Thirty-two …'

But this Laurens looked different somehow. He seemed tired, with jaded eyes, and even in his condescending disdain was less strident than we knew him. Maybe Laurens thought he had a good reason for scorn. Long ago, he was allowed to carry Joop den Uyl's bag — Den Uyl, the politician I recently criticised in *Het Parool* as being a cultureless vandal for planning to build a four-lane thoroughfare straight through Amsterdam's old city centre.* In Joop's bag was a clothes brush with which Laurens, like an exemplary paladin, discreetly swept the dandruff off Den Uyl's shoulders.

The next day we heard the news, in the very same café, that Laurens had had a heart attack in the middle of the Dam. The trauma helicopter couldn't land on the busy square, and lost precious time. Laurens didn't make it. Make no mistake: even when it happens to my self-professed

---

* Joop den Uyl (1919–1987) was a Labour politician, and was prime minister from 1973 to 1977. The proposed thoroughfare was never built.

enemies, an event of this kind does not give me the least satisfaction, and perhaps I should forgive him his condescension: he might have already felt under the weather at the moment he was expressing his contemptuous disbelief at my perceived age. I can't rule out that he wanted to warn me. A man in his mid-fifties had better not crow that he feels thirty-two.

I saw Tonio die close up. My own son, who, from just a few metres' distance, I also watched being born. Has death therefore become less of a mystery to me? No. I have seen how *easy* it is to die, but that has not yet eliminated its mystery. On the contrary. The ease with which he died has only augmented the mystery. True, I have become more receptive to death. I know that when my time comes, I shall resist it less vigorously. The ease of doing it also applies to me.

And what's more, I no longer have to stay alive for *him*. He preceded me. So what's stopping me? (Miriam, she's stopping me.)

Lola, age eleven, is acting in a play, an adaptation of Shakespeare's *A Midsummer Night's Dream*. Miriam goes with Lola's mother, Josie, to the premiere.

'So there I sat,' she said later, 'among all those proud mothers. I suddenly felt my age. Fifty. Not because most of the parents were at least ten years younger, but … because I sat there as a childless mother. Everything I saw there, the pride, the dedication, I'd gone through myself. And what for, in the end?'

After the performance, Lola could choose a Venetian mask from Miriam's glass display-case. Her choice was from a commedia dell'arte series. The girl was timid in making her selection, well aware of the grief in this house, where she had always been a welcome guest in Tonio's room.

Shortly before the premiere, she and her mother had paid a visit, and Miriam succumbed to one of her unstaunchable crying fits. Quick as a squirrel, Lola darted across the sofa and up along Miriam's limbs to help her mother comfort their friend.

32

I try to explain a condolence letter from our friend André to Miriam. He presents philosophers and physicists who regard space and time as illusory concepts.

'Everyone is everywhere, always,' concludes his letter. At first her face lights up: someone has taken the trouble to put the unutterable into words. She is grateful to the writer of the letter, but, when all is said and done, has no use for his message. The fact that 'everyone is everywhere, always' will not bring back her son. The boy will always be lost in Everywhere, Always.

'Damn it, Minchen, I can't offer you much comfort, and that drags me down. Comfort implies a promise: that a situation will improve sooner or later. Our situation will never improve. Never. Therefore I can't promise it. And ... so much for comforting.'

'But you do comfort me,' she says. 'Just holding my hand when I cry *is* incredibly comforting ... even if it doesn't bring Tonio back.'

Nice of her to say so, but it doesn't alleviate my discomfort or powerlessness. If someone who is old and sick dies, the survivors can comfort one another with 'It's better this way. He's been spared any more suffering.'

Tonio had no 'more suffering' to be spared. He had worked up a vast appetite for what would have been the best part of his life. His last days, as far as we could judge, were like a starvation diet.

33

When Dennis was here, he dropped the name Goscha a few times: the girl who had gone out with Tonio and Dennis that Saturday night. He only mentioned her in passing, as though she was only an extra. *He* had danced with Tonio, and 'dipped' him. Goscha, in Dennis's sketch, was not much more than a shadow. A girl who had waited at their table until the boys had finished dancing, and later cycled with them to Sarphati Park in De Pijp. And there her tracks vanished. Dennis said she had gone home with him, but there were likewise precious few details as to this afterparty — well, yes, actually: Goscha had fallen asleep pretty much right away.

A few days after Dennis's visit, we received a letter signed 'Goscha Bourree'. It was written in pen in adult handwriting, which hardly reminded you of that girlish swirl that so many young women retain until long after their school years have passed.

'Dear parents of Tonio …'

She wrote that she did not know Tonio well, and had in fact only met him a couple of times, always together 'with his good friend Dennis'. She explained when and where they had gotten acquainted (in early April at Club Trouw, Wibautstraat), and that right from the word go they all three felt completely at ease with one another. She shared Tonio's love of cats and photography. 'Tonio and I apparently had the same philosophy teacher at school.'

Goscha briefly described the events of that night — 22–23 May — when the three of them went out 'to paint the town red', and closed with: 'I hope this letter has been helpful in some way. I wanted you to know what a terrific evening it was. No one could know, of course, that it would be Tonio's last. I'm glad I got to know him, and sad that it didn't last long. I remember exactly what he was wearing. Fortunately I had the chance to tell him what a neat T-shirt he was wearing.'

34

The bell rang at five o'clock sharp. Miriam buzzed the door open. Goscha was a slightly built girl about Tonio's height, maybe a bit shorter. She had a sweet face, with a shadow of fatigue — thanks to the student hours she undoubtedly kept. Dark-blonde curly hair. Dressed mostly in black, with lemon-yellow tights. Her movements were light-footed but angular as she crossed the room to Tonio's spot on the sofa, where Dennis, too, had sat for some hours.

Tears came to her eyes at the sight of Tygo and Tasha: Tonio had told her so much about his Norwegian forest cats. She tried to pet them, but perhaps because they smelled her own cats (a tabby and a tortoiseshell), they kept their distance. Indeed, what did you expect, with their fine lineage and northern nobility, that they would deign to consort with cat-shelter riff-raff?

Goscha was keen to begin her account of Tonio's last evening, but as Miriam was still in the kitchen preparing the drinks, I stalled, asking her to first to tell something about herself. Miriam mustn't be allowed to miss even a word of Goscha's version of Tonio's last hours.

After graduating from high school, she 'travelled' and learned Spanish (whether during, before, or after her travels was not entirely clear). Like Tonio, she was keen on photography, but she had let it slide until Tonio … that Saturday night in Trouw.

'Goscha, could you save Tonio … for Miriam?'

'Oh yeah. Sure.' She told me she was to start a new major in the fall. Linguistics. Fortunately Miriam appeared just then with the tray, because Goscha was eager to get on with her story.

'We read your kind letter,' I said. 'Could you tell us more about your friendship with Tonio?'

'We only saw each other a couple of times,' she began, 'and Dennis was always there, too. We hit it off, the three of us. It really clicked … like we'd known each other for a long time. I met them at the beginning of April. At Trouw. We danced all night, then went back to Dennis's place. I was surprised we had so much in common … cats, photography … the same festivals. On Queen's Day, I bumped into them at Trouw again. It was terrific … everybody letting their hair down … Afterwards we were still revved up, of course, so we partied some more at someone's house. Well, "partied" … it ended pretty low-key. All of us tucked under a blanket, cups of tea, talking about cats. I lived a few blocks from Tonio, so I asked if he would ride home with me. Dennis was totally crashed under his blanket, no way was he going to wake up. That's when I saw what kind of a friend Tonio was. You don't just leave your pal in the lurch at some stranger's house. You wait until he wakes up, and see that he gets home safely. Tonio was watching over him. Whenever Dennis's blanket slid off, Tonio would tuck it back in. So sweet … so … steadfast. Meanwhile he worried whether I'd get home okay. I said I'd be fine. Dennis was the defenceless one. I left, and couldn't get that scene out of my head: Tonio carefully draping the blanket over Dennis. Really cute. He was such a sweet, caring guy.'

Goscha went on to tell us about Tonio's last evening and night — a more detailed version of what she had written. Her story more or less tallied with Dennis's , except that now she played a more central role. The three of them had made another date. It was Whitsun weekend. Now they were really going to paint the town red.

When Dennis and Tonio rang her doorbell, they had just come from a party in the Vondelpark, at Café Vertigo in the Filmmuseum. 'They were earlier than we'd planned. That was because … well, they thought it was a bit of a flop, that party. They were glad to finally meet my cats, Sieb and Mulan. It was great. We made plans to go to Berlin in the summer. Those guys were just really fun to be with. So about midnight we went to Trouw. The next night, I saw all the empty beer cans in my garbage bin … so unreal to think that by then Tonio was already dead.'

She fell silent, as though staring, dismayed, into that bin. (Cans upright on the bottom of the wastebasket, so the last splashes of beer wouldn't leak out all over the scraps of paper, it makes such a sticky mess.)

'We were all really up for it. Pity the music was kind of lame. The upside was that it gave us the chance to talk a lot. I finally dared to tell them about stuff I really want to do, but never get around to. Like photography. Being out of it for a while makes it even harder to pick up again. Tonio talked me back into it. And what do you know: after that weekend, I started taking pictures again. Tonio was really a super-nice guy. Thoughtful. He was a fantastic listener.'

35

'He got that from me,' I said. 'When I was his age, people always said I was such a good listener. But some people didn't trust it. They thought I was hiding something behind my attentiveness. That I was planning some evil deed. My willing ear made them nervous.' (Right away, I felt like a bald-faced liar. Summer of '93: I saw myself walking with the five-year-old Tonio through Pernes-les-Fontaines — the same route every day, to the restaurant in the courtyard of an old hotel. He chattered to me in melodious, complete sentences. Until he realised I wasn't always paying full attention. 'Adri, you're not *listening*.' His voice cracking: 'You have to *listen* to me, Adri. Otherwise … otherwise …' Can't make it up to him now.)

'Well, in Tonio's case it was sincere,' Goscha said. 'I can vouch for it.'

'Back to Trouw,' said Miriam. 'Did you all drink a lot?'

'All those rounds,' Goscha answered. 'It went so fast, you could hardly keep up. And I felt guilty, 'cause Tonio paid the most.'

'Didn't you dance that night?' I asked.

'Hardly at all. The music was awful. Yeah, I do remember the three of us standing out on the dance floor. Dennis gave Tonio a dip. The music was so bad we left earlier than usual.'

'What time?' I asked. (I was tinkering with time again.)

'About four. We sat outside Trouw on a bench for a while. Just to cool off. I think I was pretty tipsy.'

'If you left the place at four,' I said, 'then you mustn't have sat on that bench for very long. Tonio's accident was, let's say, imminent.'

'We biked to Sarphatipark. Via Ceintuurbaan. At the corner of the park, we stopped to chat for a minute. Dennis wanted us to go to his place. Tonio said no. He needed to be getting home. Go to bed … or no, his friend Jim was waiting up for him, I think. Did they do that much, those guys, watch a film so late? Like I said, Tonio never left anyone in the lurch, so … Normally I'd have biked back to De Baarsjes with him. But I was so tired and … well, I guess I was pretty drunk. But Dennis and Tonio weren't, really …'

'We girls just have a smaller liver, that's all,' Miriam said.

'I was of two minds,' Goscha said. 'I didn't really feel like biking all that way by myself later. It would have been more fun for Tonio, too, if I'd ...'

She shook her head with a sad smile. 'Just listen to me: *fun*. Maybe that whole awful thing wouldn't have even happened. Such a different ending. Small decisions, big consequences ...'

I asked her a few more things I'd also asked Dennis. Whether Tonio weaved about when he cycled off.

'No, I'd have noticed. Sure, we'd been drinking, kind of a lot. But he rode away completely normally.' Goscha shut her eyes tight. 'I can just see him ... riding off. My last glimpse of him. He biked over the pavement and onto Ceintuurbaan.'

'Say you *had* gone with him, Goscha,' I asked, 'what route would you have taken?'

'Oh, the usual.' She opened her eyes. 'Ceintuur. Van Baerle. Left on Overtoom and then on to De Baarsjes. Same as always.'

'So how did Tonio end up,' Miriam asked, 'at the corner of the Hobbemastraat and the Stadhouderskade?'

I had the impression that the question took Goscha by surprise: that she hadn't yet asked it herself. She glanced a bit nervously from Miriam to me, and from me back to Miriam. 'I couldn't say.'

36

Goscha had said she didn't fancy the long bike ride home on her own after that one last drink at Dennis's place. If she was telling the truth, then she had not intended to spend the night with Dennis.

'Did you and Dennis ... enjoy yourselves?' I hoped the question did not sound all too bitter.

'I still have a weird feeling about it,' she answered. 'I fell asleep pretty much right away.'

'You said you chatted more than you danced at Trouw,' I continued.

'Did Tonio mention anyone named Jenny?'

Goscha thought for a moment, and shook her head. 'Not that I can remember.'

'Nor about a girl he had done a photo shoot with a few days earlier?'

'Hmm, now that you mention it … I picked up something about a girl from an exchange between Tonio and Dennis. A photo shoot, that might've been it. But I didn't catch a name. Jenny … no.'

'Dennis told us,' Miriam said, 'that Tonio came to him for girl advice lately. You know, how to go about certain things. He'd told both Dennis and Jim more than once recently that he felt *happy*.'

'Yes,' Goscha said, her eyes downcast, 'he told me that, too, a couple of times. He obviously had to get it off his chest. He couldn't hold it in. It was as though he couldn't believe what had hit him … so intensely happy.'

I thought back on a few periods of my own irrational happiness between the ages of twenty-five and thirty-five. Once again, I had stumbled upon an intimate parallel between his life and mine. And then again, not quite, because my unruly bliss had had the opportunity to run its course.

'Tonio was wearing this neat T-shirt that night,' Goscha said, the smile returning to her face. 'A really special one. I'm glad I told him so. He obviously appreciated a compliment. He'd grin a little, shy and proud at the same time. Yeah, it feels good that I was able to tell him that, just before …'

I recalled Tonio's bare shoulders that stuck out from the sheets in the ICU. That neat T-shirt was blood-soaked from his skid on the Stadhouderskade asphalt. Goscha's compliment could not prevent them having to cut it off him in the ambulance. *Must ask Miriam if they gave it back, together with the rest of his things.*

37

'When did you hear …?' Miriam wasn't able to finish the question. She bent over Tygo, who sat at her feet, and gave him a soft rap on his nose.

'Monday,' Goscha replied. 'The next day.'

I took over from Miriam. 'Who from, if I may ask?'

'Yeah, it's a dumb story,' she said, blushing. 'I heard it from my ex. He's a bicycle repairman. I didn't know he was a friend of Dennis, but that's who he heard it from. I'd gone round to his place ... to the bike-repair guy, I mean, my ex ... and when I was back outside I felt myself go all queasy. My knees were like jelly. I had to hold on to something for support.'

Goscha rambled a bit, half to herself, timid and blushing. A comment by the bike repairman (or some other sign, it wasn't really clear) had given her the impression that Dennis was angry with her. 'Maybe because I'd fallen asleep in his room ... while he'd just crashed that time, with Tonio and the blanket ... well, anyway, I didn't hear anything from him for days. That says enough.'

She looked at the floor.

'No, wait, Dennis *did* tell me, the day after the accident, what had happened to Tonio. I got a text message from him ... or maybe it was Facebook. I don't know anymore.'

I got the impression that the dozy 'afterparty' with Dennis had given her a turn. Maybe she was wondering if it was worth it, ditching Tonio for that, and letting him ride all that way home alone ... lost in thought, a target for unexpected traffic ...

38

Since we weren't sure if we would have the stamina for much longer (those were shaky days), Miriam had emailed Goscha that an hour would be enough. When the girl got up promptly and properly after an hour, I regretted the prescribed time limit. But Goscha, thinking perhaps that we'd invited her to stay longer just out of politeness, was unrelenting — for us, for herself.

As she saw her out, Miriam showed Goscha the small photo gallery of Tonio on the landing. I heard the two talking animatedly, but couldn't catch what they said. I pondered a ruse to get her to stay longer. Aside from four fleeting onlookers (the driver of the car that hit him, his passenger, and two eyewitnesses), Goscha and Dennis were the last ones to see Tonio alive, for hours on end, half a day at least. Of the two, Goscha had spoken about him in the most detail. She had managed to present us with a warm-blooded Tonio. We hadn't heard her out sufficiently. We should have had her keep talking, until we, through her, had soaked up our boy's last bit of warmth.

Goscha came back to shake my hand. Her emotions made her jittery and timid. From where I sat, it was only a couple of short steps to the living-room door. Still, she turned around three times, her eyes wet, to say goodbye.

'Nice girl, didn't you think?' Miriam said when she got back upstairs. 'And that she kept to the one-hour agreement. When you meet kids like these, you almost feel like there's hope for the world.'

She went to fill our glasses. I suspect her of having sneaked double shots of gin and vodka in the tonic and orange juice tonight. Once she sat down next to me, she let herself go. 'The pain … the pain.'

And later, settled back down somewhat: 'If you want to reminisce about Tonio … go ahead, no matter how painful … you don't have to spare my feelings.'

39

We drag ourselves, sluggish and lethargic, through the summer, as though since Whitsun we are surrounded by another atmosphere that slows down our natural pace of movement. At the same time, there is that constant agitation, pregnant with dark thoughts: *though the worst is yet to come.* It has already started to become this requiem's refrain.

These aren't just empty expectations, because the worst, the very worst, *is* still yet to come. Not an event worse than Tonio's dying, but this: that the reality of his death will hit us head-on.

It is the fear of the pain of an eventual solution that occupies Miriam, night after night. The fear of a future that does not offer peace, nor acceptance, nor resignation, nor an answer to the pain. A future that will only knead and whittle the loss into a greater, more merciless clarity.

40

I tried to explain to a friend the cyclone of emotions we had experienced through Tonio's death.

'I'll just name a few. They rear their heads in random order, overlapping unpredictably. Either all at once or in rapid-fire succession. For Miriam, of course, it's slightly different.'

In the first place, there was that (seldom absent) feeling of being ON EDGE. It was often accompanied by rapid breathing, ditto motor functions, as though you thought something might still be salvaged (but what?).

A variant on this: extreme ANXIETY, comparable to paralysing exam-fear, or the insecurity that comes with being hopelessly in love. A sensation that Tonio's death was just a portent for some greater calamity.

PAIN, wavering between ice-cold and searingly hot, like a storm raging across the plain of your heart. Sometimes it would abate for a moment, only to surge again all the more acutely. (As Miriam put it recently: 'Just when you think you're feeling reasonably stable, the pain suddenly hits again. Unfair.')

RECALCITRANCE. To whom or to what, as long there was no authority where one could register a complaint? At the very least, to the brutal truth that Tonio would never again come sauntering in here with his sheepish grin. Without a worthy opponent, recalcitrance bashed its way inwards, wreaking havoc and destruction on the soul rather than the public domain.

41

And then a GUILTY CONSCIENCE, to be divided into *rational* and *irrational* feelings of guilt.

Irrational: that I was not there, at that very spot, to stop the car, or, in the event that I was too late for that, to be there for Tonio, to at least kneel next to him and lay my folded-up jacket under his head … hold his hand. 'I'm here. Lie still.'

Rational: that we hadn't taught him to cycle more responsibly. That I didn't see to it that his bike had a light. I should have had LED lights and reflectors sewn onto all his clothes when they were here to be washed. (This last thought might tend toward the 'irrational' category.)

Irrational: that I was unable to squeeze a second into the reality of that night, and thus prevent the collision between bicycle and car. Perhaps I should have attributed my early-morning awakening, the result of a flood of saliva, as an alarm signal, which in turn should have resulted in a warning *to him*. My mobile phone lay on the bed, within arm's reach.

'Hello?' His characteristic slightly harried voice, this time from pedalling. It also sounds a bit drunk.

'Hi, it's me … Adri. Where are you?'

'Jeez, what the … Well, let's see, I'm just cycling on the Ceintuurbaan with a couple of friends. Just crossed the bridge over the Amstel. We've been out.'

'Yeah, so I hear. Where are you headed?'

'Jeezus, you really have to know every … Okay, home, I think. Jim's waiting up for me. We were going to watch a movie.'

'At this time of night?'

'You know Jim. Insomniac.'

'And the people you're with?'

'They're going to go chill at Dennis's place, Govert Flinkstraat. I don't think I'll …'

'Yes, do! Better to bike out to De Baarsjes in daylight.

'Jesus, Adri, how old do you think …'

'I've got a bad feeling, that's all. I just woke up with a churning stomach.'

'Jesus man, take a Rennie. We're just on the Ceintuurbaan now. The others are about to turn off at Sarphatipark. I want to stop and talk to them first. Oi, oi.'

He's already hung up. Say I *did* call him, and in doing so delayed his ride across town by just a few seconds … say he nevertheless got hit by a car … wouldn't my guilt be demonstrably even greater? ('I wish I *hadn't* called him.')

And so, in the eye of the storm of emotions, I piled guilty conscience upon guilty conscience.

Let's not forget SHAME. For myself: you've fucked up, Van der Heijden, you've let him slip through your fingers. For Miriam: I begot a son with you, and he's gone, and I wasn't able to prevent his passing.

For Tonio himself: I let you loose on the world with insufficient warning, otherwise you would still be here (which itself is the proof of my failure).

Shame, lastly, before the entire world: from now on I will be the once-proud father who has lost his son. Shun him, the pariah, he stinks of grief like a wet dog stinks of dishrag. His pain is as contagious as the plague.

42

PRIDE, don't forget: for Tonio.

When I stood at Tonio's deathbed in the ICU, and watched him die, there was still, despite everything I was going through, a place for pride. He died. He did it well, too. He dealt with the task, and showed us how easy, in fact, it was. He demonstrated it to his father. See, Adri, this is how you do it.

In the weeks that followed, that pride branched out. We were proud of him: that he skipped blithely through life, had given so much love, was so helpful and generous, and kept difficulties as much to himself

312

as possible. We were proud of him because he had done his best with a life that could, on the eve of a beautiful summer, abruptly be cut short, just like that. He lived as though it would not come to a premature end. A few days before his death, as though calamity were not on its way, he reassured his parents about his future plans. Media Technology. Master's degree. Leiden. The Hague. Train.

We had the definite sense that he, and he alone, had known all along that his life would be short — and had kept quiet about it. That he had held that terrible information in solitude, so as not to saddle us with it — that thought alone filled us with pride.

ANGER: at everything and everyone, but not all at once. In the absence of a God, I unleashed my wrath at Fate. In my powerlessness I tried to unmask it by ripping away its blindfold, revealing only blind eyes. Ping-pong balls without an iris.

Other objects of my anger: daylight savings time, the manufacturer of BMW autos (because I knew for sure it was a garish BMW that had taken him down), my mother-in-law, who made a caricature of Tonio's death by incessantly announcing her own …

RESIGNATION: at times, briefly, to my own surprise. Resignation suggests something long-term, but in the present situation could not be more fleeting. It is quickly followed by a guilty conscience, because accepting Tonio's death — that just won't do.

43

FEAR in many forms. 'I'm so frightened,' Miriam said recently, her face contorting into a tearful cramp. 'I'm eaten up by fear.'

I no longer had to ask her what of.

'Before we lost Tonio, we used to discuss the problems and challenges of a novel … the series of attempts at a solution … it started to become old hat. In our day-to-day lives, too, we were always "solution people". No problem was ever too daunting. And we usually found a solution.

Problems weren't safe around us. But now here we sit with an absolutely insoluble problem … Tonio's death … and what can't be solved is scary. It scares me more than my own death. More than anything. No matter how you look at it, there's nothing you can do to make it better. It makes me claustrophobic. Like in *The Vanishing* by Tim Krabbé. Locked in an insoluble problem. And you know that nowhere in the future that lies ahead of us will there ever *be* a solution. The fear of the insoluble problem is also the fear of the future.'

Miriam could undoubtedly have added to the list of fears, just as I could. The fear of going mad from the loss. To want to follow Tonio to the grave. To be unable to write again. To be arrested for manslaughter …

I pointed out to my friend that I could expand the list with a whole bunch more emotions, and combinations of them, but that I wanted to limit myself to one last one. The feeling of utter DEFEAT. Your son has been taken from you by an unknown power that you, his father, were unable to fend off.

44

So now we'd had visits from Dennis as well as Goscha: the two friends who Tonio had spent his last hours with — a full circle of the clock, roughly the last half-day of his consciousness. (Another half a day would still come, this one *unconscious*. So that his final conscious half-day was associated with evening and night and darkness, and his final unconscious half-day with daytime and sun and operation-room lamps.) Although the emphasis they laid on certain details differed somewhat, the one version more or less complemented the other.

But we were still in the dark as to who this Jenny was, why Tonio didn't go to Paradiso with her, and what he was doing at twenty to five in the morning at the intersection of the Hobbemastraat / Stadhouderskade, so far astray from his usual route.

In all honesty, we had to admit that we had hoped for a more idyllic account of Tonio's last hours. The role his friends Goscha and Dennis played — all well and good. But where was Jenny in this story?

We were shown a Tonio who, after a high-spirited evening, said goodnight to his disco mates, who then settled down in Dennis's house. A solitary Tonio, with comradely duties to fulfil, and for one reason or another took a wrong turn — only to encounter his better in the form of blind and mute fate. We were even robbed of the illusion that he had perhaps wanted to stop in at Paradiso, either inside or out, to catch up with Jenny.

'I can't get past the moment of the collision,' I said to Miriam. 'I'm beating my brains out over it. I simply *have* to find out what happened. Otherwise I won't survive it myself. That last bike ride … the crash, out of nowhere … his battered body on the asphalt … sirens in the distance … flashing lights … It all adds up to such a devastating loneliness, Minchen … if I only knew how I *might have* assuaged his aloneness in those minutes.'

'Everything else I learn about it,' said Miriam, 'only causes more pain. But if you're determined to leave no stone unturned … then I'm with you.'

CHAPTER FOUR

Scorched earth

Grief fills the room up of my absent child,

Lies in his bed, walks up and down with me,

Puts on his pretty looks, repeats his words,

Remembers me of all his gracious parts,

Stuffs out his vacant garments with his form;

Then, have I reason to be fond of grief?

— William Shakespeare, *King John*

1

How often have I dreamt I had killed someone? I was a murderer, no doubt about it, and would soon be found out. The *ideal* murder, though, wasn't part of my dream. I swung.

There's no greater relief, of course, than to wake up from this kind of nightmare. The murder was usually sufficiently realistic that at a certain point, still deeply asleep, you began to wonder if you weren't indeed the victim of a bad dream. No, not a chance: this was 100 per cent real. I would have to accept that I was the perpetrator of the capital crime. No way out.

Only upon awakening, when the dreamer has returned to the only true reality, does the dream's decor reveal itself as though made of cardboard and styrofoam. The events surrounding the murder carry the mark of cheap, implausible fiction. 'And I fell for it!'

In another kind of nightmare, a loved one dies. Decor, details, the event itself: everything is *so* realistic. A comic-strip dreamer pinches himself, but for me that is unnecessary, for I know: this is for real. My loved one really is dead. My heart freezes.

Tonio's death, and everything pertaining to it, comes rushing at me like one of those hyperrealistic nightmares that won't be messed with. All manner of special effects are brought into play so that the dream will be indistinguishable from everyday reality. Oh, does the dreamer wish to pinch himself? Even such signs of disbelief are parried. He does not awaken. The secret of the dreamsmith.

And yet, even the most firmly quelled nightmare-sufferer retains an ice-cold place in his mind, which — gradually, and against his better judgement — registers the possibility that the reality surrounding him is the well-constructed decor of a realistic dream.

That is how I fare. My state of mind since Whit Sunday exhibits all the characteristics of a chillingly well-disguised dream. I can locate no cracks in the masquerade, nor can I shake the suspicion that the wool — a very high-quality one — has been pulled over my eyes. Only … this stubborn nightmare takes its sweet time, and lingers. The endless prolongation of the dream could also be a way of enhancing its reality level.

Let me put it this way: this nightmare is so realistic that I almost no longer feel like a dreamer.

2

Sunday morning. When Miriam enters the bedroom, I'm reading the weekend papers in bed, with the curtains and the balcony doors open. Wearing just a long T-shirt over her panties, she curls up next to me. Out of bashfulness, or maybe as a diversionary tactic, she gives me soft little head-butts, the way her cats do. Since Tonio's passing, we have fondled, embraced, caressed, stroked, squeezed — all in the service of consolation, mind you, not in any way a form of arousal or stimulation (although who knows, maybe consolation has an erotic side). For the first time in weeks I stroke, in passing, her breasts through the cotton of the T-shirt. She quickly gets out of bed.

'I'm not sure if the neighbours can see through the ivy,' she says, 'but I'll close the curtains just to be on the safe side.'

I look at the thick carpet of ivy, which for years now has entirely overtaken the side of Max Nord's house. Miriam draws the curtains and returns to bed. I resume my tender kneading, now under the T-shirt, but they refuse to become the breasts that have always provided me with a mild pre-glow of arousal. They are the breasts that fed Tonio. The nipples harden, not from the action of my fingertips, but as a reaction to the hungry wailing from the next room.

The hand that glides between her legs belongs to me *now*, but it is also the hand that, in the summer of '88, hesitantly hazarded a probe to see if the young mother was sufficiently healed from the birth to receive me. Answering my caresses, she does not show the reactions I am accustomed to with her. My hand is replaced by hers, but neither does it manage to achieve anything. When I try to take over from her, she holds me back, whispering: 'I keep seeing Tonio. On vacation.'

And from that moment, of course, I also see Tonio before me — not as an infant on his mother's breast, but as a ten-year-old. Indeed, on vacation. Miriam can stimulate and knead me all she likes, but I keep seeing Tonio as he was that summer in Marsalès. His industriousness. He approaches me with a lifelike snake draped over his shoulder. If he squeezes the tail in a certain way, the snake wraps itself around his neck.

'It's not real. It's my toy snake.'

I see him fishing at the small waterfall that feeds the swimming pond. He hauls out small, silvery fish, one after the other, which he then deftly plucks from the hook and tosses back into the churning water. Tears flow when the campground manager suddenly bans fishing because he fears for the fish stock.

'I always threw them back. It was only for the fun of it. I do too think about the environment.'

I see him with a paddle in his hand, dancing at the ping-pong table, with those phosphorescent glow-sticks taped to the back of his hands to distract his opponent. Now it's his mother who issues a veto: what if those things break, and all that chemical poison leaks out …

I hear him complain bitterly that he 'still hasn't made any friends'. I reply: 'But it's only the first week.'

'He had a nibble,' Miriam says, 'but the other boy was two years older, and Tonio didn't like that.'

Early that evening, he comes barrelling up to our property on his hired mountain bike, his face flushed with excitement. 'I made four friends at once. Playing ping-pong. I treated whoever won. And now my money's gone, so I came to ask …'

'And those friends of yours, did they treat when you won?'

'No, cos I didn't win. I'm not so good.'

'There's an envelope with some change on the dresser in the living room. Go get it.'

I dump the contents onto the outdoor table — a whole pile of French small change. I let Tonio pick out the higher denominations. 'Hey, remember: you don't have to be the only one who treats. No matter whether you win or lose.'

'Okay.'

When he gets back on the mountain bike, his trousers hang crooked, weighed down on one side from the coins in his side pocket. An hour later, he returns wearing his helmet and sunglasses, cheerful and even more flushed than before. He empties his pockets and deposits the majority of the money we'd given him back on the table. 'The other two weren't really friends. So I didn't treat anymore.'

Tonio is surprised when I say he can keep the coins. 'Because you're so honest.'

'Adri,' he says, 'the other two boys, the ones who *were* real friends, well, they asked if I could come to their tent tonight.'

'Sure. Just be back before dark.'

'What time is that?'

'I'd say: quarter to eleven.'

'How do I know when it's quarter to eleven?'

I fasten my watch to his wrist.

I misjudged the time: it gets dark early in the south of France. Miriam goes to fetch him. Tonio bikes ahead of her, and charges, laughing, onto the property, dry twigs crackling under his braking tyres. 'They're brothers.'

'Your age?'

'They seem to be the same age. I don't know which one's older.'

Tonio sits down across from me at the garden table, and sags lazily in his chair. He's got it made.

3

'With thanks to Tonio,' Miriam says with a sad little laugh. We lie next to each other, unsatisfied, without the lazy lie-ins of past Sunday mornings. Every caress and touch has become a gesture of comforting, which of course is worth something, too.

'It'll get worse,' I say. 'The living Tonio was easy to forget ... he did his own thing ... But the dead Tonio, he's here all the time. You can't just send him away. He watches over us, and has chosen us to watch over him. We three are stuck with each other until the end of your or my days.'

Miriam lies on her right side. The tear from her right eye chooses the shortest path to the pillow. The one from her left eye first has to take the hurdle of her nose before it reaches the right cheek, and only much later, the pillowcase.

'If he's always there,' she says, 'then that must mean we're less lonely, now that we ... well, now that we hardly see anyone else.'

'More than that: *he* guarantees that the outside world stays shut out. Tonio is the wedge between us and the rest. He is our bodyguard ... without an earpiece, because he doesn't need any instructions. Bodyguard, hostage, and kidnapper all rolled into one. What else could we need?'

'That.'

'What?'

'That it wasn't even necessary ... this whole isolation and all.'

'There's no turning back.'

4

An acquaintance of ours is a scent researcher, which has nothing to do with the ENT clinic at a hospital. He studies, among other things, human tears and their effect (pertaining to scent) on human interaction. He has not yet published on the subject, so his results are confidential, but he did let on that female tears can influence the male libido.

I took a stab: 'Tears are a stimulant.'

'Other way around,' he said. 'They actually impair sexual desire.'

'I've tasted a tear now and again, of course,' I said. 'But I've never noticed a particular scent attached to it.'

'Men experience tears as odourless. But the scent in fact obliterates their horniness. Tears contain pheromones. A kind of lure scent, strangely enough ... but not to attract a sexual partner.'

This surprised me. My thoughts took me back to 1973 and my farewell to a girl who had run away from home to be with me, despite the fact that I had already planned a holiday with some friends, where she would only be a fifth wheel. She had gone into hiding at a friend's. I went to say goodbye. 'It's just for six weeks.' As soon as I entered the room, she started crying, and kept it up until I left. Her uninhibited gush of tears, reinforced with watery snot, aroused me as never before — but maybe her desperate passivity played a role in it.

'We haven't yet studied the effect of the scent of nasal fluid on libido,' my acquaintance said. 'Snot from an anguished runny nose could perhaps neutralise the pheromones in tears. But that's pure conjecture.'

'When I see Miriam's tears flow,' I said, 'I mostly have an urge to comfort her.'

'Think about that,' said the scent researcher. 'I think you're very close to the function of those tear pheromones. A comfort-evoking scent.'

Life has given me a bum rap.

My background, the environment in which I grew up, always taught me that it was right to marry and start a family — even though my own family did not set a particularly good example. My father was a weekend drinker, who combated his fear of abandonment with suicide threats. I remember the time two police officers led my mother and us three children into the darkened house. The electricity had been switched off; in the kitchen, all the burners of the gas cooker hissed at their highest setting. Dad hadn't taken the trouble to hold a match to them. He had opened them with bloodied hands: on the counter, we found the shards of a smashed drinking glass.

The police found my father upstairs, lying on the bed with his head next to the open window, so that to this day we don't know who in fact he had intended that gas for — maybe for the lit cigarette lighter of the rookie policeman, or the unwitting neighbour who responded to our alarm.

Fifteen years later, I met H&NE. In the seven years that we lived together, our mothers (and fathers) kept asking about their first grandchild. It was, in actual fact, a *demand* disguised with a question mark. Apparently the family, the concept of a family, had a certain value that could not just be destroyed by a single destructive member.

I can't say I gave in to the interfering insistence of my mother and mother-in-law, God help me. But I cannot deny that family, despite an improperly used gas stove, was the model for my upbringing — a *mould* that does not let itself be renounced without a fight.

So we decided to have a child. I knew full well what I was doing in getting her pregnant. We got married, for the sake of the forthcoming child. It came, and for nearly twenty-two years made us extremely happy. Now Miriam and I are saddled, each until our own dying day, with a life-sized loss, instead of a living son. It was thus a big fat lie, the shelter and comfort that a family was supposed to guarantee. A foetid lie, the child as a buffer against the solitary chill of one's own death.

I see myself next to my mother in front of the glass wall of the Slotervaart Hospital maternity ward. Behind the glass, Miriam shows her mother-in-law the little one — and oh, how little he was — just out of the incubator. My mother looks at him, moved. It never was easy to talk uninhibitedly about sexual matters. My parents did not 'do' sexual education. ('What did we know back then?') Now she'd have to face facts.

'So, Ma, have I made a handsome little sprout for you, or haven't I?'

Since I began experimenting with sex in the late sixties, during my youth and early adulthood, I was always able to dissociate sexual intercourse and all its foreplay and afterplay from the notion of procreation. Of course, it was made easy for me, as more and more girls in my circle used the pill, and were therefore quite literally cut off from procreation. All one's attention could be focused on refining the act itself.

Sex in regard to procreation only started playing a role once we'd decided to have a child. Miriam stopped taking the pill, and quit smoking. I gave up drinking. One Sunday afternoon, I implanted, via tenderness and the tried-and-tested technique, a child in her. On Friday 13 November 1987, a pregnancy test confirmed that an heir was on its way.

The idea that with every new life you also beget a new death is an age-old cliché. They're talking about a new death that neither the begetter nor the woman who gave birth to that new life is supposed to live to see. In my case, I can safely say that in begetting Tonio I also begot my present loss. Reality cashed in the cliché prematurely.

As easily as I used to be able to dissociate sex from procreation and descendants, sex would now be forever linked with loss and absence and pain. My entire notion of procreation had been radically turned upside down. Sex, which was already an act rife with cheap-and-easy ambiguities, had now genuinely, in earnest, become something ambiguous.

The dictionary defines *penetrating oil* as 'very low viscosity oil of a certain formulation, which through capillary action can permeate hard-to-reach spots, and is most often used to free rusted mechanical parts'.

These past weeks, I have aware of my grief as a sort of penetrating oil. It permeates the capillaries of my emotional system (if such a thing exists), and loosens the tiniest details of Tonio's completed life, every forgotten and half-forgotten memory. It all dissolves into a murky soup of wistful melancholy.

Once, after a visit to my parents, we rang a taxi to take us to Eindhoven station. Tonio insisted on riding up front, next to the female driver. Miriam and I climbed in the back, and listened in amazement to what all our son told her. He was three, maybe four, and the confidential tone he assumed with the young woman almost made her blush.

'... and when we get home, Adri ... my daddy ... is going to *roughhouse* with me. We do that all the time. Roughhouse.'

Miriam and I glanced at each other, she with raised eyebrows. Yeah, I gave him the occasional playful shove, chased him around once in a while if he didn't want to go to bed, and tossed him in the air when it was convenient — but *roughhouse*, really rowdy play, no, not that I was aware of.

'So what all do you do?' asked the driver, 'have a pillow fight?'

'Tickle to death,' answered Tonio without hesitation. 'We do tickle-death.'

Oh, sweet boy. How often had he crept up on me to tickle me behind my ear or in my armpit. I'm not all that ticklish in the first place, and did my best to remain unfazed by his attempts to get me to giggle — undoubtedly to tease him (get under your father's skin? Kid, you're gonna need cruder tactics than this), but now, in the taxi, I regretted it. That wiggling finger was meant to get me to slacken, to scream, to provoke revenge in the form of a fake fight. The roughhousing he so yearned for ended in tickle-death for both parties. I'd blown it again.

Even now that he's gone, and certainly not from tickle-death, I'm still not able to scream. Inside, yes, with all the stops pulled out. Shame replays Tonio's chat with the taxi driver in my head, over and over. He was so sweet: he was satisfied with an animated description of imaginary roughhousing that wasn't to be. That way he could still enjoy it, if only in words.

6

For six weeks now, we have been living with a strangling loss. It is no idle metaphor. We have experienced, every single day, how a nagging absence can literally wrap its tentacles around your neck in a stranglehold. The scream stays stuck in your throat. Loss is a strangler who grants his victim no more protest than a hint of a gargle.

Miriam says I screamed yesterday evening, about Tonio. That would be the first time since Whit Sunday. When it comes to expressing emotions, I've often been called an internaliser — which sounds like I'm squirreling away my feelings. I'm more inclined to believe that internalising one's emotions hollows a person out. It eats away at you.

'The grief seems to trickle away somewhere inside,' I've said a few times to a weeping Miriam. 'Kind of like internal bleeding.'

I scream enough in a day, don't worry. Inner shouts of pain, which just appear out of nowhere. I have no say in the matter, but at the same time I see to it that they don't escape, that they don't pass over my lips. My insides scream.

Sometimes the inner lamentation speaks through the voices of my parents. A childhood friend, who was also the son of my mother's best friend, wrote me that his mother had said: 'Thank goodness Toos was spared seeing this.'

At once this is translated into the gut-wrenching cry of disbelief that Tonio's grandmother Toos — my mother — would have emitted (at least, before Parkinson's had taken away her ability to speak) upon hearing the dreadful news. Since receiving that letter, my mother's cry cuts sharply, sickeningly, through me. Nobody around me notices.

The way my father, reacting to Tonio's death, raises his voice within me. It's like barking, almost the beginnings of a muffled laugh of despair that ends in a coughing fit peppered with grating sobs. Oh, how happy I was to see him able to bestow on his grandson the love he wasn't able to give me. The undertone of my father's scream of dismay has something belligerent about it: this has to be undone, and be quick about it.

So yesterday evening, if I'm to believe Miriam, I let out a loud scream. I don't recall it directly. We — I, mostly — had drunk rather a lot. Could be that Miriam dared me to let it all out for once, to open my heart at full volume. My memory retains only an abstract after-image: a short-lived black vortex, perhaps of disgust, which the ever-stretching, bright-yellow tongue of a voice tries to pierce.

I only remember Miriam's faraway words — at least, when I ask her about it later.

'Go on, honey ... it's okay. It can't hurt.'

7

'How?' Miriam asks.

'By going after it,' I say. 'Not sitting around at home waiting for someone to come tell us something. Take the bull by the horns. I want to talk to the police ... have a look in their dossier ... the hospital report. I want to see Tonio's bike. The place where it happened ... maybe the yellow stripes haven't completely faded yet. I don't know if you know the feeling. You've got a bad tooth, it's a bit loose. With the least touch, like from your tongue, an awful pain shoots through your jaw. Sooner or later, you get the urge to provoke the pain. You bite down really hard ... and you're rewarded. Well, that's how I'm going to tackle my pain. Provoke it ... draw it closer.'

'And what about my pills ... d'you think I should quit taking them?'

'The pain will manage to find you, no matter what. The question is: can you handle it? Do *you* want to get to the bottom of it?'

'Whatever you do, I'm with you.'

'Okay, then we're not going to sit here having a pity party behind closed curtains. We'll get on with our own reconstruction. You know, play *CSI*. Now we know where Tonio spent his last hours ... where he came from and where the car hit him. Surely the rest can be filled in. I'll make an appointment with the Accident Investigation Unit on the James Wattstraat. If you can manage to get your hands on those photos of Jenny ... then we can question her, too.'

'I'll give Klaas another ring,' Miriam said. 'Those SD cards, those film rolls ... they can't just have vanished from the face of the earth.'

Coping with grief — we scrapped the term from our dictionary. Every form of 'coping', even considering it, removed us yet further from Tonio, and was thus taboo. We left the nerves exposed, and in doing so urged on the pain that bound us to him. That, too, was a form of grieving, but not one that allowed itself to be smoothed out — rather, one that was constantly renewed and exacerbated.

8

'If you're going to be at the Nepveustraat anyway,' I said to Miriam, 'be on the lookout for Tonio's wristwatch.'

She was going to De Baarsjes with Klaas the photographer to try to find the film rolls and storage cards with Jenny's photos. We didn't hold out much hope, because Jim and Dennis had both said that when they cleaned up his desk a week after his death they didn't find anything answering to that description. There was still the outside chance that they'd find something on Tonio's computer.

Miriam returned home morose. No sign of Jenny's pictures. Even the polaroids Tonio had showed me after the session were nowhere to be seen. They had gotten precious little cooperation from Tonio's 'best mate', Jim.

'Those polaroids,' I said. 'Maybe he had them with him. Then they should be with the rest of his things at the James Wattstraat. We have to make an appointment with those guys, not just for information, but to collect Tonio's belongings.'

'I hope the watch is there,' Miriam said, despondent. 'I couldn't find it at his old flat.'

'And their cat? How was it?'

'I didn't even touch it. It crept away, skittish. Imagine her fur crackling with static electricity ... those might have been Tonio's sparks. From the last time he petted her.'

9

He took up photography when he was fifteen — not snapshots, but striking situations and glimpses that struck no one else, combined with a natural talent for composition. I noticed that he had developed a taste for expensive photographic equipment. The lens with which he believed he could delve into the depths of the visible world's mysteries was always the costliest.

In high school, he went on a school trip to Greece to study the ruins of the old civilisation. Tonio smelled his chance to photograph the *other* Greece. The sloppy modern one. They flew from Schiphol, but had to change planes in Brussels. Tonio, far too compliant with authority, had followed too literally the airline's advice to only pack one's absolute necessities as carry-on baggage. His expensive camera got sent in the checked luggage.

Zaventem, the main Brussels airport, was in those days notorious for its corrupt baggage-handlers. Somewhere in the transfer of his bags to the flight to Greece, Tonio's photographic equipment was stolen.

I remember how upset I was when, after a bus trip to Luxembourg, where I was to go camping with a group of friends, my new set of miniature pots and pans (a gift from Grandma) had vanished. My homesickness fitted precisely in the void left by the missing camping gear. I was twelve. In my bag I found only the plastic tub of soap for treating the outside of the pans so that the aluminium didn't go black over the campfire. The adventure was spoilt.

Tonio reported the theft by phone. He held up well. We heard later from the chaperones that he participated fully in all the planned activities. They didn't notice a thing, but I knew better. He carried the humiliating loss of his equipment with him the whole time. Everything he'd have taken a picture of was reduced to the square made by two thumbs and two index fingers.

When, in these days of despondency, I feel myself tied up in knots, I picture the fifteen-year-old Tonio in Greece, around his neck the stone where his proud camera should have hung. Just as a loud alarm bell can have an effect on someone's full bladder, the thought of the stolen camera affected my mood. Tears, at last — two of them, but enough for now.

10

'All those details … I don't know if I can take it,' Miriam had said a few days earlier.

'All right, I'll go on my own,' I replied. But now that the day had arrived, I wondered whether *I* could handle it all on my own. I suggested she go with me anyway, and leave the room as soon as it got too much. 'Then at least there's someone waiting for me out in the hallway.'

An officer from the Traffic Infrastructure Control Service, Serious Traffic Accidents Unit, had offered to go to a police station in our own neighbourhood with a colleague, so as to lessen our burden. So the appointment was made for three o'clock at the Koninginneweg bureau.

'Let's take the car,' I said.

'What?' Miriam exclaimed. 'It's practically around the corner.'

'Minchen, I can't face the thought that people might stop me on the street to offer their condolences.'

Fortunately, the car was parked right out in front, so that we were only steps away from safety. Miriam went back inside to fetch Tonio's mobile phone, which he'd had on him at the time of the accident and which had been handed to us, sealed in plastic, at the AMC. The officer from the Serious Traffic Accidents Unit said he wanted to check whether the victim had been using the phone on his bicycle at the time of the fatal accident. Miriam replaced the phone in the transparent bag and handed it to me.

'That plastic,' I remarked. 'Do you want them to think we haven't handled the phone? It's obvious the bag's been opened.'

She shrugged her shoulders and started the car. We had gone through that mobile a good twenty times. Incoming calls, with and without caller ID. The text messages. The voicemail messages, like a few from a timid-sounding girl (who turned out to be the Jenny we were looking for), her voice going higher and thinner with each message, the last one beseeching him to get in contact with her, either by phone or on Facebook. She didn't leave a phone number, and there was no 'Jenny' under any of Tonio's saved contacts. She hadn't sent any texts. We had made a note of everything, and phoned all the numbers we didn't already know. The identity associated with that girl's voice remained untraceable along those channels.

She was right — it was just around the corner. We parked at the end of the Van Breestraat. On the corner of the Emmastraat is our regular pet store, which provides us with sacks of dry food for the Norwegian forest cats. Although the sky was uniformly grey, the shopkeeper sat with friends on a bench outside his shop, smoking and drinking. He greeted us, amiably and with curiosity, but luckily didn't strike up a conversation. I shoved Miriam across the street, between the parked police cars, toward the late-nineteenth-century former coach house, now a police bureau. This is where they had interviewed the driver of the car, still unknown to us, who had hit a cyclist, then unknown to him, on the morning of Whit Sunday.

The small reception area was shabby and dated, with one of those drop ceilings; one of the pressed-fibre tiles was hanging askew, behind which, judging from the bundle of wires, the electricity had been repaired. Even now I couldn't help letting my eyes wander, in aid of the scenes set in the police bureau in my new novel. In the corner, an officer stood at the coffee dispenser, cursing quietly, and balancing several dripping paper coffee cups in his hands.

The receptionist knew of our visit. The agents from the accidents unit were in another part of the building, and he would personally let them know we were here. 'One moment.'

From Miriam's pallidness, I could guess how pale I probably looked myself. I had been here twice before. The first time had been in 1995, when I had left my bag in the train on the way back from Berlin, and was directed by the railway police to my local bureau to fill in a report. (Eventually the bag was delivered, without any police intervention, to my home address by a young Romanian man who had been in the same train, and was here in Amsterdam for a summer course in economics. He had taken the bag under his wing 'to do something in return for the hospitality he encountered here every summer'. I invited him in, and fixed him up with food and drink.)

The second time I came here was the result of an official appeal to do so. A friendly officer informed me that there had been a complaint lodged against me, for assaulting a café patron. I couldn't recall any recent incident in that genre. According to the policeman, the incident had taken place at Café Welling, and the victim was a Canadian tourist. He gave me a few descriptive details of the man. When he got to a height of 2.2m — almost 6'8"! — well, that rang a bell. After opening night at the Uitmarkt 2000, a phony poet managed to rile me no end. As far as I could see, I only had two choices: give him a wallop, or leave the café. I opted for the latter.

I wasn't even out the door when I heard an excited voice next to me: 'Sir, sir, do you have a moment … are you a writer, sir?'

Why the madman suddenly addressed me in English, I didn't know, nor did I give a damn, but enough was enough.

11

In a blind fury, I turned and grabbed the pest-poet by the lapels. I hurled him in a single flowing motion — oof, standing up he turned out to be quite tall and heavy — straight over an empty bicycle rack on the sidewalk. Only once I saw the man sprawled out on his fakir bed of curved metal tubes did I realise my mistake. He was not the poet who had been vexing me, but — as I soon found out — a Canadian student of Dutch literature. His Amsterdam friends rushed to his aid. I offered him my hand and, accompanied by a thousand excuses, pulled him off the bike rack. While explaining my mistake, I brushed off his clothes and asked if he was hurt. Oh, no, not at all. Could I offer him a drink? Certainly. I ordered a trayful of drinks at the bar, including for the Canadian's hosts. We drank round after round (I paid), to the brotherhood between our parts of the world, separated by distance but related by migration; we drank to the literature of both our countries, and toasted our friendship, which was growing more intimate by the minute.

'How lucky,' spake the Canadian, 'that our little tussle was just a small misunderstanding.'

I gave the policeman an account of that evening and enquired as to how this could have led to charges of battery. He quoted from the police report: the Canadian had discovered bruises on his back the next morning while showering, which led to the decision to press assault charges after all.

'You don't say. Doesn't it mention the hangover I caused him?' I asked the desk officer. 'I mean, all those rounds I stood them … I might have been out to poison the Canadian tourist with alcohol.'

'Hearing your version of the incident,' the policeman replied, 'his charges don't stand much chance. My colleague has your statement in the computer. I'm pretty sure this is the last you'll hear of it.'

All the same, a few weeks later, when I figured the whole business had blown over, I received a three-hundred-and-fifty-guilder summons in the mail. For that amount, I could buy off the assault charges. Having no desire to embark on an idiotic court case, I was pathetic enough to pay it — something I will never do again.

So here I was at the Koninginneweg police station for the third time, this time to hear precisely how my son had died in a traffic accident.

From this very bureau, a police van with two young officers drove off toward my house on the Johannes Verhulststraat early that bright Whitsun morning. The female officer later sent me a condolence card: how awful she felt having to bring us news that would possibly change our lives forever. It was the most difficult moment of her still-fresh career, she wrote.

12

The receptionist reappeared at the counter. Another bureau staff member led us up some stairs and past bare walls to what was perhaps once the hayloft for the coach-horses. We were introduced to officers Hendriks and Windig.

The officer who had accompanied us offered us something to drink. Miriam and I asked for a glass of water; the men from the accidents unit chose coffee. There was a plate of assorted butter cookies on the low table, the kind of mix that fancy bakeries call a 'mélange'. Miriam and I passed. Perhaps that was why the policemen also left it untouched, even though everybody knows how delicious a butter cookie is with a cup of coffee.

Agent Hendriks, four stripes per shoulder, took the lead. He asked if we had any questions. I glanced at Miriam, who, with glistening eyes, nodded almost imperceptibly — a sign that I could go ahead.

'The car that hit Tonio ...' I began, '... is there any evidence that he was speeding?'

'No, that's still being investigated,' Hendriks answered hesitantly. 'The driver came here immediately after the accident for questioning. He spent a short while in a holding cell. I happened to be on duty that night, and came straight over here. A colleague and I questioned him. He'd already done a breathalyser test, which showed that he had not been drinking. The man had come from his job, something in the café or restaurant business. He was terribly shaken up by the accident, and when he heard the next day that it was fatal … well, you can take it from me that he was crushed.'

'Back to that questioning,' I said. 'Did the man deny that he was speeding?'

'Not categorically,' Hendriks answered. 'But he said he had kept to the speed limit. This is corroborated by his passenger, but he's what we call an unreliable witness, because he might be biased in favour of the driver. There were other witnesses. A pedestrian and a taxi driver. They gave first-hand — that night, I mean — accounts, and will be questioned again in the course of the inquiry.'

'Might technical investigation reveal any new facts?' I asked. The smell of the cookies started intensifying. 'You warned me yourself over the phone about those yellow outlines drawn on the road surface … so I assume …'

'Oh, certainly.' Officer Windig took over. 'The force of the impact, the angle at which the bicycle and the automobile collided, these things still have to be thoroughly investigated. The results might take some time. The car has been impounded, and is in the lab together with the victim's bicycle, where they're being subjected to a battery of tests. For instance, the bike may have left an imprint in the car body. A detail like that can help up fit together the pieces of the puzzle.'

'Moreover,' continued Hendriks, 'CCTV films have emerged from a security camera on the Max Euweplein. From Holland Casino, if I'm not mistaken. They're in our possession, and are being studied. We're talking about images taken from quite a distance, but they still might shed some light on the situation.'

'As long as I don't have to see them,' Miriam said. 'I cherish the very first photo taken of our son, when he was in the incubator. A faded Polaroid. I hardly even dare look at that …'

With security-camera images in the back of my mind, the kind you saw on TV family-search programmes or of jeweller or petrol-station robberies, I tried to envision the last moving documentation of Tonio's life. Jerky images of him cycling into view — only to be obscured by the equally jerky images of a charging BMW. How did I know he'd been hit by a BMW? Because I'd always hated that vulgarly expensive make.

'By the way, what kind of car was it?' I asked, in fact only to have my BMW suspicion confirmed.

'A Suzuki,' officer Hendriks said. 'A red Suzuki Swift.'

Hendriks took a folder out of the leather bag he had wedged between his feet, and laid it on the table. In order to make more room, he slid the plate of cookies in my direction, which made the buttery smell all the more penetrating. He opened the folder and thumbed through a stack of papers, until he found a situation sketch of the Hobbemakade/ Stadhouderskade intersection, complete with a childlike drawing of a red compact car.

'My responsibility for this accident only seems to be getting bigger,' I said.

The officer gave me a quizzical look.

'He's writing a book about the murder of —' Miriam began. I looked at her and shook my head. It did not seem like an opportune moment to inform the Amsterdam police force of a novel about the murder of a female officer in Amstelveen. 'You tell them,' she said.

'I'm working on a novel,' I explained, 'in which three Suzuki Swifts play a role. Right before the story begins, a red Suzuki Swift is repainted black. Just because. To add to the suspense, throw the reader a red herring. The red Suzuki in your drawing is about to be dunked into black paint.'

'No, really, I think you're mistaken …' It was all a bit too non-explicit for officer Windig. 'Oh, you mean … or …'

'The gentleman is referring to the hearse,' Hendriks said softly. He spread a number of photos of the intersection out on the table. They were Google Earth printouts, taken by daylight. 'Just to give you an overview of the traffic situation. Don't worry, there's nothing upsetting in them.'

In order to study the satellite pictures more thoroughly, I had to lean forward in my chair, bringing my nose right above the plate of butter cookies. No matter how fresh they were, if you had no appetite (for instance, because the situation sketch next to them had arrows pointing to where your son was killed by a car), the sweet smell at once turned rancid.

13

A Holland Casino security camera had captured Tonio's fatal fall on CCTV, while inside, the Wheel of Fortune spun, and then came to a standstill. *Rien ne va plus*. And so the end of his conscious life was immortalised on film. Just like the violent death of Tonnis Mombarg, from *Homo duplex*, was registered by a traffic camera of the Department of Public Works and Water Management.

I was reminded of the first time Tonio was filmed. He was two. Having just returned to the city from that cursed Loenen, we resided on the Leidsegracht. I was to be interviewed in the living room by a team from Flemish television. The interview hadn't begun yet; we were still working out the details. Tonio sat next to me on the sofa, to all appearances interested only in his bottle of warm chocolate milk, which he sucked with dozy, sighing satisfaction. As soon as they gave the 'roll 'em!' sign and the camera began to hum (television cameras still hummed back then), Tonio rose theatrically from the sofa. More or less obliterating his seated father from the eye of the camera, he gaily flung back his curly head, his bottle planted almost perpendicularly in his mouth. It was a film role he had thought up all on his own.

With the Holland Casino images, his career as a spur-of-the-moment film actor had come full circle.

14

In my fantasy, I had seen Tonio career recklessly toward his fate over the Max Euweplein footbridge so many times that, as gruesome as it was, I could hardly shake the image. It was even harder to get used to a *new* situation sketch, even though it was nearer to the truth.

Tonio did not come from Paradiso, not from Jenny, and did not cycle down the footbridge on his way to the Vondelpark entrance across the road. His accident took place at the row of traffic lights a full curve further, with him coming from the opposite direction: from Zuid, from Hobbemastraat, back from club Trouw.

Likewise, the image of a flashy BMW with tinted windows held tight in my mind's eye, not willing to be replaced by that beefed-up shopping cart, a Suzuki Swift. This car (in black) become a national icon due to the incessant replays on television of an attempted attack on the royal family — repeated shots of that wrecked little car, with its shattered and bulging windows, looking as though it was wrapped up in a cobweb, rocking with its sprung bonnet like a broken-winged crow. It had rammed blindly into the eyeless De Naald monument.*

15

The death of a boy we thought we had done such a fine job of protecting — didn't this fact provide irrefutable evidence that the world was a life-threatening whirlpool of chaos?

Tonio perished in the middle of one of western civilisation's safest

---

* The attack on the Dutch Royal Family occurred on 30 April 2009 at Apeldoorn, Netherlands, when a man drove his car at high speed into a Koninginnedag (*Queen's Day*, the national holiday) parade. The vehicle, a black Suzuki Swift, drove through people lining the street watching the parade, resulting in eight deaths (including the assailant) and ten injuries. It missed the royal family's open touring bus and crashed into a obelisk-shaped monument, The Needle, at the side of the road.

cities, on a nearly traffic-free night, surrounded by signs meant to rein in disorder: arrows and crosswalks painted on the asphalt, traffic signs, flashing stoplights, speed limits. After Tonio was run over like random road kill, the quasi-organised world immediately resumed its course.

I pointed to the stoplights. 'I understand these are turned off at night. Is that a money-saving measure?'

'No,' said Hendriks, 'it's got nothing to do with economising. It's a question of safety. At night it can be more dangerous at certain intersections to leave the traffic lights functioning. The cyclist gets impatient waiting at a red light, wonders why he needs to wait for green when there's nothing coming, and ... he goes ahead and crosses. And, sure enough, a car unexpectedly approaches, which accelerates to make it through yellow. No, trust me, they've thought this one over.'

'Were the stoplights turned off altogether,' Miriam asked, the only one of us with a driver's licence, 'or were they flashing?'

The policemen glanced at each other. 'That's not entirely clear,' Windig said. 'We would expect them to be flashing. But that's being looked into. You'll be given a definitive report of all the results of the investigation ... in due course.'

The discussion turned to the details of the collision itself. It was clear that Tonio had not been run over; he was hit and thrown. Out of the corner of my eye, I could see Miriam cringe every time the description became too graphic.

'The victim,' officer Hendriks said, 'had a ... well, he was pretty badly wounded all along his left side. We gather this from the photos taken by the forensic photographer directly after the victim's death.'

'That'll be where the crushed lung came from,' Miriam said. She shook her head. 'His insides were totally mangled.'

'And his spleen,' I added. 'It had to be removed. First, half of it, then later the rest.'

The police officers seemed surprised that we were so well-informed as to the details of Tonio's injuries. 'The AMC always tells us as little as possible,' Winding said. 'They assert their oath of medical confidentiality. Professional secrecy.'

'But you've got the pictures from the forensic photographer,' I said. 'What is your conclusion, based on the photos, of Tonio's injuries as a result of the accident?'

'We suspect,' Hendriks said, 'that the victim collided with considerable force against the car door-frame. There's a dent in the body that appears to confirm this.'

'Was his death a case of pure bad luck?' I asked. 'I mean … taking a particularly bad spill?'

'It doesn't take a car going more than thirty kph to make an accident like this — hitting a bicyclist — a fatal one,' said Windig. 'Let's say he was going fifty.'

'There are experiments with air bags for cyclists,' added Hendriks, 'but that's still some way off.'

His remark brought about a silence in which the sickly-sweet smell of the biscuits became almost unbearable.

'What sort of lad was Tonio, actually?' Windig asked suddenly, addressing Miriam. The question was so out of context that she drew into herself, embarrassed. For some time, all she did was stare down at her knees.

16

'Oh, just, you know …' Miriam said at last, 'just the kind of kid you'd least wish this kind of accident on. Sweet, handsome, talented. Always ready to lend a hand, sometimes endearingly lazy. A son you never argued with. Even if we'd wanted to, he'd never let it get that far. I love movies, so if Tonio would show up on my birthday with a couple of DVDs, that in itself would have been sweet and all. But, no, he included a book with all the films of the past century. Twice as thick as a phone book. That's the kind of boy Tonio was. A bag of contradictions, sure. One time, he would show up on his way to a party wearing his tux jacket. The next time, also en route to a party, he'd have two week's worth of beard, and his hair in a ponytail. No pigeonholing him. He and I, we were buddies … real friends … cohorts, if necessary. Strolling through town together. On the lookout for men in shorts with the ugliest calves. "Where's my calf-shooter?" we'd chime out, each trying to outdo the other. One day, he was just turning into an adolescent, he decided we had to go and get ourselves a calf-shooter at the Bijenkorf. His disappointment when it turned out there was no such thing! But to go shooting spitwads with a rubber band at ugly white calves … no, he was above that. He was just sweet and friendly and helpful, and proud if he could help someone out. Yeah, what can I say? Just the opposite of all those antisocial creeps you guys have your hands full with here. And to be run over on the street … in the middle of the night, just like that … Such a waste.'

Miriam just let the tears flow. The men from the Serious Traffic Accident Investigation Unit reminded us that, despite our initial refusal, we were eligible for Victim Assistance. The driver of the red Suzuki had been offered it as well, and he'd accepted.

As for the investigation, it would take some time. Once everything had been examined, we would come back for an 'evaluation'. Before then, too, we were welcome to come back 'for a bit of counselling'. We could have complete access to the photos of Tonio's injuries, although they suspected we would only be ready to see them in a year or so, at the earliest. Miriam and I looked at each other: she shook her head, almost imperceptibly.

I turned to officer Hendriks. 'You said on the phone that they'd taken some of Tonio's blood for tests. Does it appear he'd had too much to drink?'

'We don't have the exact details yet,' he answered, 'but that alcohol was involved, yes, that much we know.'

I recalled what Goscha had said about the rounds in quick succession, and I remembered hearing Dennis say: 'With one shot of tequila in between …'

'He just wasn't paying attention,' Miriam said. 'After a night on the town …'

Tired, *beat*, a bit drunk, with that techno-boom still ringing in his deafened ears — add it all up, and no one could stop me adding to it that as he pedalled along he was also lovingly musing over Jenny.

17

It appeared that no one was to blame for Tonio's death, at least in a legal sense. (My self-incriminations were another story.) But was I required to go along with the vision of blind, dumb fate as the cause? Or could I, instead of taking a fatalistic stance, occasionally feel *wronged to death*?

My son, my only child, goddamn it, had been mown down like a dog on the street, on a public thoroughfare. Men at conference tables had determined, supported by statistics, that at that time of night it was better to turn off certain traffic lights, or set them to warning flashes. It was all about statistical probability.

Had Tonio's safety been optimally guaranteed? Granted, as a twenty-one-year-old cyclist, he had his own responsibilities — but still relative to the traffic scheme of the city of Amsterdam, which ultimately was the responsibility of the traffic controllers. Otherwise we could just as well run amok across a bare asphalt surface minus the lines, arrows, signposts, and lights, we could play bumper-car without the rubber bumpers, and end up, all of us giggling, scattered about the graveyard.

An accident like Tonio's — it was the statistician's calculated risk. According to their calculations, more nighttime accidents happen at certain intersections with a fully functioning traffic light than with only a yellow flashing light. But ... *someone*, in this case Tonio, had to absorb the minimal risk of a switched-off traffic light.

Fate? He has been torn away from us. A kid like him flung dead on the pavement must never be categorised as 'one of those things'. You must not accept it, ever, even if fate wears a blindfold, and is led and prompted by the laws of probability.

18

Hendriks and Windig accompanied us out to the front hall. They were the most courteous and attentive policemen I had ever encountered. I could not help thinking that they knew much more about the progress of the technical investigation than they had let on. They had learned this, of course, at their division of the police academy: feed the truth to the shocked survivors *in phases*, also when it concerns the victim's own errors.

We crossed the street back in the direction of the pet shop, where our supplier was still seated on his bench, smoking and drinking, now on his own. I was so lost in thought that I reached for the door handle of a green car that resembled ours parked in front of his shop. I opened the door on the passenger's side: on the seat lay stacked-up bags of cat litter.

'Go on,' called the pet-shop owner. 'Take it, it's yours. As long as I can have your house in return.'

I raised my hand in a sign of apology, and followed Miriam to our own car, just around the corner of the Van Breestraat.

19

'So is this civilisation?' I said to Miriam, summarising my disgust. 'A society, a community, a city … is supposed to be a *triumph* over disorder. It is an organisation that is supposed to leave nothing to chance. Chaos always manages to find a chink to squeeze through. But managing, organising, containing chaos is supposed to be the main goal. Right? I can accept that at night a flashing yellow light is less risky than red and green. Human psychology … Of course, there are always risks. With Tonio and that Suzuki, it didn't work, that experiment with the flashing yellow. Tonio was a victim of the exception to the rule. The system suffers a lesser defeat for the greater good. The terrible part is that society accepts its loss as a matter of fact … silently … It's just part of the calculation. And as a result, no one bothers about us. No apologetic word, nothing. Ice-cold silence. We just keep paying our taxes for the nighttime operation of the traffic lights. No one loses any sleep over it. We are expected to accept our loss just as they accept theirs. As an industrial mishap.'

What had happened here descended on us like such an unspeakable horror that it proved impossible to adopt a fatalistic attitude. There was no way to go on without an answer to the question of guilt. Someone or something — a responsible authority — had to have this on their conscience. Since I couldn't find anything or anyone that fitted the bill, I landed upon myself. *I* was the guilty party.

20

'What happened to us,' I say once we get home, 'most resembles a *miracle* ... in the iniquitous, Catholic sense of the word. Minchen, it's so unfathomable, so far removed from everyday events, that it is no less than a miracle. Your son is sent heavenwards with a massive thwap. You're struck rigid by disbelief. You run back to the village pump, and everyone else reacts just as incredulously. Flabbergasted. Dismayed. Some of them try to explain the miracle in terms of physics. Even if the car had been going thirty, the cyclist still wouldn't stand much chance. *Quod erat demonstrandum.* But for us it remains a wonder. Our One and Only grabbed out of our midst, never to return. An event that has no parallels, except for previous morbid fantasies. And that is what makes it so obscenely miraculous. A vision come true. It can't be. It mustn't be.'

Because my words remind her of the situation's irrevocability, Miriam suddenly starts to cry — loudly, too, like only a child who has fallen flat on its face can. But unlike that child, nothing can cheer her up. Only when she calms down somewhat do I repeat my own lament: 'I would so like to comfort you, Minchen, but the damn thing about comfort is that it always offers some kind of promise: "Everything will be all right." I can't promise you that.'

'The fact that you're here, sitting next to me, is enough.'

343

After Miriam has picked up her father from Beth Shalom and dropped him off at home (side-by-side grief in an old Renault), we sit on the sofa and drink a far-too-strong long drink. I use a small kitchen knife to open envelope after envelope of condolences. We take turns reading them, until Miriam can no longer stand it. It's the letters from Tonio's old schoolmates that break her up the most. We try to eat something. A bit of French bread with some egg salad — but I can't swallow it. Miriam's hands are clamped, motionless, onto a cup of chicken soup, into which her tears fall — silently, thank God.

When I abandon her to go to sleep, or at least to get into bed, she is lying on the couch with leaden eyes (Valium, vodka), not-watching a thriller. I kiss her goodnight.

'Night, sweetie,' she says with her tiniest voice.

21

This afternoon, Miriam went back to the Nepveustraat with our friend Klaas to search Tonio's computer for those photos of Jenny. She came home in a bitter mood.

'Doesn't he get it?' she snarled. 'That a mother clings to every last thing her dead child left behind?'

She was referring to Jim. After her insistent ringing, he finally staggered to the door, torpid and disoriented, in a cloud of pot smoke.

'It's starting to dawn on me,' I said, 'that all those stories of his chronic insomnia are all about sleep, sleeping, and sleepiness. Maybe we've misjudged the problem.'

Jim was being intentionally unobliging. He told Miriam and Klaas he was busy putting all the pictures he found (but none of Jenny) onto a hard drive, but that there was 'something wrong' with Tonio's computer. He literally told the mother of his dead best friend: 'You can't just keep dropping by whenever you like, y'know, I've got my own stuff to do.'

Surely Jim had forgotten that he shared the flat with Tonio, and that we, Tonio's parents, still paid half the rent. He also seemed to have lost sight of the fact that Tonio, on account of his permanent absence, was not able to keep an eye on his belongings.

'Jim,' Miriam had said, 'you and Dennis were going to make a selection of the photos for us within two weeks. It's now been two months. Adri and I have lost our son … Can you imagine, Jim, that we regard everything that was Tonio's as a keepsake … including his computer?'

'I'm working on it,' was his answer. Jim did, though, show a far more engaged interest in Tonio's laptop. He didn't have one of his own, at least not a functioning one, so if he might be able to take Tonio's with him tomorrow, when he went on vacation with his parents … the message was clear: no laptop, no vacation.

Tonio's laptop was a souped-up one, with a digital tablet that you could write on with a special electronic pen. There are few memories these past weeks that pain me as much as the shyly proud Tonio who came up to my workroom to demonstrate this birthday gift, inviting me to try my hand at writing something on the tablet. (At long last, this techno-moron made his first foray into the world of computers.) Goddam, that sweet kid … in all his maturity, he was still a child who could get a genuine kick out of the gimmicks and gadgetry of a present. It was the summer before he was to start his Media & Culture studies.

'It's handy, this tablet … for in the lecture hall. I'm really pleased with it.' And off he went. 'Back to work, oi.'

What would have been more obvious than to give Jim the laptop, as a memento of his best buddy? Well, now that he'd behaved so boorishly to his best buddy's grieving mother, he could forget it.

When Miriam rang him later that afternoon in an attempt to lay it on the line, he hung up on her in mid-sentence. A while later, he rang back.

'Come get the computer,' he growled, with a tone that implied it was *his* job to put an end to all this kvetching. 'I've put everything on a hard drive.'

I was sitting on the veranda with the evening papers when Miriam brought me this message. I didn't have an immediate response, except an expression of sadness: that the whole world, including Tonio's best friends, had calmly glided back into their day-to-day routine — and so thoroughly that promises made in the immediate aftermath of Tonio's death had faded, or were even, apparently, voided.

The sky turned black as ink. 'They're predicting thunderstorms,' Miriam said. 'I'll run out to the liquor store before the rain starts. Vodka, gin … we're fresh out. Now, of all times, when medicine's what we need most.'

I cranked up the awning, and brought the newspapers into the living room. It was as dark as a late-December afternoon. I turned on all the lamps and switched on the television. The six o'clock news reported heavy storms in Brabant and Limburg, as far north as Gelderland. 'Trees snapping like matchsticks.'

A quarter of an hour later, after so many evenings under the clear sky, we sat drinking in semi-darkness. Some herring on rye bread: our meal would not consist of any more than this. I could finally mix my Bombay Sapphire gin with London Club tonic, which had more bite and was less sweet than that spineless, weakly carbonated Schweppes. Somewhere on the edge of town, the flash and rumble of the storm had begun.

'Y'know, when I think about it …' Miriam shook her head. 'Those two, Jim and Tonio. The way they spent Friday nights here in their pyjamas in front of the TV. They used to think it was so cool that I let them watch that police show. *Baantjer*. Plate of chips on their lap. You were always off at the pub, Welling or De Zwart, but I loved being around those kids … their laughter, their banter and snappy comments … A while ago, I heard a snippet of the theme song. Toots Thielemans on the harmonica. Then it all comes back, and I can almost touch them. Their warm little flannel-wrapped bodies …

She let out what I'd call a weep-sigh. 'That hard-headed scorn of his … it's killing me. Of course, I understand he's angry and upset by Tonio's death. But that's just it. I'm Tonio's mother. We used to take him everywhere with us. Spain … Nerja, Lanzarote … the aeroplane trips, the apartments, the restaurants. No expense spared. The Golden Owl

346

awards in Antwerp a couple of times. They had a suite to themselves in the Hilton, remember? The sky was the limit. They were brothers. They belonged together. And now … what a shitty, awful day.'

'I'm noticing,' I said, 'how our patience with people is wearing thin. Our relationship with the outside world is changing at full speed. Maybe for good.'

That evening, Miriam had one of her worst crying bouts since Whit Sunday. 'So … *so* damn cruel that he's gone … that he'll never sit there anymore' (she waved a floppy arm at the corner sofa that we never used) 'in his usual spot with a bottle of beer … and Tygo on his lap. *So* unfair.'

At a certain point, her face become so bloated from the incessant crying that anyone but me would not have recognised it.

'If fate is so unfair,' I stammered, 'what's the point of expecting even a *little* fairness from people … I mean the people having to do with that fate?'

'That hard drive with Tonio's photos,' Miriam said, suddenly harsh, 'if needs be, I'll sic a lawyer on them. I don't want those boys fooling around with it anymore. They've had two whole months. Now it's our turn.'

'Ach, Minchen … don't let it come to that. Tonio chose those two as his best friends. We owe it to him to keep treating them nicely, even if they let us down. If they were out to misuse those photos somehow, then that would be another story.'

She nodded and rubbed her face dry. I guessed that my bitterness was greater than hers. Theirs was not a generation of rich promises — or perhaps they were rich after all, but, like a rich piecrust, promises are made to be broken.

22

Before he entered the gymnasium, Tonio managed to wheedle an 800-euro boulder of a watch out of us. On his skinny wrist it resembled a deep-sea instrument that could withstand depths greater than its wearer's heart could. Tonio was as proud of his cadging-trick as of the watch itself.

He wore it always. But unlike his wallet and mobile phone, the watch was not among the things the AMC returned to us. Later, we enquired at the Emergency Room. They hadn't come across it among the rest of his belongings. In the ambulance they had snipped off his clothes, which were then turned over, together with his shoes, to the Accident Investigation Unit. Maybe the watch was there, at the James Wattstraat, with the clothing.

<h1 style="text-align:center">23</h1>

Dr. G., the traumatologist who had led the operation team on Whit Sunday, had given us his card, with 'for follow-up appt., if nec.' jotted on the back. I had sent him Tonio's photo and the death notice, with a handwritten note of thanks for his efforts.

Now, weeks after Tonio's death, we were anxious to learn all the details of his injuries and the operation. Miriam wanted to confirm her intuition that Tonio was already beyond help upon arrival at the AMC. I wondered if a query like that was really appropriate for a surgeon who had fought to the bitter end for Tonio's life. Miriam was plagued by the uncertainty as to whether Tonio had suffered despite the artificially induced coma, even if it was in the deepest recesses of his consciousness.

We lay in bed arguing until it was time to get ourselves tidied up for the appointment with Dr. G.: half past one at the AMC.

The argument was about that one painful question, and whether or not to pose it to the traumatologist. 'You're really pulling the strings here, Minchen.'

'You wouldn't be happy either if I left it entirely up to you.'

Except for the funeral, since our last visit to the AMC I hadn't worn anything but my faded jogging pants and shapeless lumberjack shirt. Now it was time I put on normal clothes for a change. My appetite might have fallen by the wayside these past weeks, but not the pain-numbing alcohol consumption, so that my sports jacket had gotten too snug for me.

The sun had been beating down on the car, so, despite the air conditioning, I spent the first half of the trip in a sweat. The same route as Whit Sunday. Then, in strangling uncertainty; now, in stifling certainty. On our way to the same doctor. After thirty-six hours in the saddle, he had been forced to go home to rest while Tonio was still alive. Exhausted, he came to say goodbye to us while there was, theoretically at least, still hope. In just a short while he would receive the now-childless parents. Among all those involved, a huge certainty had descended, as immoveable as a rock. How did that feel for *him*? As a defeat?

The traumatology department is located on the first floor of the same wing as the outpatient clinics. We reported to the reception desk. The receptionist had been made aware of our visit, and showed us to a seat in the waiting area. That anxious feeling reared its head while we waited: the unspeakable worst was still yet to come, and soon Dr. G. would tell us what that dreadfulness entailed.

The tension momentarily rekindled the morning's argument. 'We said we would get to the bottom of it,' I said. 'Well, here we are.'

'And that's why I'm going to ask him.'

'He'll take it badly, you'll see.'

Dr. G.'s assistant brought us to his consultation room. He was tall, but much less so than I had remembered from Whit Sunday: in my imagination, he must have grown to the fearsome stature reserved for messengers of doom. He was in his early forties, tops.

I said: 'Thank you for seeing us, doctor.'

'Don't mention it. Please take a seat.'

He sat down behind a small desk. We took the two chairs opposite him, alongside each other. I had the impression that the doctor, despite all the authority he exuded, was still a tad nervous. We could well be there to unload a heap of reproach upon him. He thanked us for the personal note, together with Tonio's photo, that we'd sent him. 'How are you both doing, after all that's happened?'

'Pretty bad,' said Miriam. 'But we haven't had a complete breakdown. Which is something, I suppose.'

He nodded. I related to him what we had heard thus far from the Serious Traffic Accident Investigation Unit, and what we had managed to find out on our own. I amended the previous facts of the case: Tonio had not come from Paradiso, but from Club Trouw on the Wibautstraat. Dr. G. nodded again.

24

'If you have any specific questions,' Dr. G. said, during a lull in the conversation, 'then I can address them.'

'You and your team,' Miriam began, 'operated on Tonio the whole day. Didn't you know right from the start he wouldn't make it?'

So she asked anyway, and not really with the wording we had agreed upon.

'Do you feel we carried on operating for too long?' Dr. G. asked, taken aback. He braced himself.

'If I might explain,' I said. 'Miriam's referring to her intuition on the day itself. When the police came to our house that morning, they described his condition as "critical". Miriam thinks she knew already then — instinctively — that Tonio wouldn't make it. And when you came from the ER to brief us during the operation, Miriam was still certain he would die … was dying already. For me, it was different. You know how often you hear that someone is in a critical condition … and still the person pulls through? My thought was: as long as they keep operating, there's a chance he'll survive.'

For a fleeting moment, I was back in the waiting room on the twenty-third of May, a Sunday that could still end well. I even felt, with clenched fists, a resurgence of the dread of Tonio's wounds, the brain damage he would have to continue to live with. I shook off the thought. Tonio

350

has been dead for six, seven weeks now. A certainty that we have been sidestepping, with stubborn disbelief, all those weeks.

'I suspect,' I continued, 'that Miriam's question is actually more a medical-ethical one. She wants to know if you're obliged to *continue* operating as long as there's a modicum of life in the patient. Right, Miriam?'

Miriam's question to Dr. G. betrayed an element of her dilemma. If there was no way to save her son, she'd have strongly preferred that Tonio was relieved of his pain and suffering right at the beginning of the operations.

25

A recurring question from visitors is: 'Did Tonio suffer?'

I hear myself reply: 'He was unconscious from the moment of the collision. They reanimated him in the ambulance, which he responded to well. But according to the doctors, he never regained consciousness. In the ER they kept him anaesthetised, just to be on the safe side. So, no, he was unaware of the situation.'

Am I being truthful? I am reminded of a passage from 'Anecdotes on Death', in which Harry Mulisch quotes Thomas Mann's reaction upon awakening from anaesthesia after a lung operation: 'It was much worse than I thought ... I suffered *miserably*.'

In *Die Entstehung des Doktor Faustus*, Mann wonders: 'Might there be a certain depth in man's vital existence where he, in a state of completely extinguished consciousness, still continues to suffer? Can one completely separate "suffering" from "to endure suffering" in the deeper layers?'

Mulisch then writes: 'If the extinguishing of my consciousness does not relieve me of my pain, then there is little hope that my destruction will ever pass. It will not pass. It will never pass, it catches on itself and continues to falter in an endlessly petrifying world — my demise will know no end: *my destruction is everlasting*.'

One's hair stands on end at the thought that this might be true. My poor Tonio, tethered to his destruction for eternity … For sure, his destruction carries on *within us.* Miriam and I will, until our last breath, continually endure the devastation of his life.

And if I assume that Miriam, eight years younger than I, will be the last of us to die, will her death finally do away with Tonio's destruction?

26

Miriam nodded. I could see in her eyes that she was at a loss for words.

'I'll give you a brief summary of how the operation progressed,' Dr. G. said to Miriam, 'which I hope will answer your question.'

'Can I ask you to begin with the ambulance?' Oh, how I tried, desperately, to sound like a hard-nosed interrogator and investigator, especially for myself. 'I understand that a *second* ambulance was called in.'

'In keeping with noise restrictions, we're not allowed to employ a trauma helicopter at night,' said Dr. G. 'Therefore we equip an extra ambulance with a surgical team and additional supplies.'

Perfectly plausible, isn't it, that in our out-of-control hedonistic society, human lives are sacrificed for the benefit of a good night's sleep? We're forced to endure the screams of boat bacchanals as they putt-putt through the canals at night, but a trauma helicopter: No. It wasn't safety that was sacred, but boozing.

'Was Tonio reanimated at the scene?'

'Let me put it this way,' said Dr. G. 'Reanimation activities were carried out. For instance, he was put on a ventilator. His lungs, after all, had stopped functioning. And there was an immediate blood transfusion. He had lost a significant amount of blood at the scene of the accident … But comprehensive reanimation, no. Even with exhaustive reanimation efforts in the ambulance itself, the victim is often dead on arrival.'

I felt a lump of misplaced pride in my throat. 'So Tonio was, so to speak, still strong enough that it was worth a try?'

(He still died, didn't he? What did I expect?)

'After your son was brought in here,' continued the doctor, 'I first attended to his spleen. He had suffered a powerful impact to the left side of his body. As you might recall, I first removed half of it. When the remaining half continued bleeding, I removed that as well. He had coagulopathy, that is, severely impaired blood clotting … Meanwhile the neurosurgeon was tending to his brain. The right side had started to swell. Therefore we detached the skull on that side, so as to drain the fluid and blood.'

Dr. G. relayed the information with such clarity and detail that only now did I truly experience Tonio's agonies in the OR. The operation lamps glaring into his insides, altering the natural colour of his blood … The green, fenestrated surgical drape … *Did* he actually have one of those sheets with the cut-outs draped over him? They were working all over his body at the same time. At most, only his legs would have remained covered.

My boy, my son, that beautiful product of my loins … wrecked … His mother's pride, literally the fruit of her womb … already so distant at that point in time, and unable to return of his own accord, nor able to be brought back by the united efforts of the trauma team. He still had a chance, then and there, no matter how negative the prognoses.

'Meanwhile I'd turned my attention to his lungs,' Dr. G. continued. 'A great bleeding mass. They had simply stopped working. When they brought him in, his blood pressure was alarmingly low. We gave him one transfusion after the other. That was the situation, more or less, the first time I came to brief you. After that, the left side of his brain had also begun to swell. The neurosurgeon then set about dealing with that. And all the while his other functions were rapidly worsening. So, what with the drop in blood pressure, the lungs, which no longer produced any air, and the problem with the clotting … his condition became more and more hopeless. And yes, at a certain point you have to make a decision. He's not going to make it. There's no point in continuing treatment.'

And after a short pause: 'I can assure you, as long as there's any hope of achieving something, we keep trying. Especially with someone his age.'

Tonio, who, still very young, assembled a vehicle out of technical Lego, his eyes glued to the diagram spread out on the table, and his worm-like fingers independently executing their work.

Tonio, who, after visiting my parents, demonstrated (oh, tender white lie) how my mother was slightly less hunched from the Parkinson's than a few weeks previously. 'First she stood like this …' (Tonio bent way over.) 'And now like this …' (Nearly upright.)

Tonio, who …

'If I might ask *you* something,' Dr. G. said, 'because, whatever happens, we can learn from it … Is there anything we could have done better?'

'We're laymen,' I replied. 'Who are we to correct or criticise you and your team of experts?'

And then I made the mistake of bringing up the nurse at Tonio's deathbed, when the alarm went off and I asked if 'this was the end', to which she had blithely replied: 'Oh no, there's even a bit of improvement.'

What possessed me? Did the fact that I still brought it up mean that her careless words really had given me a sliver of hope?

'Of course I knew better,' I hastened to say, 'but I *can* imagine that a family member might take false hope from a remark like this, and then shout: "Don't turn off the ventilator! He's recovering!" I don't want to put her in a bad light. It was just clumsy.'

Dr. G. concurred. Miriam had wept during most of the conversation, and at a certain point I believe I saw the doctor's eyes glisten as well. He asked whether his observation — namely, that the accident had occurred at a dangerous intersection — had been confirmed by the traffic police.

'Well, not exactly,' I said. 'There was a survey in *Het Parool* where it was mentioned as particularly hazardous.'

I pointed to the file the doctor had consulted a few times during our discussion. 'Might we have access to that sometime? I'm considering writing a kind of prose requiem for Tonio, and perhaps … I wouldn't be able to read it now, of course … but later …?'

'You can ask me for it when the time comes,' Dr. G. said. 'I'll warn you, though, it's full of medical terms. The reports are succinct, here and there staccato, because, well, sometimes … in life-threatening situations … you have to be quick.'

'If I do request it,' I said, 'I'll treat it with the utmost discretion.'

'Oh, I don't doubt that,' said Dr. G.

I thanked him for the clarity of his explanation. 'We might have expressed ourselves awkwardly now and then, but rest assured we have the greatest admiration for the efforts of you and your team.' Miriam and I got up. 'We'll let you get back to work.'

'This is also my work.'

27

If I am to take Dennis and Goscha at their word — and why shouldn't I? — they had put away a good deal of alcohol that night. I don't know if it was enough for a hangover the next day. Tonio spent 'the morning after' on the operating table. If it was true that pain could not be entirely suppressed by anaesthesia, then what about a hangover?

And: what were the consequences of all that alcohol on the operation? Dr. G. had said that Tonio's clotting was disastrous. Could that, in this case, have had something to do with drink? I remembered that soon after his birth, before being placed in the incubator, Tonio had been given a shot of vitamin K in order to boost his coagulation, premature newborns being susceptible to poor blood-clotting. Later, I met the man who had discovered provitamin K, Professor Hemker, in Maastricht. He was also an avid collector of oboes. I did not neglect (also on Tonio's behalf) to thank him for his scientific efforts.

If I wanted to immerse myself in shame, I could imagine how the operating-room surgeons commented on the patient's booze-breath.

That Thomas Mann quote kept haunting me. 'It was much worse than I thought …' If it's true that even under anaesthesia, consciousness continues to experience pain somewhere *deep down*, then Tonio spent the last half-day of his life in immobile, excruciating suffering — first on the asphalt, then in the ambulance, later in the operating room, and lastly (with his parents finally at his side) in intensive care.

I have always told myself that the worst part about pain is the *further effect* of suffering. One remembers the source or cause of the pain, and cringes with shame for allowing it happen or for having brought it on oneself. One feels the pain ebb, and experiences the added fear of a sudden resurgence of the torment. One is afraid that the pain could well be the harbinger of approaching death. And so on.

I have always reassured myself with the thought that pain quickly eliminated by death, no longer able to be replayed and reconsidered in one's consciousness, in fact never existed.

But *what if* the pain, before being absorbed by death, is allowed to run riot for half a day, as with Tonio? Was that pain also nonexistent? How far back does death's power retroactively function as a pain remedy?

A boy of six falls out of an upstairs window and is skewered by the spikes of the garden fence. The child survives by the skin of his teeth. It takes neighbours half an hour to free him. If that boy lives to be eighty, does his eventual death, all those decades later, still, in retrospect, erase the pain of the then-six-year-old? If so, we can just as well posit that death 'retrospectively' erases *every* feeling experienced throughout a human life — indeed, erases that life itself, as though it had never existed.

It is thus precisely in my most lucid moments that I am convinced that Tonio, like the author of *Tonio Kröger*, must have undergone, in the depths of his vital being and for hours on end, the ruination brought on by the collision and the scalpels. If that is true, then I owe him, many times over, my own present pain.

We drove from the AMC, where he died, to Buitenveldert, where he was buried — but at the last moment, just as Miriam was about to turn onto Fred. Roeskestraat, I managed to forestall a visit to the grave.

'Sorry, Minchen, but I can't face it, not after that medical talk. Damn it, let's just go to the Bos.'

'I figured you'd say that. The goat farm has always been the perfect refuge … I mean, if the cemetery's too much for you.'

'Aside from our back porch, there's no better place to talk about Tonio.'

Later, during lunch at the outdoor café, Miriam shared with me her latest discovery: on that fatal night, Tonio was not riding his own bike, but Jim's. 'Somebody brought it up when Jim and his parents were at our place, two days after the accident. But like so many things, it totally slipped my mind.'

Nor could I recall it being mentioned. So soon after the incident, countless details ricocheted off our armour-plated denial. The eagerness to learn *everything* only arose after the funeral, when we tried to sneak him back into our midst.

'Then it's time we returned Jim's bike,' I said. 'Or … well, what's left of it. Mangled or not, it's still his property. Or maybe we should —'

'His parents have already bought him a new one. He said to his mother: "Mum, you don't think I'm going to ride that thing now."'

'The police said they were still busy studying the bike and the Suzuki.'

'The bike's in storage at the James Watt bureau,' Miriam said. 'I checked. There's even an appointment to go collect his things — bike, clothes, the lot.'

'Hey, all this behind my back, how come …'

'You stay home. Write. I'll go with Nelleke.'

'Don't forget to ask about the watch.'

'I'm dreading the shoes even more.'

We sat for a good, long time in silence at that café table, looking past each other at the chickens and roosters, but even they weren't all that active this day. A bantam was having a wash in the fine, grey sand under the octagonal bench that encircled a tree.

'What about his own bike?' I finally asked.

'At Central Station,' Miriam answered. 'As usual. They've already carted off so many of his bikes from there.'

29

'Oh, I might take a puff in the bar now and then,' Tonio had told me months ago, when I asked him if he smoked. 'You know, just to be cool with the guys. Don't know why, really.'

In retrospect, it occurred to me that he'd seen the question coming (which, incidentally, sounded too much like: not *you!*), and had prepared his answer in all its nonchalance. He wanted to spare us. If he'd just admitted that it was *more* than just the occasional drag in the pub, then I could in turn have said: 'Listen, Tonio, I've been able to keep you away from smokes until you turned eighteen. I still think it's dumb, but now it's up to you. Go ahead and light up, if it'll make Miriam's screwdrivers taste better. So we'll open a window later.'

From a conversation between Jim and his father, who shortly after Whit Sunday were pondering the riddle of Tonio's nocturnal detour, I picked up a snippet about 'stopping at Leidseplein for cigarettes', which could just as well have meant: picking up a pack for Jim. Photos that surfaced on the Internet showing Tonio theatrically holding up a lit cigarette (or joint) struck me as no more than a pose, but Dennis and Goscha had more or less confirmed that Tonio was a regular smoker. Another friend had placed, as a kind of salute, a film roll, a can of beer, and a pack of cigarettes at Tonio's grave.

He wanted to spare his parents, damn it, and in doing so had more than once denied them his company. Now I suspected that his restlessness after a drink or two-and-three-quarters of a portion of chow mein at our house meant he had to have a smoke, and didn't want to put us out. Courteous to a fault.

I found myself fretting over that smoking of his. Until he was nearly twenty and moved to De Baarsjes, I'd never once seen him light up. All right, let's say he did so when he was out of the house, at parties, 'just to be cool with the guys'. At home, he always backed me up whenever I pronounced on this pet peeve of mine. His beloved Grandpa Piet, a smoker from the age of eleven, was felled at the age of sixty-seven ... his Aunt Marianne was now struggling, post-emphysema, with lung cancer ... No tobacco user could pretend anymore that he would simply get off scot-free.

I armed myself with strategies that would help him quit. For starters, I would talk to him, not in a fatherly way, but more like an old friend ... Smoking was deadly — that warning wasn't put on the packet just to deface the product design.

Suddenly there was the image of the lanky Dr. G., who had given Miriam and me a discreet but frank report of Tonio's lung trauma. In a fraction of time, his still healthy lungs had been transformed into untreatable blood-sponges — and in that same fraction of time it happened again now, interrupting my train of thought. Here I was, whingeing that Tonio had, despite all my good advice, started smoking. His lungs would never even get the chance to be destroyed by nicotine.

30

If Tonio had survived, badly injured, and had remained in a coma for an extended time, he could have one day regained consciousness, wondering in horror: what's happened? Where am I? What am I doing here?

A damaged brain, too, can still produce such questions. At the very least, there's a battered command centre that registers the puzzling and the elusive. At best, it begins to dawn on the person, in fragments, what happened, or what might have happened.

Immense regret, perhaps. Shame.

Miriam and I appear at his hospital bed. Whether he recognises us or not, there is at least a consciousness that may or may not *be able* to recognise us. He is alive.

In one of his novels, the Dutch writer Alfred Kossmann touches on the great scandal of human existence: that a person cannot experience his own death. Tonio is already on the other side of that scandal.

Now that he is irretrievably dead, he does not have access to an authority (namely, consciousness) that informs him: 'Listen here, Tonio, your life has come to an end, you cannot finish what you have started.'

Tonio knows *nothing* now. Miriam and I, and a few others, do know. We are well aware of what's denied him: that the future he envisaged — partly clear, partly cloudy — is now out of reach.

Events experienced in the past remain in one's consciousness, thanks to mental rumination.

You're walking carelessly down the street, eyes wandering, and bang your head against a beam sticking out of a window. The smack is followed immediately by a brief, blindingly bright flash. Then anger: who in their right mind sticks a beam so far out the window? Embarrassment: how could I be so stupid? You look around: did anybody see? You walk on. Besides pain on the outside, shame burns under the skin of your face. The collision nestles in a variety of guises in your consciousness, which continues to illuminate every aspect it, over and over.

Of all possible incidents, death is probably the most serious thing that can happen to a person. But … it is life's only self-terminating event. For the one who experiences this unique event, reflection is impossible. Anger, shame, guilt, cause and effect, consequences … none of these count. Dead is dead.

31

I had asked my editor to come by so we could discuss when (and if) I might resume work. I was looking, first and foremost, for a strategy to keep from going mad, to fend off the fear: the fear of a future not only without issue, but also (as either a direct or indirect result of which) without a steady pursuit.

'The bothersome, no, the paralysing part,' I said, 'is that in the past few weeks I've had to visit a whole list of locations from my new novel. Hospital, police station ... Even the car that plays a crucial role in the book is the same make and colour as the one that hit Tonio. A Suzuki Swift. Red. It's not very stimulating to have reality literally take over my meticulously made-up world.'

It was another brilliant summer day. We sat on our back terrace under the expanse of the spent golden rain, and I told her that Tonio had taken a break here with his photo model a few days before his death, in the same resplendent sunlight.

The editor suggested I first write about Tonio, and then later, when it was out of my system, to pick up where I left off on *Kwaadschiks*.

'A requiem-like book could go one of two ways,' I said. 'I could write it two, three years from now ... or five ... by which time it will take on a retrospective character. Looking back, some years earlier, on a terrible event. A reassessment of the grief. How the lives of those involved have changed. Or, if I write it *now*, this summer, it will be an account from within a situation that took place such a short time ago ... straight from the mishmash of emotions ... Writing then becomes part of the struggle, and vice versa. The distraught parents reconstructing the last days and hours of their son ... because everything is imperative ... they cling to every detail ...'

Poetical bullshit. I have no choice. I cannot *not* write about him, for him, *now*, because at this moment nothing else matters. It's either write about Tonio, or not write at all — it's not a matter of choice. Without even having thought about it, without consciously setting out to, I was *already* doing it. From the minute the doorbell rang on Whit Sunday, and a police officer uttered the words 'critical condition', I was composing my requiem — at first as an incantation, in the desperate hope of keeping him alive, and, later that day, with incredulous acceptance, in the desperate hope of conjuring him, in words and images, back to his former life.

Even in my vilest nightmares, I couldn't have predicted that I would one day have to devote myself to a requiem for my own son.

32

'If there's nothing more left of that bike than scrap,' I said to Miriam, 'then just take a few pictures of it for our archive. Ask the police to junk it. If we put it here in the hall … I don't think I could stand the sight of it. And the photos: put them in a sealed envelope until I can face it. Remember to ask about the watch.'

Since Miriam was too nervous to drive, Nelleke took them in her car to the Serious Traffic Accidents Unit near Amstel Station. It was a police domain, so there were lots of broken parking meters. After finally coaxing a ticket (or half of it) out of one of the machines, Miriam rang officer Windig, who had promised to accompany her to the depot. His colleague Hendriks answered the phone and came downstairs in his place.

Later, Miriam and Nelleke described a labyrinthine trek through corridors, stairs, rails, reinforced steel doors, and walls adorned with rolled-up fire hoses and extinguishers. All of a sudden, they found themselves in a lofty space that felt halfway between an aeroplane hangar and a parking garage.

'I was so nervous,' Miriam said later, 'that I only saw that one empty passenger car in the middle of an immense open space.'

She couldn't say whether it was a red Suzuki Swift. There were racks of damaged bicycles and scooters, and the sweating Miriam made a beeline, as though by radar, for Jim's bike — not that she recognised it, but she saw Tonio's shoes dangling from the handlebars in a plastic bag,

362

their toes sticking out of the bag.

'Nelleke, that bike ... it's still intact,' Miriam exclaimed. I can almost imagine her misplaced triumph. 'Surely a bike doesn't come through a fatal crash looking like this ...'

'That bike is going with us,' Nelleke said resolutely. 'Not to the junk heap.'

Shoes absorb part of the soul of their wearer. It's in the slight distortion of the opening ... that walked-in warp ... the nuances in the grey tint of the X-ed indentations the laces leave on the tongue. It was this shoe portrait that Miriam suddenly discovered, and that broke her up.

Officer Hendriks led Nelleke and Miriam back through the labyrinth to the exit. So this is where the belongings of those caught off-guard at an intersection at night, of the flung and fallen, end up. Bits and pieces, often smeared with blood or mud, waiting for their rightful owner, sometimes surrogated by his or her next of kin.

Hendriks shook hands with the women, and reminded Miriam that she could always call. They walked to the car: Nelleke with one hand on the handlebars, and the other arm around Miriam's shoulder. Miriam phoned me before they got in.

'Those horribly empty shoes, Adri ... without his feet ... without *him* in them. Gaping at me with their terrible emptiness ...'

'And the bike?'

'Not a scratch. You could ride off on it as is.'

Miriam said she wanted to take Nelleke to the garden centre, to get her something as thanks for her support. 'Retail therapy.'

'And the watch?' I asked.

'It wasn't there,' she answered. 'It *could* still be somewhere in his flat ...'

'He always wore it,' I said. 'Certainly when he went out.'

'It might have come loose during the accident ...'

I was reminded of an incident from my youth, which made its way into my book *Vallende Ouders*. One day, my mother, riding on a narrow bike path that cut across the meadow, collided with an oncoming cyclist and landed in the ditch alongside the path. Her left wrist was bleeding, just where her metal-link watchband was torn loose by the lip of the bike bell. The watch must have ended up in the murky, rust-brown ditchwater. We rode to my grandparents, who lived nearby. My father and I returned to the scene (me perched on the baggage carrier), armed with a skimmer. He stirred in the sludge with the kitchen tool until the sun, blood-orange red, rested just above the heath. The watch was nowhere to be found. He did fish out a long, narrow screwdriver, though, which would perform many long years of service as an aid in opening and closing defective electrical plugs and sockets.

I tried to recall Tonio's wristwatch. 'Did it have an elastic metal band,' I asked, 'or a leather strap?'

'It had a kind of buckle clasp that clicked shut,' she said. 'I remember that it wasn't really a boy's model, and it was way too loose. So they took out a link at the jeweller's, and later, when Tonio's wrists got fuller, I had it put back in.'

'A buckle like that,' I said, 'could easily have sprung open from the collision. It was probably left lying there on the street, and got picked up by an early-morning passerby.'

'That person didn't arrive home with a clear conscience, then,' Miriam said. 'The intersection was painted with yellow accident-scene stripes. If you find a watch lying there, chances are it belonged to the victim.'

She was already starting to talk in James Wattstraat jargon.

'And what did the Control Unit have to say about the accident itself? Was the Suzuki driving too fast?'

'A bit too fast,' Miriam said, 'but Tonio shouldn't have crossed the street right then.'

'And the blood tests?'

'Yeah, he'd had quite a lot to drink.'

'There must be a couple of thousand drunk students cycling through Amsterdam at that time of night. Doesn't mean you have to get run over.'

The bike did not have a light. In his pockets they found the small lamps that could have been attached to his clothes or wrapped around his arms.

They needed recharging — which is maybe why he didn't have them on.

33

I lie on my sweat-drenched bed reading the paper, with the balcony doors opened to the cool morning air. It is moderately sunny. I read that the actress Patricia Neal has passed away. Yesterday it was announced that they found a notebook of Roald Dahl's containing his account of the death of his seven-year-old daughter, in the early 1970s. Patricia Neal was the mother of the little girl.

When Miriam brings breakfast, she seems slightly panicked. When I mention it to her, she is very much surprised. 'I've just taken a pill, but I guess it hasn't kicked in yet.' (Recently, she takes her pills only in the late afternoon.) 'Klaas is coming at nine-thirty … to transfer the photos of Jenny. I still have to shower.'

34

At five o'clock, a delegation of Tonio's college friends: a guy and three girls. They've brought a large bouquet with them, on behalf of the whole class, in a vase — there had been a collection — and a big card signed by all of them.

One of the girls tells us how she met Tonio last September, in a grand café on the Max Euweplein. It was at the end of orientation week, which Tonio had missed part of because he still worked full-time at Dixons. They would finally meet their missing classmate. (There, too, our histories overlap. During orientation week in Nijmegen, I was working at Daf in Eindhoven to rake together enough money to furnish my student digs. I only arrived at the university on 1 October 1970, just in time for the first day of classes, and to discover that the rest of the class had meanwhile become great friends. My social life never recovered.)

Because Tonio, true to tradition, was late, his waiting classmates wondered out loud what kind of guy they should keep an eye out for, out of all the people that came into the café. They pooled their expectations of the newcomer, and arrived at a sort of composite profile — which, apparently, was spot on.

Our four visitors, especially the girls, gush enthusiastically about Tonio's helpfulness, and not only in class-related matters.

'He was *so* nice … *so* friendly.'

They shook their heads dejectedly as they reminisced. I asked about that 'parents evening', which we had missed. They groaned with embarrassment. Yeah, something really did go wrong. The organisers decided at the last minute to change the dinner venue, and the email with the new information never reached Tonio. 'Although,' one of the girls said, 'I did see him later that evening at the Atrium café.'

Miriam told them how our evening had panned out. 'It was a pity to have missed you and your parents, but we had a wonderful evening. In retrospect, even more so. It was the last time the three of us had such an intimate dinner together … without knowing, of course …'

Perhaps because of the tears in her eyes, the students all stood up at once, as though on cue. I didn't want them to leave. The boy, Jörgen, was the only one to have accepted a beer. I tried to coax him to stay for another, but he politely refused.

'I guess we'll be going,' said one of the girls.

'Just one more question,' I said. 'Did any of you hear Tonio mention a girl named Jenny recently?'

'Jenny …' The name was repeated a couple of times. They looked inquiringly at one another, hesitantly shaking their heads.

'Not that I know of,' Jörgen said. 'At least, there's no Jenny in our class.'

'She was, how should I put it, *new* in his life,' I said. 'No one in Tonio's circle of friends appears to have met her. We get, well, the impression that in the last week of his life something might have been brewing between Tonio and this Jenny.'

It was irritating that I couldn't show them a picture.

'We didn't see Tonio that week,' one of the girls said.

I was beginning to look like a fogeyish matchmaker, but one with a very specialised mission: to couple Tonio posthumously with a woman. Tonio's classmate Claire offered to have a look on Facebook or some other social media to try to find out about Jenny.

'It's okay, don't bother,' said Miriam. 'I've finally managed to reach her by telephone. She's willing to come by. We're just asking around, you know, what kind of girl she is. And especially, well, how serious they were.'

35

Us and our detective work. At times, I watch from a distance as Miriam and I make the rounds, knocking agitatedly on doors. Our mouths move, we gesticulate. I know we are asking about Tonio in his last days, but without the sound it looks more like we're going door to door demanding our son. 'Give him back ... we know he's in there.'

After the students left, Miriam and I dove for the bottles, which we did not dare to do in the presence of the cola-drinking girls.

'I'll order a couple of pizzas,' Miriam said.

We talked even more greedily than we drank. Every day, three times a day, theories having to do with Tonio's disappearance spun around in our heads. They all had to be put to the test.

'Minchen, have I already told you about my variant on the scorched earth?'

'Doesn't sound pretty.'

'Everyone makes mistakes in their life. It's all about what you do with them.'

'Learn from experience,' Miriam said. 'That's what they say, anyway.'

'For now, I'm thinking about how you look back on them, those mistakes. Even if I've long redeemed myself, I can still cringe with embarrassment at the memory. The incredibly stupid things. Even totally on my own, I want the earth to swallow me up, let me tell you. As a kid, I had the tendency to obsessively repeat to myself the hideous blunders I'd let loose in adult company. Just to wallow in the shame. Maybe I was out to punish myself … to better my life.'

'Gee, makes me almost want to forgive all the stupid things you've done to me.'

'Since Tonio's death … if I look back on my life, I see nothing *but* mistakes, gaffes, idiocy. Even things I wasn't dissatisfied with back then, that other people complimented — now they don't stand a chance. And why not? Because everything I ever undertook, even long before Tonio came along, could count as the groundwork for his death.'

'Don't be so hard on yourself,' Miriam said, now without sarcasm. 'It's inhuman.'

'I've got no choice. This is the way I see it. The death of my son is *proof* that my life has been nothing but one big blunder. When I look back on my past I see a vast, charred expanse. My memory has applied the scorched-earth tactic. Every blessing I've ever thought I'd counted has been burned. It's all out of reach.'

Miriam gave up protesting this morbid take on things — perhaps (but I hoped not) because she shared it. Her glance drifted more and more toward the corner sofa, Tonio's regular spot. I knew the tears wouldn't be long in coming.

'Whenever I think of … of how he always sat over there,' she said, not for the first time. 'With Tygo on his lap, writhing around under his hands.' She was already crying. 'The thought that he'll never come walking through that door again, ever …' She stamped her feet on the floor and yelled: 'Adri, it hurts so much. Help me. Please just help me.'

The pizza menu, where the phone number of the delivery service was printed, was downstairs in the front hall. Miriam left the room to place the order. I sat there, exhausted with grief, more from hers than from mine, staring into my greasy glass, when suddenly the living-room door sprung open. I started, as I used to do when Tonio dropped by unexpectedly. First came the vague, dark reflection of a figure in the white paint of the door, and then Tonio stepped through the opening. He always gave me that childlike grin of his, like when he had hidden himself to tease his parents, and suddenly reappeared.

('Say, have you seen Tonio?'

'Nope, not for a while.'

'I'm starting to worry.'

'I've looked everywhere. Nothing. Nowhere.'

'Well, I guess we should make some calls then.'

This was always the moment when he would leap out of the laundry basket, gleefully blurting out: 'You *really* thought I was missing, didn't you?')

Miriam had once again neglected to close the door properly behind her, so that one of cats only had to jump up against it to shove it open. I sat with bated breath, waiting for the arm that would push the door further open. Fooled again. Our ginger tomcat, Tygo, came zigzagging into the room.

36

Summer 1990. Having fled the war zone in Loenen, I turned in desperation to De Pauwhof, a doomed artists' colony in Wassenaar (where you were expected to take tea with the widows of the sculptors who had drunk themselves to death) to finish my book. I had left Miriam and Tonio behind in the Veluwe, where they were at the mercy of the fickle landlord/neighbour, who would sometimes just switch off the electricity for an entire weekend. I was so afraid Tonio would forget me that every other day I went to Wassenaar's only toy shop to buy him a Matchbox car, which I then sent off to Loenen, accompanied by a drawing or postcard.

The shop had a limited range. How many could I send before running out of models? Miriam subtly let me know over the phone that Tonio had received the stretch limo twice already: grey with a black roof.

At De Pauwhof, I made friends with the musicologist Albert Dunning and the elocutionist Maud Cossaar. Miriam and Tonio were planning a day trip to Wassenaar, so Dunning's wife, Jeanine, bought a small gift for the boy — from the same toy shop. It was beautifully wrapped, but when she presented it, Tonio grudgingly unwrapped the gift and reacted with the vaguely bored comment: 'Oh ... a car.'

Jeanine was slightly miffed, but Albert had a good laugh over His Lordship's ho-hum reaction. From a balcony somewhere above our heads, Maud Cossaar exclaimed, with the diction of an interbellum diva, her arms outstretched: 'Don't *you-ou* have a charming little family!'

What Jeanine did not know was that Tonio had been sent the very same car, in the very same colour (yellow) by his father, identically gift-wrapped. Sigmund Freud claimed that children had the tendency to throw a toy out of their crib every time their mother left the room — to give themselves the feeling it was *them* who had showed mama the door. Freud does not go into expelling the father in this manner. And yet it seemed that this is precisely what Tonio had in mind when he flung, with a decisive and potent gesture, that yellow car into the rhododendrons that surrounded the Pauwhof terrace.

No matter how thoroughly we combed the dark inner reaches of the bushes, destroying a good number of flowers in the process, we were never able to find that little yellow car. Tonio watched our fruitless efforts with amusement.

37

It is Friday afternoon. Miriam and her friend Josie take Josie's daughter Lola to a party. Jenny is supposed to come pick up her portfolio photos at four o'clock. Miriam has agreed to give them to her: I don't want to be there. Just to be on the safe side, I've left the door leading from my workroom to the landing ajar so I can hear the doorbell if Miriam's not back by the time Jenny arrives. In that case, I can buzz the girl in and ask her via the intercom to wait for Miriam downstairs.

Four o'clock, four-fifteen: no doorbell, and no sound at all drifting up the stairwell when I go out to the landing to check. I dial Miriam's number. Voicemail. She rings back a bit later.

'I'm just having a drink with Josie at a café. Jenny cancelled. Bladder infection, just like that afternoon with Tonio. Tomorrow she's going on holiday for three weeks. She'll come fetch the photos when she gets back. Promised to, anyway.'

The cancellation rankles me. I say: 'Don't let it get to you, Minchen. Jenny probably can't handle it yet. Every photo she sees bears witness to Tonio just out of view. Evidence of that afternoon together in our house.'

'To be honest, I was dreading it, too,' Miriam says. 'I'm relieved she cancelled.'

She says she'll pick up some sushi from the Japanese takeaway, to nibble with a cold glass of something. I have a sneaking suspicion that as far as dinner goes, that will be it. 'See you later.'

That evening, out on the veranda, we wondered what good it had all done — the talks with Tonio's friends, nosing around, going to all that desperate bother.

Mostly a bit of distraction from the — in reality — insoluble problem. And yes, now we knew that he'd spent his last night in the company of Goscha and Dennis, and not with Jenny. And that he did not come from Paradiso, but from club Trouw, and after that he had cycled off on his own to his flat in De Baarsjes.

Why the date with Jenny didn't go through: unclear. *What* had brought Tonio to that intersection of the Hobbemastraat and the Stadhouderskade: no one had the foggiest idea. Nor the precise circumstances of the accident itself: the police investigation was still underway.

All right, after a lot of digging around, we had managed to unearth the results of the photo shoot, but Jenny had still not picked them up. Jim and Dennis were supposed to organise a small exhibition of Tonio's other photos, but we didn't hear a peep out of them. Jim's brazenness to Miriam only drove us deeper into despair.

We had wanted to defend and protect Tonio, in his now-defenceless position as a dead person, but we hadn't counted on the indifferent, run-of-the-mill betrayal of the living. If this sounds bitter — it *is* bitter.

The heavy-duty envelopes with Tonio's photos of Jenny lay there between us. His last earthly task. Neither of us had the courage to look at them, because we knew as well as Jenny that on each and every print, conspicuously invisible, was Tonio's presence. His keen eye, peering straight through the glossy paper. What was in that envelope was a collection of snapshots etched in Tonio's memory on Thursday, 20 May 2010 — a memory swirling with Jennys.

'So. Here we are,' said Miriam. 'Photos located, model AWOL.'

'Just look at us,' I said. 'Too shit-scared to open a packet of snapshots. And Jenny? She wouldn't be able to see a single print without getting Tonio's squint into the bargain ... the top of his head as he bent over his Hasselblad ... No, she didn't dare. Actually, I find it kind of touching that she's now claiming the same ailment as the day of the photo shoot. Maybe she had the jitters then, too.'

'Then I'd just as soon she didn't come by three weeks from now either.'

'We'll just wait and see. If it takes too long, we'll make contact ourselves. We have the right to hear her account of the whole business.'

38

Since Black Whitsun, I have cursed, more than ever before, the vulgarity of what opinion leaders call *low culture*, and in the expression of which I find nothing that even obliquely reflects or clarifies my present situation.

I was wrong. Miriam's encouragement, some time ago, to 'let it all out', scream out my misery, apparently shook something loose in me. This morning, I heard the old song 'My son, my son' by Vera Lynn on the radio. My mother used to sing it now and again, fumbling through the English lyrics. It starts out with a rather ripe male chorus, but then suddenly you have Vera Lynn, with her swelling belt voice.

The song hit me right in the gut, and relieved me of a cramp located somewhere between my head and my heart. Two weeks ago, Miriam had coaxed a dry scream out of me, but now it all came pouring out, complete with heavy sobbing and an unstoppable stream of colourless snot.

It felt liberating, but it did not liberate me. It is a short number. When it was over, the catharsis went no further than a damply whispered: 'That's it … that's it.'

My son, my son
You're everything to me
My son, my son
You're all I hoped you'd be
My son, my son
My only pride and joy
God bless and keep you safe
My own, my precious boy

For all the care and heartache
    life has brought to me
One precious gift has made it
    all worthwhile
For heaven blessed and with
    great joy rewarded me
For I can look and see
My own beloved son

My son, my son
Just do the best you can
Then in my heart I'm sure
You'll face life like a man
My pride and joy
My life, my boy
My son, my son

CHAPTER FIVE

A second brood

1

The fact that he is no more, and will never be again (but remains as indelible as ever), is more evident to us now than in the beginning. After the funeral, well-meaning people suggested that 'the loss, the grief, would wear off, one way or the other'. The accident is now six weeks behind us. The only thing that has worn off is the surreal feeling that keeps the possibility open that one day, today or tomorrow, the nightmare will end. This unwelcome process of erosion takes place for the sake of reality, which, wielding the hard truth like a battering ram, drives itself ever deeper into us.

Were it a nightmare, it should have been long over by now. Typical of nightmares is that the dreamer wakes from them with a jolt. A nightmare is not a soap opera that can be stretched out infinitely for the sake of 'to be continued'.

The pain. It has only just started.

'Sometimes it *seems* a bit less awful than at first,' Miriam said this morning. 'It no longer feels like a bad concussion, but my brain is still a sieve. Especially with names and words, and the order of things ... things, you know ... dates. Events. And shopping is still a disaster. I drift through the shops, and have no idea what to buy. At home, I first go to make up a ... a, what do you call it, a note, a list ... and it's just blank, because ... what were we going to eat again? Sometimes I'm scared it'll never get any better.'

'Think of all those other functions that have stopped, Minchen. Hoping for. Yearning for. Praying … begging. They still exist, but have been switched off. They're arrows you have nowhere to aim at. No bulls-eye on the target. You can hope for Tonio's return as much as you want … believe in the miracle of his survival … pray, beg, threaten. Come back! Here, you! Or else! Pointless. Functions just as redundant as the appendix, the wisdom tooth, the coccyx …'

2

The tiring part is that every morning, awakening from the stale flush, we begin a new life, and that very evening grope the old one back. Every day, the same old ritual of resuming the pain management.

It is a quarter to seven, still early evening. Miriam has fetched her father from Beth Shalom and dropped him off at his house, where she administers his eye drops. Five minutes later, she is home. I sit on the sofa in volatile sombreness. The evening news and feature stories are over. Sometimes Miriam catches me in the living room seething at an instalment of *RTL Boulevard*, the Dutch celebrity-gossip show, with its vapid blather about weddings, divorces, and babymaking by members of the species who, probably due to their spiritual bastard status, are known as 'Dutch Notables'. Every once in a while there is a guest crime journalist, who offers commentary on the pictures of Joran van der Sloot in a Peruvian jail. I am always struck by the resemblance of this young murderer to Frankenstein's monster, but with the scars neatly airbrushed out.

Miriam asks if I want something to drink. I respond petulantly.

'Weren't we going to quit? This morning we swore we wouldn't go tempting each other.'

'Who's talking about booze? I'm just having mineral water.'

'Me too, then.'

A few minutes later, we sit chewing, with utter aversion, a glass of Spa. In silence. Without looking over, I can hear from Miriam's breathing that she's going to go to pieces. I ask: 'Did you take your pill on time?'

'Just did.' She's already crying. 'Bit too late.'

'This is no good.' I set the water glass down on the coffee table with a smack. 'Pour me a real drink. I won't make it through tonight otherwise. A gin and tonic, yeah. A generous one.'

Even before the first swig that makes everything lighter, a load glides off our shoulders. Miriam, crying, goes into the kitchen, but not dragging her feet. I hear the rattle of glasses, bottles, fridge drawers. The crackle of ice-cube trays. The tinkle of the ice cubes. This has to stop — sooner or later, this has to stop. Miriam's esophagus has been acting up again, because she pours pure vodka down it. It also gives her painful heartburn, which she combats with Rennies. For the time being, relief has the upper hand: we have managed to put off complete abstinence for yet another day.

Miriam returns to the living room carrying a tray with, in addition to the drinks, a plate of pata negra (or slices of mackerel, or toast with paté). 'This will have to do for tonight.' She has fixed herself a screwdriver. I get an extra-large glass with a double shot of gin watered down with tonic. My favourite brand: Bombay Sapphire.

Whenever Tonio dropped by unexpectedly he would have either one or the other: a G&T or a screwdriver, and usually left it at just one. Miriam and I clink glasses. She drinks through the lump in her throat, and shakes her head.

'That he'll never again sit here holding a tall glass … it's incomprehensible.'

3

One motif in the novel I was working on up until Whit Sunday involved the double suicide of two lovers (in this case, to put an end to a mortal fear of abandonment).

Have I ever raised the idea of doing ourselves in, together, to put an end to the pain? No. The thought hovers unspoken between us. We did not give in to it. Or did we? There are long-term forms of suicide, such as allowing insidious self-destruction to take its course. It is still too early to conclude whether or not we have caved in irrevocably to this offensive event. It's entirely possible that what we see as a fight for survival are really the spasms of an inevitable downfall.

Someone wrote: 'Would Tonio have wanted your lives to go to pot because of his death?'

Although he probably never gave the question much thought, because his joie de vivre did not permit it, I answered the correspondent: 'No, Tonio would not have wanted that. We are persevering in his spirit.'

On the other hand: what else can you do, as parents, than go to pot over the destruction of a boy like him? We *say* we're resisting our downfall, and keep telling ourselves that Tonio didn't intend to drag us along in his own destruction, but maybe, resistance or no, that is precisely where we're headed. It would mean that our love for him is stronger than our survival instinct, our craving for self-preservation.

Miriam and I are either in a process of recovery, or we are up to our necks in auto-intoxication. Does it matter? The booze bottles in the hall once contained either medicine or poison — they are, however you look at it, empty.

Keeping our heads above water won't bring Tonio back, nor will going belly up. In *life*, Tonio was worth surviving for, with every bit of our strength. Precisely because we experienced the live Tonio in all his vitality, it is tempting to destroy ourselves over the dead one.

4

When a new Bombay Sapphire needs to be opened, Miriam brings me the bottle, because she can't get it open herself. The only drawback to this superior brand is that the screw cap has no knurling, so the fingers cannot get a grip, especially when they are wet from the ice cubes. Even my dry fingers don't manage without chafing. I begin to believe that the designers of this bottle (square, the glass light-blue as a spring sky) intentionally opted for a slippery-smooth cap, in order to create in the user an additional moment of reflection. I clench my teeth, twist and wring, while my left hand, clamped around the bottle, goes numb from the cold. I am inclined (if not likely) to think: *What's the point of this mock relaxation if it requires so much exertion?*

Follow Tonio's destruction with my own: it remains, in its desperate irony, an appealing thought. A moment later, I resist it again. This one, irreplaceable life of mine must be lived to the very end, developing all my strengths and skills.

But … if I choose the latter option, I must also live on behalf of Tonio, who no longer can live under his own power. I must apply all my achievements to show how extraordinary his life was, and how extraordinary its significance still *is*. It means that, in addition to my existing capabilities, I must develop new techniques — not to simply describe him with verve, but to bring him back in all his vitality.

5

You can shut out the world as much as you like, but there will always be cracks, chinks, leaks that cannot be filled. Family bonds, for instance, cannot be ignored. Hinde is available on demand, but she does not interfere. I notice that, once in a while, I am in need of my brother's willing ear. Since Miriam told him this, he rings regularly. Natan, ever modest, sometimes waits for weeks to hear from me, and then telephones himself — always briefly, afraid to take up too much of my time. And then there's my mother-in-law.

6

The relationship between Miriam and her mother has been quiescently poor for forty years now. It did not improve with my entrance on the scene, thirty years ago, but thanks to my (then-) conciliatory disposition, the animosity went underground. In retrospect, I would have been better off fanning the smouldering fen-fire: it might at least have brought about — if need be with a great brouhaha — some degree of clarity for all parties.

The arrival of Tonio distracted mother and daughter from much as-yet unmined conflict material (although Miriam claims that her breast-feeding abruptly ceased when she withdrew with the baby to her old room, which was so thin-walled that as a child she could hear her parents coupling and fighting — not necessarily in that order — in the next room). Tonio was often entrusted to the care of his grandparents. Only some fifteen years later, when Miriam began writing about her youth, did the mudslide break loose. In her search for poems dating from her childhood years, she overturned a good deal of poisoned ground. Their relationship worsened rapidly, and not only below the surface. Wies made desperate attempts, in my presence, to explain away her daughter's angry outbursts as no-nonsense efficacy: 'Miriam can be harsh sometimes, but she's quite the organiser.'

One of Miriam's most vehement reproaches was that her mother had a knack for knowing exactly when to go to pieces: immediately before her husband or daughters had an important event. I remember having booked a hotel for eight weeks in Positano in order to work on a book. My mother-in-law had a breakdown the day of my departure: Natan, pale as ivory, came to tell us, he himself nearly on the verge of collapse. Last year, when she heard that Miriam and I had rented a house in Lugano, she had to be admitted to the Valerius Clinic. I don't want to suggest that she faked her mental condition, but she certainly could manoeuvre it well enough to achieve the maximum theatrical effect. Her nervous system was the theatre animal in her: a shrill, handwringing tragedienne.

In between earth-shaking breakdowns, she kept her nerves honed by a continual series of mini-collapses. In fact, she typically behaved like someone who could be swept away by the black wave of melancholy at any moment. Year after year, if Miriam and I ate at my in-laws on a Friday evening, Wies would interrogate me as to my labours, and in particular what they achieved in a material sense. My job, after all, was to support her daughter, preferably in a comfortable and cushy manner. Seated on the edge of her armchair, she subjected me to direct questions that were, to put it bluntly, doozies. The tricky part was that as soon as I began to formulate an answer, she flew out of her chair and into the kitchen to turn down the chicken soup or stir the latke batter to keep it from going lumpy.

Her return to the edge of the armchair, too, followed a regular pattern. With her right hand she would make a quick rubbing gesture over her nose, like you see certain adorable rodents do, but usually with both front paws at the same time. This nose-polishing rub was always a preamble to the same utterance: 'You *know* …!'

And thereafter followed a half-hysterical harangue about life's perils and pitfalls. The answer she had required of me a few moments earlier had apparently become entirely irrelevant. If I ever managed to get a word in edgewise, so as to assure her that my pursuits had indeed led to a certain level of prosperity, she would drown me out with the whine: 'Oh well, as long as you can keep it up … heaven forbid you should hit a slow patch!'

When, some years later, I tried to impress her with the offhand remark that two-thirds of my income went to the taxman, she began caterwauling that I could never in a million years earn that kind of money. Without allowing me to say a word, she declared me bankrupt then and there.

7

Since Tonio's funeral, Miriam has no desire to see her mother. This is only partly because of the way Wies insulted me during the post-funeral reception.

'My attention is focussed on Tonio, and no one else,' Miriam says. 'I'm trying to survive.'

Despite my aversion to the woman, I do feel sorry for Wies, so I occasionally ring her up. If she doesn't answer, there's no point in leaving a message, because she does not know how to retrieve her voicemail. If she does answer, she immediately begins wailing and screeching, so that I can hardly understand her. Her voice squeaks and cracks and grates.

'Tonio, such a good boy … why? why?' That part I do understand, every time.

I'm torn, I'll admit it. I see before me the brazen face with which she shunned her ex-husband at the funeral, and at the same time I think: Tonio was her only grandchild, she took care of him, Tonio took care of her yard (for a price), Tonio got her mobile phone in working order.

Her endless repetition of everything means I gradually pick up pretty much all of it. 'And you … you probably can't write anymore, can you?'

I assure her I that I am writing. About Tonio.

'I hope you'll be able to write again someday. And Miriam, how is she coping? Are you two holding up together? I never hear from her anymore …'

'Miriam's mind is entirely on Tonio. She needs to focus all her energy on dealing with this terrible event.'

'I understand that … I do understand. But she'll have to come see me *once*, at least. When I die.'

This she repeats, almost triumphantly, in each telephone conversation. She often says: 'I don't want … don't want to live anymore. I'm going to Tonio.'

Hinde came by the day before yesterday. Her mother has decided to let herself die, and soon. She has chosen to wither away. No more medicine, only morphine for the pain. She refuses food and liquid.

Miriam is beside herself. 'She's using Tonio's grave as her final podium … to give one last theatrical performance, to go out with a bang. Doesn't for a moment think of me … that I'm trying to come to grips with Tonio's death. She just bashes her way through the whole grieving process. It's blackmail, that's what it is. I put our contact on hold temporarily, so now she's going to *force* me to visit her. How did she put it? "Miriam will have to come to me *once*, at least. When I die." Uh-huh. Now I'll have to. One last breakdown. Right between Tonio and me. Then she'll be satisfied.'

Suddenly, the accents are shifted. Intense discussion between the two sisters. Consultation with my mother-in-law's psychiatrist.

'She's done it again,' Miriam exclaims. 'Once again, she's got me spending my whole day thinking about *her*. Instead of about Tonio and that I miss him so goddamn much.'

8

Since Miriam, despite her mother's languishing, still does not want any contact with her, I ring Wies a little more often, say once a week. If she doesn't answer, I get her voicemail, on which she announces herself with only the sound of her breath, which is undeniably hers. In this way, I discovered that human breathing, too, also contains a non-exchangeable fingerprint.

If she does answer, and I say my name, she begins at once to cry and shout.

'Not a minute goes by when I don't think of him ... I get up with it and go to bed with it ... I don't want to live anymore. I want to be with him. I hope I die soon. And you two ... will you be *all right*? Miriam doesn't want anything to do with me. It upsets me, but I do understand. I only hope ...'

On top of it, she has come down with shingles.

'Shingles is also called St. Anthony's fire,' I say, just to say something, and then she really breaks down.

'That darling Tonio ... he's there somewhere. He's hiding ... he gives me all kinds of signs. St. Anthony's fire. I hope I'll be joining him soon.'

9

I know no one who takes her dreams so seriously, and often so literally, as Miriam. She is quick to dispel daytime misunderstandings, but not nighttime ones. This morning, she reproached me, half in tears, that she had had an 'awful' dream about me. When she says it like that, in that tone, what she really means is that *I* caused her to have a bad dream.

'Now, of all times,' she snarled. 'How dare you.'

'Be a little more specific,' I said, 'so I can confess to my crime.'

'You'd left me for another woman.'

She gave me a dirty look. There was no doubt in her mind that I was fully responsible for my behaviour during her REM sleep.

'Well, think about it,' I said. 'It's simply the fear that, now of all times, I could start on a second brood. I hate the word, but that's what Flip called it when I bumped into him pushing a baby carriage. "Second brood, y'know …"'

'Oh, so that's what you're thinking about. A second brood. You see? Once again, my dreams speak the truth.'

I followed Miriam with my eyes as she crisscrossed the bedroom with choppy, agitated steps and a wiggling bosom (no bra on yet). That nightly drinking of ours had led both of us to start puffing up. I'd been having the problem for years now, but now Miriam's belly was starting to protrude more and more. I had to be the one to set an example, and be the first one to leave the glass untouched.

'Come on, Minchen, wait a sec.'

'I'm going to shower. I have to go over to my mother's this morning with Hinde, yeah? You go fantasise about your second brood.'

My mother-in-law had meanwhile been put in hospital with her shingles. They had decided to admit her after finding her stark naked and completely disoriented in the hallway of the retirement home. I knew this was a tall order for Miriam, who since Tonio's death had come down with a severe case of matrophobia. Too much baggage there. She went mainly to shore up her sister.

After the chaos of conflicting feelings in the weeks immediately following Whit Sunday, I had decided to be as merciless as possible in my self-reflection — an unsparingness that over time might bring some clarity to my present and future situation. In the context of this introspection, the notion of a second brood, like Flip's, had not yet come up. Was my desire for an heir, now that this, in the person of Tonio, had fallen by the wayside, so strong that I could attach myself to a young, fertile woman? Apparently I needed my wife's dreams in order to ponder the question myself.

I followed Miriam by ear as she went from the shower cell to Tonio's room, where she got dressed. Ten minutes later, the strident doorbell: Hinde. Women's voices, cut off by the echo of the front door. I had hoped she might come say goodbye, just to show that for her, too, it was only a game, posturing, put-on indignation. But, no, you didn't mess with Miriam's dreams.

10

'How was your mother?'

'Completely disorientated. At least that's how it looked. She mainly lay there, staring into space. Once in a while, she spewed out an incongruous word. The doctors think she's got temporary aphasia. I have my doubts. At a certain point, she snarled something like: "You've gotten fatter ... are you pregnant or what?" Hard and tactless, but to the point.'

'She's really something,' I reply. 'Her fifty-year-old daughter is grieving the loss of her only child, and then she just asks offhand if you're pregnant. Way off the mark, but you're right, it's got nothing to do with aphasia.'

I look at my darling Minchen, who stares from the back of her eyes, deep in inscrutable thoughts. What she sees, I wish I could reconstruct via her facial expression, without asking. If she is so far away, there is only one place she can be: with Tonio. I imagine her taking stock of her life's biological history. All those preparations in the flesh ... The changes in a girl's body. Her first period, and all of those that followed. The ever-ticking clock of ovulation. Sexual blossoming. Unrequited loves. Lovesickness. Requited loves, and, finally, again the lovesickness.

True Love.

All the sperm delivered but rebuffed by contraceptives. And then all the sperm that is *not* sabotaged by contraceptives. The negative tests. That one positive test.

The various stages of pregnancy, for three-quarters of a year. The worry about miscarriage. Decorating the nursery. The countdown. Labour. The pain. The joy. The fear.

And all of this just to be able to hold *that one* in your arms, to later take by the hand and to help grow up. And all of this effort just to lose *that one*, forever, so that the entire process of nature and spirit only served to create an illusion, and then to destroy it.

She looks up, meets my speculating gaze. 'What?'

'What were you thinking of?'

'What do you think?'

I first got chatting to Miriam at her twentieth birthday party. This fall she'll turn fifty-one. I have experienced her in all available moods, period or no, just as she has been subjected to all my states of mind, hangover or no. How many times does a man, in the course of three decades, ask his wife, noticing her angry or teary face, what's wrong?

'You look so sombre.' How many times in the course of all those years has she said that to him? 'I'm not going to sit here looking at some sourpuss all night.'

Since Black Whitsun, I no longer need to ask Miriam this question at every brow-furrow, nor she me if my mouth happens to droop. This will hold true for the rest of our mutual future: we know exactly what's wrong with the other. Mind-reading is not that difficult when the mind is fixed on one thought, for forever and a day.

'Minchen, years ago we saw a documentary on TV about that Italian gynaecologist … remember? He ran a kind of posh clinic where he managed to get post-menopausal women pregnant. Sixty, sixty-five years old, they were all welcome for fertility treatments. At first, all hell broke loose among the medical-ethics people, but women came to him from all corners of the earth. Women who, after a busy career, still wanted children … or only met the love of their life at a more advanced age …'

'I get it,' Miriam says. 'You feel so sorry for my mother with that blunder of hers about me being pregnant … now you want me to go to that Italian clinic for therapy. I wonder if it still exists, actually. I'll look it up online.'

'It's just a daydream, Minchen. I only want you to dream with me … about what it might bring us.'

'A lot of pleasure, and even more misery.'

'I'd get to see a child reach its twenty-first birthday before I turned 80,' I say. 'You'd only be in your early seventies. Think about it.'

'I *am* thinking about it. We would get to go through every stage of Tonio's development one more time. Great. And then? We'll never see what Tonio's future had in store. No graduation, no career, no wedding, no grandchildren, no … nothing. But what about when we're old folks, how much of Tonio's successor's future will we get to see? Not much, maybe. Thanks a lot for the offer, Adri, but I'll pass.'

I don't have an immediate response to this. And she hasn't yet brought up the inevitable fears that would go along with a new case of dangerous-growing-up. Oh, it would be far more fraught than with Tonio, because after him, our fears would be completely justified by his fateful death. The newcomer would be made to suffer twice over because of the unknown predecessor, the missing brother. The child would have a hell of a life with two bodyguards posing as parents.

'Well, nice of you to consider it anyway, Minchen. Consider the appointment with Dr. Antinori cancelled.'

'Oh, so you'll go for a second brood in another nest after all.'

'Quit it about that second brood, will you,' I say. 'It takes two to tango. Doesn't it?'

'Where there's a will, there's a way.'

'I don't want that *way*. I don't even want that *will*. Listen, Minchen

... the fact that Tonio is gone for good feels like complete emasculation. With his death I've lost so terribly much. A great love, my best friend, the heart of my future. A masculine muse. And yes, my progeny, too. The grandchild I might have been able to hold someday. There are, at least as far as I know, no apocryphal Van der Heijdens roaming around anywhere. The single outcome of my manly efforts here on earth was Tonio.'

'Remember what you used to say, when Tonio was little, when people asked if we were planning to have more children? "No," you'd say, "fatherhood doesn't suit me, but I had to try it out once. I could never die without ever becoming a father." That's what you said.'

'Try it out ... if I said that, then with hindsight it does sound kind of sinister. As though it was a one-off experiment that could either succeed or fail. Depending. All right, I *did* try out fatherhood. And with brilliant results. Now he's gone. The boy, the man, who was supposed to take it all over from me. He has left me without heirs. Here I am, a retrospectively sterilised father ... Don't think that I often thought of myself as a future grandfather. Seldom, in fact. Through Tonio, the way he acted around me, I could consider myself still young ...'

'Second brood,' Miriam says. 'You're dodging the issue.'

'Minchen, once and for all: I don't have the instinct of a tribal leader that offers up three, four marriages for the sake of producing, at long last, a first-born son ... and subsequently only thinks eight generations ahead. Honestly, I am not going to go build a new nest. I could give you a whole slew of reasons why not. For example, that back in '88, at the age of thirty-six, I was already a belated father. Or that for a new child I'd already be a grandpa ... No, the real reason is because I want to stay with you. That I want to live out my life with you. Our names will soon be joined together on Tonio's gravestone. We have a dead son together. We will both die childless.'

'I'm so frightened,' says Miriam.

'Childless ... and not, either. You can't erase the fact that for nearly twenty-two years we were Tonio's parents. Until the day we die, our job is — no, not to keep his memory alive, but to keep *him* warmly alive. I need you for that. And you need me. We are the heirs of the person he was. The executors of his life, his works, his words … But the most important thing is that we keep him wedged in between us forever. Only that way will he let himself be nourished. With love, with memories. No way, a second brood. Tonio remains our progeny.'

11

I ring my mother-in-law in hospital. Today is her eighty-fifth birthday. Contrary to my expectations, she answers the phone, but her voice is nearly inaudible. If I stylise the bits I think I understand, I come up with: 'I'm old. I don't need to go on any longer. You all are still young … I hope you'll pull through … that you'll be able to write again someday …'

After the umpteenth repetition of suchlike phrases, she says, suddenly perfectly intelligible: 'Well, I have to hang up now, I've got visitors … and there's someone waiting in the hall, too. Thanks for the flowers.'

That visitors are clamouring to get in is not entirely plausible. Perhaps it's her way of showing her displeasure at our absence on her birthday. And as far as starving herself to death goes: Hinde reported recently that her mother had announced that she 'rather felt like some bonbons' again.

12

Fortunately, it wasn't necessary to track Jenny down and press her to tell us her story. Exactly a month after the cancelled visit, and a week after returning from her vacation, Jenny rang Miriam. They made a new appointment.

'I'll make sure the photos are ready,' Miriam promised.

'The photos aren't the main reason I'm coming,' Jenny said.

13

As though the summer had resurged just for the occasion: it was that kind of day, bathed in swirling light, when we finally made Jenny's acquaintance.

Despite the heat, almost unbearable under the flat roof, I had spent most of the day upstairs working on this requiem. More and more, it was taking on the form of a detective-like reconstruction, albeit without a private eye or a Commissioner Maigret. You could hardly call it a whodunit. Yes, if you could eventually single out fate as the perpetrator. The desperate parents had thrown themselves into a case reconstruction. The *what*, the *how*. In that order.

I had described the uncertain hours preceding Tonio's death, the dying itself, the consternation, the funeral, the discussions with friends who had been with him on his last night, the accounts of the police and the trauma surgeon. I had reported on the search for his bicycle, his clothes, his watch, his camera, his photographs. Everything had been checked off, except a chat with the girl from the photo session.

I turned off the fan, tired of constantly picking up sheets of manuscript paper that had fluttered out of place. I had briefly considered plundering Tonio's glass display case of volcanic and other stones in order to have enough paperweights, but I was afraid that, at the sight of all those minerals and semi-precious stones Tonio had collected and displayed, I wouldn't get a single letter set to paper. For the same reason, I did not open the awning on the balcony: too many associations with the last time Tonio and I spoke.

Today at five o'clock, we would, if all went as planned, finally get to meet Jenny. No wonder writing was such a chore this afternoon. I could blame the heat, but it was Jenny I needed in order to move on. If she was able to answer a few questions that were still troubling me, I could perhaps round off my requiem for Tonio, before it crushed me.

At the same time, I dreaded the meeting with a distaste bordering on revulsion. Who could guarantee that what Jenny had to say wouldn't cause me to cave in altogether?

The piano jingle of my mobile phone. Miriam. 'Not too hot up there?'

'I was just about to come down.'

'I'm taking my father to Beth Shalom a bit earlier today. So I'll be home in plenty of time to let that girl in.'

'I'm having a hard time of it.'

'Me too.'

It was a quarter to four. I'd been sitting up here, sweating and stinking, for long enough. Under a tepid shower, I thought of Tonio and girls. Of what Dennis and Jim had revealed about it: that girls had been on Tonio's mind a lot recently … that he'd come to them for advice … Once again, I was fretting about something that no longer concerned him. Quandaries that could no longer trouble him.

There had been no lack of sex education. But the attendant difficulties, had I prepared him sufficiently for them? There had never been any prudishness between us, although we never overdid it and turned our house in to a nudist colony. When, as a toddler, he occasionally saw me naked, he would prance through the house, gleefully exclaiming, over and over: 'Whoa, what a big one … whoa, what a big one.'

Once, he must have been about eleven, Tonio burst into my workroom, panting from the three flights of stairs. He positioned himself next to my desk, and without preamble dropped his trousers and underpants. Arching his back, he held out his organ between thumb and index finger. Being the son of a Jewish mother made him technically a Jewish boy, but he had never been circumcised.

'It hurts like crazy,' he said, pointing to the reddened foreskin, which, like mine, was rather elongated, but apparently not very loose, perhaps too tight. 'Mama said I should show you.'

'It looks a little inflamed,' I said. 'You have to wash the spout on the inside, too, not just the outside.'

'That's what makes it *hu-u-u-rt.*' He shivered theatrically, imitating a cartoon character getting a prolonged electric shock. 'It's way too tight.'

'What you have to do is, every time you wash it, soap up the spout really well. Try to slide it back a bit more each time. Until one day it's gone as far back as it can. Plenty of soap. *Tons* of soap. It takes practice. You'll see that the spout will loosen up over time, and won't hurt anymore.'

'Yeah, but ... yeah, but,' he whined with a put-on small voice, 'if my hand's full of soap, then I can't hold onto anything.'

'Goodgawdalmighty ... then keep a pail of sawdust handy.'

Wearing the most solemn expression in the world, he pulled up his trousers. Before he turned and left the room, he gave me a tense, and a tad glum, look.

'So what're you going to do now?'

He could no longer contain himself, and guffawed it out. 'Soap up my spout, of course. Soap up my spout, what else?'

And off he went. I heard him laughing as he skipped down the stairs. At first I thought: he is going to tell his mother. But he stopped a floor below me, in the bathroom, where a while later you could hear water running. For the first time, I wondered if it might have been better to have had him circumcised at birth. If he indeed had inherited my foreskin, genetically speaking, he could, owing to the wrong kind of sensitivity, encounter lovemaking problems later. If pain won out over lust, then impotence lay in wait.

I turned off the water and stepped out of the shower stall. About six months later, Miriam had told me, a bit embarrassed but also laughingly, about a television evening with Tonio (twelve, by that time) and the sisters Merel (thirteen) and Iris (fourteen). Tonio and Merel had been an item for years, but the hyper-intelligent Iris was indispensable to this constellation: she was the most creative of the triumvirate, and managed, by inventing new games and adventures, to drag the other two out of their lethargy. On the evening in question, they were all watching the 1973 film *Turkish Delight*. They had missed the titles, but were treated to a bruising opening scene with Rutger Hauer, dumped by his wife and feeding his longing with nude photographs of her glued to the wall.

'Shit, goddamn it,' Rutger exclaimed, trembling, 'shit for me ... then I'll lick the shit from your arsehole.' (Or words to that effect.)

Tonio thought it was hilarious, but the girls were bewildered. 'What's he doing?' asked Merel.

'Jerking off, of course,' Tonio answered, laughing. 'He's jerking off.'

'What's that?' asked Iris, who was always the one who had to explain things to the other two.

'Jerking off, Iris,' Tonio exclaimed triumphantly. 'You mean you don't *know*?'

My shower was just a bit warmer than cold, but no matter how much I dried myself off, the sweat just kept streaming down my body. It couldn't only be the heat of a summer day. I'd have given anything to put on my baggy shirt and jogging pants and sit out on the veranda, the doorbell turned off, so as to slowly drink myself into oblivion. I perspired from things I did not want to know about.

Oh God, please let Jenny have a relapse of the kidney infection ... well, not too seriously, please, the poor thing ... but bad enough to have to cancel at the last minute ... maybe the antibiotics didn't do the trick last time ... say we just post her the photos ...

Tonio was thirteen. It was a regular school day, but he had showered at an unusual time of day: in mid-afternoon. As I needed to use the bathroom myself, I lay on my bed waiting until his poorly dried feet crossed the landing with a sucking, slurpish sound to the door with the poster GENIUS AT WORK. The bathroom was steamy and humid. A generous scent of pine gel, stuff I never used myself, filled the air. I never liked showering right after someone else, but hey, come on, this was Tonio. I pulled aside the nylon shower curtain. A classic still life: on a bed of matted dark hairs, a bird's nest in the making, that clung to the drain, lay a large white glob of Tonio's freshly shed semen.

Good, I thought, intensely satisfied, that's taken care of. God, kid, I hope you enjoyed that with majestic embarrassment.

14

With everything that annoys me about him, in literally unguarded moments, I can immediately point to something corresponding to my own student days. The reckless drinking, the cycling without a light, the bungling perseverance with girls, an unshaved look, neglecting grandparents (except when it came to extra pocket money), late nights, sleeping in, a trashed house, a chronic lack of money, a chronic shortage of study hours and course credits ...

In fact, I cannot think of *anything* of which I say: I did that better when I was twenty-one. Maybe I went to bed with more girls, but that was only partly thanks to my seduction tactics, which suffered greatly under my innate shyness. Those were different times. Sexual revolution? Nah, it was just the pill. You didn't ask a girl if she was 'on the pill': she would warn you if, on the outside chance, she was not. Crabs and the clap were the fifth column of 1970s student life, but being the pre-AIDS era, the turn-on was never turned off by the talcum scent of a freshly unrolled condom.

It was now 2010, and AIDS had still not been licked, and for the remaining venereal diseases they'd thought up a collective name: so much transmittable misery threatens the love life of young people these days. Once again, one has to negotiate, or at least confer, and never since Mr. Condom saw a profit in a tied-up lamb's intestine has there been as much fussing with rubbers as there is today.

This is not going to be an unauthorised biography of Tonio — more like an unauthorised requiem. Am I sufficiently aware that Tonio's take on some events might be different from mine? Would he prefer not to have seen certain facts in print at all?

He was two, or nearly. The three of us were in the train, perhaps en route to my parents' in Eindhoven. Tonio had a sketchbook and coloured pencils with him, but he'd stopped filling the page with scribbles, so I amused him by making simple drawings. Sucking intensely on his pacifier, he watched my doings with sleep-laden eyes. After rendering a cat in a variety of positions, I then drew a portrait of Tonio, with his long locks, the pacifier like a clown's mouth, and the security blanket he kept pressed against his ear. I showed it to him. His face cleared. He laughed.

All right, then, next portrait. The big eyes, the sumptuous curls. I folded the paper in half lengthwise and tore out a small hole where the mouth was. After flattening the paper back out, I took Tonio's pacifier out of his mouth and stuck it through the hole in the paper. I held up the portrait. Almost the same as the last one, which had made him laugh so heartily, but now adorned with a real-life pacifier. Quoting from 'Nader tot U', I exclaimed: 'Is that true to life, or is that not true to life?'*

Tonio looked at his likeness for a few seconds, his little face scrunched in earnestness, and then burst into uncontrolled wailing. I hurriedly removed the pacifier from the paper, and tried to give it back to him. He wouldn't take it. I tried to wedge it between his lips, but he kept intentionally letting it fall out of his mouth. For the rest of the journey, he was inconsolable.

I still wonder what had upset him so much. Was the pacifier, incorporated into the drawing, too realistic a detail, whereby the little boy in the picture seemed to have made off with *his* privilege? When Tonio was about fifteen, sixteen, I related this anecdote to him. I asked if he had any idea what exactly had caused such intense dismay. The tricky part was that at this age he seemed to regard every query from me as an exam question.

'Really, I don't remember *anything* from when I was little,' he said, attempting to balance a small stack of coins on his jiggling knee. 'Maybe I just thought the drawing wasn't much *good*.'

15

On the cupboard in the hallway lay a small stack of post, which from halfway up the stairs I could already see were condolence letters. Even in the most killing of circumstances, a person was apparently still capable of learning new things, even if it was to distinguish between envelopes containing sympathy and those containing a demand for payment.

---

* 'Nearer to Thee' (Gerard Reve, 1966)

I carried the post out to the veranda, stopping in the library on the way to pick up a letter opener. Miriam had already put the cushions on the garden chairs. There was a fresh tablecloth, fastened with clips, on the round table. Of course: Jenny needn't see how, every night, to wash down a morsel of food, we sloshed and spattered our rosé and red wine.

Ten past four. I still had almost an hour to myself. What I'd like the most is to have the rest of my life to myself — myself and Miriam. Finish my work, for what it was worth, and talk to Miriam about Tonio, until my last breath — or hers. This would be sufficient.

Children's voices from three, four houses up wafted over the backyards. Harmony. I opened the first envelope. Two female friends, teachers, recalled a talk I gave at Rhoon Castle in the early nineties. They enclosed a photo of Tonio, smiling shyly, as he scribbled his name in one of my books. He had his dark, smooth hair (just a few years earlier they were tight, light-coloured curls) in a pageboy cut, the fringe touching his eyebrows. Seeing that five-year-old while the twenty-one-year-old was still alive would have tested even the strongest heart. Now I held a photo in my hand of a boy who, you could say, was doubly gone.

I read letter after letter, looked at card upon card. Kind, impotent words of comfort. Mothers of Tonio's primary-school classmates recalled playground anecdotes, where they so often stood waiting in clusters until the kids had finished playing. Many colleagues or journalists with whom I had locked horns in the past stepped over the vague border of the dispute to offer words of support. Now that the stream of sympathy had continued unabated for all these weeks, I began to realise that there hadn't been a word from the television world. The producers and hosts of literary talk shows were the first ones, of course, to be your best friend and go into raptures over your indispensability for this very item — at least, as long as you hadn't yet committed to an appearance. But even after the show they were not too averse to having a drink together, and, in passing, to praise your contribution.

And then the son of the esteemed guest dies, and … not a word. Perhaps I shouldn't be too hard on the TV folks. The guests on their shows are no more than light rays in motion. There might be a person of flesh and blood at the table, but what matters is their presence in the living room: the image recreated in light, which the broadcasting company hopes and prays the house tyrant on the couch does not surf away from. Mutatis mutandis, this also applies for the talk show host: he, too, thanks his existence to the rays given off by a television. As the interviewer of a guest, he is not a person of flesh and blood, and therefore does not have to act outside the show like a real person with compassion.

16

The doorbell. We still hadn't gotten around to having the Brom people install a friendlier jingle. This bell still sounded just as it did on Whit Sunday, bypassing your ears and going straight for the nerves.

That must be Jenny. Five o'clock already? I did not have a watch or clock at hand, but my instinct told me that not even a half-hour had passed since I'd started going through the post. I pricked up my ears to hear if Miriam was going to open the door: she could easily have been back from Beth Shalom for twenty minutes already.

The bell echoed in the empty marble hallway. When Miriam answered the door you could hear the rattle of the glass inner doors, shut to keep the cats from escaping, but that, too, was absent.

The bell rang for the second time. If Miriam hadn't returned from the seniors' canteen by five, when she was expecting a visitor at home, something must have happened on the way. As I walked through the library to the hall, I tried to quell visions of Miriam and her father, strapped into their seatbelts, their necks snapped and their heads flopped against one another. The cats stood in angry expectation on the stairway landing, their fur already critically on end.

On the stoop stood the girl I recognised from Tonio's Polaroids.

'I'm really sorry,' she said. 'I'm way too early. Stupid of me.' She extended me her hand. 'Jenny.'

As I took Jenny's hand (small, dainty), I saw Miriam behind her, in the row of parking spaces, get out of her car. 'Was I mistaken about the time?' she exclaimed, half-panicky. 'It's a quarter to five. I thought it was at five o'clock. Oh, this head of mine ... a mess.'

While I led the way to the terrace, behind me the women apologised profusely back and forth for their negligence. I offered Jenny a chair, but she stayed standing for a moment with her hands on the railing, looking into the garden: for the first time since 20 May, she saw the place where Tonio had photographed her. Even when she finally sat down at the round table, she regularly cast oblique, almost furtive, glances at the small arbour with the white bench.

Miriam asked what we wanted to drink. Jenny first asked for mineral water, but upon hearing I was having gin and tonic, changed her mind: she'd have that, too, 'but not too much gin'. Miriam went to take care of the drinks.

We sat slightly awkwardly opposite each other. *A real Tonio girl.* Those were the exact words that came to mind, even though I had never pegged anyone as 'a real Tonio girl', let alone knew what characteristics a Tonio girl was supposed to possess.

'Were you nervous about coming over?'

'Yeah, a bit. But at the same time, no. On the way, I kept thinking: *Oh gosh, I won't know what to say ... and then?*'

Was it my despair that so wanted to see that this Jenny was ... would have been ... a match for Tonio? (Verb tenses, too, played their game of life and death.) Across from me sat a frail girl with a delicate face, whose expression altered continually under a painful nervousness, which had also taken hold of her arms and shoulders. She cast another quick sideways glance at the wooden loveseat up against the pink-stuccoed wall. She was exactly the kind of girl I would have wanted, when I was twenty, to defend, cherish, caress. She wore lightweight clothes, which allowed her body heat to penetrate fully: perfect for Tonio while dancing. Or was the 'Tonio girl' my own invention?

Come on, I'd *seen*, hadn't I, that Tonio felt the same way. The bashful pride with which he showed me those Polaroids … His downplaying remark that I shouldn't just go on these practice snapshots. He would soon show me the proper prints.

Miriam was gone for quite a while. I could hear her puttering about in the kitchen up on the first floor, where the windows were open. Fixing some snacks, no doubt. I'd have to say something now, it didn't matter what, otherwise the poor girl would die of nerves.

'Of course, I've got all sorts of things I want to ask you,' I said, 'but I suggest we wait for Miriam. She wants to hear everything, too.'

'Fine.'

Yes, she was pretty, but didn't have the refined beauty of a model — I had suggested as much to Tonio, to his slight irritation. It was, after all, just a way for a student to make some extra money via a modelling agency.

'So what are you studying?'

'Art history. I'm in my second year.'

It's been like this for weeks now: every time I saw anything attractive, I tried to see it through Tonio's eyes, since his retina has permanently *gone black*, to use TV jargon. But my attempts to share with him the beauty of whatever it is I'm looking at are starting to backfire. Each thing, each image that I believed would have met with his approval, reduced, in equal measure, my *own* enjoyment of it. Instead of enjoying something doubly, 'for the two of us', the eye-catchingness that Tonio was now eternally deprived of became lessened in my own aesthetic experience.

To put it another way: I could keep on enjoying something until I fully realised that Tonio *would have* enjoyed it just as much. The profit-and-loss sum of my visual enjoyment thus came out to exactly zero. As regards Jenny's attractiveness, this afternoon was no different.

Relief: Miriam arrived with the tray.

'Have I missed much?' she asked, placing the glasses on cork coasters. 'Here's the one without much gin.'

On the middle of the table she put a platter with prepared Melba toasts: salmon, sardines, meat salad.

'We haven't gotten any further than Jenny's bike ride over here,' I said. 'She was afraid of being tongue-tied.'

We raised our glasses. 'To our absent friend, then,' Miriam said. We each took a gulp.

'It was so weird,' Jenny said, 'to stand out there on your doorstep. And on as beautiful a day as back in May. For a moment, everything seemed the same ... and still it was all different, because ... well, yeah, of course I knew he ... Tonio ... wouldn't answer the door. In May, he appeared at the door wearing a really smart shirt ... something with red stripes ... and that broad smile of his.'

She shook her head and quickly brought the glass to her mouth. I was reminded of my blind date with Marike A., organised by her sister in the spring of '69. How I stood at the mirror practising the right smile, followed by a snappy opener: 'Who'd have thought it would be something so charming ...' ('Something', was that okay? Or did it make her sound too much like an object? And then 'charming' ... would a fifteen-year-old girl want to be called 'charming' these days? After an endless round of corrections, I could only come up with 'such a charming something' — and I think I even said that. The rehearsed smile had long dissolved into a grimace.)

'His favourite shirt,' Miriam said. 'He pretty much forced me to wash and iron it beforehand. Not what you'd really call work clothes. He must have had a good reason to want to wear it. Now he's got it on in ...'

She shook her head, smiling, without finishing her sentence, as though pointing out that Tonio had been buried in that shirt might detract from the compliment he had made Jenny by wearing it for the photo session.

Now was the moment to ask Jenny about Tonio — how they'd met, how the photo shoot went, why the date at Paradiso didn't go through. Weeks ago, when we had begun putting together something like a reconstruction of Tonio's last days, I had admonished myself not to overlook a single detail. Otherwise there would be no point in it all. I was surprised at how cold-bloodedly, through all my despair, I dared to look the facts straight in the eye. Strange: now that the missing link, the reluctant Jenny, was sitting opposite me, my old fear of the truth grabbed the chance to rear its ugly head. The man who left the post unopened because it might contain bad news (or otherwise unwelcome tidings) was back with a vengeance, when I needed him least of all.

The problem that I identified right after Tonio's death: Jenny could impart one of two possible truths, neither of which I wanted to hear. First truth: Jenny had chosen Tonio as the photographer for her portfolio, making the session no more than a business transaction, with perhaps a friendly lining at most. Second truth: an unspoken mutual attraction had, via request or offer, taken the form of a lengthy photo shoot, whence a budding romance had unfolded or was about to unfold.

Truth No. 1 meant that Tonio had to say farewell to life without one last romance, which gave his death an inhospitable starkness.

Truth No. 2 would always torment us with the thought of 'what might have been'.

Neither truth deserved to be preferred over the other. The impossibility of a choice made it all the more painful. I did not want to hear it.

'Jenny, would you mind telling us,' I asked, 'how you and Tonio met?'

'It's no secret,' she said, with a brief chuckle.

17

One day in the summer of 2009, Jenny's mother went into the Dixons computer shop on the Kinkerstraat to inquire about new photographic equipment. She was assisted by a courteous young man who switched effortlessly to English when he realised his customer was Canadian.

'I live with my mother in that part of town,' Jenny said. 'She came home all excited. "I was at Dixons, and the nicest young man helped me," she said. "So friendly and helpful. Good-looking, too. He explained everything so patiently ... demonstrated cameras ... without being at all pushy." You should know my mother has an eye for young men. I don't know if she bought anything then, but she went back often. Usually she got the manager, a guy called Kantorovich.'

'Kantorovich,' Miriam said. 'Yeah, he was Tonio's tormentor at Dixons. The guy ringing Tonio at home when he'd overslept again, that was one thing. But he kept pestering him in the shop, calling him lazybones and sleepyhead. He really gave the poor kid a tough time.'

'My mother always asked the manager if Tonio could assist her. And then she had another hundred questions for him, which he always answered patiently. "You should come with me sometime," she said once, "then you'll see for yourself. He really is an awfully nice boy." Of course, she was matchmaking. Okay, so one day I think: I'll go over to Dixons with her. And sure enough ... Tonio. We chatted some. Me about college. Him about his passion, photography. I went back to the shop a couple of times after that. Without my mother. I think we, you know, kind of hit it off. But it never got as far as a date.'

You only heard a faint trace of English in Jenny's Dutch if you knew her mother was an English-speaking Canadian. I wanted to shout at Tonio: go on, ask her out, what are you waiting for ... say that Kantorovich needs you, but that you'd like to pick up the conversation after you've closed up shop ...

'Why not, do you think?'

'One day he'd disappeared,' Jenny answered. 'Just like that. It was last fall. The boss told me Tonio had quit because he felt he couldn't combine the Dixons job with college. Of course, I knew he had started his Media & Culture course at the beginning of September, but ... well, yeah, he kept working at Dixons. Until late autumn. And then ... he just disappeared. My mother didn't know about it either. I had no phone number, no email address, didn't even know where he lived. The Dixons people couldn't help me either. So we lost touch.'

Damn that Tonio. He blew chances just like his father did at his age. (The sun-drenched St. Annastraat in Nijmegen. The blonde who cornered me with her bike. 'Tea? You can see my new digs.' And me, doofus, who couldn't manage anything, except: 'I was just on my way to the employment office across the street. I'm broke.')

Jenny drank her gin and tonic. She took too big a swig, which appeared to burn her throat; tears came to her eyes. She thumped her chest.

'But not for good,' Miriam said. 'Well, yes, now … for good, I mean … but not yet, then.'

'This past spring,' Jenny said, swallowing continuously, 'I found Tonio on Facebook. I was a second-year, had debts, needed to make some extra money. Yeah, I know it sounds horribly vain, but I toyed with the idea of modelling work, playing an extra in TV or film, something like that. What I needed was a portfolio with decent photos to take around to casting agencies. So when I saw that Tonio had a Facebook page, I remembered his enthusiasm for photography. I got in touch. Surprised him, of course. A photo shoot, he saw no reason why not. I offered to reimburse him for his materials, and pay him for his hours. The indignation! What a way to start, if I wanted him to photograph me … He wouldn't hear of it. It was up to me. Okay then, fine, of course. You know the rest. We had an appointment for the Thursday before that weekend. He would ask if he could do the shoot here in your house. He didn't seem to think it would be a problem. "It wouldn't surprise me," he said, "if they cleared out for the day. That's how they are." He was right.'

If I couldn't fend off her version of the truth, I had to ask Jenny if she hadn't actually used the portfolio as an excuse to get in touch with Tonio. I opened my mouth, but Miriam beat me to the punch. 'So, Jenny, how'd that afternoon go?'

'I think we pretty much hit all the rooms in the house,' Jenny said. 'The living room, his old room, the library … out back, of course … Tonio even photographed me up on the roof. Those pictures were his least favourite; mine, too. Not much ambience up there. He wasn't able to do anything with the view.'

'Wait a minute,' I said. 'If you two were up on the roof … the only way up there is via the fire escape on the third floor. You'd have to have gone through my workroom.'

'Shooting off my mouth again,' Jenny said. 'I know he wasn't allowed to take pictures in there, with all those papers and such. Tonio kept up his

402

end of the bargain. All we did was cut through on the way to the balcony. No, that's not entirely true. I did have a peek around. There were various maps spread out on that long table ... maps of Amsterdam, Amstelveen, Valkenburg ... Tonio told me they were for a novel you were writing. About the murder of an Amsterdam or, no, an Amstelveen police officer. Something like that. What Valkenburg was doing there, he couldn't say.'

'Ah, now I know why the awning had been rolled shut,' I said to Miriam. 'You can't get up the ladder if it's open.'

'You've been racking your brain about that for weeks,' Miriam said.

'Now that we're solving mysteries,' I said, turning back toward Jenny. 'The father of the main character was a travelling vacuum-cleaner salesman in the sixties. Sometimes he brought his son with him. Once they went to Valkenburg. Hit the row houses with the latest model. The son has a sixth sense for which of the housewives his father has developed a special kind of rapport with. Beyond the "cup of coffee" stage, you might say. So there you are. On Thursday, Tonio gives you a summary of my new novel, and three days later the book, thanks to him, is destroyed, and he forces me to write a totally different one. The tyrant. A benevolent tyrant, I'll give him that.'

'Tonio was suddenly in a hurry,' Jenny continued. 'A rooftop shoot: waste of time. He insisted on photographing me out back, before the sun went down. I was still wearing white clothes. I also wanted a series in black. So I changed quickly in his old room. Neat, really, the place where he'd spent his whole youth ... that gave it a special feeling ...'

If she kept up such a light-hearted report of that afternoon's photo shoot, we'd be confronted with neither the one truth nor the other. Fine, then, the truth would be somewhere in the middle. That's actually what we wanted, wasn't it? Well, then again, not really. We'd still have to get to the bottom of it.

'From age four until he left home at nineteen,' Miriam said.

'And?' I asked. 'Had you changed into your black quickly enough to take advantage of the light?'

Jenny turned her head toward the arbour again, this time less surreptitiously. 'We even had enough time left to sit in the sun on that bench. Tonio brought some iced tea out from the fridge. Nice and cold, straight from the freezer. He said he hoped the beautiful weather would hold … all summer long … he kept repeating it. It was so nice sitting there, face to the sun, eyes shut. And Tonio saying: "I really hope it stays like this."'

I thought back to that brisk spring evening in '69, after the party in Eindhoven, when I brought Marike A., who I had only known a few hours, to the designated spot where her father would fetch us in the car. He wasn't there yet. Shivering, we paced back and forth along the sidewalk, and I kept repeating (because I thought it was what one was supposed to do, and also because I kind of meant it): 'Let's make a great summer of it.'

The girl looked up at me with a pale and frightened little face. She had those big light-grey eyes, really special, but terrified. Not really a stayer.

'Agreed?'

Only then did she nod. Exactly ten years later, she put an end to her life, but that was another story entirely. My first requiem experience.

'Apparently, Tonio didn't know you well enough to know what you like to drink,' Miriam said. 'He'd jammed the fridge full of iced tea and fruit juice. Bottles of soft drinks, too. Stuff we never have in the house. Took us weeks to get through it.'

Jenny laughed. 'Just iced tea would have been fine.'

18

As a teenager, I used to watch the television series *The Long Hot Summer* while doing my homework at the dining room table. My parents sat with their backs to me, unaware that I was closely following the plot, with all its forbidden content. Most of all, I sank into a reverie at the title itself. A *long hot summer* — this was my plan, too, once exams were over. Together with Marike A., who I was still seeing.

I recognised my daydream in the words of Tonio, via Jenny: how, even though it was still just May, he openly yearned for a real summer. I could just hear him say it.

Now I knew what kind of guise a long hot summer could assume: days of tropical temperatures helping you sweat out the grief. This *long hot summer* was mainly an emotionless one, a summer that shut Tonio out and refused to mirror our melancholy.

'I've only seen two Polaroids,' I said, 'but Tonio was satisfied most with the photos he took out here.'

'It's hard to judge on such a tiny screen,' Jenny said. She turned her upper body to take a better look at the garden. Tonio had photographed her here for a whole afternoon. His concentrated gaze must still have been palpable everywhere she looked.

'Would you like to see them?' Miriam asked her. 'There's quite a lot. And of pretty uneven quality. I had them all printed, though, just to be sure. You can make your own selection.'

The girl became very uneasy. 'Later, thanks,' she said.

Understandable, I thought. Although he was out of sight, Tonio was looking directly at her from each photo.

'Later's fine,' Miriam said, undoubtedly thinking of all the trouble she had gone to in collecting the photos.

The conversation flagged. Jenny stared more or less constantly at the little arbour and its white bench. In her hand, she held the empty long drink glass, occasionally bringing it to her lips, but it couldn't have provided much more than a sour droplet from the lemon slice.

'Another gin and tonic, Jenny?'

19

It had been a warm day, but it did not end in a sultry summer evening. As twilight fell, the temperature quickly dropped. Not that there was a breeze to speak of, but little puffs of chill began to rise from the backyard. We sat for a long time in relative silence. Tonio was with us, that was for sure, and each of us sat there grieving for him, but why in God's name didn't we *break down*? Why didn't we crumple onto the veranda floorboards, screaming as we slid off the chair? Wasn't what had happened enough for that? How Jenny dealt with all this, I couldn't rightly say, but Miriam and I — why, for whom or what, were we putting on a brave face?

'Jenny, if you still want that G&T,' Miriam said, 'then I suggest we go inside. It's getting chilly out here.'

'Easy on the gin then,' Jenny answered. 'I'm starting to feel it already.'

We went upstairs; Miriam disappeared into the kitchen. Jenny went into the living room and sat down (without prior knowledge) in Tonio's regular spot. I realised I now had to broach the subject of Paradiso: the date that didn't happen. Once again, I was forced to wonder whether I really wanted to know how fate had taken advantage of the U-turn.

'After the photo session,' I began, when Miriam had returned with the tray, 'Tonio told me he was going to go to a party at Paradiso on Saturday night. With you. That you'd invited him. I understand it was an Italian-themed affair. Italian hits from the eighties. Eros Ramazzotti and so on.'

'Oh, that.' Jenny flicked her hand in a dismissive, somewhat embarrassed, gesture. She took a sip of her gin and tonic, which made the skin on her forehead rumple. I wasn't so sure Miriam had 'gone easy' on the gin. I was well acquainted with her portions.

'In the end,' I continued, 'later that evening, around midnight, Tonio went to a disco called Trouw. With two friends, a boy and a girl. Dennis and Goscha. We've talked to them both. They were with him the whole time, Dennis since that afternoon. You don't figure in either of their stories. They hadn't met you, although, yes, Tonio had mentioned you. That much he did. But neither had heard anything about a date at Paradiso. If you don't want to talk about it, Jenny ... that's perfectly okay. But we'd so very much like to know ...'

'Of course,' Jenny hastened to reply. 'Although I'm still not quite sure why the date fell through. Tonio and I had chatted on Facebook that afternoon. He suggested going dancing at Trouw instead of at Paradiso.

I'd heard of it, a new place in an old printing works. Techno. I told him I'd rather go to a quiet café, where you can at least hear each other. Without all that loud music. Tonio wrote back that he was still pretty beat from the previous night. *Beat*, that's the word he used. He'd been in Terzijde, on the Kerkstraat, with friends until really late, and he was still beat. I think he preferred to dance out his beatness at Trouw rather than go back to another café.'

'I get the picture,' I said, more grimly than I'd intended. 'A quiet café … He couldn't face having to rely only on conversation.'

'That's putting it pretty bluntly,' Miriam said.

'I was the same way at his age,' I said. 'In the noise of the disco, with the distraction of everybody dancing and all, I thought I'd have a better chance with a girl I didn't know so well. I've never seen *more* of myself in Tonio than these past two months.'

'We didn't argue or anything,' Jenny continued. 'It's just that … we didn't see eye to eye about how to spend that Saturday night. So we just left it, and decided we'd get back in touch after the holiday weekend. Also to talk about the photos.' She leaned forward, her forearms resting on her knees, no longer looking at us but at the glass on the coffee table. 'The thing is … I wasn't part of Tonio's circle of friends. None of them knows me. I didn't hear anything. Whit Monday and the Tuesday after that … Tonio didn't answer his phone. Wednesday, still nothing. I saw that his Facebook page had been dormant for days. Not a single visit. I had a funny feeling about it. On top of it, my mother was in Morocco the whole week. I was home alone. I was sick, couldn't keep anything in. Everything I ate came back out, and not just "up". I did talk to my mother on the phone, but I couldn't make it clear to her exactly what was wrong. I didn't know myself. When she got back a week later, and saw the state I was in, she went straight to Google. She found a site where someone had put pictures of Tonio. With an obituary. Then we knew for sure.'

She did not cry, but when I looked more closely I could see her lower eyelashes glisten — as though the moisture belonged there, as part of her make-up. So that was it: the digital quarrel on Facebook had unhinged the plans — and how. So fate, too, made use of social media these days.

20

Jenny sucked down the last drops of her drink and stood up. 'I've overstayed my welcome. I really should be going.'

'But you haven't seen the photos yet,' Miriam said.

'Can it wait till next time?' she said, almost begging. 'Right now it would be too much for me.'

Miriam stood there, holding a large cardboard envelop, bulging almost to the point of bursting. 'You can just take them with you ...'

'Can I leave them here? If you don't mind, we'll make another appointment. I might be able to handle it then.'

'Of course,' Miriam said, 'The modelling agencies can wait ...'

'Oh, that.' Again that dismissive gesture. She took a few tentative steps toward the living-room door, and hesitantly turned to us. 'Would you mind if ... I'd really like to go up to Tonio's room.'

21

'That stupid dilemma I kept talking about,' I said to Miriam. 'Now I know it wasn't a dilemma at all. Whether or not there was something going on between Tonio and this Jenny ... for me, it was bad news either way. Actually, I didn't want to hear either version. I almost didn't show my face this afternoon. Now I know, more from what Jenny *didn't* say than what she *did*, that it did indeed go deeper than just that photo stuff. It's just *that*, I now realise, it was exactly *that* version I didn't want to hear. There *was* no dilemma. If Jenny had told us that as far as she was concerned, it was nothing more than a professional transaction ... something between a model and a photographer ... then I might have felt at most, on Tonio's behalf, slightly snubbed. No last hurrah just before his last farewell. That

408

in itself would have been lonely enough. But *this* … a potential opening nipped in the bud … it's more than I can take.'

Miriam, next to me on the sofa, only nodded. After Jenny left, Miriam refilled our glasses, but we didn't touch the drinks. A few days ago, after Jenny had phoned, I still harboured a secret hope that, contrary to all the dark thoughts, my heart could leap at the news that at least some amorous feelings were at play, mutual ones. I sure missed the mark there: the soft, modest voice of a girl had just formulated our worst nightmare.

The nightmare of what might have been, and what will never be.

'This is one of those moments,' Miriam whispered, 'when it *really* hits me that he's gone. We've lost him.'

22

The morning after Jenny's visit, I went up to my workroom, now looking at it though the eyes of Tonio and Jenny, in the spring light of the twenty-first of May.

'We'll do one last shoot up on the roof,' he might have said. 'You'll have to climb a ladder to get there, though.'

She was rather excited by the idea. He led the way up the stairs. 'This is where my father works.'

Jenny had, so she said, nosed around a bit. The long table was full of newspaper clippings and manuscripts-in-progress. She had asked Tonio about the maps of Amsterdam and Amstelveen and Valkenburg, which lay unfolded in a row on the table. 'What have these got to do with his work?'

I could imagine their voices in complete clarity.

'All I know,' Tonio replied, 'is that he's working on a novel about the murder of a police officer. True story — it happened a couple of years ago in Amstelveen. I guess he's plotting out routes on those maps or something … See, here's the ladder.'

He showed Jenny an aluminium ladder attached to the side wall of the balcony, and leading to the flat roof.

'I'll have to raise the awning first.'

After Tonio flipped the electric switch, to the left of the balcony doors, the awning hummed upward. 'Funny.' He nodded at a pile of wooden planks against the balcony railing. 'Pieces of my old bunk bed.'

'You slept in a moss-covered bunk bed?' Jenny asked.

'When I took it apart, because I decided it was time to sleep in a real bed, the slats were still natural wood. And varnished. Just look at 'em now. Gone all green from the rain. Dunno why my father leaves them … Okay, now we can go up. You first?'

'No, you go ahead. Those rungs are pretty far apart.'

Laden with equipment, Tonio climbed the ladder.

The photos he had taken up on the roof were the only ones he was dissatisfied with. Jenny said the surrounding rooftops, with the occasional terrace, didn't offer much of a backdrop. Soon enough, they went back down — to Tonio's old room, where the bunk bed had once stood, at times with Merel in it.

23

I couldn't stop myself. Just as on Whit Monday (but now better informed), I kept retracing Tonio and Jenny's route through the house. From the backyard to the living room on the first floor, and from there to his old room on the second — and then another flight up to my workroom.

The styrofoam light reflector, still propped in the corner of the living room, indicated where Tonio had photographed her: right next to the glass display case with his rock collection. No matter how hard I sniffed, the used-ashtray smell had disappeared. The first time I nosed around, that Thursday after we got back from the Amsterdamse Bos, I had concluded to Miriam: 'She's a smoker.'

Now I knew it was Tonio. Again I regretted not encouraging him to come clean about his smoking habit. There had been a nicotine smell in his old room that afternoon as well.

For the umpteenth time, I circled my long sorting table, repeating Jenny's questions and Tonio's answers.

'I don't see a computer.'

'Don't get me started ... my father's so stubborn. He's got, like, three antique electric typewriters. See that empty desk there? Twice there was a beaut of an Apple ... all the bells and whistles ... never used it. The first one, it was when I was still living at home, I slowly but surely smuggled it to my room. The second one's now in my mother's study. You see that thing? An old-fashioned photocopier. If he's not satisfied with the order of a text on a sheet of paper, he snips it into strips. Then he lays them in another order on the glass plate, and ... how inefficient is *that*? I've explained to him, I don't know how many times, that it's so much easier on a computer ... without scissors and copy machine. I'd offer to teach him. He paid me — twice! — for the computer-lesson fees we'd agreed on. And every time he gave up after a few pointers. "I'm attached to my old stuff," he'd say. "Just let me tinker." An impossible man.'

'And the lesson money?'

'I kept it, of course,' Tonio said. '*I* wasn't the one who dropped out.'

The balcony doors. I turned on the electric motor that lowers the awning, for the sole reason of raising it once again and thus freeing up the aluminium ladder.

The dismantled bunk bed. I assumed its mystery remained in his mind for a few days. (He did not ask about it that afternoon — undoubtedly to cover up the fact that he'd been in my workroom.) A moss-covered child-sized bunk bed. Here he rose, via a fire ladder, above his earliest youth, with a pretty girl following him. He was going to take photos of her on the roof. Through various camera eyes, he could examine her with impunity.

Even though my dodgy back really couldn't take it, I climbed up the too-widely spaced rungs. I imagined that, while Jenny was on her way up, emitting feigned squeals of trepidation, Tonio was studying the surroundings with the eye of a professional. Near him, the glass-enclosed stairwell belonging to neighbour Kluun, leading to a future roof terrace. No, that had to stay out of view. He wanted the expanse of the urban horizon as a backdrop to Jenny.

Tonio walked to the edge of the roof, as close as he dared. The Obrechtkerk with its twin spires, like a slightly stumpy cathedral, might be an interesting decor. But he couldn't get her to stand close enough to the edge.

'I've got vertigo.' For the first time that afternoon, her voice had a slight squeak to it.

Tonio looked out over the jagged stone labyrinth, the grooves filled in, here and there, with cloudlike greenery. He could still see the Rijksmuseum, with its red façade, as simply a backdrop for a photo shoot. For me, the building was now a beacon that announced: *Here, in my shadow, at my feet, a few days after that photo session, Tonio perished.*

24

I went back down the fire ladder and closed the balcony doors, but instead of going downstairs I stayed in my room, shuffling aimlessly about. The material for the work-in-progress was bundled neatly in Leitz ring-binders on top of the filing cabinets. I pulled one or two out at random and thumbed through them. Everything I read crumbled before my eyes. Even the act of putting the thing back in place was in fact no longer worth the effort.

When we moved into this house, the third floor had been divided into three rooms: two boys' rooms (one with corner bar) and a cork-padded maid's room. In '97, I had everything torn out, leaving behind a large L-shaped room. Once the builders had left, I stood speechless on the gleaming parquet floor, while Tonio, letting out little bursts of cheerful laughter, wove around me, his arms spread into aeroplane wings. I had always dreamt of having a workroom like this, and he knew it.

I inspected the dozens of locks on the filing cabinets and drawers. A key stuck out of each lock, its duplicate dangling from the ring threaded through its eye, swaying gently in the breeze that Tonio had created.

'How am I going to tell all these keys apart?' I said more or less to myself.

'I know,' Tonio cried. He ran down two flights of stairs, and then all went quiet. I stood out on the landing, listening. From the kitchen came the sudden sound of clinking bottles. Then the fridge door closed. Tonio came charging back up the stairs carrying several sheets of self-adhesive mini-stickers in various colours — the kind you stick on freezer food items, with the date. Like lightning he began sticking labels on the keys, spares, and locks to the filing cabinets, after notating a numeric code per lock. Yellow, green, red, blue … He carried out his operation laughing, with a vague undertone of scorn, because his father hadn't come up with the idea.

'There, Adri. See?' He was already finished. 'Easy-peasy.'

Now, thirteen years later, the freezer stickers, numbered in his handwriting, were still attached to those locks and keys. I made good use of them, especially when I was travelling — no one, after all, needed access to those cabinets during my absence. I walked along the cabinets, flicked the dangling spare keys with my index finger, and chided myself grimly that Tonio's labelling of the locks was the only meaningful work that had been carried out on this floor since its renovation.

25

In Louis van Gasteren's documentary film *Hans, het leven voor de dood*, there is a scene with Hans van Sweeden's mother. When she received the news of her son's suicide, her first reaction, she said, was: 'My child is dead … now no flowers will ever bloom again.'

I recognise that expression of heartbreak. But in my case, this deathliness refers to the past as well. Wherever I look on the life that lies behind me, I see only failure and futility. Every attempt to achieve anything, no matter what, can in retrospect count on my disdain and disgust. Everything, every action, was, after all, a direct or indirect rehearsal for my greatest failure ever: the accidental death of my son, which I was unable to prevent.

I look back on my past, and what I perceive is not the necessary passage of time; no, I see only a needless waste of time. A pointless botching of days and months and years.

I suspect that I am doing opponents of my work no greater favour, but I confess that since Black Whitsun, no single book of mine (including this one) will enjoy a whit of mercy in my own eyes. I once defended my work with the ferocity of a lion. Now I throw it all to the lions. Whatever I have produced and undertaken is, in retrospect, besmirched by the loss that gapes at the end of it. Tonio was one of my foremost reasons for writing, even for the many years before his birth, because I already had more than a portent of him. I knew he would come, and what he would mean to me, and I prepared myself thoroughly for his coming.

He came, and then vanished, and now everything with which I aimed to give him a full-fledged life is tarnished and sullied. His untimely death is proof that I have gone about things the wrong way, with too little commitment, and that I overlooked important matters. For Harry Mulisch, if a writer is hit by a meteor as he stands waiting at a tram stop for line 2, that's proof he has no talent. I have allowed my son to be struck in the dead of night by a similar projectile — precisely what I had been trying, with all my written efforts, to prevent.

Ergo: no talent.

26

Tonio's father was a writer. As a youngster growing up, Tonio couldn't grasp the blatant revulsion, even hate, that this could evoke. Once, at a school party — he had proudly put on his best sports jacket for the affair

414

— he was actively shunned. A few of the girls who he had bravely asked to dance said: 'I'm not dancing with you, sicko.'

It looked as though it had been a deliberate plan. A small-scale conspiracy. When he got home, he put on a brave face: oh yeah, great party. But his friend Alexander spilled the beans: 'It wasn't so great for Tonio. No one would dance with him. The girls called him a sicko.'

Then it all came out. I dare to use the cliché that my heart bled for him, at the thought of the smartly dressed Tonio, complete with burgundy bow tie, being rebuffed: 'No, sicko, not with you.'

Further questioning revealed that it probably had something to do with the recent broadcast of a literary talk show, in which an intellectual lady, a Romanist, had spat out the words 'intensely disgusting' to describe my latest work. I hadn't even followed the broadcast, but the 'intensely disgusting' epithet that had adhered to Tonio's father had somehow made the rounds of the Dutch Notables and their brood at the Cornelis Free School.

A few years later, in late August 2000, Tonio sat next to me at a bookstall at the Uitmarkt, held that year along the Amstel. That fall he would start at the gymnasium, but he still liked the ritual of appending his own name to his father's signed books. He now wore lightweight glasses and had cut his hair short, so he looked younger and more vulnerable than a few months earlier at his graduation from the Cornelis Free. He appeared timidly aware of the significant leap forward that was expected of him — even with the lump behind his cheek from the lollipops the publisher had fed him at regular intervals.

At her request, I had set up my portion of the booth as though it were a corner of my workroom at home. With Tonio's help, I had even put together a few fake manuscripts, drawing on my supply of misleadingly yellowed counterfeiters' paper. We tied the bundles up with string, putting the titles of *Homo duplex*, a cyclical novel-in-process, on the flyleaves. Tonio enjoyed it more than I did. I completed the decor with old inkpots and other writing implements among the nonchalantly placed 'manuscripts'. Those afternoon signing sessions at the Uitmarkt always terrified me: author on folding chair in a bookstall, waiting for that one client. Regardless of your demeanour, you always felt that it came across as slightly desperate.

On the sheets of yellowed paper, I wrote out aphorisms from the work-in-progress, and added to them mysterious Chinese stamps — well, you had to do *something*. Tonio, ever good-natured, smilingly helped me stamp and hand out material.

When, later that afternoon, things quieted down some, I noticed a small group of young men nearby. They had been loitering there for some time, but only now did I sense their hateful glances cast in my direction. There was clearly something that irked them. Finally, one of them approached the stall. He stuck his fingers under the string holding the blank manuscripts together, and started slamming the packs of paper onto the tabletop, without a word, but with a constant, fierce anger in his eyes. Tonio got such a shock that he recoiled, chair and all. It was most of all the loud bang of the 'manuscripts' being slammed onto the wooden trestle table that was so intimidating, combined with the boy's silent rage.

Now I think: a band of aspiring writers wanting to unmask me. But still, Tonio was quaking in his boots.

'Why'd he *do* that?'

It was probably the last time I'd seen his lower lip tremble. And the last time he joined me at a book signing — but that also had to do with school and age.

27

Tonio, because of you I've lost everything. My life. The thought of having you at my deathbed. Worldly goods were for your benefit. Since there is no longer any reason to strive for them, I shall lose them. (I will try to salvage this house, because your mother is so attached to it. She was, after all, born in this neighbourhood.)

My goals, my work, my attempts at maintaining something resembling a personality … my whole world has drained into your grave. Melted snow, and Tonio is the sun.

As a beginning writer, I pretended to live recklessly beyond my means, grazing the edge of bankruptcy, in order to force myself in to productivity. *Het bankroet dat mijn goudmijn is* [*It broke my goldmine*] was the title of a bibliophilic booklet I later published. That bankruptcy has now arrived, with your demise, and now that it's here, it has proved hardly a goldmine: it is barren and infertile. I *was* rich. You were the capital of my existence. I hadn't even taken out life insurance on you, certain as I was it would never have to be cashed in. Or perhaps my superstition couldn't bear the monthly premiums …

All that I've gained from your disappearance is freedom — of a dubious kind, to be sure. I am now free of responsibility. No one has to remind me of old, unfulfilled promises. They were all made null and void on Black Whitsun. Ever since those two angels of disaster from the Amsterdam police appeared on my front stoop that twenty-third of May, I laugh at every summons-server.

I feel free to spend what is left of my life exactly as I please. If I do not succumb entirely to idleness and torpor, it's because I want to continue caring for your mother. It is the only responsibility I still accept, also on behalf of her son.

28

So, with Tonio's death, my life has demonstrated its uselessness. By dying, he has carelessly cast off his father like a cloak. The one thing I am still good for, by way of ritualistic and associative writing, is to preserve as much of his life as possible. I am almost obsessive in the composition of my requiem for him, about him. His brief, beautiful life must not simply sink into oblivion, just like his beautiful, broken body has sunk into the earth.

And after this? Tonio was, as I have said, my most compelling reason to write, even before he was born. A muse of the masculine sort. In recent years, I have noticed wanting to show him what I was worth, in the hope that he would want to show me what he *was* worth.

One of the last things he said to me, a few days before his death, was, with that endearing, slightly mocking smile: 'So, up to your ten pages a day yet?'

Less recently, he told me, recalling from when he was twelve and was about to begin high school, that I had predicted (or, rather, promised) I'd have *Homo duplex* finished before he graduated.

So I still have a lot to show him.

The next moment, I sweep aside these ambitions as redundant.

Now I am an orphan *and* childless. As that quarrel with Miriam confirmed, I am not the type — as many of my dissatisfied contemporaries are — to want to start on a second brood. I will have to die, when the time comes, without living descendants. And considering that literary works are unlikely to outlive their maker these days — the maker himself might even outlive *them* — one can conclude that when I reach the end of this journey, all I can expect to see is a gaping oblivion.

29

Tonio's demise has, more for Miriam than for me, brought a lot of life's issues into focus. Sometimes I notice in her an absoluteness that scares me.

Miriam was a daddy's girl. As I've said, as a youngster she frequently locked horns with her mother, but at that age possessed the gift of blissful withdrawal. The cramped quarters of her room were in no way an impediment: more than into her physical space, she retreated into herself.

Just *how* bad her relationship with her mother was, I only realised when I read an account, in novella form, that Miriam had written about her youth. Her mother had already suffered numerous nervous breakdowns and had threatened suicide, but only after she ended up in the Valerius

Clinic did her younger daughter's rage erupt. Miriam was no longer able to be in the same room as her mother and remain calm. Going for a spin in the car with her became a risky undertaking, even for a confident driver like Miriam.

Now that, with Tonio's death, the family bonds are dissolving faster than ever, I tried to salvage whatever I could by phoning my mother-in-law at St. Vitus, the old-age home where she returned after her hospitalisation — even though I knew it would only depress me even more.

'Will you two pull through … are you there for each other? No, will you *pull through* … I'm asking: will you *pull through*? Oh, as long as you're there for each other.'

I repeat, a second and a third time, that we will more or less pull through, and that we really are there for each other, but that we have to get through this strictly on our own. No third parties, for God's sake. Sooner or later, she brings up her own imminent death, or at least the yearning for it.

'I don't want to live anymore. I hope the end is near. I want to go to Tonio … I want to be with Tonio.'

What she probably wants is for me to scold her, and say that we need her, now more than ever. I can't summon up the energy, and say: 'Yes, Wies, I understand.'

'They say here that I have keep on living for you two. I've already told them … no more medicine, no more food, no more water … but they won't, not without a reason. Even though I don't want to go on … I want to die. I want to go to Tonio, that sweet Tonio. He's here. I feel him. I talk to him.'

I feel genuinely sorry for her. I don't doubt the sincerity of her grief. But Wies, could you just — please! please! — take into consideration the period of mourning your daughter has to go through? Do you appreciate how unbearable this is for her, all your death announcements, while she's not even by a long shot worked through that one death announcement from Whit Sunday?

I'm too chicken and too broken to say that to her.

'How is Miriam, anyway … Oh, I realise she doesn't want any contact with me right now. I really do understand. But I *so* hope to see the two of you again. Later … later.'

She asks me to pass on her greetings to her daughter, but that's just the problem. She assumes that I'm going to tell Miriam I've spoken to her, but then I have to relate all of her mother's death wishes, and, really, that's the last thing she wants to hear.

'Could you give me your number?' Wies asks at the end of the conversation, not for the first time. 'Only in case of an emergency. I won't abuse it.'

I promise her, also not for the first time, to send a card with the number, in the hope that my promise, and preferably her request as well, will have been forgotten by the next time I ring. I still remember her previous attacks of phonesickness, and that we had to change the number several times.

Well, just for emergencies — I believe her — all right already, it would be heartless to keep her emergency exit locked. After we hang up, I write my mobile-phone number on a card, addressed to St. Vitus.

Two days later, it starts. At first I don't recognise her number on the caller ID screen, so I don't answer; but, sure enough, it's my mother-in-law on the voicemail. It is a nearly literal repetition of all our earlier telephone conversations. More messages containing sighs, advice, and demands follow, all of them true to form. I don't return the calls, nor does she ask me to.

One Monday morning, just as I'm starting work, my mobile phone rings. It's the voicemail; Wies's voice, bossy as in her heyday: 'Will you call me back …' No question mark. An order. It does not sound like an emergency, more like matter-of-fact abuse.

Miriam's voicemail, too, is overflowing with messages from her mother. Wies pursues her daughter by all possible means, via her mobile and her landline work number. Within a few days, we all — Miriam, Hinde and I — have new phone numbers. Peace and quiet.

30

I applied the pain management a bit too rigorously tonight. At two-thirty in the morning, I awoke on the living-room sofa, sitting upright, my hand tightly screwed to a whisky glass filled with vodka, and the ice all melted. Miriam had gone up hours earlier.

I drag myself up the stairs. The door to Tonio's old room is ajar. Light falls through the door opening, clearly not from a regular bulb — it's too white and cold for that. Back in 2008, Tonio left his hide-a-bed (once intended for overnight guests) behind, which Miriam has since used to escape from my snoring or the hiss of my CPAP machine.

I stand on the landing, holding my breath, and listen. The cats, curious, emerge from the room. They sit in front of the half-open door. The light behind them seems like the dawn light that pours into the room through the open curtains. But that can't be — it's half past two in the morning.

I push the door open a bit and look around the corner: Tonio's dismantled room, where Miriam plans to move her study, furnished as much as possible with his things once they've been moved here from De Baarsjes. She has already installed her new computer on a writing desk. The wide-screen monitor bathes the room in a cold, numbing light. Miriam lies on the bed, the comforter pulled up to her navel. She lies as she seldom does: on her back, with her sumptuous dark hair fanning out over the pillow.

My eyes returns to the computer monitor, where I see a blue block and some text in white letters. I cannot read it from here. Surrounding the blue block is a pearl-grey area, the source of the deathly light. Words jostle each other in my head, until just one ghoulish term remains: FAREWELL NOTE.

The cats have slid noiselessly back into the room, and now stand in a symmetrical pose in front of the bed, glaring at me. I take a few steps back to the landing, where I stand trembling as I stare at the half-open door — until the light in the room goes off by itself. I find my own bed, where for the rest of the night I do not get a single moment of shuteye.

Like every morning, Miriam brings me breakfast at around eight-thirty. I tell her I saw a light in her room at a quarter to three.

'Oh? Didn't notice. The cats do that. At night they traipse over the keyboard, which can make the screen jump on. I sleep right through it.'

> O paradox! Black is the badge of hell,
> The hue of dungeons and the school of night.

Generations of scholars have racked their brains over these lines from Shakespeare's *Love's Labour's Lost*. What could the 'school of night' be? I'm no Shakespeare analyst, but thanks to all those nights that have passed since Black Whitsun, I think I do have an inkling. From what I have learned in these past months of night school — I wish I could reflect even a fraction of it in this requiem.

31

Yesterday, Hinde checked the voicemail on her new mobile number. There was a message from St. Vitus. A staff member informed her: 'Eh … well, it's like this … this afternoon your mother tried to … jump in front of a car, to, you know … Some passers-by managed to restrain her. They took her to the police station, and the police brought her back to us. Judging from her condition, we're considering taking her back to the Valerius Clinic. Could you give us a call to discuss the situation?'

Aside from upset, Hinde was, of course, livid. You don't go and plop that kind of message onto someone's voicemail — you ask them to ring you back, adding, if need be, 'It's urgent.'

Yesterday evening, Miriam came home with the mobile phone at her ear, listening to a voicemail message. 'That was Hinde … wants me to call her back. She sounded pretty down. I hope it's not about my mother.'

Miriam called her sister. I kept an eye on her face, which was as tense as could be. 'Oh no!' she cried, after listening for a bit. I could hear Hinde's unamplified voice, but couldn't make out what she was saying. I knew there was indeed something seriously wrong.

The previous evening, Miriam had gone inside with her father after bringing him home from Beth Shalom. He complained that he'd been rung a few times by his ex-wife — something she had never done, except anonymously, in the seventeen years since the divorce. She insisted ('It's an emergency') he give her Hinde's new mobile-phone number, which had just been changed, along with Miriam's and mine. Natan, taken completely by surprise, did not see through her ruse quickly enough, and gave her the number.

While Miriam was in the living room with her father, the telephone rang again. 'Let me,' she said. And, sure enough, it was Wies, who was shocked to get her other daughter on the line.

'So you visit Papa,' was her first reaction, 'and not me ...'

'Think about it,' Miriam said.

'And you won't phone me either?'

'Nope.'

'Then I'd rather be dead. Do you hear me? I'd rather be dead.'

'You ... you fling death wishes and death threats as though ... as though it's Sinterklaas candy. Don't you realise, woman, that you're just crying wolf? Every time you get Adri on the phone, you want to die ... the sooner the better ... and he's supposed to relay the message to me. It's the middle of August, Tonio hasn't been dead even three months, and you announce you're thinking about passive euthanasia. Pining away, whatever. Do you ever just once think about *me*? My son got ploughed over in the middle of the street, okay? I'm trying not to let it ruin me. And you ... you just bulldoze your way through my grief with your disgusting death wish. Leave me in peace. You've never cared about me.'

At that point, the receiver went down on the old-fashioned telephone.

My mother-in-law escaped from St. Vitus yesterday afternoon. She ran to the nearby Nassaukade, where she tried to throw herself under a moving car. Passers-by held her back. Hinde did not know whether she tried to wrestle loose from their grip, or if she went calmly with them to police headquarters, which is nearby. She also did not know if the police had made an official report of the incident. All she knew was that they brought Wies back to the old-age home.

Miriam was dejected after that phone call. She didn't say much. I could tell she was furious. Miriam had relived the terrible accident that had cost Tonio his life thousands of times in the past three months. And now her mother had decided to go the same way: to throw herself under the wheels of a passing car, in order to, God only knows, find the secret passage to Tonio. Hundreds of times she had moaned on the telephone that she had no need to live, that she wanted to die, and that she wanted to join Tonio — and still her suicide attempt felt like a knife in the back.

'It's like one of those copycat crimes,' I said.

'She's trying to punish me,' Miriam said quietly. 'She knows exactly where she can hurt me the most.'

32

I only went downstairs after I heard the moving van drive off. From the second-floor landing, I could see Tonio's furniture spread randomly throughout his old room. Boxes with smaller belongings were stacked in the downstairs hall. Miriam looked woebegone.

'Less than I'd expected, fortunately,' she said.

'Any sign of the watch?' I asked.

She shook her head. The thought crossed my mind that maybe he had been negligent with it, or had taken it to a pawn shop. After all, two weeks before the accident we'd promised him a new one (owed to him ever since his final exams, along with the cost of driving lessons). Tonio was chronically short of cash. On the other hand ... material objects, especially gifts from a loved one, had a sentimental value — he wouldn't just go and pawn them off.

'Let's just say, shall we,' I said, 'that it got lost during the accident.'

I thought back with shame on the LP records my mother had gone to a great deal of trouble to get me for Christmas, and which I unloaded for far under their value because I thought my turntable arm had ground an unpleasant hum into them. If that wasn't negligence, then I don't know what was.

I had recently discovered so many parallels between his student days and my own, thirty-five, forty years ago, that the pawn shop was not entirely out of the question.

33

At long last, before the apartment on the Nepveustraat was turned back over to the diddler who had sublet it to the boys, someone found Tonio's watch on top of the dividing wall between the shower and toilet. The wristband was broken. The watch itself was still set to standard winter time. Daylight saving time started at the end of March. In our ongoing reconstruction fever, we concluded that the band had broken at least two months before Tonio's accident. He had probably noticed the watch hanging loosely on his wrist during a visit to the toilet or shower, and had put it up on the divider to free up his hands. It lay there unused for five months, or longer, passively extending winter time.

'The idea that half-asleep or in a drunken stupor, who knows, he left it lying there ...' I said to Miriam, 'and forgot where he'd put it ...'

'That does shed new light on the purchase of that new watch,' she replied. 'Who knows how bad he felt about it.'

'Well, we never got around to it.'

'He was too *beat*.'

Miriam had the watch meticulously repaired, shortening the wristband to fit her own arm, which is (was) far more slender than her son's. Since picking it up from the jeweller, she wears that watch — with its extra-masculine look, thanks to the little buttons on either side of the twistable outer dial — constantly, day and night.

CHAPTER SIX

Nourishing hunger

1

Shortly after she cleared out Tonio's flat in De Baarsjes, Miriam refurnished his old room in our house with all his original things. For days, I dared not enter the room, but when I once unthinkingly went in, I was struck by his good taste — pricey without being lavish.

Even the oversized train-station clock, which he himself had gotten the biggest kick out of, was back.

Two weeks after Whit Sunday, the photographer Klaas Koppe brought round an envelope full of blow-ups in which Tonio happened to feature, such as a few taken at a recent Book Ball: Tonio with his parents, Tonio with Klaas's daughter Iris. Miriam framed them at once, and hung them in a much-used curve in the stairwell. Not long thereafter, she came in, teary-eyed, to say she'd packed up the photos and replaced them by less-recent ones. Later, I discovered a paper bag on the landing with the framed photos. I pulled one out (Tonio and Iris) — and took a blow to the gut, which then nearly got wrung out. Tonio had not been so tangibly present since his visit on 20 May. I quickly slid it back into the bag — which is still there, propped in the same corner.

In the midst of Tonio's completely reconstructed teen bedroom, Miriam still *does* manage to breathe. She sits there all day long at the computer, with Tonio's laptop within reach. When I want to talk to her,

I tend to stay out on the landing, and conduct the conversation through the half-open door.

2

Miriam gets up at 5.00 a.m. every day to go to work in Tonio's room. Around nine, as I lie reading the paper in the next room, she brings breakfast. We eat and talk, side by side, propped up against the pillows. Radio 4 is on.

This morning, she came into the bedroom without the breakfast tray. A light slap on my legs told me to scoot over, so she could sit on the edge of the bed. She was not crying, but her face was taut.

'Able to get anything done?' I asked.

'I was suddenly so afraid of losing you, too,' she said testily. 'And there I'd be, mourning Tonio all on my own.'

Then the tears came. When there was no other way out, I took refuge in literature.

'The end of *The Trial* … remember, Minchen? That Josef K. believes the shame will outlive him? Well, my grief for Tonio will long outlive me. I don't know how long *you* think you'll outlive me, but you'll always be able to share your grief with me … until your last breath … it's strong enough for that. Even after I'm dead.'

'I didn't mean I think you'll die soon.'

'That I'd start on a second brood after all, is that it?'

'Y'know … just the plain fact that I could end up alone, and be the only one who …'

'Minchen, there's no morgue tag hanging from my big toe yet, nor is there a guarantee for longevity. There's no tag hanging on your big toe either. Let's take it day by day. Together. Let's do our best to guard each other against sickness. If that's asking too much, then let's at least try not to *make* each other sick. Or crazy.'

3

When Rimbaud wrote *Une saison en enfer* (*A Season in Hell*) at his parents' home, after his disastrous sojourn in Paris, his sister listened at the door of his room, behind which she could hear his anguished sobbing. As a seventeen-year-old with writer's itch, this intrigued me no end: the concept that reliving, in poetry, one's own experiences could have such a powerful effect on one's disposition. I should from now on mistrust every word by my own hand that is not well-nigh illegible from grief and melancholia.

Since I have started working on this requiem, Miriam complains (her computer being situated directly below my writing table) of sudden bursts of noise above her head. She says I regularly slam my chair backwards, curse loudly, then stomp to and fro, at times ranting unintelligibly.

I am not, at age fifty-eight, going to hide behind poetic torment, but while I am not always conscious of my blasphemous work interruptions, I have to admit she's right. When Tonio used to do his homework in the very spot she now occupies, he never complained of falling plaster dust fluttering onto his computer. Except once, when he proudly and amusedly announced during dinner: 'This afternoon, all of a sudden, I heard you start cursing and throwing things.'

I would give anything to know what possessed me, with my small family still intact, that afternoon. Maybe I realised, in an unbearably lucid moment, how fragile we were, the three of us, and that our bliss could fall to pieces without warning. It could have led to the paroxysm of impotent rage to which Tonio, a floor below, was an acoustic witness.

Ach, of course not — this would be too pat. I probably quaked with anger in search of a word balanced on the tip of my pen, suddenly blown away by the switching on of a leaf-blower out on the street. Some such thing.

4

'There will always be a *before* and an *after*,' one condoloncer wrote. As the months tick on, I appreciate each day how true those words are. A deep scar has been drawn straight through my life. 'Before', my existence was worthwhile; 'after', it is worthless — I can't put it any more simply than that.

I will probably continue to write, and if I do indeed find the strength to do so, I will give it my all, for otherwise there's no point. But actually *believing* in the craft, as when I was Tonio's protector and breadwinner — that is a thing of the past.

In my darkest moments, I am even capable of thinking that a bit more professional effort on my part might have saved Tonio — even though I realise at once that greater concentration on my work during his life would have meant less attention for him. So there you are: the sombre surges of my constricted brooding.

5

The *letselschadeadvocaat* on the Tesselschadestraat (this phrase is begging for a limerick)* had managed to get his hands on the Serious Traffic Accidents Unit dossier, including the CD-ROM with images of the collision recorded by the Holland Casino's CCTV camera. The public prosecutor handling the case offered to meet with us.

Forensic measurements, police officers at the accidents unit had told us earlier, confirmed that the driver of the Suzuki had been driving 'a bit too fast', and that Tonio had drunk 'a considerable amount'. According to the files obtained by the personal-injury lawyer, the Suzuki was going between 67 and 69 kilometres per hour in a 50 kph zone. Blood tests showed that Tonio had 0.94 mg/ml of alcohol in his body, corresponding

---

* A *letselschadeadvocaat* is a personal-injury lawyer

to six or seven beers. (For motorists, the limit is 0.5 mg/ml, the equivalent of three beers.)

'Six beers,' said the personal-injury lawyer. 'Not much, in fact. That's how an evening usually *starts*.'

I was surprised by the results. All this time I'd told myself, grudgingly, that Tonio must have been pretty drunk. After all, he and Dennis had been at a party in the Vondelpark that afternoon, and after that they'd had a few beers at Goscha's place. At about midnight they rode off to Trouw, where, Goscha had said, the rounds 'kept coming'. In recounting the evening, she regretted that Tonio was always a step ahead of her, picking up the entire tab. Dennis said that Tonio had had a shot of tequila between beers. So how could all that drinking result in a blood-alcohol content equivalent to just six beers?

'Don't forget,' the lawyer reminded us, 'that the accident occurred at 4.40 a.m. The alcohol from that afternoon and evening was long out of his system by then. And don't overestimate the rounds at a club like Trouw. At that hour, the place is jam-packed — the bar, too — so buying rounds wouldn't have been a speedy affair. If there had been six of them, and Tonio got them all, he'd have been awfully busy. Six times three is eighteen ... work that out at nightclub prices. I do understand that Goscha felt guilty, and that at the end of the evening Tonio only had five euros on him. Let's say that he'd long burned off the beer from that afternoon and evening, that he biked off into the night with five, six beers and a tequila in him. Then he'd have been a little tipsy at most, but certainly not drunk.'

Miriam went with the lawyer to the public prosecutor's office on the Parnassusweg. They were told that it was up to us whether to sue the driver for involuntary manslaughter as a result of reckless driving. The man would certainly be fined for speeding — nearly twenty km above the speed limit. Miriam, speaking for both of us, did not want to prosecute. She did want to know, however, whether the police had dissuaded the driver from seeking contact with us, or whether he himself had taken the initiative (to do so or not).

As far as the cause of the accident was concerned, the prosecutor's view was that both parties were guilty. Neither bicyclist nor driver was paying attention at the moment it happened. Tonio should have yielded to the car. The driver could have been chatting to his passenger and had perhaps glanced the other way. He was on his way home from a job at a café, but had not been drinking.

In the past weeks, I have often told myself that Tonio was a clumsy cyclist; that, when he was a youngster, I should have taught him better. This was my daily routine, day in day out: fattening up my guilty conscience. That notion of careless cycling was contradicted by the memory of Tonio on his bike, about two years ago (he had just gone to live in De Baarsjes). I was sitting outside at Café De Joffers, right near the intersection of Willemsparkweg and Cornelis Schuytstraat. Suddenly, I saw his orange granny bike swerve onto the Cornelis Schuyt from the Willemsparkweg. Leaning languidly back, pinkies on the handlebars, he meandered entirely at ease between the backed-up, honking cars — quite elegant, actually, as though city traffic were his natural habitat.

He cut up onto the sidewalk across the street from Joffers, raising his backside to take the curb. I'm sure I saw Tonio park his bike in front of Van Dam's bistro and go inside. I paid hastily and rushed across the street to 'catch' him red-handed. In the bistro: no Tonio. In the bike rack: no orange bicycle.

Maybe there were no tables at Van Dam, and he had continued on to our house. Against our front wall: no orange bike, nor had Miriam seen him inside.

Had I imagined it all? No, when I spoke to him some time later, it seemed I had not. A reckless ride through the Cornelis Schuyt and among the idling cars? This and that day? Could be, but he hadn't been inside Van Dam. 'What on earth would I be doing at Van Dam?' Oh yes, of course, he had nipped into Mulder's bookshop, a couple of doors down from Van Dam, to buy a photography magazine, and in order to avoid the traffic jam he continued on his way via the sidewalk. His destination was not his parents' house, but somewhere else — he couldn't remember where or for what.

I drummed it into my head that whenever I thought of Tonio as a clumsy cyclist, I should try to see him as I did that day on the Cornelis Schuytstraat, with his elegantly reckless cycling style. And this is how he, in the wee hours, had shot out of the Hobbemastraat, heading for — yes, heading for what? For something that justified, at such a late hour, his purposefulness.

6

I do not believe in a soul that is released from a body after death, and subsequently lives on in some rarefied way. There are those who, after a significant loss, see the light, and convert to one religion or another. As much as I would like to believe in the presence, somewhere, of Tonio's soul, it is not enough: I want evidence that his soul exists, so that my words do not fall on deaf ears. I would so very much like to inform him of my anger: that he has not been allowed to go on with his life.

'To tell you the truth, Tonio, I'm pissed off at the whole world. For me, it's been one huge conspiracy against your future. My anger is all-pervasive. Your mother's rage is purer. She does not blame anybody in particular. She is just livid on your behalf, because you no longer have the means to express your indignation at the brazen theft of the years you still had ahead of you.'

Show me that his soul is still there somewhere, and I will lay bare my still-living heart to him: my shame for his death, my complicity therein, my shortcomings during his life.

His soul need not respond to my unburdenings, as long as I know it's *there*, as a listening or otherwise registering substance, if need be as a cosmic black hole from which not even a faint echo of my confessions will ever return.

'The few times anyone has had the nerve to ask me these past few weeks if I was working on something, I have answered: "A requiem about Tonio." Should have been: "*for* Tonio." I write it first and foremost for you. No, not for the serenity of your soul. I *hope* in fact to attract your soul's attention. I want to rile it. Via your soul, I want to you to know that we have adopted the pain you endured for half a day. "Rest in peace": nothing doing. We are united in that pain. You, Miriam, and me. And should souls exist — ours, too — then, when we die, we'll be united for eternity.'

7

Come on, Tonio, be honest: didn't it bother you that instead of cycling back the De Baarsjes with you, Goscha chose to stay behind and keep Dennis company? You didn't *have* to leave alone. You were also invited to hang out at Dennis's. You usually didn't turn down an invitation to extend the festivities.

Or did you have the feeling that Dennis and Goscha would have preferred to be alone together, and insisted you stay only out of politeness? Maybe there had been signs earlier that night that something was brewing between them … Did you feel like a fifth wheel? Did you want to be discreet, and let Dennis and Goscha have the rest of the night to themselves?

Jim, who wasn't in bed yet, said you had promised to be home by about four o'clock to keep him company. Dennis and Goscha told us something about you guys watching a movie, even at that late hour. Goscha, who was the most tipsy of the three of you, wasn't sure: 'Maybe he was just too tired, and wanted to go to bed. We did put away a lot that night.'

She told us that she'd fallen asleep 'pretty much right away' once inside Dennis's house. She thought that Dennis, perhaps because of that, was angry with her afterward.

The three of you stood there for a bit, bikes between your legs, on the corner of Sarphatipark, just near the intersection of the Ceintuurbaan and Van der Helststraat. In the seven years that I lived on the Van Ostadestraat, I walked past this corner nearly every day, in total many

433

hundreds of times. I imagine you standing at the spot where, before I had my own line, my regular phone-booth stood, where I took care of business and appointments. Here, one Saturday in the spring of '78, I had desperately called every medical emergency service in the city, reaping only answering machines, while the first droplets of bright-red blood dripped out of my pant leg onto the granite floor of the phone booth: a case of an unstaunchably torn foreskin.

What did you all talk about, with the beat of the Trouw DJ still banging in your ears? I hear your laugh waft across the quiet intersection, but cannot make out what you're saying, except for a quasi-indignant: 'But Dennis, jeez man ...', followed by more laughter.

From where you stand, you can see the church tower on the corner of the Tweede Van der Helst and Van Ostade as it juts into the night sky. If you had taken a left there, within a few turns of the pedals you'd be at the small row of houses (now a modern block of flats) where your history — not yet in the flesh — began. There, in front of the school next to number 205, your mother and I first met. She was on her bike, and kick-scooted along the sidewalk, greeting me as she passed. She was wearing a hand-me-down raincoat from your future grandpa Natan — such a filthy piece of clothing, totally black with grime on the lapel and between the buttons, that I subconsciously forbade her on the spot to ever wear it again. Of course, I had already seen what a dark beauty lay concealed behind that ratty, formless skin.

More than thirty years ago, and there, in that run-down, pre-gentrification street, is where the Tonio design had taken root.

8

All right, so Goscha does not bike back with you, and you don't go to chill at Dennis's. According to Goscha — and I specifically questioned her about this — you did not ride off swerving like a drunkard. You rode normally, straight ahead, onto the Ceintuurbaan. I imagine you glancing back one last time, waving: 'Oi!' (Unless you shouted at something or someone along the way, this would have been your last word — more a sound than a word, your signature goodbye: 'Oi.')

I follow you on your last bike ride. A few things are still unclear to me. Maybe, if I keep a close eye on you, I can solve them as we go.

The Ceintuurbaan, the main artery of my years in De Pijp. The intersection with the Ferdinand Bol. The metro station construction site. In case you have a change of heart: you can't turn right again to rejoin Dennis and Goscha on the Govert Flinck.

The bridge across the Boerenwetering, with the Hobbemakade on either side and the mini red-light district to the right. The night is high and clear. Daytime is not far off: it promises to be a splendid Whit Sunday. I suspect we share a distaste for whores. Can't count on a lifesaving stopover on that front.

Roelof Hartstraat. The traffic lights at the intersection are flashing yellow. Individual responsibility. There is almost no traffic. The occasional taxi. To the right, the College Hotel, whose loutish owners chopped down the trees. To the left, the road becomes the Coenenstraat. On the one corner, the local branch of the public library, where you and Miriam used to go to check out books. And on the opposite corner, Huize Lydia, where as a child you went to see your grandparents, when it was still a neighbourhood community centre (Grandpa Natan was treasurer).

Along Van Baerlestraat, too, trees were sacrificed during the recent 'restructuring'. But right now, urban-planning atrocities are not on your mind as you pedal further on Jim's bike under the streetlights. Still a ways to go until the Nepveustraat. You're tired after two nights of hard partying. After all the euphoria of the past few days, the Jenny fantasies, visions of the long weekend ahead, you bike home all on your lonesome — a thought that drapes a dull melancholy layer over everything.

You ride past the Van Baerle/Nicolaas Maas junction. There, on the corner, my colleague K. Schippers lives. (I gave you his novel about photography as a present.) Once, I stood chatting with him on the sidewalk in front of his house a little too long for your pleasure. Out of impatience, or attention-seeking, you crawled under the unbuttoned back panel of my raincoat. If you walked backwards a bit, I was transformed into a variant on a circus horse, a kind of baggy-clothed centaur. Your excellent performance, while embarrassing me, pleased Schippers, who was a fan of clowns and patchwork animals.

'As half-man, half-horse, you're free to piss on the street ...'

At least fifteen years ago, this incident. You approach the intersection in front of the Concertgebouw. Behind the buildings at your left, two blocks of houses deeper into the De Lairessestraat, the Jacob Obrechtstraat runs parallel to your route. You spent the first years of your life in the large apartment building called 'Huize Oldenhoeck' — those precious years of which you have no recollection (me, all the more). It occurs to me that on your final bike ride, you keep frighteningly close to the houses of your youth. You cycle, with a few zigzags here and there, along the images and settings of your earliest years. Look to the right, across Museumplein. You know better than I do where the hangout spot was, where the older boys gave you your first drag on a cigarette. You secretly hope that the Dutch football squad goes far next month — not because you really care all that much about the sport, but because of the festivities on the Museumplein grounds.

9

At the Concertgebouw, I know you're always reminded of your boyhood friend Jakob, who was run over by a truck on the corner of Van Baerle and De Lairesse. The truck did not have a blind-spot mirror. Jakob was cycling to the Vossius: it was his very first day at the gymnasium. He only barely survived. That same week you started at another gymnasium, the Ignatius, so the news of Jakob's accident didn't reach you right away, you heard it on the grapevine. It was one of the few times we really lit into you: you told us the news far too late, and almost in passing: 'Oh, guess what I heard ... y'know, Jakob, right? Well he was ...'

Now I think you didn't appreciate the seriousness of the incident, the lethal danger. And anyway, Jakob and primary school, those days were long behind you, a new life was opening up. And yet you kept apologising, with tears in your eyes, for your negligence: you were starting to cotton on.

The traffic light changes to green. Now we have to talk turkey. I advise you — no, I beg you — to turn left here onto De Lairesse. A few blocks further, past the Jacob Obrecht, turn right onto the Banstraat. Then just a tad to the left — to your old house on the Johannes Verhulst. The whole front stoop is free to park your bike.

Kid, you're tired, you've been drinking, you're about to keel over, bike and all, from fatigue. Forget that whole trek out to De Baarsjes. Sure, Jim will be disappointed, but he'll figure it out for himself, and sooner or later he'll go to bed. You'll explain it to him tomorrow.

You *think* you've got your wits about you, because you're brooding about Jenny, but in fact it's just sluggish, lovestruck daydreaming. Granted, there's hardly any traffic at this hour, but … you also have to take that Eerste Constantijn Huygens / Overtoom crossing … a left turn … the taxis drive like maniacs there at night.

You've got a key to the house. (It's hanging, if I remember correctly, on the same ring as the key to your bike lock.) You always manage to slip noiselessly up the stairs. You won't wake us, I guarantee you. Besides, I'm wide awake anyway, thanks to a churning stomach from having eaten way too much garlic last night; I'm sitting upright in bed like a cat retching itself free of a hairball. It's nearly half past four, I see on my watch. There's no light yet coming through the curtains.

Go lie down on the living-room sofa. The afghan that Mama was curled up under last night while watching TV must be there somewhere. Pillows galore. You spent sixteen years of your life in this house. After graduation you were in no hurry to leave — you stayed under your mother's wing for another two years. So what's another night? Do it for us. You're bound to move back in this September anyway, when you have to leave the Nepveustraat. The census people say statistics show more and more young people living at home again after a few years on their own. The demographists call them 'boomerang kids'. There is no generation gap anymore.

C'mon, there's no shame in it. Sleep in tomorrow morning as long as you want. Mama will make you a fantastic Whitsun breakfast.

10

For a moment, he seems to hesitate, but that's his unsteady way of biking. He stands, his buttocks off the saddle, nearly motionless on the pedals, and almost falls over. He could still turn left just past the Concertgebouw, along Café Welling, where as a child he put in so many pub-hours with his father.

Tonio goes straight ahead. His is a fixed route. Van Baerle, past the Stedelijk Museum, over the Vondelpark viaduct, Eerste Constantijn Huygens. Left on the Overtoom, continuing on to De Baarjes and the insomniac flatmate.

At the next intersection, too, he can still reconsider. Left on the Willemsparkweg, and he'll be home in a jiffy. His manoeuvres suggest he's going to turn right onto the Paulus Potterstraat, but he quickly corrects his course, returning in a gentle curve to the Van Baerle, where he cycles past the old music conservatory, now being renovated into a chic hotel.

If he turns, now focused and resolutely, onto the Jan Luykenstraat, then at once I'll know what's possessed him.

You know, Tonio, sometimes I worry about your eating habits. Your friend Jonas, himself a good eater who never gains an ounce, says you've shed many kilos these past two years by systematically skipping meals and quashing your appetite with cigarettes. Take today. You nibbled at some snacks at that duff party in the Vondelpark this afternoon, and that's it. The three of you drank beer at Goscha's place, and later, in club Trouw, Goscha could hardly keep track of the rounds. Food — no thought of it.

For years, you would make your rounds past the work tables in my study. Once a manuscript lay there entitled *Voedzame hunger*. You asked: 'What's that, Adri, "nourishing hunger"? You can't eat hunger, can you? How could it be nourishing?' I explained that the story was about love, and that love resembles hunger, but the kind of hunger you and your lover gorge yourselves with. 'Look at it this way … being madly in love makes you forget to eat. With lovesickness, it's even worse. You live on your own reserves, until you don't feel hunger anymore. That's what they mean when they say that someone is consumed by love. It guts you.'

Miriam says I completely lack didactic talent, and my wise lesson will not do any good today, either. I don't know how things stand with your feelings for Jenny, but I do know they haven't suppressed your appetite to that of a sparrow. You've got what, forty years ago, we called 'the munchies'. The only place in Amsterdam you know where you can satisfy that urge at this time of night is in the neighbourhood around Leidseplein, with its fast-food automats and shawarma joints.

It won't be a banquet. You've only got a fiver in your grey wallet, plus a fistful of coins.

Your hunger might persuade you to make a U-turn after all and plunder our fridge. As I said, you wouldn't wake me, because my recalcitrant stomach already has. And your mother, she's such a deep sleeper that you'd have to let a jar of pickles slip through your fingers to rouse her. Go on. The cats will come sniff at you, rub along your calves with their thick, furry tails.

Now I understand why you nearly turned onto the Paulus Potterstraat. So far, all north-east-heading streets here lead in just one direction, to Leidseplein and the snack bars. But for sentimental reasons you took the next street, Jan Luyken, where you went to school. The playground of the Cornelis Free School, completely vacant in the clear night. Aren't you tempted to stop for a moment, rest your foot on the curb? You used to holler and cavort on this paved patch of courtyard. There are your old teachers … the cheerful Loes, the somewhat mysterious Jeanine … They were crazy about you. In that now dark, impenetrable building, you learned to read, write, and do sums. You built a Viking ship there and, dressed up as Dorus, you performed *Er zaten twee motten*. Day after day, a Moroccan kid waited for you on this playground in the afternoon, first sweet-talking you and then making off with your first mobile phone.

Jakob lived a ways further up the street. His father still lives there. One afternoon, there was a misunderstanding between Mama and Grandma Wies. Grandma was supposed to pick you up from school on a different day than usual and take you to play at her place on the Eemstraat, because she had already left Grandpa Natan. Someone must have made a mistake, because no one came to fetch you. Jakob's dad, who came to pick up his son, waited with you for a long while.

'So where does your granny live, Tonio?'

'On the Eenstraat, I said so already, *jeepers*.' And more vehemently: 'The Eenstraat, Joost, the *Eenstraat!*' Do you remember, Tonio, how the incident turned out? All right in the end, apparently: we didn't have to put out an Amber Alert, or whatever the missing-child alarm was called in those days.

Oh, so you're cycling further? I notice I'm still trying to tinker with your timing. A second here, a second there. You're now passing Joost and Jakob's house on Jan Luykenstraat. They hosted the reception after the school play that marked the end of primary school. While the parents drank cocktails in the living room, you and Jakob and your classmates retreated to the basement. It was so quiet down there, contrary to all our expectations, that after a while one of the mothers, maybe Afra's, went to make sure you hadn't all been asphyxiated in the closeness of the basement. She came back nonplussed.

'They're sitting there, crying. All of them.'

From that moment on, a group of mothers periodically descended to the cellar. When the door opened, the bawling could be heard above the adult hubbub upstairs; the sobbing persisted shamelessly. Miriam returned, pale, from the basement.

'Incredible, what a pity party,' she said. 'I've never seen so much childhood anguish in one place.'

'Tonio, too?' I asked.

'Yeah, what do you think. They've just realised they might never see each other again. I don't know who it started with, but they've set each other off.'

Once in a while, a mother herded her big baby into the living room, where he or she, red-eyed, could cool down before being allowed to return downstairs to the orgy of blubbering. When Miriam decided it was time to take you home, you came to say goodnight to me with a face withered by prolonged crying. You couldn't muster up a smile anymore. It was for real.

11

Are you grinning right now, on your bike, as you think back on that bawl-fest? Or does it make you wistful, because time has so bitterly confirmed your classmates' cellar-snivelling? That was goodbye. From that basement, you split up and swarmed to high schools across the city. In the course of the past ten years, you bumped into an old classmate from the Cornelis Free now and then, but these were mostly awkward encounters. The old camaraderie had been left behind in the Nijsen family's basement.

At the end of the Jan Luyken, the massive, dark-red Rijksmuseum looms to your right. You've always thought it intriguing that the largest and most valuable of the city's treasures just hang there in the dark, unseen, their fate in the hands of a soulless security system.

Left onto the Hobbemastraat. The asphalt glistens with embedded bits of glass, as though the road surface is mirroring the starry night above, but you're too tired to lift your head and cast your eyes upward. You do see, in a flash, the book stalls set up on either side of the street for an Uitmarkt some ten years ago. You and I stood behind the table at my publisher's stand, signing books together.

You've got other things on your mind now: a döner kebab from the Turkish snack bar. It was your favourite lunch when you worked at Dixons — plenty of shawarma joints in the Kinkerstraat neighbourhood.

Heading toward your destination, you cycle between the tram rails of lines 2 and 5. You pass the leather-goods store where we bought Mama that red-brown set of bags for her fortieth birthday. You always managed to send costs skyrocketing with your expensive taste. You enjoyed giving presents even more than getting them. 'She's sure to want a toilet bag, too … don't you think, Adri? Look, it's made of the same leather. And here, this carry-on bag, the same leather, too.'

No, the leather-goods store doesn't ring any bells with you tonight. Your thoughts have narrowed to Jenny and döner kebab. The traffic lights at the crosswalk at the corner of the Park Hotel blink lazily. Ach, that Jenny. How she turned a quarter-turn, at your request, in order to benefit more from the reflector sheets … and you, bent over the tripod with the reflecting umbrella above your head. More like a parasol … You might still have the presence of mind to cast a glance to your right, past the yellow flashing lights. A taxi is just driving over the crosswalk. On that side, the Stadhouderskade is otherwise empty.

And to the left? If you didn't first look left, was it because there was no *sound* coming from that side? Or were your ears still pounding from the beats of techno-animal Carl Craig?

Maybe you were a bit dizzy from doing those dance dips with Dennis.

12

We provided Tonio with plenty of toys. He had a way of charming us out of anything his heart desired. Grandma Wies once said: 'You always get your way in the end.' She made a fake-suffering face to go with it. From that moment on, Tonio seemed to see it as his job, refining his charm as he went, to get his way. A teary eye was often more than enough.

The expensive problem was that once Tonio had figured out the mystery of a toy, he got bored with it. He could put together, one-two-three, a technical Lego set intended for age groups far above his own, but the then secret formula had been cracked. At best, the resulting construction could be expanded with accessories and attachments, which kept costs down. But usually his eye fell upon an entirely new challenge, complete with flashing lights, rolling caterpillar tracks, and an electrical transformer.

He constructed a power-driven Ferris wheel out of a K'Nex building set; it was so tall he had to use the kitchen stepstool to reach the top. When I pointed this out, he replied: 'The Ferris wheel on Dam Square is higher.'

Roller skates. A super-manoeuvrable silver-coloured kick scooter. The radio-controlled jeep with tractor tyres. Warhammer armies, complete with half a paint studio to decorate the miniature soldiers and their arsenal.

Computers and laptops, the toys of the growing adolescent. The games that went with them. The software.

After he turned eighteen, he expanded his playing field to the cafés where you had to be seen. Club Trouw, where he spent his last night: wasn't that, with all its techno music, his final plaything? The outcome of a lifetime of toys? And there had to be a bicycle, too, on which to ride home, spaced out. From technical Lego via a headful of technopounding on his way to a Media Technology degree — somewhere in the process, at a crucial point, he was scooped up and thrown down. Then came the ambulances, and *he* was subjected to medical technology, with which they had hoped to piece him back together.

13

Even murder serves a purpose, no matter how perverse. It is, after all, the aim of the murderer to bump off his victim. There is, likewise, apparently, a point to a soldier felled on the battlefield: he does it for his fatherland; he is cannon fodder in service of the triumph over Evil.

And the victims of a terrorist attack? At least in the eyes of the person who gave the order, their death had a purpose. The more casualties, the more successful the operation. Not only suicide terrorists, but their victims, too, die for their country, judging from the memorial services and plaques organised from higher up.

I can see no point, unearth no purpose, whatsoever in Tonio's death. He was on his way home, and felt like a bite to eat on the way, and encountered an unwanted and unintended force in his way, which killed him. The operator of the deadly projectile did not know, until that very moment, that he was operating a deadly projectile. He had left his job, and was driving home with a friend. Silent night, holy night.

Tonio's death was the result of the collision of two forces. The devastation they were capable of causing, should they meet, was calculable before the fact with scientific probability. The destruction they eventually caused was able to be established, after the fact, with scientific certainty.

Tonio's death could thus be reduced, in both point and purpose, to a physics formula. Our dismay was all the greater when we realised that our flood of emotions had run up against an ice-cold formula, hard as rock. There is no guarantee that emotions are able, in the long run, to wear away even the hardest stone.

14

In *Asbestemming*, I described once seeing a statue of St. Sebastian, who in a sort of death-leap is hit by the shower of arrows. They are thick, cast-iron arrows, and they pierce St. Sebastian's trunk according to a very precise geometrical pattern: as though a square harrow had been rammed in its entirety straight through the martyr's chest from behind.

Tonio, your fatal accident will continually pierce me in the same way for the rest of my days. My God, you dear boy, why did this have to happen? Why, goddamn it, did everything have to be ruined — you, us, the future, everything?

Sometimes, to put it bluntly, I'm pretty pissed off at you. A bit earlier

homeward, a few less beers, a light on your bike, look before you cross
… and it wouldn't have happened. You little bastard. You told Jenny on
Facebook that Saturday you were still 'beat' from the previous night.
Beat — your favourite term for hung over. Doesn't that give you the
responsibility to get a good night's sleep for once? You three wanted to
'paint the town red', as Goscha put it. Well, you did paint it red — with
your own blood, you fool.

Why this? Why this irrevocable death, which nothing can correct?
Goddamn it, Tonio, I was prepared to face *every* problem with you, no
matter how terrible. Your worst misery would still have been a formidable
adversary for me. I would have fought down to my last drops of sweat
and blood to find a solution. Anything for you.

The problem is: your death *isn't* a problem, because there is no
solution — even one that doesn't stand a chance.

15

No, I blame *myself*. I do not reproach you, in your groundwater-deep,
breathless sleep. Your stillness is one massive indictment of myself, even
without you wanting it so, because you can no longer want. Your death
speaks the truth about my failure. Your death is the sum total of my
negligence. There is always the possibility that your death was the result
of that *one* act of negligence — which one, I don't know, and that only
makes it worse.

Your whole childhood long, I regaled you with signs of attention,
large and small; caring gestures; soothing words. These, however, do not
hold up against the all-pervasive sensation, in retrospect, of guilt and
negligence. If I wasn't able to create for you a situation allowing for a safe
nighttime cycle route from De Pijp to De Baarsjes, then I should at least
have *been* there, halfway, to throw myself in front of the enemy vehicle
and force it to stop. A persistently gurgling stomach on its own does not
offer much resistance.

I acknowledge my defeat, which cannot be parried, not even into eternity.

16

Sundays are Miriam's darkest days. The pain is at its worst — partly because the huge loss happened on Whit Sunday, of course, but also because if Tonio dropped by, he usually did so on that day. This afternoon, some three months after the accident, she rang me in a panic.

'There's a trauma helicopter above the Hobbemastraat.'

This morning, she got up at five and worked until nine-thirty, after which she fell into a deep sleep in bed with a book in her hand, until noon. Just now, she woke up from a pitch-black dream to the pulse of the rotors.

The telephone pressed to my ear, I opened the streetside window of my workroom. If I bent far enough outside, I could indeed see a yellow helicopter with red-blue stripes off to the north-east, hovering approximately above the Rijksmuseum, whose position was marked by the asymmetrical cross of a building crane. It did not rise or descend, did not circle; it just hovered motionlessly like a bird of prey. against the steely-blue sky — at most, swaying gently.

'If you need some company ...' I said. A few seconds later, she was upstairs. I was still leaning out of the window. The helicopter swung in our direction now, slower than a police chopper, banked steeply to the west, and then returned to its initial position above the Rijksmuseum, staying there for a time, again like a bird of prey.

'A stand-by, I reckon. He's waiting for instructions. There'll be an ambulance down at the scene.'

I comforted Miriam with the thought that even if it had been allowed to fly at night, a trauma helicopter wouldn't have saved Tonio. 'He was in good hands. An extra ambulance with a trauma team replaced the helicopter. The kid just didn't stand a chance.'

No, that wasn't it. The sound of the propellers had roused her, and then she saw the chopper hovering above The Spot, as though someone was trying to rub it in that the nightmare was for real, even after she'd woken up. 'I'm okay now.'

Later, when I went downstairs, Miriam was sitting uncomfortably on the sofa, with one leg tucked up and her head leaning back. Red-rimmed eyes staring into nothingness. 'I miss him so much,' she kept repeating in a whisper. Her head rolled slowly back and forth over the back of the sofa, in a sort of resigned denial. 'I miss him so *terribly* ... it's just inconceivable ...'

At moments like these, I had no answer other than to hold her cold hand until it warmed up and she pulled it away because I squeezed it too tightly.

17

My self-recrimination is not limited to Tonio's gruesome end. I have also brought this on Miriam. I robbed her of her youth on her twentieth birthday, a bottle of whisky under my arm. Later, I saddled her with a child, which put paid to her childhood once and for all.

I not only saddled her with a child, I also saddled her with death. I had sworn to her I would protect that child with my life, if need be with my dead body. I was not able to honour my promise. The boy slipped through my fingers.

Her life as a girl is finished, and her life as a mother is finished. It is a miracle that she wants to continue her life with me as my wife.

18

A Sinterklaas celebration at Arti. Finally — you were almost the last one — Santa called you up to the stage. You'd hardly made it there before launching into a little dance on the red carpeting, turning your back on the good saint as you skipped in a circle. Your dance was loony and stiff, hands flapping and rotating like miniature propellers. Your eyes sought me out. I was sitting at the bar.

'Gotta poop,' you called out to me. To salvage the situation as best you could, you made an idiotic face. Sinterklaas looked on, flabbergasted. I have seldom loved you as much as at that moment.

I asked Ria the bartender for the wooden stick with the key, and yanked you from the stage.

There is no doubt that I loved him, from the first to the last day. As often as I said it to my mother ('I love that boy'), or silently to myself, it was mostly an unspoken, matter-of-fact love. No proof necessary. (I sometimes dreamt of a God who would command me to sacrifice my son to Him. I was prepared to believe in such a God, but only in order to make a fool of Him by sparing Tonio.)

The binding and convincing evidence of my love for Tonio was presented, unasked-for, by his death. The ice-cold black hole into which my life plunged, from the one moment to the next, proved how much I loved him.

Since Whit Sunday, Miriam and I talk about Tonio, surprisingly consistently, in the past-perfect and imperfect tense. Only, 'I loved him' is something I can't get out of my mouth. Even my pen baulks. Of course, I can replace the wretched past tense with '… how much I love him', but I am still tempted to add: 'as he *was*'.

My love for him is still there, and more intensely than it used to be. Grammatically, it makes no sense at all. If, under duress, I say, 'I love him', then what *him* am I talking about? Tonio no longer exists as *him*. He exist*ed* (and how!) in what now is past tense. And yet I love him, like I used to love him.

My love is genuine and sincere, but it has to make do without an object. It is love desperately in search of an untraceable lover. A talk-show

448

editor once warned his colleagues against inviting me as a guest: 'Right away, he'll open up a can of old Greeks.' Well, now that the can is open anyway: the old Greeks at least had the myth of Orpheus and Eurydice to hold on to. An exceptional miracle — by the grace of the gods. I have to make do with a love meandering in the present imperfect tense, forever cut off from the beloved in past imperfect.

Seeing that language is so uncooperative, how can we expect to keep Tonio alive in words?

19

To be abandoned by a lover, by the woman in your life — even *that* I'd braced myself for. 'You never come out of it unscarred,' a colleague once said. I was prepared for the shame of being dumped. All the love still left over for someone who just slammed the door behind them ... the wastefulness of so much longing ... well, all right, that passes. Time would do its work.

At most, I had braced myself for the death of my son by allowing my fear to make a pact with my imagination. That I might *actually* lose him never really entered my mind. I let my imagination, fed by fear, do the work — the work of warding it off.

Someone had abandoned me, my own son, without my love for him being *able* to pass. Time would show me what longing was. A lover who abandons you can transform your pain into hate. With the loss of a child, this was impossible. I moped around like an utterly betrayed lover whose love only grew and grew.

CHAPTER SEVEN

Pantonioism

1

His passion for rocks was sparked in Brussels. Miriam and Tonio were there in the mid-1980s, visiting her friend Lot. The boy immersed himself in a book belonging to Lot's husband on minerals and semi-precious stones. Back home, he begged us for a subscription to a rock collectors' magazine. In every city we visited, he managed to wheedle a handful of special collectors' items out of us. Soon, stones had no more secrets from him; he developed an infallible memory for types, colours, names.

Once he heard me mention a forthcoming book-cover design to Miriam. I had decided that midnight blue would make a nice background, but couldn't find the right colour swatches, either at the paint dealer or elsewhere. Tonio darted off to his room, and reappeared a little while later, opening his fist in front of me. 'D'you mean this?'

A stone of the most splendid shade of blue glistened at me. Maybe not exactly midnight blue, but more useable than what I was looking for. I took the stone in my hand.

'What's this?'

'Lapis lazuli,' he exclaimed. 'Lapis lazuli, of course. The real thing, lapis lazuli.'

He accompanied the announcement with a triumphant little dance. He went with me to the publisher, where he unwrapped the lapis lazuli from its dustcloth. His face radiant, he observed the effect his magic stone had on the publisher and his staff.

'Lapis lazuli,' he cried gleefully. 'For Adri's book.'

Unfortunately, it was not feasible to use this unique colour for the cover. With every proof I received, Tonio fetched his stone for comparison. It wasn't even in the ballpark.

'You know what,' he said, 'just take a whole bunch of colour photos of it, and snip out the lapis lazuli from each one … then you paste all those lapis lazulis together on the front of your book. Easy.'

When we had the living room renovated in '97, we had two glass display-cases built in on either side of the fireplace: one for Miriam's collection of Venetian masks, the other for Tonio's rocks. He kept his smaller specimens in foam-rubber powder puffs, which were in turn enclosed in transparent hard-plastic boxes. The larger minerals were placed among them on the glass shelves. Every visitor was brought to come see *his* cabinet.

'That blueish stone there, Tonio, what's it called?'

'It only *looks* blue. Because of the light. It's really grey. A labradorite.'

And then he'd look over at Miriam or me and shake his head. How could people be so ignorant?

In a town in Sicily, Tonio found a small, dusty, forgotten shop (he seemed to have a sort of rock-radar) where a little old lady dressed in black, and as wrinkled as a desiccated apple, had a glass case full of minerals and petrified seahorses. While we drank ice-cold, nearly red rosé in the shade of a nearby café, Tonio nosed around that shop. When he came to show us his purchase, he put on his most pathetic face: 'They've also got an agate. Not even that expensive.'

When I gave him the money, he howled with a sort of mocking triumph. He regarded every gift as a victory over his parents' didactic restraint. The other café patrons got a kick out the way he instructed us to guard his newly acquired booty, returning post-haste to the shop with a fistful of freshly wheedled money, as though he were afraid that other buyers, who of course didn't know the first thing about rocks, would snap up his prize.

Ten minutes later, he was back. The old woman had packed up his agate, complete with a blue ribbon, like the Sicilian bakers did a tart. Tonio tore open the paper with nimble fingers. 'Just look at how nicely the manganese left its mark ...' He spoke like an article out of his collectors' journal, in a deep voice. 'That grain ... and this here, that's a dendrite print. Just like a Christmas tree, huh Mum?' And after a brief pause, looking at me in desperation: 'The lady also showed me a few pieces of jasper. They're her last ones. Red and green. I don't think they're very cheap.'

'The money's run out.'

'Yeah, I *know*, but ...'

Today, Miriam and I are going shopping for a stone for Tonio. The last of his collection, with an inscription.

2

Two p.m. Continuous alternation between sunlight and wind-driven cloud cover has always made me nervous (it was the same weather the Saturday that my father drove his motorcycle into a ditch and was brought home by ambulance, unrecognisable through the mask of clotted blood), but today it's worse than ever. We've got an appointment at the stonecutter's at five. I draw the curtains against the intensely raking light, then whip them back open at every interlude of darkness.

Work is out of the question. At three, I decide to go ahead and shave and shower, meticulously and at my leisure, so I'll be in tip-top shape when Miriam comes to get me. Seeing my bed on the way to the bathroom reminds me how tired I am. To regain my strength, I lie down with the first bit of reading material I find on the headboard: a booklet on Shakespeare. It informs me that the bard's work contains some sixteen thousand question marks. As I lie there half asleep, my finger between the pages, wondering whether that's a lot or a little, sixteen thousand spread over forty-some plays, Miriam peeks around the door.

'I'd like to leave at four-fifteen at the latest, okay?' she says, slightly harried. 'Friday-afternoon traffic, you never know.'

Shave, shower, wash hair — the thought of it puts me off entirely. I lie there on my bed until four, not even reading, and without resolving the issue of the sixteen thousand question marks. If I get up now, there'll be just enough time to get myself more or less dressed. Every day, I still wear what I pulled on the morning of Whit Sunday: jogging pants and a flannel lumberjack shirt. Well, not always the exact same ones, because things do have to go in the wash once in a while. The raking light has definitely made way for a slowly passing cloud cover, for the strong winds have subsided.

Crossing the street to the car, I realise the gout in my left foot has returned. I walk so little, and not at all outside the house, that I hadn't really noticed the pain until now. The conventional wisdom that foot gout can be caused by eating red meat and drinking red port was recently debunked in the science section of the newspaper. I don't care for red meat or red port, but do enjoy clear alcohol, which indeed appears to play a role in the formation of painful crystals around one's joints. I finally dare to leave the house after all these weeks, and the whole neighbourhood gets to see me stagger to the car.

'You're limping,' Miriam says from behind the wheel.

'I'm forgetting how to walk, that'll be it.'

Cornelis Schuytstraat. Willemsparkweg. Koninginneweg … the streets are indeed crowded with Friday-afternoon traffic, but it never comes to a standstill. Only at the main intersection with the Amstelveenseweg does traffic move so slowly that we have to let four green lights pass.

The Zeilstraat drawbridge is open. There is such a confusion of gulls flying every which way above our heads that it's as though they've just escaped from a great big box, of which one flap is propped open. It is a long while before the bridge begins to swing shut.

'I'm curious how far they've got,' Miriam says. 'I asked them to wait with the lettering. It looked good on the computer, but we have to see it with our own eyes first.'

'Did you remember about the hyphen?'

'There wasn't *supposed* to be a hyphen ...'

'That's what I mean, no hyphen. But did you check?'

'Now that you mention it ... My mind is such a chaotic mess. I wonder if it'll ever get better.'

'You can go.'

The barrier arm jerks upward. We cross the Schinkel canal, heading toward Hoofddorpplein. When we cross under the motorway, entering Slotervaart, Miriam says: 'This is the same route we took the day Tonio was born, in the midwife's little Fiat. Keep an eye out ... there, off to the left, Slotervaart Hospital. That's where he was born.'

I have not been back since 15 June 1988, but I recognise the building at once. Miriam was so caught up in her contractions that morning that she only realised we were at the wrong hospital once we got to reception. Tonio never tired of hearing this story.

'Sorry, honey, sorry,' the midwife kept repeating. 'My fault. Stupid of me. Sorry.'

It was clear, Tonio, that there was no way we were going to turn around and go to the VU, where you were supposed to be born. The midwife pushed the wheelchair with a groaning Miriam down the hall to the lift. Your father wobbled alongside, one hand on your mother's neck. The wrong hospital. Miriam a wrung-out wreck in a wheelchair. This couldn't possibly end well.

'But it did!' he'd exclaim. 'Just look at me!'

3

From Plesmanlaan, we turn right into the bland monotony of Osdorp.

'Jan Rebelstraat,' Miriam says. 'Have a look at the map. I was here once with Nelleke, but that was sleepwalking. It's close to Westgaarde.'

In a north-west corner of Osdorp, I locate the Jan Rebelstraat, indeed not far from the cemetery.

'Turn left here.' This autumnal summer sky makes me just as nervous as this afternoon's uneasy grazing sunlight did. 'There it is.'

Miriam drives past what looks like a normal shop window. LIEFTINK BROS. STONECUTTERS - SINCE 1913.

'Just a sec.' Miriam turns off the engine, closes her eyes. 'Help me muster up some courage.'

I undo her seatbelt and pull her close. 'Think of last time, Minchen, when you were here with Nelleke. You pretended it was a garden centre … shopping for a little something for our back terrace. A bargain from the sale section.'

'That was then,' she whispers. 'It's harder now.'

The door, complete with jangling bell, makes me think of one of those old-fashioned general stores. The left side of the shop has been made into a life-size imitation graveyard, like on a film set. What doesn't tally is all that marble, flamed pink and striped pearl-grey, so glossy and unweathered. Nowhere is there a patch of moss or a sprig of grass between the stone chips that fill up the plots.

Grass markers. Slants. Uprights. Combinations of these. I wonder if the names inscribed on them, some of them with gilded letters, have been made up. If so, what about the portraits sunk into the marble — or are they computer composites? The novelist's ideal playroom.

To the right, a display of pink marble hearts, and toy animals (teddy bears, bunny rabbits) carved out of light-grey marble. Behind that, two desks with computer equipment. On the wall, large boards with typeface examples.

A man of around forty gets up from one of the desks. Miriam apologises that we're early. Handshakes all round, which we don't normally do at the garden centre. We assume he recognises our names from the gravestone.

'No problem,' the man says.

Early. He leads us to the workshop behind the showroom, where a second man is at work in a hazy cloud of dust. Maybe they're brothers, but not the 1913 ones. Suddenly, before we've prepared ourselves for it, we are looking down on a gravestone, lying flat on its back and supported by wooden trestles — with our surnames on it.

'I'll just go get the paperwork,' says the man who received us. He goes back to the front room.

TONIO

ROTENSTREICH —

VAN DER HEIJDEN

I point out the hyphen to Miriam. 'You see how these things take on a life of their own? It's as though Tonio, maiden name Van der Heijden, was married to a Mr. Rotenstreich. One little hyphen, and he's lying in his grave with another identity. With a different gender, even.'

'Stuff for a thriller,' Miriam says. 'Alfred Kossmann coined the term "identity fraud" — that's where it all started, right? Without my thesis on him, we wouldn't have come up with the name Tonio.'

'All right, the thriller opens with an exhumation,' I say. 'Reason: an erroneously chiselled hyphen, giving the buried person a mistaken identity. I'll leave the rest up to you. After all, it's your last name that ...'

'That what?'

'That doesn't belong there.'

'You can still have them take it off.'

'Not on your life. Not now that I can finally make good on an old promise.'

The three names, and Tonio's dates, are printed on a sheet of paper, which is taped to the stone. Everything can still be amended, shifted. The man returns with the paperwork. 'Check along with me, if you will ... The headstone is made of Belgian bluestone ... one hundred centimetres high, eighty wide, and eight thick. How do you want the photograph?'

The rectangular plaque with Tonio's self-portrait as Oscar Wilde etched onto it is, I see only now, is lying loosely on the stone. 'What are the choices?' I ask.

'Anything you like,' says the man. 'From medallion to recessed. My personal advice would be: half-sunken into the headstone, so it's still in mid-relief.'

I look over at Miriam. She nods. The man has understood, and makes a note of it. I bring his attention to the extraneous dash. I needn't explain; he knows the story. How the hyphen still found its way into the design, he couldn't say, but he assures us it will not end up on the final product.

'Otherwise it's at our cost,' he says.

Back in the showroom we pick out the definitive typeface. We choose 'Albertus Bold'. We watch as the man changes the headstone's lettering on the computer.

I draw his attention to the excess space between the components of the dates. He trims it. Out comes a printout of the definitive text, with the photo in place. I point out the misleading hyphen again. Without a word, he removes it from the computer screen as though it's a fleck, and I get a new printout.

I am reminded of the young woman at the registry office, to whom, bundle of nerves that I was, I neglected to give Tonio's middle name. Granting Tonio his complete name has taken more than twenty-two years. I have waited until it had to be etched in stone. The shame I now feel is infinitely greater than back then, on 16 June 1988, when I stood outside the registry office with an incomplete birth certificate. ('How am I going to explain this to my wife?')

'The stone,' the man says, 'can go into production this week. We'll place it in a fortnight. Just as a reminder: Belgian bluestone weathers over time … it's supposed to. Gives it a nice effect. The gravel will be refreshed every four years.'

He motions us to wait for a moment, and goes back to his colleague in the workshop. After a brief exchange, he returns. 'We won't start on it until next Monday at the earliest. So … if you change your mind as to the lettering or the photo, you can always call us first thing Monday morning. If we don't hear from you, we'll assume we can go ahead as planned.'

Miriam wants to leave, but I linger in the doorway separating the showroom and the workshop until the man has run off his own printout (without the hyphen) and taped it to the gravestone of Tonio Rotenstreich van der Heijden.

My feet feel uncomfortable on the cement floor. It's Tonio's feet that should have been standing here, in shoes that have gained a size, the flesh having got looser and fatter after two, three decades. I would have preferred to see him here at forty-something, in which case I would have been the eighty-something deceased for whom he was ordering a gravestone. 'Belgian bluestone.' Maybe he would think to print out one of the photos he'd taken of his father over the years, and incorporate it into the monument.

I imagine him pacing impatiently, with or without his mother, as he attended to this necessary evil. A gravestone for his father. Even if I were that age, it would, if he still loved me, be a defeat for him.

This, me in *his* shoes — now *that's* defeat. For him and for me. God, kid, I wish we could have skipped this, and leap forward to, say, 2034. Me, dead at a respectable age; you, living on toward that age.

4

Since beginning this requiem, I have tried to find solace from other writers who have lost a child.

Shakespeare's son Hamnet, the male half of twins, died at the age of eleven. If traces of this loss can be found in his work, they are only indirect. The filicide in *Macbeth*, perhaps. 'Give sorrow words ...' Maybe, with the portrayal of the young hero in *Hamlet*, Shakespeare created an idealised version of his own son, and disguised himself as a voyeuristic ghost.

Ben Jonson lost his eldest son at age seven. 'My sin was too much hope of thee, loved boy, / Seven years thou wert lent to me, and I thee pay, / Exacted by thy fate, on the just day.'

Descartes never got over the death of his young daughter, but whether her death played any role in forming his philosophy, I couldn't say. Klaus Mann, eldest son of Thomas, committed suicide. In his diary entries from the time the lad was twelve, the father wondered if he could fall in love with his sailor-suit-clad son. Klaus's funeral in Cannes had to make do without the sacred presence of Thomas, who was on a speaking tour of Scandinavia.

Anna Enquist lost her daughter Margit to a traffic accident on the Dam. How she (Margit) sang and played and beamed at the twenty-fifth anniversary party of *De Revisor*. The infant daughter of P.F. Thomèse became a 'shadowchild'. Mauringh, the eldest son of Jean-Paul Franssens, jumped in front of a train (his father died a year later). One of Jan Cremer's sons was murdered. A son of Jeroen Brouwers died of an illness. Not long thereafter, I sat across a restaurant table from the father, and could see, close up, the pain in his tired eyes.

The list is long. Writers are not spared. Perhaps they are asking for tragedies, being so tied up with them professionally. After the publication of George Simenon's *The Disappearance of Odile*, his own daughter vanished. She was later found to have committed suicide. Simenon wrote a thousand-plus-page memoir in the form of a letter to her.

I have not been able to take any comfort from my colleagues' pain. Shared pain lessens nothing. It only augments.

5

On the return trip through the scattered building-blocks of Osdorp toward the land of the living, Miriam again points out the high-rise main block of the Slotervaart Hospital.

'Want to stop?' And since I appear to take it as a joke: 'I'm serious. For your book.'

'Another time. The stonecutter's also got to go in the book.'

As we ride past the hospital, I keep my eyes glued to the tower block. Somewhere, on an upper storey, I watched my son being born. Looking out over Amsterdam from that height, and becoming a father at the same time — oh, that gave me the most majestic feeling. The urge to take the still-unwashed babe to the window, to show him (to) the world ... I didn't dare.

I have just seen his gravestone. His photo will come just under the arched upper edge. He'll be looking out over a patch of gravel about as long as he was tall, from a height of less than a metre.

'I don't know quite how to put it,' Miriam says, 'but I have the constant feeling that Tonio, well, is living in me. Permanently.'

'In us both,' I say. 'And since Whit Sunday, we, with Tonio in us, live permanently in another world. Hasn't anybody sent the change-of-address cards yet? It's a world we never imagined existed. Take the stonecutter, for instance ... Just drive over there, walk in and order a gravestone ... two months ago, we'd never even considered it. Another world, other doors, other interiors. The curious thing is that we behave as though it's the most normal thing in the world ... stroll around, shopping basket in hand, choosing accessories for Tonio's grave ... like at the corner grocery. The way back to our pre-Whitsun existence is gone, cut off, forever. You see something of the world this way, at least.'

We've passed the hospital now. I turn back for a last look at the ugly tower block. A couple of days after Tonio was born: I stand with my mother at the glass window, behind which Miriam has appeared wearing a nightgown, with the baby in her arms, her face fatigued, but all smiles.

'Yeah ... yessir, you sure made a good one there.' She claps her hand over her mouth. 'Oh dear, what *am* I saying?'

6

Last week, Miriam got a phone call from Lieftink Bros.: the gravestone had been put in place. They didn't have quite enough gravel to fill the plot, but it would be taken care of ASAP.

Miriam made a telephone-round of the family straightaway, to find a suitable date for us all to visit the grave together, for you couldn't call it an unveiling anymore. Natan thought it was strange that they hadn't done it in the presence of the family. Surely that was a widely held tradition? But, naturally, he wanted to accompany us to the gravesite, also to see his own, endangered surname chiselled into stone.

My father-in-law, my sister, my brother, with wife and child: they were all free on Monday 12 July, the day after the World Cup finals. My mother-in-law, who had so vociferously refused even to shake her ex-husband's hand at the funeral, would have to go another time. Even then, we couldn't discount that she would raise a stink about the name ROTENSTREICH on the gravestone. Dealing with her was a matter of never-ending, and usually fruitless, diplomacy.

7

Before the finals, Miriam served deep-fried calamari with the drinks.

'The guy at the Albert Cuyp market said it was one of Paul's tentacles. Y'know, the German octopus that predicts football results. By … how'd he do it again? … picking mussels out of the right box, something like that.'

'And you just toss a tentacle of the oracle into a deep-fryer? That's tempting the gods.'

'Nah. Octopus. Paul predicted that Spain would win. Now he's been rendered harmless. At the Cuyp, they cut the bad mussel out of him and threw it to the gulls. Spain's gonna lose.'

'These rings have an alarming crunch to them.'

'I sprinkled coarse sea salt on top.'

Every moment that, thanks to a bit of diversion, I don't have to think *My life is ruined for good* is a plus. At the same time, right after such a moment of distraction, I am convinced that I cannot let go of the thought of my ruined life for even a second. This would be my permanent tribute to Tonio. His life cut short for good, and his future definitively behind lock and key? Then I must be continually confronted with the ruination of my own existence. My focus must not be allowed to waver.

In that duplicitous frame of mind, I take my place in front of the TV.

8

I could keep telling myself that I couldn't care less who won, but I was at least conscious of the subdued atmosphere after the anticlimax. I had expected the spectators to leave Museumplein in a jeering protest as they made their way to various flashpoints throughout the city: the Spanish consulate, for instance, and any number of Iberian restaurants. I pricked up my ears, but the streets were quiet — there was no noisy grousing by streams of passersby, no vuvuzelas.

The image arose of a crowd, stunned and silent, remaining behind en masse.

'I'm just going out.'

Herds of dejected football fans were indeed hurrying home: mute, on whispering and lisping shoe soles. In this anonymous darkness, which had erased our national identity, I dared to walk unguarded outdoors. I ambled against the stream to the end of the street. The interior of Café Welling, where the television had already been switched off, looked so sombre you'd think they'd just come from the funeral of one of their regulars. A small group sat outside, smoking.

Museumplein made me think most of one of those third-world garbage dumps, where paupers send their kids to root around for usable rubbish. But these manure pits are usually not lit up at night by floodlights and giant projection screens (now imageless). The place was nearly entirely deserted. A ragged, glittery carpet of trash (beer cans, water bottles, lots of light-blue plastic, crates, orange bits of clothing) concealed what used to be the grassy commons. You looked up almost automatically to check for buzzards. Only nose-diving gulls.

Two amateur scavengers, about ten years old, were collecting discarded vuvuzelas, perhaps in the hope of creating a last-minute market in the run-up to the team's homecoming welcome the day after tomorrow. They were clever enough to try them out first, braving the residual spit of strangers, just to make sure they could get a lugubrious honk out of the thing.

The sound of crushed aluminium and splintered plastic underfoot had not entirely dissipated: here and there, groups of hangdog supporters were leaving the area, aware that despite the profound loss, in four years' time there'd be the opportunity to get even. I was immune to it. What did hit me was the *setting* of the disgrace: it only reminded me, together with those ten-year-old scavengers, of my own loss. Missing Tonio could be augmented in myriad ways and with myriad attributes.

9

Today, the 12th of July, we would add the newest acquisition to Tonio's rock collection. Not in the glass display-case in our living room — its dimensions did not allow for that. This monster of Belgian bluestone was to be exhibited in the open air, at Buitenveldert Cemetery. I had wanted to have them incorporate a piece of lapis lazuli, Tonio's favourite, into it, but this was problematic for the stonecutters, so we dropped it.

The municipal sanitation department had already started clearing the debris from Museumplein that very night. When I took my timid early-morning walk, they were still busy cleaning — anything to provide a spotless foundation for the next day's homecoming, so that a new carpet of garbage could be laid. Win or lose, the screaming must go on. Even the city government had already decided there would be a canal parade. This way, they hoped, by some alchemistic trick, to convert defeat into victory. Bring a million orange-clad provincials by train to the capital. Have them throng the players' boat, from bridge to bridge, and from canal wall to canal wall. All that honking and orange smoke will magically transform disgrace into triumph. The new mayor cashed in on it: his inauguration was ratified with two streetfests in a single week. Public misconduct, provided it was cloaked in the national colours, was okay.

10

'Say you lost your wife or your son. Would you keep on writing?'

If someone asked me this before Whit Sunday 2010, my answer would be: 'Of course not. They are both my muse. Tonio a male one. I do it first and foremost for them. Aside from the question whether there would still be any point in writing, I wouldn't even be *able* to.'

And yet, since the end of May, it's Tonio who in fact *keeps* me writing. Every day, from ten-thirty in the morning till five in the afternoon, without a lunch break. It is more an obsessive ritual than voluntary labour. Writing for and about him is the best way to get as close to him as possible, the person he was and the absentee he now is, to talk to him and sit in silence with him. In this way I keep him alive, and when my work is finished, this requiem can, in a dialogue with the reader, keep him alive a while longer.

But after that? Of course, I can say: it's my job, and seeing as we've decided to stay alive … It can never be solely a matter of breadwinning, otherwise I'd have chosen a different profession, with a bit more to show for itself at the end of the workday.

The real question is: *what* to write after this? My current subject is a kind of pitch-black marvel that has crossed my path. A one-off thing, seeing as there are, thank God, no more children of my flesh and blood to be sacrificed. It seems likely that this will overshadow all subsequent topics.

Maybe I should just wait and see. A fruitless void or …

I have no other answer to this terrible loss than to write about it — only to discover along the way that writing is no answer either, because there was no question. It makes the loss all the more chilling: that no question has been formulated, only an exclamation mark like a razor-sharp icicle.

You could turn things around, and bury the loss, but that does not provide an answer either.

11

At ten o'clock, I went upstairs to work on my notes. It was stuffy. I had the window next to my desk wide open. There wasn't much point, as it was windless outside — and now the air lay thick and motionless against the houses, not even syrupy, because that would suggest a kind of current. Just when you thought the sky had never been this dark during the day, it got a shade darker. Everything to bring out the effect of the lightning. The muffled thunder reminded me of the drums muted with black cloths in a Neapolitan funeral procession, like the one I saw in Positano in 1980 when I left Miriam behind 'to observe my happiness from a distance'. We couldn't have picked a more suitable day to inaugurate Tonio's gravestone.

Just when I thought there would be no cloudburst, I became aware — rather than actually seeing the rainfall — of a violent drumming on the flat roof above my head. I shut the window to keep the raindrops from spattering from the windowsill onto my papers.

The events of the past seven weeks were (with the exception of a single passively grief-drenched day) meticulously notated in telegram style: material that could be useful as the groundcoat for the requiem. How to actually start it? Should I, owing to the unpredictable turn of real events, impose a rigid structure upon it? Or could I make the most of the chaotic whirlpool of feelings and experiences we'd been dragged into, so that the story of our grief could be flung every which way?

My heart felt like a pincushion — so many short jabs punctured it whenever I thought back on this afternoon's mission. It was like the pins and needles when your foot goes to sleep, but then in the region of the heart.

Hinde arrived by bike at half past one. She was supposed to go with us in the car, but at the last minute decided she'd rather cycle to the cemetery. Miriam and I drove to the Lomanstraat. Natan's arm appeared slowly above the half curtains, waving — a sign that he had seen us. We knew it would be quite some time before he opened the front door.

Ninety-seven. He was old and wizened. His friendly face was pale, with pink half-moons under the eyes. I helped him cross the street, shuffling along with him to keep to his tempo. In the past two months, he had aged years. He was over a hundred now.

12

We arrived at the cemetery just as Hinde did. My sister was waiting on a bench inside the gate, with a bunch of flowers on her lap, short of breath just from sitting. She still wore a wig, because her hair had fallen out from the chemo. She had a cut on her chin, which bled. I hugged her.

'Did you fall? Bang into something?'

'I was trying to pull out a hair,' she said, 'and the tweezers slipped.'

I almost laughed, because this was her all over. The perfect motto to sum up her life: tug a single hair out of your chin, and injure your face with the tweezers. I asked about the therapy.

'Well, I think they've done all they can do.'

I got a fright, but she meant that she was 'kind of' finished with chemo. 'The tumor's still there, but it's dormant. Sure, I'd rather be rid of it altogether, but they say *that* could take another three years. On top of it, I had a chest infection. That's why I'm wheezing like this. I've only got 50 per cent lung capacity.'

'Isn't that the emphysema?' Again, I caught myself being concerned about Tonio's clandestine smoking — until something like an X-ray of his wrecked lungs popped into my head.

'Yeah, that, too.'

Then I saw Frans and Mariska walk up with their son, Daniel, now sixteen months old. They had come by tram, or a combination of bus and tram. We all hovered around Daniel's pram until the poor little guy started bawling from the excess attention. ('So big!')

We walked together to the grave, slowly, Natan setting the tempo. And again, the cemetery proved itself to be a modest labyrinth, where you always managed to take a wrong turn somewhere. Everything was still wet from the midday thunderstorm, but the ground had not been turned into a swamp. Nor was it all slowly drying out, for the sun was hiding behind a low cloud cover. The rabbits had resumed their darting through the hedges, which still glistened with raindrops.

Usually we got lost because Miriam insisted on relying on the map. Today, though, we all just trudged alongside one another, more or less following the route we remembered from the funeral.

In the end, we reached the grave from two sides, in two groups: Natan, flanked by the women, had taken an earlier turn than Frans and I, but we all converged on the grave at the same time. Frans was pushing the empty pram (Daniel dangled in his mother's arms), and parked it next to a neighbouring headstone. The old provisional sign, including the plot number 1-376-B, still marked Tonio's grave. We stood in a semi-circle around the gravelled plot.

TONIO

ROTENSTREICH

VAN DER HEIJDEN

15 JUNE 1988   23 MAY 2010

What a relief, now that I could confirm with my own eyes that the hyphen was gone. I laid my hand on my father-in-law's arm. 'So, Natan, there's your name. How about that?'

His doleful face wrinkled into an insecure smile. I didn't think the moisture on the pink half-moons under his eyes had been brought on only by the puffs of wind from between the hedges.

'Fine,' he said quietly. 'Fine.'

His life had been quite a journey. He had already had three nationalities before leaving his home and undertaking the trek through Europe. Born in 1912 under the Habsburg monarchy, he became a Pole after World War I. With the Stalin–Hitler pact of '39, Natan's part of the Ukraine (Lemberg) fell under Soviet rule, and he was conscripted into the Red

Army. Thus began his long march to the Netherlands, and finally to this graveyard in Buitenveldert. He had served as an interpreter in the Red Army: he knew his languages, including Russian. He helped raze Berlin, and after the German surrender he returned to Poland — only to find that anti-Semitism there had only gotten more rabid after the occupation. He volunteered to assist Jewish war orphans, of which a few hundred were to go to Holland to be adopted by foster families.

Once in the Netherlands, he met Wies, a Jewish nurse who had gone into hiding during the war with a family of market gardeners in Sint-Pancras, where she spent long hours in an underground dirt shelter. They got married, and in the fifties had two daughters.

I never did manage to figure out how an incorrect birth year (1916) got into Natan's passport. Had there been a mistake when he first arrived in Holland, lowering his age by four years, or did he purposely disregard the oversight in order to be more eligible for a residence permit? Even to his wife and children, he maintained that he was born in 1916.

At her birthday party in 1979, Miriam burst into tears when I enquired as to her father's age.

'He'll turn sixty-three next month. He's probably not long for this world.'

She, just twenty, seemed slightly ashamed of having 'such an old father', but was mainly afraid of losing him to old age. In the mid-'90s (he and his wife were already separated), Natan informed us that his year of birth was not 1916, but 1912, suddenly obliging us to add four years to his recently reached milestone of eighty. His daughters took it badly. All of a sudden, they had a father 'in his eighties'. As though to prove his staying power, he had now managed to stretch it to ninety-seven. He lived on his own, and cared ably for himself. Four days a week (Monday through Thursday), Miriam drove him to the Beth Shalom cafeteria for his dinner, and picked him up an hour-and-a-half later.

The tragic disadvantage of reaching — and thriving at — such a ripe old age is that, already being the only surviving member of his immediate family (his parents and sisters were murdered by the Nazis), he had also outlived his one and only grandson. Natan was more than three-quarters of a century older than Tonio. When Natan was born, the century was just twelve years old, and at Tonio's birth that century still had twelve years to go. In between those two births lay three world wars — two hot and one cold — and the remaining filth of the twentieth century. Perhaps it says something about my perseverance that only now, twenty-two years after my visit to the Amsterdam registry office, I managed to bequeath his name to his only grandson — on his gravestone.

Despite his affability, Natan was a closed book. I couldn't guess what he really thought of seeing his surname in such an awkward position, wedged between 'Tonio' and 'Van der Heijden'. We might even be doing something illegal. Rotenstreich was not registered as his middle name, nor as an appendage to the family name, because that, too, needed to be vetted by the authorities, with a price tag.

13

The sky started to darken again, like earlier in the day, but without the same threat of cloudbursts.

It can happen late at night, after a few drinks, in the semi-sleep of early morning, or at moments of sudden fatigue after a day's work: if I'm in a foggy frame of mind, Tonio's role in my life tends to disintegrate. He no longer seems like my full-fledged son, but rather someone who at irregular intervals drifts in and out of my life … who drops in from time to time … a somewhat unpredictable family friend. The more muddled my mood, the more I see Tonio's presence in my past dissolve.

It's not that he is becoming less important to me — on the contrary — but he seems suddenly elusive. It's as though I haven't spent as much time with him as I had wanted to. Thoughts like these drive me to despair, because this makes his perfectly contiguous life susceptible to erosion.

It is not surprising that such a state is the creation of an exhausted brain. It forms, subconsciously, my answer to Tonio's demise, to the unfathomable decomposition he is undergoing in his grave. Somewhere in the depths of my soul, I want to see his past, as it intertwined with my own, retrospectively decompose.

Not when my brain is working at full power, though — then I know better. Tonio fills my life again: the present life, *and* what it once was.

Don't think about his decomposing body underneath that gravel right now. His living, mobile body was here with me, in me, enlivened and driven by my knowledge of its every aspect. His motor functions were in my muscles.

The thunderstorms might revisit us soon. But, unlike Frankenstein, I did not need lightning to bring my boy back to life. My science was different from Frankenstein's. My knowledge of Tonio was itself the life-giving lightning bolt.

The potted plants, half-eaten by the rabbits, had been placed at the edge of the patch of gravel. Between them was a can of beer that one of his friends had set there shortly after the funeral, together with a pack of cigarettes, now heavy and rain-sodden. I looked at the bottom of the can: a long way until its use-by date. I put it in the pocket of my raincoat, intending to drink it one evening on Tonio's behalf.

14

The coarse gravel on Tonio's grave brought me back to a small Greek gravel beach on the Pelion Peninsula.

In the spring of '95, Tonio's grandmother took him to the carnival on Dam Square. He was not yet seven, and the rules were clear: no under-sevens on the bumper cars. But watching them close up, how they bashed and ricocheted, was not forbidden, and that's what he did, running back and forth along the ledge surrounding the rink. The spot where the cars were most congested, and the crashing the most violent, attracted him the most, and he was determined to get a good look. And eventually he tripped on the ledge, took a bad spill, and broke his wrist.

His dismayed grandmother brought him by taxi to the emergency room, where his arm was encased in plaster, or rather a sort of waffled armour, the kind that was mighty difficult to fill with signatures. It happened at an awkward moment for us, because Tonio's spring break had just begun, and we were about to leave for two weeks' holiday in Greece. We were to visit my German translator and her husband in the coastal town of Horto. The hospital gave Tonio a waterproof plastic sleeve for the cast, so he could swim.

'Yeah, those bumper cars, Tonio …' I said. 'Risky business.'

Angry: 'They wouldn't even *let* me ride them.'

Whenever he was really indignant, he would cross his arms, with the back of his hands arched upward — which now, because of the cast, was impossible. By the time we got to Horto, he had come to grips with his handicap. He couldn't wait to get into the water. It was endearing to see how Tonio braved the blue-green marbled bay. It was shallow, so he could easily gain a foothold on the bottom, kicking up silty little clouds. To give his motions the semblance of swimming, he executed a sort of crawl stroke with his good left arm, while his plaster-cast right arm, engulfed in its oversized and inflated sleeve, stuck upwards like a sail.

Miriam and I stood watching him from among the rocks. The spring breeze rippled the surface of the water like silver foil. From time to time, Tonio interrupted his swim stroke and stood chest-deep in the water to wave at us, then tipped back to his prone swimming position.

If that inflated lump with its illegible lettering was so comical, why did Miriam take my hand and squeeze it? When I glanced over at her, I could see that her eyelashes were wet with sea spray — even though the wind was as mild as could be, and the waves, if you could call them that, did not send up spray. Looking straight ahead again, at Tonio jerkily under sail, the gentle breeze told me my face was not entirely dry either.

Remembering how the beach pebbles crackled under our feet, I almost took a step forward, over the stone edging enclosing Tonio's grave, so as to feel the freshly laid gravel under my soles.

471

15

In Horto, we rented a bungalow in a holiday park, but it being low season — the first half of May — we had the place to ourselves. Helga, my translator, and her husband, Wolfgang, an architect, had built a house with a sweeping view of the sea a stone's throw from our cottage.

Along with her elderly parents, Helga had a niece, Inky, staying with her. Inky and Tonio were about the same age. They did not speak each other's language, but Tonio tried to impress the girl by clambering up the olive tree in Helga and Wolfgang's yard. Considering he could only use his left arm, Tonio developed a remarkable agility. Upon reaching the uppermost branch, he would sit and, nonchalantly ignoring Inky, stare out to sea as though he expected a ship to appear on the horizon.

Helga and Wolfgang were in Horto when Tonio died. Still in shock from the news, they planted an olive cutting in his memory near the tree he had climbed all those years ago. We received a colour photo of the sapling by email. If I say we were moved, that is perhaps the best neutral description of the pain, joy, and disquiet we experienced while looking at it. Helga and Wolfgang care for the new offspring, and we hope someday to be travelworthy enough to water it ourselves.

16

During our second week there, we (Helga and Wolfgang, Miriam and me, Inky and Tonio) took a day trip on Wolfgang's sailing yacht. Dolphins swam along, some distance from the boat, to the children's delight. The way the animals, five or six at a time, lifted themselves above of the surface of the water in agile curves, sending out entire Milky Way galaxies of silver bubbles out of the dark-blue water as they dove back in … Tonio leaned against the mast, looking excitedly back and forth … port, starboard … he didn't have enough eyes. A complete, infinite dolphinarium, and we were sailing straight through it.

Wolfgang, assisted by Helga in executing the more complex manoeuvres, moored the boat at a small, uninhabited island, which was dominated by a dilapidated chapel with an exclusively feathered parish. A forgotten set of Hitchcock's *The Birds:* they had taken up residence in every niche, every windowsill, and were in a raucous conclave on the altar. As we approached, they shifted restlessly back and forth, shoulder to shoulder, but, as though guarding their colony's lodgings, did not take flight to join their brethren circling above what used to be the roof. Tonio and Inky were awestruck, but in a slightly fearful way, perhaps because the birds sat there mumbling in chorus, as though they had abandoned themselves to a mussitated vespers.

On the way back, Tonio was allowed to man the rudder. Captain Wolfgang demonstrated how to plant your feet wide apart, to avoid falling over in case of an unexpected lurch. Since Tonio could only steer with one arm, Wolfgang stood behind him, but so unobtrusively that Tonio could maintain the illusion that the yacht was entirely under his control. As we didn't know beforehand how much spray we would encounter on board, Miriam had fastened Tonio's waterproof cover onto his arm, and it whipped sinisterly in the wind. For one reason or another, we weren't able to keep the air out of the sleeve when fastening it, so I began to wonder whether the constant back-and-forth of the balloon was doing Tonio's wrist any good.

Of course, I was touched to see my little boatsman at the helm, so serious and manly in his role, so secure in his task, one-armed like a Captain Hook … but at the same time …

'You're mulling over your new book, aren't you?' said Helga, sitting down next to me. 'I can tell.'

'Oh, do you miss translating?'

She had me figured out. There, surrounded by white seagulls and silver dolphins breaking through myriad tints of blue, all I had to do was luxuriate in my immediate happiness. Miriam, up on the foredeck with her face turned to the sun … Tonio, with the rudder in his little fist, occasionally enclosed in Wolfgang's grown-up hand, steering the

473

yacht through Greek waters ... and next to me, the imaginative translator of *Advocaat van de hanen*, about to be published after the summer by Suhrkamp ...

And me, instead of counting my blessings, sitting there in my own world, piecing together the fragments of the new manuscript ... this here, that there, and in between, for now, a blank page ... I was back in my workroom, the ship where I was captain, coxswain, and galley mate all in one.

17

Now I stood at Tonio's grave, wondering why I hadn't simply prolonged that Greek idyll. Sell the expensive house in Amsterdam, live modestly in a village like Horto ... Tonio at school in a neighbouring town ... I really did not need an eighty-square-metre office garden, sumptuously planted with technical vegetation, like I had in Amsterdam, in order to write. An eyebrow pencil and a roll of toilet paper would do the job just as well.

Upon take-off from Thessaloniki, there was no turning back. I had definitely chosen the confines of the writing table and the faux relaxation of the urban café. Since Whit Sunday, there was a new punishment, which would taunt me for the rest of my days: look up from my work and see the nearly seven-year-old Tonio at the rudder of a sailing yacht, cleaving its way through the deep-blue Greek waters ... laughing nervously, but he does it ... yes, he does it ... the ship obeys him.

18

I consider myself to have been a writer since the summer of 1972, no matter what a failure my first novel was. I have published since 1978. Writing has become second nature to me. After Black Whitsun, I was apparently not so devastated that I was unable to make notes on the dirty trick fate had played on us. I now write this requiem. Say that, after fulfilling this duty to Tonio (for this is how I regard this undertaking), I am able, one way or another, to continue practising my profession and to succeed in completing the various pending projects — then, no matter how good they turn out, for the rest of my life I will be, at least in my own eyes, a *failure*.

Once again, I quote from the poem Ben Jonson wrote upon the death of his seven-year-old son:

Rest in soft peace, and, asked, say here doth lie
Ben Jonson his best piece of poetry.

Likewise, I have the feeling that my best piece of prose is now behind me, and that it is dead and buried, and can never be outdone.

On second thoughts, I'm a little disappointed with the likeness of that etched photo of Tonio as Oscar Wilde. Too blotchy. Maybe it's because a larger, true-to-life print of the portrait, in a waterproof frame, was still there. (The men who placed the gravestone had anchored the frame firmly in the gravel.) There was some discolouration from the damp — the bottom of the photo had gone violet — but otherwise it reflected Tonio's clear glance admirably.

So here he lay all that time, without an audience, without anyone. The boy was with me the entire day, in every guise between zero and twenty-one years old. I lived with him, spoke to him, wrote about him — and yet treachery once again slithered into my soul: I had left him here all on his lonesome for weeks on end, in slow decay.

Frans scuffled about, taking photos of the group. He also bent over the plot a few times, twisting himself into contortions in order to get a legible shot of the text.

Natan stood motionless and deep in thought. Maybe he imagined Tonio in all his vigour, like the last time he had dropped by for a visit, the Wednesday before Whit Sunday. Just as with us later that afternoon, he probably told Natan of his future plans. His visit to his grandfather was likely not entirely selfless. There was a holiday weekend ahead, and he wanted to go out with Jenny. In the end, he drank up grandpa's money with Goscha and Dennis. That night in Trouw, in a sentimentally philosophical confession, he had shared with Goscha (as she told Miriam and me) his guilty conscience regarding his grandparents: that he was slack in keeping in touch with them, and then pocketed a tidy sum once he went around, only to squander it on booze.

I looked over at Natan, and caught a glimpse of him as he was back in 1993, in the Catherina Hospital in Eindhoven, where he and Wies had visited my dying father. Two men from such radically different worlds, one on his deathbed at sixty-seven and the other eighty-plus and still going strong ... the one sometimes hard to follow with his Brabant drawl, the other sometimes impossible to follow with his East European brogue. After the (final) goodbyes, my father called out to Miriam's father, in his failing voice:

'Natan!'

Natan turned around for the last time.

'Our grandson, Natan — *what a* ... !'

And with that, my father, worn out and gasping for air, raised a wobbly arm in the air and stuck up his thumb.

'*Ja ... ja*,' was the only thing that Natan, moved and embarrassed, managed to utter. He, too, stuck his thumb in the air, although this was not part of his normal repertoire of gestures.

Daniel had made a drawing for Tonio, which Frans had rolled up and tied with a ribbon. The little boy thought it entirely normal that his gift be left on the grave, but the ribbon had to be untied. They unrolled the drawing and weighed it down with a large chunk of gravel. Scrawls of red and blue, and, in Frans' handwriting, the word 'meow'.

'When I asked him what it was,' Frans explained, 'Daniel said, without hesitating, "meow". His word for cat. So I guess it's a cat.'

As I said in my brief speech at his funeral, Tonio would go out of his way not to argue with his parents. Even that one time when my nagging him about his lack of ambition threatened to turn into an argument: this, too, fizzled before becoming a real showdown. He simply asked for the time to prove his mettle; what else could I answer but 'I can count on you.'

He took a job, and enrolled at the University of Amsterdam. I had no reason to raise the matter again.

In recent days, I have caught myself inventing, in my daydreams, terrible conflicts with Tonio. They always occur in moments of fatigue and mental disorientation, when the truth about his death takes on less-defined contours. A head-to-head clash, followed by deadlock, could have driven father and son apart. But no matter how terrible the conflict, even if it lasted for years, there was always the opportunity for rapprochement.

My pride in our stable relationship was now equalled by my unbridled ingenuity in fantasising conflicts between us. Nothing was too harrowing. The key point of the visions was that the son turned his back on me, *lived* — at whatever inaccessible distance. And then, one day, we buried the hatchet. The scope of the conflict coloured the reconciliation. It surprised us both that, after years of our gruelling feud, our embrace had remained so strong.

In my most horrific daydream, I envisioned a fight with Tonio about ... his death. We hurled the most awful accusations of neglect at each other. Then we exhausted ourselves with self-censure.

'I take the blame, Tonio.'

'Cut it out. I screwed up.'

'If I hadn't ...'

'Quit it! It was my own stupid fault.'

It ended with us reproaching each other's self-reproach, and forbidding ourselves from blaming the other. When the mist of the daydream cleared, there was no longer a life-threatening conflict. He was dead. Only a hyena dragging around a carcass makes himself think he is still fighting with his prey.

20

On the way back to the exit, we rambled a bit through the cemetery, in search of the grave of the musician Hub Mathijsen. He had been a violinist in the salon-music 'Resistentie Orkest'* and often played the violinophone, which had a metal resonator much like a gramophone horn, rather than a wooden sound box. Its melancholy sound would have been quite apt now, here.

If you wander around this small cemetery long enough, you'll eventually pass every grave. Hub, I had forgotten, was buried next to his brother Joost, the pianist he had performed with all those years. His widow had told me Hub was deaf in one ear: she had him lovingly laid to rest with his good ear facing his brother.

21

The family came back to our place for refreshments. If Mariska held Daniel on her lap, then she, Frans, and Natan would fit perfectly on the back seat of our car. The buggy could fold up and go in the boot.

Halfway home, the car began to fill up with the smell of rot — no, not a dirty diaper or dogshit-packed shoe treads. Rot.

When we got out, Miriam held the earthenware pot in her hand that, filled with moss, slime, and the strands of sodden tobacco from the waterlogged cigarettes, had stood for weeks next to Tonio's grave. It must

---

* A play on the name 'Residentie Orkest', the resident symphony orchestra of The Hague. Prior to founding the Resistentie Orkest, Mathijsen was 2nd concertmaster of the Netherlands Ballet Orchestra and was active in the Amsterdam 'provo' movement of the 1960s.

have all started decomposing, together with the half-unrolled film spool that someone apparently wanted to give Tonio on his way to eternity.

'That rotten-egg smell,' she said. 'Here's the culprit.'

She put the stinking pot on the curb, but, remembering that we were forbidden to throw away anything having to do with Tonio, picked it up and put it back on the floor mat of the car. 'So let it rot.' I wanted her all to myself at that moment, if only for that expression of hopeless embarrassment.

The party had already gone upstairs when Miriam came out of the library. 'I've just been out back. The veranda's beautiful at the moment. The sun's going to come out.'

A little while later, we were all sitting under the spent golden rain, which let loose a flutter of brown shreds at the least bit of breeze. Frans pointed to the huge growth of ivy, which, a good metre thick, was still covering the entire side wall of the houses on the Banstraat. 'I don't want to get on your case,' he said, 'but you really should think about trimming that thing. Otherwise ...'

'Not now,' I said.

We ate and drank. As quiet as everyone was at the grave, they were now boisterously chatting. Except Natan. Seeing him sit for a while with his hands covering his eyes, Hinde asked if he was all right.

'I'm thinking,' he said, in his customary, somewhat singsong tone. Soon after that, he had Miriam drive him home.

I talked mostly to my brother, who was sitting next to me. He couldn't remember a thing of the telephone conversation we had had the night before, after the football finals. His explanation was that the unexpected loss had made him twice as drunk as he really was.

Daniel swung like a monkey from chair to chair, never taking a moment's rest. His blonde hair made me think of Tonio at that age, although there was a difference in energy level. O, horror ... this little boy was in all things Tonio's successor and surrogate. I hoped I could continue to love him as I now did, divorced from all thoughts of my own son.

The sky had gradually gone pitch-black again. I suggested moving the gathering indoors, to the living room, and started rolling up the awnings.

The upstairs television was on: it was nearly six o'clock. The news showed footage of the effect of thunderstorms in the east of the country — uprooted trees and collapsed party tents (there were festivals all over the place). The rest of the news was dominated by The Grief At The Defeat: a dejected Museumplein, which I had seen with my own eyes the previous night, and the arrival of the Boeing with the Dutch team, escorted by a pair of F-16s.

'A dubious honour,' Frans said. 'This is how they usually escort a hijacked aircraft. The enemy of the people brought to the ground. Get down, you. Lie, dog.'

22

'So. The stone's there,' I said after the visitors left. 'Firmly anchored in the earth. *His* patch of ground.'

'And, most importantly,' Miriam said, 'his second name is on it. Or, what's it called ... his *middle* name. Oh, my poor sweet father ... he was really broken up.'

How do tears of compassion differ from tears of grief? They both leak out of the same ducts. It must be the facial expression that goes with it. It's been a long time since I've seen her simply moved to tears, rather than destroyed by grief.

'Well, let's see,' I said, counting on my fingers. 'We've found the bike, his watch, the photos ... Jenny has been traced, and now she's got her portfolio ... the stone's in place, his name is complete ... Now all we need to do is visit the site of the accident.'

'Do we have to?'

'Yes, we have to. We owe it to Tonio. At that spot, he had his last thoughts of us. Of you and me. The word "dumb!" probably flashed through his mind, and that says it all. Also that he did something dumb to *us*. That's how it must have gone. "Dumb!" To himself, to us. There, at that intersection, before he lost consciousness.'

'All right, I reckon we can handle anything now. When?'

Today, nearly two months after Whit Sunday, it has finally got through to me that Tonio is dead. Until now they were just suspicions, followed by denials. Signs posing as the truth. Disbelief still held sway.

Everything is different now.

23

Acquaintances of ours, a couple, had repeatedly offered us a jaunt on their motor punt as a diversion, but until now we had not taken them up on it. On the morning of the team's homecoming, the woman rang us. They were planning to take their boat out that afternoon, to meet the Dutch team's boats out on the IJ harbour and, if possible, tag along through the Amsterdam canals toward Museumplein. Would we ... on account of the historic aspect of the event ... be interested ...?

Miriam promised to confer with me and ring them back. We had already decided to keep half an eye on the TV broadcast of the whole travesty, not to spare the screen our ridicule and to wash down the taste of national duplicity afterwards with a glass of strong stuff. I suddenly saw the chance to break through the cast-iron bands that grief had forged around our house, and finally brave the city and visit the place where our boy had had his fatal accident.

Under cover of a dubious festivity. Incognito among the sham-jubilant crowds. No one would pay us any notice. Just what the doctor ordered.

'Tell them we'll go.'

Miriam arranged with the friends that we would drive to their place later that morning. They lived on KNSM-eiland, a residential development in the IJ, near where their boat was moored. We could watch the team's reception with the Queen on television, where we'd see for ourselves when the players left The Hague for the Amsterdam canal procession.

I rang a neighbour who I knew wouldn't miss a minute of the broadcast, and asked if he would record the whole charade for us — Noordeinde Palace, IJ, Herengracht, Museumplein, the lot. He was so surprised at my sudden patriotism that he promised to run off a disc for me.

24

It's the unguarded moments that have a monopoly on our true feelings. The brain is still under the spell of semi-sleep, or a daydream, or a bout of fatigue. At such moments of doziness or inattention, it appears that I still, or more than ever, consider the possibility that Tonio will return to our midst. The unguarded moment gives a glimpse at a more primitive layer of the soul, where the hope is fed that we will get our son back one day. We need that latent expectation, apparently, in order to survive the loss.

Wide awake, we appear, albeit with self-destructive revulsion, to accept the hard facts confirming the irrevocability of Tonio's fate, and in doing so we embrace, apparently, our own fate. But deep in our heart we still preserve the animalistic disbelief that he has vanished from our lives forever.

This requiem, too, if it is a requiem, has its own unguarded moments. The reconstruction of Tonio's last days and hours loses its predetermined futility, and is transformed into a search for the lost and forsaken boy himself.

'He's not dead; he's woken up from the dream that was life.'

What we are reconstructing is nothing other than the closing moments of this dream — from which Tonio, according to the poet, has now escaped. It is the escaped Tonio we are searching for. This requiem serves no other purpose than to track him down and retrieve him.

Before we got in the car, I browsed through *de Volkskrant*, which, like yesterday's paper, was all about Dutch football. Patriarch Cruijff had nothing good to say about his great-grandsons' playing. Disgraceful, is what it was. In Uganda, a bloodbath took place in a bar where godless fans were watching the finals. The severed head of the suicide bomber still rolled around amid the dozens of dismembered bodies — which was at least a change of pace from the Dutch misery of a badly behaved soccer ball on the screen.

Anyway, our boys, who did first have to reach the finals in order to lose, would be soon cheered rather than jeered. It was the will of the people. Triumph had already nestled itself in everyone's consciousness nationwide: it was the spark that illuminated every empty-head from within, like the candle in the hollowed-out beetroot on Shrove Tuesday.

At eleven o'clock, Miriam came to get me. 'I'm not even sure we'll get through the crowds with the car. They're streaming in from far and wide, I heard, and not all by train.'

She was wearing a new summer dress, brightly coloured and with an African print. Its length and width nicely camouflaged her waistline, enlarged by our evening pain-relief. Unlike with me, drink did not at all leave its mark on her sweet face. The fingerprint of grief in her features: that was another story.

25

The football squad and their bigwigs were still inside Noordeinde Palace having tea with the Queen. Screaming hordes of supporters rattled at the gold-spiked gates. A NOS helicopter filmed the players' bus waiting for them behind the palace. But first the terrace scene. The palace doors (whose narrowness always makes them look uptight) opened, and the losers spilled out onto the stairs, positioning themselves around their queen. Self-conscious shuffling.

'The cabinet formation is complete,' our host said, to kick off the mood. 'One less worry.'

'The Queen's the only one smiling,' the hostess said.

'Can't say I blame her,' her husband replied. 'She's just been treated to the sight of the family colour being supported by twenty-three pairs of muscular, hairy legs.'

The players and their coaches were wan and sickly by comparison. Indeed, not one of them could muster a smile. Maybe they were all hung over. Their loss had been celebrated until the wee hours in Huis ter Duin, Noordwijk, where they were fêted by our other national losers, De Toppers.*

Eventually, here and there, a cagey grin passed over a player's face. So this is how they faced each other: the Queen with her disgraced football cabinet on one side of the gilded gates, the triumphantly howling herd of cattle on the other.

Then they turned and followed the Queen back inside. Later, we were shown a bird's-eye view of the players and their entourage stepping into two helicopters on the Waalsdorpervlakte, on the outskirts of The Hague — for a half-hour flight to Amsterdam. Our host switched off the TV and suggested we walk to the mooring.

26

On the IJ we joined a slapdash flotilla of smaller and larger boats, from motor punts to speedboats to seaworthy yachts. The water police, ever vigilant, kept all of us at a safe distance from the players' and VIP boats. We needed our captain's binoculars to make out the Museum Boat moored at the marine base, festooned as it was with orange-red flowers and guarded by a fleet of motorised police super-pedal boats.

We kept our eyes peeled for the arrival of the team's helicopters, but seeing as it had been at least an hour since they left the Waalsdorpervlakte, the guys must have already long arrived at the marine base.

---

* The three-man pop music group that represented the Netherlands in the 2009 Eurovision Song Festival. They competed in the second semi-finals, but failed to reach the final round.

Miriam and I would watch it all again that night on TV. The players had changed clothes, trading their blazers for training gear — blue with orange trim, to distinguish them from the monochrome uniforms of their supporters. They marched, in a barely orderly single file, across the dock to board the Museum Boat, fidgeting and jostling like schoolboys on a class outing.

'Well, well, look who we have there,' our host said, passing me his binoculars. 'Our brand-new mayor himself.'

With difficulty, I could make out the newly appointed burgomaster, Van der Laan, who, sporting his official mayoral collar, somewhat worriedly greeted the entourage. Later, in the rerun, we would get the details. All those overtrained football machines went straight for the beer, provided by sponsor Heineken in green slurp-bottles, regular glasses, and goblets the size of the World Cup itself. This was their way of bracing themselves for the shameful ticker-tape parade.

Once both boats, surrounded by the police water-scooters, were well past the fans' flotilla, there was no stopping the crush. It was like Sail, when everything that could float came out to welcome a Russian cadet ship as it reached the IJ. Despite the police, our little punt could now get quite close to the players' boat. The whole chaotic armada set out in the direction of the Westelijke Eilanden.

The goalkeeper appeared at the railing and brought an oversized World Cup tankard of beer to his mouth. Dirk, Robin, Wesley … what a bunch of little boys they were, really, when you saw them horsing around on the deck like that. They became more and more rambunctious. The mayor stood there, a bit out of place in his water-spattered suit. None of the players seemed to want to trade words with him.

I crouched at the bow of the boat. I looked back at Miriam, who, seated alongside our friends on the thwart, was holding on tightly to the gunwale. Her face was wet, but it could just as well have come from the spray sent up by a passing boat. On the other hand … in this open expanse of light, surrounded by bobbing boats all hurrying in the same direction, it was impossible *not* to think of Tonio. She knew, as I did: we were heading, via an enormous detour, for the spot we haven't dared visit since Whit Sunday, the day we stood at his deathbed, kissing him goodbye for eternity. But a confrontation with the crossroads where he had lost consciousness for good early that morning, we hadn't been able to face. We'd still have to wait and see if it would happen today.

We bobbed to the left of the players' boat. There was a gap in the water police's cordon, which a floating camera crew from the popular show *RTL Boulevard* took advantage of by cruising right up alongside, so close they could almost touch. The TV glamour-programme crew did its work until Wesley Snijder recognised the presenter's mug and dumped the contents of a ten-litre beer stein over him. There: payback for the tendentious reporting on Wesley's fiancée.

The armada sailed past one of the harbour islands.

27

When I woke up that morning, I realised I was wearing my apnea mask. Usually, if I went to bed tanked up — as was certainly the case after that visit to the cemetery — I'd neglect to put it on, sometimes out of forgetfulness, more often because I fell into a deep sleep the minute I lay down. Last night, even though my mind was a blank, I apparently did think of it.

I dreamt of Tonio. As I lay there half asleep, listening to the quiet murmur of the CPAP device, I tried to recall the dream. Tonio cried at the end — no, he was *still* crying. You could barely hear it above the sound of the machine, but it was unmistakable. He did not cry like a young adult man, no, but like the two-, three-year-old he once was. He cried, quietly and inconsolably sad, as he occasionally did on Thursday evenings in our Leidsegracht days, when Miriam had her regular night out with a girlfriend. I would babysit Tonio, and if he woke up, perhaps because he knew (or felt) that his mother was not there, he cried. If I went to have a look, he would stand up in his crib, which only just fitted in the nook of the roof. Upon seeing his father, he said, with a sniff and a wobbly voice: 'I want Mummy.'

I couldn't offer him Mummy, because she was sitting in a restaurant with Lot, or they were having a last drink at Café Schiller. 'I want Mummy.' His singsong weeping made me all the more nervous, because on Thursday nights we usually received a couple of anonymous calls. If I answered, it was silent on the other end of the line. Sometimes I thought I heard vague pub noises in the background. I have to admit that at first I suspected it was Miriam: checking whether I was at really at home with the little one. Our relationship was not at its best in those days (even though Our Man in Africa was not yet in the picture). When I brought it up with her, she hit the roof. Never, *never* would she do such a thing. Didn't I remember that back when we lived in De Pijp, ten years before, she had been the victim of anonymous telephone terrorism? Whenever she answered, the caller played a German march, or the Horst Wessel. Later, we discovered that the caller was a neo-Nazi in the neighbourhood, a civics teacher at the high school where my sister taught English. A nostalgic anti-Semite.

We assumed that the Thursday-evening caller was a Schiller regular, who wanted to let me know he'd spotted my wife, or wanted to suggest that he himself was in her company — in short, that he had me in his grip. But this suspicion did nothing to relax me in my duties as babysitter, and Tonio was well aware of it, so that he kept on whimpering, almost apologetically softly — a full-out sob session just wasn't his style. 'I want Mu-u-u-ummy.'

Meanwhile, that morning, the thirteenth of July, he went on wailing as a continuation of my long-forgotten dream, as only the very occasionally inconsolable Tonio could. For a moment, I thought it was the neighbour's youngest child, whose early-morning cries I heard from time to time through the open windows. But no, the neighbours were on holiday. And besides, it was unmistakably the weeping of the three-year-old Tonio — so real, so near, that it frightened me. The sound was dampened by the hum of the CPAP machine. I wanted to hear Tonio cry in all his unadulterated misery, so that I'd know what he needed …

I tore off the apnea mask without undoing the plastic hooks. I yanked the elastic bands over my head and hurled the thing, tube and all, onto the floor. The apparatus lay there for a few seconds, making that slurping and sucking sound, and then … silence. The child's hushed crying had vanished.

In its drowsy state, my brain must have converted the singsong hum of the CPAP into Tonio's long-ago disquiet. I wanted it back. I wanted to be able to listen to it for hours on end. I groped in the dark next to the bed, found the tube, and pulled the elastic bands back over my head. The apparatus resumed automatically, softly pumping air into the mask, guarding its wearer against suspended breathing. The puffs of air sounded the same as before, but the weeping was gone. I'd driven it off.

All day I tried to call to mind that real-life crying. I am not a great believer in supernatural incidents, but I could not avoid the notion that Tonio, via my apnea machine, was trying to tell me something. Perhaps the terrible, unutterable truth about his end. The suffering he must have endured after being thrown to the asphalt, or later, in the ambulance or on the operating table. Or, declared brain-dead, on his deathbed, when all he was given was air through a breathing tube. Maybe there he felt his parents' presence, their kisses and caresses, and heard their choked words of farewell. This morning, Tonio tried to say something back. But not comforting. Only how awful it was. The pain. The farewell. And in doing so, he used his most anguished child's voice. Its melancholy, wordless melody.

28

Much as the police in their bumper-boats tried to keep the pursuing fans' fleet at bay, our motorised punt remained in the front ranks. We jounced our way into the labyrinth of the city. The very first bridges were already thronged with hysterically bleating supporter-sheep. Compared to June '88, when the blandness of everyday duds still dotted the red-white-blue, the fans were now far more exuberantly decked out in the colour of their religion. Many of the supporters wore shapeless, bright orange angel-hair wigs, some of them a good half-metre across. The costume director of the film *Amadeus* would have been jealous.

Seen from a distance, the frizzy offshoots of the wigs bled seamlessly into a powder-like orange mist produced by spray cans. As it hissed out of the valve, the smoke was still a clear day-glo orange; but as it wafted out across the water, the mist quickly took on a grubby tint. It made me think of the crayon I used as a child to colour in a pencil-outlined rooftop. The crayon always dragged some pencil graphite with it, smudging the orange into a dirty grey-red — quite realistic, you could say, but today it only made me sad.

As we turned onto the Brouwersgracht, I felt Miriam poke me in the back. I was being beckoned by the host, who sat at the stern, manning the rudder. He shouted that he wanted to bypass the Herengracht and try to approach Museumplein via Prinsengracht and Spiegelgracht. That would give us a head start.

I nodded, and wondered if I could get to the Hobbemastraat/ Stadhouderskade intersection without running into a barricade. We hadn't told our friends that, for us, that spot was the actual objective of this trip.

The Melkmeisjesbrug was, in all its slenderness, a living triumphal arch, rising up out of a dense, unearthly orange mist. The red-white-blue mass that swarmed over it had a thousand legs and waving tentacles, and it screamed wordlessly from a thousand throats.

The players' boat, followed by that of the officials, turned left onto the Herengracht directly after passing under the Milkmaids' Bridge. Our captain picked up speed. The bow of the punt lifted slightly and cleaved the water of the Brouwersgracht. Straight ahead. I glanced to the left. The Herengracht was, for as far as the eye could see, a tunnel formed by a canopy of trees and a mass of writhing arms, all waving flags, banners, and pennants.

If you didn't know better, you might mistake the monotonous

hollering for a mass lament. The bridges over the Herengracht appeared to be covered in a rusty orange sort of teeming moss, kept in undulating motion by maggots. And then there was that layer of red-brown mist lying low over the water of the canal, like the vapours emitted by heavily polluted wastewater from a chemical factory. The team boat would soon be out of sight.

I thought back on the idyllic Loenen in the Veluwe, where the manure was brought out in thick winter mist. As the morning progressed, the low-lying haze took on a filthy yellow colour, like London smog above an industrial zone. Poor Tonio, who I had brought to the unspoilt countryside to protect him from urban grime. The windows in his room had to be hermetically sealed against the stench of the liquid fertiliser, which, absorbed by the ground mist, could only escape horizontally ... across the road ... through the yards and into the houses ...

We cruised past the West Indies House, situated on the Herenmarkt on the right bank of the Brouwersgracht. That's where we were married on 24 December 1987, while Tonio was already taking shape inside Miriam's belly. Here, on that frigid winter morning, my father nearly fell into the water from a sudden attack of dyspnea. After the marriage ceremony, he wobbled, hacking and gasping for air, over to the water's edge to hoick a gob of bloody saliva into the canal. I saw, in the nick of time, from the way his eyes rolled back into his head, that he was having a dizzy spell, and just managed to prevent him from teetering into the canal. Pulmonary emphysema. He was just sixty-two, but half of those years had been spent chain-smoking. He never did quit. Secret chemical substances in each cigarette insured that his lungs, overgrown with glasslike slime, would open up — until the next cigarette.

We were planning to go to the Sonesta Hotel, next to the Koepelkerk, for champagne, but the upshot of the palaver was that I went to the reception desk to cancel the reservation while the rest of my family helped my half-dead father into a taxi. I did not want to write him off as a bad fairy in drag, but it was clear that the ceremony, intended to legitimise the foetus, had been jinxed.

29

The new gravestone had not provided closure. More than any single day between 23 May and now, today, the 13th of July, was one of *pantonioism*. This was, of course, also because we hadn't left the house just for a trip to the goat farm or Buitenveldert Cemetery, and were back in the city proper for the first time since that dinner on the Staalstraat. Tonio was everywhere. Everything exuded Tonio. Even the most insignificant objects, the most unimportant occurrences, revealed a trace of his soul.

30

'If he keeps on like this,' Miriam shouted into my ear, 'I'm going to be sick.'

The punt hardly slowed in the frothing turn that took us onto the Prinsengracht, lurching sideways without interrupting its Japanese bows. Miriam grabbed onto me and said: 'I'm really gonna throw up.'

When we had passed under the bridge and straightened our course, I turned halfway toward our friend at the rudder and motioned to him to slow down. Maybe he only understood my signal when he saw Miriam retching.

July 1994. The boat trip from our village on the Ibiza coast to Ibiza Town was scheduled to take an hour. En route, said the brochure, we could enjoy views of the rocky coast as we sailed past. A mirror-smooth, deep-blue sea ... white lassoos of sea foam around the megaliths jutting out of the calm waves ... cold drinks on board included in the price ...

The Spanish skipper tore to Ibiza Town in less than half an hour, while the man who was supposed to provide the drinks had already positioned himself with the fire hose, ready to rinse away the gall of passengers who had gotten seasick within the first ten minutes. The bow slammed against the water surface with a force that a whale's fin couldn't have matched. Miriam was the first one to throw up, immediately followed by Tonio (out of solidarity with his mother). Grinning, and adopting a fiendish routine, the steward stood there, legs spread, hosing down the deck. The boat lurched so violently that Miriam and Tonio were unable to aim their puke, and consequently sullied themselves.

Later, as we walked along the quay (still sick to our stomachs), we saw the crew lounging on coils of rope, thoroughly enjoying a leisurely lunch thanks to the extra half-hour they had robbed from the tourist riff-raff.

The six-year-old Tonio was so horrified at having to witness his own mother vomit that he went into a panic at the thought of the return voyage.

'I don't want Mama to throw up.'

In the end, we took a taxi back to the bungalow — an hour-and-a-half trek, including inexplicable traffic jams, over winding inland roads. At first, the driver only sniffed with distaste, but later he launched into an all-out rant against his sour-smelling passengers.

Once home, the hardships were soon forgotten. Before dinnertime, Tonio and I thought up a new chapter for our book *Reis in een boom*. The boy had climbed into the chestnut tree behind his house and refused to come down, despite the pleas of his father and mother. Yes, at night, when his parents were asleep, he did climb down — to fetch tools and planks with which to build himself a treehouse. He carried out the construction during the day, doing his best to imitate a woodpecker with his hammer and nails.

'… to mislead his parents.'

'What's a woodpecker?'

'You know. Woody Woodpecker.'

'Oh yeah.'

'When the treehouse is finished … a kind of cabin … then he can start his travels.'

'Yeah, but Adri … a tree … how can you travel in it? A tree doesn't have wheels. It has roots … way deep in the ground.'

'And *that* is the secret of our story. A secret only you and I know. Omigosh, just imagine, if *everyone* knew the secret … then every Tom,

Dick, and Harry could write a story like this. Uh-uh, this is *our* story. Yours and mine.'

'Will my name be on the book, too?'

'Of course — the author's name is always on the front cover. And the title page. So there'll be two names. Yours and mine.'

If I were worth my salt as a writer, I would be able to describe Tonio's expression at the realisation that he might write his own book. With me. His face darkened a bit, perhaps as he realised the hurdles of such an undertaking.

'Yeah, but Adri … I don't even know the tree's secret. Does he turn it into a ship?'

'No, the tree stays put, with its roots anchored firmly in the ground. And the boy still travels.'

'So what's the secret?'

'When you get onto a train or a boat, and you go travelling on it, what's the first thing you notice?'

'That you're moving … or sailing.'

'Exactly. You move forward, and that means your surroundings change. First the train chugs past the houses, then fields and meadows. The secret of our tree is that it never leaves its spot, but that it keeps getting new surroundings. So it's as though that boy in his tree travels all over the world. With a constantly changing view from his treehouse.'

31

What was I doing here, in the middle of all this mass hysteria? Wanting to finish off what I started on 26 June 1988, when I made an about-face because I didn't dare abandon the newborn any longer?

My intuition had not deceived me. I got home and found Miriam in panic. The maternity-support worker had given Tonio his bath, whereby a plaster on her finger came loose. She showed Miriam the cut, which had opened up again in the warm water and was bleeding profusely. The silly woman had mentioned in passing that she had also been nursing a terminal AIDS patient for several months. After my phone call to the clinic, she was recalled from our employ and fired on the spot. We were told that the nurse was a chronic fantasist, and that she never should have been placed with us, but this only augmented Miriam's (and my) disquiet. I should never have gone to the football homecoming that afternoon.

32

Grasping the gunwale, I crouch-walked to the stern. I had to step over two cross thwarts along the way. The host-captain made a beckoning gesture at the handle of the rudder, assuming, apparently, that I wanted to take over from him.

'The Pulitzer's mooring is just up ahead,' I said. 'Could you let us off there? Miriam and I want to go into town on foot.'

He looked disappointed, but nodded, ticking his finger against the brim of his cap. At the Pulitzer Hotel, I helped Miriam out of the boat. We thanked them for the enjoyable cruise, and watched as the punt cut its way, razor-sharp, through the khaki-coloured water.

Via two side streets and the bridge over the Keizersgracht, we approached the Herengracht as quickly as the unflagging stream of thronging supporters allowed. We needn't have hurried, as the Museum Boat still had a couple of hundred metres to go before reaching the jam-packed bridge, where we tried to find a spot. The place was swarming with silver-white wigs, spray-painted to look like cloudish versions of the Dutch flag. Under the wigs, faces were caked with orange gunk, with mini-flags in red, white, white, and blue on their cheeks and foreheads.

The Revolt of the Clowns. They hung in clusters on lampposts. Something tickled my face: an orange wig, generously adorned with the kind of sticks you get at the herring vendor: a toothpick with a little Dutch flag at the end. The players' boat appeared under the next bridge. The animalistic braying, which you thought couldn't get any louder, only increased in volume. Again I noticed the lack of anything triumphant in the sound of the cheering. You only had to shake your head and it sounded like a mass yell for help, a crowd crushing itself to death.

The boat had now emerged from under the low bridge, and the blue training outfits all stood back upright, bottle or glass in their raised hand. The police force's motorised waterbikes hastened to resecure the cordon. People jumped, or fell, into the canal, reminiscent of old black-and-white cinema newsreels of The Beatles on their canal tour through Amsterdam. Then, too, it seemed to me as though people were screaming in protest, because there was a fake Beatle, complete with signature haircut, cruising along as a stowaway.*

The trio of young men who jumped into the water right in front of us wore orange life vests, ruling out a joint suicide born of desperate adulation. The boat drew nearer, and the cheering got even more deafening. Orange gorged itself on Orange, but the screaming suggested insatiability.

I held Miriam tightly, with her back pressed against me. We were now looking straight at the boat, insofar as the frizzy orange wigs allowed. Van Bommel's goofy hat. A black player, whose name I didn't know, wore a gold-coloured Roman victory helmet, I suppose in order to dispel any residual doubts. Another player was being interviewed on camera.

The spray-can orange mist thickened as the boat approached. Now, showers of orange confetti rained down upon the deck.

'Heads down!' cried the MC. The players crouched obligingly, just to be on the safe side — a pity, because after their scandalous performance against Spain, I thought they all, down to the last man, deserved a good head-butt. The boat glided under the bridge. I took Miriam by the hand and pulled her behind me.

'What are you doing?' she called out.

'They'll be going down Leidsegracht next.'

---

* Drummer Jimmy Nicol replaced Ringo Starr, who had taken ill with tonsillitis, on the group's June 1964 tour.

Despite colliding constantly with other spectators, we managed to keep ahead of the team's boat. On the Leidsegracht, we found a surprisingly uncrowded spot across from number 22, where we had lived from November 1990 to July 1992. As if I hadn't stopped here on purpose, Miriam pointed to the house across the canal, her finger singling out the second floor. I looked at her. It was the first time today I'd seen tears in her eyes.

Hysterical cheering along the canal wall broke the relative quiet. Through the arch of the bridge, led by two police boats, sailed our national pride.

33

With every tourist boat that turned the corner from Herengracht into Leidsegracht, we heard the loud honk of a ship's horn. In time, it drove Miriam and me completely crazy, but Tonio ran excitedly to the window with each new blast.

'Boat … boat!'

And then he watched contentedly as the flat, glass-topped vessel passed through the canal below, and the passengers' heads turned from left to right on cue from the tour guide.

One pleasant spring day during our first year at that address, I knelt at the low windowsill and looked out the open windows to see if Miriam and Tonio were yet on their way back from nursery school. There they stood, on the stone steps leading to the front door. A rare sight: Tonio in tears. He kicked the lowest stair angrily while Miriam spoke soothing words.

'No … I want to go to Bibelebons!'

He wasn't faking it for effect. His crying seemed heartrendingly sincere in the serernity of that spring afternoon. 'I want to go back to Bibelebons. Bibelebons! Not home.'

He plonked himself down at the bottom step and refused to go inside.

Eventually she sat down next to him, an arm around his shoulder. I couldn't make out the words, but the snivelling continued, softer now.

Sweet poppet. He was the only one of us who missed the Veluwe. A tour boat tooted its horn. Tonio wasn't interested. He shook his head vehemently. Bibelebons — his beloved Veluwe nursery school. And we had just yanked him out of there, without asking his permission.

34

Tonio called me by my first name from the moment he could speak. If he wanted to indicate our familial relationship, he'd say: 'This is my Adri. My Adri.'

And with it, he'd tug at my sleeve.

I sit in the small living room at Leidsegracht 22, with the glass door open to the short hallway and the stairs leading to the dining room. Reading on the sofa, I watch Tonio scuffle past, bearing a large bale of blankies. The entire house is laid with the same soft, thick, grey carpeting, including the stairs — it is Tonio's greatest pleasure to climb up the stairs on his bare knees. From behind the pacifier comes a combination of humming, mumbling, and gentle groaning as he conquers the stairway. When he reaches the curve and is nearly out of sight, the ruffle of his limbs against the treads stops, as do the noises from his nose and mouth. I turn a page of my book, and observe out of the corner of my eye how he hangs motionlessly on the stairs, the pacifier now in his free hand. He is looking at me. I focus on the page, but have stopped reading. Each of us as stock-still as a grasshopper, we eye one another: he, straight at me; me, indirectly.

I can't hold my pose any longer, and turn to him, looking straight into his wide-open eyes, which glisten teasingly.

'Adri, you're my fa-a-a-a-ather, right?'

'Whether you like it or not, yes, I am your father.'

Before I've even finished my sentence, he sticks the pacifier back into his mouth and continues lumbering up the stairs. His panting laugh has something triumphant about it: as though he's unmasked me, or at least has coerced a confession out of me.

I stare motionlessly at my book awhile, without reading.

35

When the homecoming boat had passed and the players crouched once again for the next arched bridge, we stood looking at the gable of our former home. All the way at the top, at the back, was Tonio's attic room, which he proudly showed to every first-time visitor. 'This is *my* house.'

I pointed at the wide canal-green door, which shone like a mirror. Next to the door was a lantern that would have gone down well at a brothel. 'You think that lock is still the same?'

Miriam didn't know what I was getting at.

'Remember, that time you locked me out ... and were hiding inside with Our Man in Africa?'

'Oh, that. I'd lost my keys. I only wanted to keep thieves out.'

'Maybe I was the thief.'

Having had enough of the noxious orange fumes, I suggested to Miriam that we take a short cut through Leidsestraat to the Leidsebosje, and wait for the parade there. We took a left onto the Keizersgracht. Leidsestraat and Leidseplein were less packed than otherwise on a warm summer afternoon. As we approached the square, I caught myself peering down side streets in search of the shawarma joint that Tonio might have been heading for that night, in order to put some solid food in his beer-ravaged stomach.

By the time we got to the Korte Leidsedwarsstraat, I could no longer contain myself. I walked over to the door of a Turkish snack bar, and examined the colour photos of the various dishes. Sure enough, they did a döner kebab, Tonio's favourite late-night snack. Was this the image he had in mind, and for which he allowed himself to be lured into a detour

— off the Van Baerle, to Jan Luyken and, finally, Hobbemastraat?

Yes, a person can meet his end as unheroically as this. I recently came across an old postcard, sent in the summer of 1978 by Jolanda, who was vacationing on the island of Terschelling with a girlfriend. 'I miss you + shawarma sandwich'. I had spent a few intense weeks with her, both of us so in love that we forgot to eat, but not to drink. Late at night — I lived in De Pijp — we would end up at the shawarma joint on the Ferdinand Bolplein. The streets were just as deserted as now in the early morning. I never considered those nocturnal meals life-threatening.

36

We passed the Hotel Americain's new fountain. From the sudden cheering around the corner, we reckoned the players' boat had reached the Singel. For those on the bridge, the boat still had to take another curve, so here the howling only started a few moments later. Miriam and I found a spot at the far end of the bridge railing. The sunlight shone on the deck and on the players, a few of whom were being interviewed. The TV helicopter hovered above Leidseplein, taking the bird's-eye footage we would soon be watching at home.

No sooner had the boat nipped under the wide bridge than the entire herd of supporters rushed across the tram tracks to the other side — in order to see their heroes reappear. The stampede looked just like thirty years before: the giddy panic with which hordes of squatters and their supporters were scattered by riot police. The tear gas was now orange, and the tears were not chemically induced, but brought on by the confused mix of triumph and defeat.

Miriam and I cut straight through to the Leidsebosje. We were approaching The Spot, but were in no hurry to reach it. We preferred to be pushed or washed there by the hordes of clowns that were now heading our way. Hundreds of them swarmed further up along the raked wall of the Singel canal, in order to get as close as possible to the boat, which was just emerging from under the bridge. It cruised down the short stretch of Leidsekade where Harry Mulisch lived. From where I stood, I couldn't see if he was watching from his workroom: there was too much reflection in the window. He might well have been there. Usually, he'd have retreated to his favourite hotel on the Lido in Venice right now, but it was closed for renovations. The day after the accident he had walked over to The Spot, and was shocked by the bright yellow lines and symbols that illustrated the brute force of the drama, as yet unaware of who it had happened to.

I recognised the player now being interviewed as Robin van Persie. I pointed it out to Miriam, who nodded sadly. Without having to say it out loud, we both pictured the six-year-old Robin leaning up against the wall of our rented schoolhouse in Marsalès, watching sullenly as his sisters taught the one-year-old Tonio to walk. Even the flat-bottomed flagship of Dutch football could not escape from pantonioism today.

The pedestrian bridge linking the Max Euweplein to the Stadhouderskade (the bridge I had once believed had played such a crucial role in Tonio's unhappy end), too, was chock-a-block with screaming fans who were already wastefully dumping fistfuls of orange confetti into the canal while the boat was still no further than the old Lido. My eyes glided along the front façade of the Holland Casino, trying to locate the security cameras that had registered Tonio's last deed in this world. I wasn't able to find them. Of course, being a system designed to foil burglars, they wouldn't make them overly conspicuous.

On the other corner of the entrance to the Max Euweplein was the grand café where, not even a year ago, Tonio had first met his future classmates. The small delegation that had brought us flowers at the beginning of June explained how it had gone. August 2009: because Tonio was still working at Dixons, he missed the beginning of intro week. When he finally made a date with his 'group', he showed up much too late. Trying to kill time while waiting for him, his classmates — who had never met Tonio or even seen a photo of him — tried to picture what he was like, based solely on his name and date of birth. The game got more and more serious. Based on just those two bits of information, they put together a profile, a sort of intuitive composite sketch. Theories on his personal attributes like hairstyle and weight were posited and dismissed. A small majority came to the conclusion that he was 1.75m at most. Another small majority saw him with long, dark hair and thick eyebrows that grew toward each other a bit just above the bridge of his nose. Finally, they all more or less agreed: this, and only this, was how the newcomer looked.

Just then Tonio walked in, certain of his anonymity. He scanned the tables in the full café for what could be his group. How on earth was he to recognise them? All at once there were ten arms waving in the air, and ten voices calling out as one: 'Yoo-hoo, Tonio! Over here!'

They had democratically conceived just the right picture of him. If I try to imagine his surprise at that moment — his shy grin (that started somewhere between his shoulder blades) — I could just cry. Just nine months later — a stone's throw from that very same café, on the other side of the canal — he would be dashed to the pavement by a car.

I imagined him walking over to his classmates' table. 'Jeez, what the … you guys …'

Laughing, with jerky gestures, he would make a round of handshakes. 'Shit, how'd you know …?'

37

The team's boat approached The Spot, where the Singel canal curves to the left toward the Rijksmuseum. Supporters still slid down the sloped, overgrown canal wall, either on their back or in a crouch walk, toward the water's edge, as though they were prepared to wade out to the boat, up to their neck in brown muck if need be.

'Come with me.' I pulled Miriam past the undulating wall of orange backs and wigs. The Hobbemakade/Stadhouderskade junction was deserted. High above, a helicopter hovered, but not to guard The Spot.

The crowd faced away from the intersection, cheering hysterically. No more yellow outlines, which the desk officers had warned us about, were to to be seen — worn away by cars that *hadn't* suddenly found a cyclist on their front bumper.

I pointed to the place. 'Right about there.'

Here he had been slammed out of life. Life itself not yet entirely out of him, but what ensued was mostly just a last-ditch attempt to save what, in the end, couldn't be saved.

The boats, accompanied by whoops and roars, followed the curve. Vuvuzelas bellowed their heavy tones. Entire hordes advanced en masse toward the Rijksmuseum, so as to enjoy, for another few moments, a view of the players, or to be at Museumplein on time for the actual tribute.

Miriam shook her head, crying inaudibly. 'Just like that ...' I thought I heard her say. 'In the middle of the road ...'

What struck me all the more was the *loneliness* of what had occurred here. After a bike ride on his own ... blind fate grabbing him by the horns ... being flung into the air and smacked against the asphalt. How long did he lie there like that? Did he groan, or were his lungs already too wrecked to provide sufficient air to cry out?

I studied the area carefully. The curve in the Stadhouderskade, the mouth of the Hobbemakade, the crosswalk from the Park Hotel to the Singel ... indeed, it really did look, as Dick had said, open and orderly. Blindfolded and all, fate had had quite a chore bringing together a cyclist and a car right here. Exacting work in the early-morning darkness.

In my imagination these past weeks, The Spot had gradually shrunk — until it became a narrow, indistinct, one-way tunnel in which a bike and a Suzuki simply *had* to have a fatal encounter.

38

Tonio, the finest thing you gave me is the sense of self-esteem. Before you made your entrance, I always had to *act out* a form of confidence, such was the low self-regard I secretly harboured. As I watched you develop, so too grew my sense of pride — in you, of course, but also in myself. I was, for a not-inconsequential part, in you. Whoever could have a hand in producing such a magnificent creature, must certainly be worth *something*.

Now that I'm forced to release you so abruptly, my self-esteem is in a sorry state, as though it was not only created out of you, but has vanished along with you. I begat you, but was unable to preserve you. I'm not worth crap anymore.

39

It is a night
you normally only see in films

Night was apparently a thing, an object, which could usually only be made visible cinematographically, but also occurred once in a blue moon — in the form, for instance, of the Brabant balladeer Guus Meeuwis. He was on stage at the far end of Museumplein, rounding off his act for the rapturous mob. After this, the national team would be given its official tribute; the players were now just about stepping off the boat at the pier across from the Rijksmuseum, in order to be reunited with their loved ones.

On the floor there's an empty bottle of wine
and clothes that could be either yours or mine

My Dutch grammar teacher would probably take more umbrage at that 'empty bottle of wine' than 'there's clothes'. Gerard van der Vleuten is no longer with us in this life, but through the years I often hear his undaunted voice: 'A bottle of wine, Guus, is a bottle full of wine. If the bottle is empty, Guus, the wine is finished, leaving us with an empty wine bottle. An "empty bottle of wine", Guus, is like "the corner of a round table": a *contradictio in terminis*. Got it? Guus …?'

Meeuwis closed with *the* stupidest number to ever emerge from the history of Dutch song: 'Kedeng, kedeng', the title offering an onomatopoeic depiction of a train chugging along the rails. The audience hollered the refrain in over-the-top ecstasy, enriching it with an improvised arrangement for a thousand vuvuzelas. Here a loser lifted up the hearts of the losers — and necessary it was, too.

The players were now allowed to take the stage. Van Bronckhorst, the captain, announced each of his men one by one, all twenty-two of them. The cheering from below elevated the athletes ever further above their flop. The *vox populi* had the last word.

40

The neighbour who had recorded the live broadcast for us warned me that the video and sound quality was 'godawful', with pixelated block faces and wrung-out heads.

Filmed from the air, the fans looked even more like a herd of cattle at round-up time. If they got squashed hard enough against the bridge railings, their fervour would get squeezed out by itself. This mass display of rapture about absolutely nothing — this can't be what life, civilisation, Tonio's death, was all about. It was not so much that people sought out emptiness — they sought out *echoing* emptiness, so they'd feel less alone. Nothingness had to be an echo chamber. You tossed in a bass, and got back an ass, without having to do any more than scream at the top of your lungs.

The boats disappeared under the Marnixstraat's wide bridge at the end of the Leidsegracht, and stayed under it for so long that one might think they had just evaporated into the darkness. The helicopter's camera could only film the fans who desperately raced from one side of the bridge to the other, in disbelief that their heroes might be gone for good.

And yet the team boat re-emerged into the full sunlight, and turned left onto the Singel toward Leidseplein and the Hotel Americain. Before the vessel once again vanished into the darkness of the bridge alongside the hotel, you could see Robin van Persie being manoeuvred into an advantageous position for his turn as interviewee. Again the helicopter filmed as the herd galloped from one side of the bridge to the other. I knew that we, too, had crossed the road — not to the railings on the opposite side, but to the Leidsebosje, but I wasn't able to make us out: it was filmed from too high up.

The broadcast switched to the camera on board the boat and the interview with Van Persie. His handsome face had become, as the neighbour said, a Picasso cubist image, and his ear bled into a series of coloured squares.

'So how does this all make you feel?'

'Yeah, great, fantastic. All these people. This sea of orange. I'm starting to believe we actually won the championship.'

The boat cruised past the Holland Casino, under the footbridge. The helicopter briefly filmed the dome of the casino from above. Armando has written of the 'guilty landscape'.* Well, this here was a 'guilty cityscape'. Security cameras, meant to guard the casino's lucre, had registered the last moments of Tonio's life. The disc with the film was in the CD-ROM tray in Miriam's computer. I should try to convince her — and myself — to watch it together: this, too, we owe to Tonio.

'So, Robin, does this lessen the loss any?' the interviewer attempted again.

'I don't believe in "loss" anymore,' Van Persie replied. 'These people lining the canals, on the bridges, it's their call. If they want to act like we've won, then we've *won*.'

'In other words,' I said to Miriam, 'the national fan-club has unilaterally elected the Dutch football team world champions. If the hoi polloi want a shindig, they'll twist the facts as long as they need to, until they come up with a *reason* for one.'

---

* Armando is a Dutch painter, sculptor, and writer.

Miriam shrugged. The interviewer mumbled something about second place.

'When you see this,' Robin said, 'coming in second's not so bad.'

The boat parade approached the scene of the disaster.

'Second place is just the first-place loser,' I said. 'An American sports slogan. The Dutch spin on it is: a first-place loser is still in first place. A water-tight argument, if ever I've heard one.'

Miriam shrugged her shoulders again, this time shaking her head, too, but without taking her eyes off the TV. Where the Singel followed the curve of the Stadhouderskade, the team's boat started manoeuvring to the left.

'Minchen, don't you feel like shouting at them: wait here ... stop ... out of respect ... throw some of those flowers up onto the street ... do something ... have somebody say something ... even if just a moment of silence ...'

'With a city full of Dam Screamers?' Miriam said. 'Fat chance.'

The interview with Van Persie had come to an end. The camera mocked him once more by deforming his good-looking head and turning a close-up of his torso into a motif of brown-and-pink squares, a sort of *Victory Boogie Woogie*-ised portrait. I suddenly realised that the images of Tonio's accident would show the same kind of jerkiness — not due to sloppy camera technique, but to frugality. Like all that surveillance-camera footage in *Crimewatch*. I didn't know if the fragmentary images of his last deed on earth would make it easier or more difficult for me to watch them.

Now the broadcast switched to bird's-eye-view shots from the helicopter we'd seen hovering above us this afternoon, when I'd had the confident certainty that we were being filmed as we stood at the spot where Tonio had been killed seven weeks earlier. That pair of flecks, separated from the crowd, was that us? Miriam and I sat tensely on the edge of the sofa, as though we were expecting Tonio's resurrection, filmed from the air.

'Do you see us?' Miriam asked.

'Helicopter's too high.'

The yellow accident-reconstruction lines on the asphalt, the chalked outline of Tonio's body, would have been the only thing you could make out from that distance, if they hadn't been washed away by rain, by car tyres, or maybe by one of those high-pressure hoses spraying a chemical cleaning agent, the kind they used to get rid of squashed chewing gum from the cobblestones of the Kalverstraat.

Miriam and I were not visible on the film images. The camera swung back to the Singel, where the team boat, surrounded by motorised police waterbikes, glided around the curve.

'Think of that schoolhouse in Marsalès, back in '89,' I said. 'Those two little boys in our yard. Tonio, who was learning to walk behind his buggy … and Robin, who glowered through it all. And you see? — their histories graze each other, there in that curve.' The camera showed us the back of Paradiso. If Tonio had gone there with Jenny that Saturday night, he'd still be alive; but, according to a whole lot of well-meaning and well-disposed people, we 'mustn't think like that'. And what if this is the only way I *can* think? Thinking is like forms of government. In some places, there is a regime of freedom; in others, one of suppression. The subject has no choice but to go along with it.

41

I thought back on that day, in the same summer of '89, when we lost track of Robin while his sisters were immersed in Tonio's attempts to walk. Despite Robin's reputation for recklessness, or maybe because of it, the girls brushed it off, but Miriam and I were uneasy, so they decided to go looking for their brother after all.

I saw Robin again later that afternoon, at the campground happy hour, where the keg contained Heineken to make the Dutch guests feel more at home. I sat at a table with Robin's mother and a friend of hers, another divorcée from Rotterdam, and the friend's young daughter. The former Mrs. Van Persie was an extraordinary person, not exactly pretty, but with looks that stuck on you, or rather: they imprinted themselves in your brain like a seal in wax, indelible.

Lily and Kiki played with Tonio on the lawn. His buggy was next to me, empty. In her marvellous Rotterdam accent, Mrs. Van Persie told me about her job, her life, her family. Of the three children, Robin had taken the divorce the worst. Even when treating serious matters, her words alternated regularly with a brief, melodious giggle, or just the beginning of one — a kind of punctuation in the conversation.

Meanwhile, the children had congregated near the washroom block. Lily put Tonio back in his buggy and raced with him over to Kiki. My attention was distracted by the daughter of Mrs. Van Persie's friend. The girl, maybe ten years old, wanted to sing me a song she'd learned, using a pop bottle upended on a broomstick as a microphone. She put on a guttural voice vaguely reminiscent of Louis Armstrong, but the featherweight variant. Her performance was interrupted by screams from the Van Persie sisters, who had come running from the washrooms in our direction. In tears.

'Mama! Mama!' they cried. 'Robin! It's Robin! He's bleeding! He fell into barbed wire!'

'Well, that's about it,' the mother said, rounding off her summary of the Van Persie family. Her daughters leapt around her like frightened puppies. 'Come *on*, Mama! Robin's bleeding like crazy!'

She stood up, slow and dignified. 'Robin again.' It was not the first time this had happened. That carpenter's square in his forehead a while ago was indeed serious business, but pretty much every day there was a wound of some size to be patched or bound.

As though to demonstrate the proper lifesaving tempo, the girls ran ahead, looking back anxiously at their mother — who walked, straight as an arrow and unhurriedly, toward the washrooms. I had to keep an eye on Tonio, so I remained at the table, which in any case was littered with various small items belonging to the Van Persies. I watched the mother. The crowd of children parted for her, and the ruckus died down. A little while later, she led her son, pushing him gently forward, past the tables toward their tent. She greeted me with a gesture signifying: this is just how it is. Robin held his wounded arm outstretched, tilted slightly downward, so that the trickle of blood, having originated in the neighbourhood of his armpit or shoulder, wound its way to his wrist. He frowned as sullenly as that morning in our yard, but he did not cry.

42

Early that same fall, the Van Persie sisters came for a visit with their mother (without Robin, who by now was living with his father). Adults who meet during summer holidays should avoid renewing the acquaintance afterwards, when everyone has re-immersed themselves in day-to-day life. Awkwardness and tongue-tied embarrassment take over. Kiki and Lily, however, were oblivious to all this, and their need to cuddle Tonio had not dwindled.

But something else had changed. Tonio, now two months older, ran around the house as though he had never done otherwise. I don't remember if we had prepared him for the girls' visit, and if so, whether he understood *which* girls. The visitors' voices drew him out of his room. There he stood, in the doorway between the bedrooms and living area of our apartment, with his blue-cotton elephant under his arm. I don't hold with the cliché of the beaming bride, beaming faces, or beaming babies, but just this once I'll admit it was the truth: when he saw Kiki and Lily, he radiated an almost iridescent joy. Out of pure bliss, he gathered up a fine gob of spittle on his drooping lower lip, which soon hung in a quivering strand halfway to the floor. Tonio had not only recognised their faces but their body warmth, their eager and secure arms, their scent.

Squealing with delight, the girls pounced on the little boy. 'Tonio, can we see your room?' He waddled proudly ahead, down the hallway leading to his private domain. Miriam brought them snacks every now and then, but otherwise we didn't see the trio for the rest of the afternoon. When I took a peek around the doorway, I saw Lily with Tonio in his crib, singing to him. He giggled, listened, and giggled again — as though every verse contained a punch line, and he wanted to show he had caught it. Meanwhile Kiki worked on constructing a tower out of Tonio's colourfast, drool-proof building blocks.

If I think back on these and later situations, I'm surprised how often he, as an only child, was surrounded by girls. Isoude, Femke, Merel, Iris, Alma, Pareltje, Jayo, Lola … Tonio loved women of all ages, and women loved him, ever since he was a tyke. Amazing that a boy like this would later worry about girls.

Love, not woman, was problematic.

43

Here, in the curve now being shown, Tonio was killed. 'Run over like a dog,' I once said in one of my worst bouts of anger. Two metres below street level, following the same curve, cruised the boat carrying football hero Robin — on his way to the tribute on Museumplein. My recollection of the two boys at the Marsalès neither added to nor detracted from Tonio's death or Robin's triumph. It was what it was.

A camera, set up on the mooring across from the Salt & Pepper shakers,* filmed the players' wives, some of them with children, as they waited for the boat. One heavily made-up face pulled itself loose from its Modigliani neck, disintegrated into little coloured blocks, and was rebuilt from these same blocks as though they had imploded back together.

'So this is what she got herself all dolled up for,' Miriam said.

'Minchen, I think after all this jerky camerawork, we can handle the Holland Casino footage, don't you?'

Miriam switched off the TV. 'I don't know. When the policeman from

---

* Notoriously ugly 1970s twin buildings across the Stadhouderskade, on the Weteringschans, so nicknamed because of their boxy ungainliness.

the accidents unit told me on the phone what that film showed, I was sick to my stomach for days.'

'Come on, that disc has been lying in your computer for long enough now.'

'I don't think I can watch it. Later, maybe. Someday.'

'Remember when we took Tonio to see *The Lion King*? When the buffalo went wild and stampeded over the lions, he couldn't bear to watch it anymore. He got down on his knees in front of his chair, laid his face on the seat, and plugged his ears. You're free to do exactly the same if it gets too much for you. But at least come sit next to me.'

'I'm afraid I won't even dare close my eyes.'

'Listen, Minchen. Back at the AMC we watched him die, close up. If we can do that, we can do this, too.'

44

Two small figures danced with goofy, wooden leaps across the crosswalk between the Max Euweplein footbridge and the entrance to Vondelpark — apparently to dodge a vehicle approaching jerkily from the west side. I know nothing about cars, but from the documentation for my novel I recognised it as a Suzuki Swift. The car might have slowed down some for the pedestrians and, once past the crosswalk, sped up again, but from the jerky images it was impossible to tell. The Suzuki jolted around the wide curve of the Stadhouderskade, toward the next crosswalk. At the same time, a cyclist approached the same spot from the Hobbemastraat, thus more or less from the south. The traffic lights at the intersection appeared not to be on.

The collision between car and bicycle took place precisely between two consecutive frames — as though someone had snipped out, in an act of censorship or for some other reason, the collision itself. So we had a result but no cause. The CCTV film showed a stopped Suzuki Swift with a bicycle lying in front of it, and a more or less prone, slightly curled up figure behind it. The driver got out of the car, wooden as a marionette.

Miriam stood leaning over me from behind, her bosom tucked into my neck, and I could feel her gasp. Her fingers, lying loosely on my upper arm, now dug into my flesh. The driver jumped to his next position — and then the film went dark. I set the video back to the beginning, and replayed it.

'No, not again,' Miriam said, crying. She hid her face in my neck, and I felt the warm wetness of her tears.

'Oh yes, now I want to know everything.'

That quasi-discreet omission of the *moment suprême*. The tidy division of oncoming figure into cycle and cyclist, split between front and rear bumper. Head and shoulders of the passenger getting out of the car. Strange: in the rerun, the CCTV film went on for longer. The driver's leap led to the victim. And with another such leap, he was back at the car door.

I pushed the pause button. The driver had a hand to his ear. Perhaps the Forensic Institute could make a giant blow-up of this frame and see what number the man had dialled. I knew already: 1-1-2.

Again the screen went dark. I scrolled back. It was as though I expected the images of the collision itself would, sooner or later, come into view.

'Minchen, see those running pedestrians? … they could have distracted Tonio. Coast clear for them? Then for him, too. Ride on through.'

Miriam had stopped watching a while ago. She hung heavily on me. I replayed the film a number of times. More eagerly, it seemed, the more I got used to it. As though I had found a way to erase the images of the accident from my memory by overfeeding them. It's true, the replays gradually became numbing. The video, with its jittery figures and all, suddenly started to resemble Tonio's very first video games, which he operated with deft little fingers. Except that *this* game could not be manipulated. No matter how often I replayed it, the car hit the bike every time.

'Adri, stop now, will you, please.'

'Look, there's more.'

If I let the video play on through the blank, black screen, four rotating lights, jerky and flickering, suddenly came into view: two from police cars, two from ambulances. The jolting images made it look as though the victim was being literally thrown, stretcher and all, into one of the ambulances.

Miriam had lifted her head off my shoulders and watched the last images, sniffling quietly. 'Our sweet Tonio … why did this have to happen?' (I'm almost certain she said '*does* this *have* to', using the present imperfect: it happened, after all, at that very moment, in front of her own eyes.)

The ambulance with Tonio in it jerked into motion, leaving behind a flea circus of uninterrupted, hopping mini-figurines. With something in between a sob and a sigh, Miriam nestled her head back onto my neck, murmuring the words she'd used since the first night, when all other expressions of grief seemed to be depleted: 'Our little boy.'

With my arm stretched back tightly around her neck, I sat there staring at the screen. The running clock at the bottom of the screen said 05:09:14. Was the Holland Casino still open at that hour? I imagined that behind the high front wall, on which the security cameras were mounted, the balls on the roulette wheels just rattled on. A tired croupier raked up a fortune in chips. The mysterious yellow-eyed customer finally dared to loosen his necktie a bit.

The solar eclipse

The more awayness stings,
the more despairingly its traces,
until what sometime needs completing,
become besotted with the missed.

Time and again the instant a shiver runs
along the blossom-twined stem
still keeping his tomahawk in check,

the little lunar disc behind his heart,
be it extremely briefly, still mists over,
at which any second every sleeper
attempts to pay off his blood-debt
in wrongly faltering mirror script.

— Hans Faverey, from *The Missed*

1

August is drawing to a close. Tomorrow is the first of September, the beginning of meteorological autumn. This morning, the in-house philosopher at *de Volkskrant* wrote a piece about hope. I quote: 'Hope is out, fear is in. Hope and fear are twin brothers, born of the unknowableness of the future. We hope for the best, but we fear the worst.'

Hope may be a form of self-deception, but we can't live without it, even though it means hoping against all odds. 'Hope is a reflex.' But if it's true that the terminal patient keeps hoping for a cure, and the death-row inmate for a reprieve, what does that — reflex or no — leave Miriam and me to hope for? 'A person cannot evade his hope any more than he can his fear.'

The hope that Tonio might one day return to us has been obliterated. The fear that this icy truth will pierce us, deeper and more obscenely than before, only augments. What should we hope for? That sooner or later the sense of loss will fade? That is an idle hope, for the loss will be there, with a lifetime guarantee, forever.

2

It is as though we have landed in a dimension of reality where different laws of nature apply to us than to others. If I can go by all the well-meant predictions, most people see the date of the fatal accident as a point in time from which we move forward, marking various calendric milestones (a month now; three months already, soon four; before you know it, six), while loss and grief undergo an organic process of erosion.

Miriam and I (varying somewhat on each other's perception) experience the situation much differently. Whenever, having just managed to catch our breath, we glance back, we see the events of 23 May racing toward us at an unpredictable (and incalculable) speed. Instead of standing still, and thus falling further behind us, the date and what it represents keeps nipping at our heels — without actually nabbing us. We are like fugitives on the run, being chased by a hyena or some other predator. With every glance over our shoulder, the pursuer appears to be catching up, but it holds back, bides its time — its shadow, moreover, adding to the illusion.

We will be relentlessly pursued for the rest of our days by a nightmare in the flesh — Tonio's dead flesh. Nothing doing, the waning of pain and grief. The only thing that wanes is not what is behind us, but that which lies ahead: what's left of our lives.

3

In a half-hearted attempt to do something about my physical condition, I mounted the exercise bike for the first time since Whit Sunday. I lugged it from a dark corner of the bedroom to a spot near the balcony doors, so that I could read the paper by daylight while pedalling. The machine is set to its maximum resistance. The last time I used it, in May, this setting felt easy. Now the pedals are sluggish and heavy. Now it's my joints that, after months of sedentary brooding, are threatening to seize up.

I drape the newspaper over the handlebars so as not to have to watch the odometer. I concentrate on my unwilling legs. Each rotation of the pedals is another step in my recovery. Soon we'll initiate Prohibition. My brain has long since become immune to the pain-killing effect of alcohol. Booze is back to what it always was: simply a way to get blotto. With the difference that it now augments the pain, rather than numbing it. The grief-variant of a bad trip.

As far as the physical boundaries of Prohibition go, there's not much area to patrol: the two large seat cushions on the sagging living-room sofa, and the 40x40 centimetres of cocktail table, which, thanks to its special construction, can be slid back to divide the sofa into two parts.

If I quit, it is primarily to no longer drag Miriam down with me. She regularly complains of a burning sensation in her throat after drinking her favourite herb vodka. Diluting it with orange juice works for the first two glasses, but after that even the sweetest fruit juice has a bitter edge. Neat, then, either straight up or with an ice cube.

That little table, by the way, as handy as it seemed when we bought it, is beginning to get on my nerves. The veneer, which once gave it the impression of being made of solid wood, has started to peel and chip under the rings of sloshed alcohol; but the worst is that, in its function of sliding in a C-shaped embrace around the sofa seat, it forms an annoying barrier between Miriam's grief and my comforting, and between my grief and her comforting. Every time we nevertheless reach out with an impotent gesture of support to the other, we risk knocking over a glass or bottle in the process.

So away with that wheelless ServeBoy trolley, that clinking witness of our most intimate death-disgust — and all those bottles along with it.

A muscle pain soon develops in my legs that seems more appropriate to hours of daily jogging than a few minutes on an exercise bike. What's more, the image of Tonio on this same apparatus keeps forcing its way in, to the point of paralysing me. He has deposited a bag full of dirty laundry downstairs, and wants to take advantage of the opportunity to enjoy a decent shower. (The shower in de Nepveustraat does not produce much more than 'a weak dribble'.) Looking for his parents, he goes around opening doors. Miriam isn't home, and he eventually finds me in bed, reading. He is cheerful, full of energy.

'Hi. Taking the day off? You gonna shower?'

'In a bit.'

'Mind if I go first?'

'Learn once and for all not to toss the wet washcloth over the edge of the tub, okay? I really don't feel like wringing out your used washrags.'

He chuckles and climbs onto the exercycle. I don't know how the conversation turns to the Coen brothers, his favourite directorial duo, but as he loosely pedals he gives me a brief lecture on Coen cinema. 'So tricky.' He's just seen their latest, *Burn After Reading*, and groans as he recalls the roles played by Pitt and Clooney. 'A pitiful pair, those two.'

Brad Pitt, I understand, plays a babytalking personal trainer at a gym. And Clooney ... too pathetic for words: 'What a sucker.'

'In the roles they're playing, d'you mean, or the actors themselves?'

'Both. That's exactly the Coen brothers' mean streak. By giving them those roles, they're totally typecasting them. Really sneaky.'

'Forgive me, Tonio, but you kind of remind me of a gullible theatregoer from the old days. Someone who waits at the stage door for the bad guy in the play, to punch him in the nose for the evil stuff he did on stage.'

Tonio quit pedalling and looked at me, shaking his head. As usual, I just didn't get it. 'Why do *you* think the Coen brothers ask superstars like that to act in their movies?'

With an expression that said 'Just think about it', he dismounted the exercise bike. He took a towel and washcloth from the linen cupboard and disappeared into the bathroom, where I would later find — not on the edge of the tub, but on the washbasin countertop — the washcloth, unwrung, and saturated with frothy shower gel. I lay in bed pondering whether from now on I should regard every Coen brothers movie as a sort of garbage grinder or paper shredder for disposing of mainstream celebrity reputations.

This morning I had already taken Tonio's imaginary place on the exercycle when Miriam came into the bedroom. It was clear she'd been crying — not dramatically, not for a long time, but nonetheless noticeably, even though I couldn't put my finger on what made it so. I'd been with her for more than thirty years, and in those three decades we'd had our share of crying behind closed doors, me less than her, but never *more* than these past three months. By now I could put together an encyclopedia of the many categories of crying, complete with gradations in intensity, that the death of a child can lead to. My internal weeping, too, could be itemised, at the very least into the trickle and the gush.

'I just thought of something,' she said, and her eyes started glistening again. 'My father is ninety-seven; I'm fifty. I take after him. Say I also live to be ninety-seven, or even older … that means I've got another forty-seven years to live without Tonio. A half a century. Isn't that an unbearable thought?'

My legs had come to a stop, but I stayed sitting on the machine. I laid a hand against the side of her face. 'Minchen, what did we decide? *Not* to resist the grief. More than that: we'd keep the nerve open and raw, preferably let the pain get even worse, because that's our last link to Tonio. If we can keep him alive via that searing pain, then we have to do our best to live to a ripe old age. We can't let death cut us off from our pain too early — that won't do Tonio's survival any good. Dying deadens the pain, you know, for good. Regard that pain as the eternal flame on Tonio's grave. It'll go out one day, that's for sure. Half a century from now, that's soon enough. Deal?'

Miriam nodded, smiled, wiped her face dry.

'Then we have to quit boozing, and soon,' she said. 'What d'you say to an official last glass tonight? Really, that when we go to bed we can say … uh … finito, over and out, enough is enough. Y'know, I don't really even like the taste of it anymore.'

'All right, one last toast … to our longevity.'

'To the longevity of all three of us.'

4

(Diary entry, Wednesday 19 May 1999)

8.00 p.m. Tonio home. Observe him surreptitiously as he plays, kneeling on the floor, wearing his drab olive outfit: the picture of health. 8:30: he goes up to the third floor with me and sits on my chaise longue reading something. Later he gets up quietly so as not to disturb me. Out of the corner of my eye I see him walk around the long sorting table. He inspects the manuscripts, arranged by chapter in small stacks. Here and there he reads the summary on the top sheet.

'It says here: "Movo in the Burn Centre." Why is Movo in the burn centre?'

'He stuck his head in a deep fryer full of scalding-hot fat.'

'Oh. Why?'

'To punish himself.'

'Oh. What for?'

'The terrible things he had done.'

'Yeah, but here it says he got twelve years in prison.' (Laughs.) 'Then you don't have to go and punish *yourself* ...'

'It's for other things than the judge punished him for.'

'Oh. Why does he get to go free after eight years? It says so here.'

'That's how it is in this country. If you behave, you only have to do two-thirds of your sentence.'

'Oh.' He gives me three big kisses, and goes off the bed. 'Work hard, okay?'

5

I have long searched for a memory of Tonio with which I might close this requiem.

In a work of fiction, a few recollections of the lead character's past, provided they are well chosen, are sufficient to recall his entire youth. This document dedicated to Tonio would only be complete if I could include in it *all* my cherished and less pleasurable memories of him, plus all those gleaned from third parties. Loss makes one insatiable. In order to combat the unattainable yearning for completeness, I have let my memory take its own associative course. I have worked the material so gathered into a structure similar to that of a novel, in the hope that Tonio, despite the gaps, will emerge as multifaceted as possible.

I stumbled on my diary notes from the summer of '99, when the three of us vacationed in Marsalès for the third time (for Miriam and Tonio, it was their fourth visit). The date: Wednesday 11 August 1999. I do not quote the diary entry verbatim here, but fill it out so as to get to the heart of the situation.

The previous weekend we had visited the publisher Dick Gubbels and his wife Elly in the Corrèze, and our return to Marsalès marked the last week of our holiday. On the morning of the 11th, the three of us are sitting in the yard of the rented house, which we use only for sleeping, and occasionally to take refuge in from the fearsome Dordogne thunderstorms. The yard is surrounded by a tall hedge, but the sun has already long risen above it. Miriam and Tonio recline in plastic lawn chairs, while I sit at the metal office table the landlord put there especially for me: a frame in peeling army-green and a desktop of grey linoleum, which has been scratched by so many penknives that if one were to smear it with ink and press a large sheet of paper onto it, the result would undoubtedly be a Baroque linocut.

I write using a portable electric typewriter, which is powered by way of a long, rodent-safe, heavy-duty cable leading to the house. Since my compulsive nature is in no way put on hold during vacations, I make notes for one of my works-in-progress. The main character, Movo, is being treated at the Beverwijk Burn Centre, where he has been taken after immersing his face in a pan of hot oil, in an act of self-mutilation. There, too, it is the morning of 11 August 1999, and it's getting on to 11.00 a.m. Movo is sitting in the hospital garden, guarded by a nurse, awaiting the solar eclipse. Around him are the victims of a recent fire that burned down the Roxy discotheque in Amsterdam. An indoor fireworks display following the funeral of the fireworks artist Peter Giele had set the disco ablaze. Movo, who has undergone a series of plastic-surgery efforts in Beverwijk since the end of April, recalls the tumultuous arrival of the ambulances from Amsterdam.

My worktable is in the shadow of a densely crowned tree. Miriam and Tonio's deck chairs are in the full sunlight, which now, at almost eleven o'clock, is still just bearable. Miriam is reading a book by Patricia Highsmith. I can't see the cover from here, but I think it's from the Ripley series. Tonio sits stock-still, his knees tucked up, against the back of his chaise longue. Now and again he puts on the cardboard eclipse glasses he bought at the campground store. The lenses are made of green mica, or of ordinary plastic. He looks briefly at the sun, and removes them again. His face does not betray any impatience; rather, stoicism.

The Roxy victims around Movo are all wearing protective eclipse glasses. Some of them have the earpiece stuck in the gauze bandage in which their head is swathed. The nurse asks Movo if she shouldn't go buy a pair for him, too, from the kiosk in the lobby:

What's to protect? I'm as good as blind. Well, okay, three-quarters. All the better to see the solar eclipse with, and no need for those dumb glasses.

From the timetable printed in the 6 August edition of *de Volkskrant* (also for sale in the campground store), I note that the eclipse will be visible in the Netherlands, depending on the location, somewhere around ten past eleven. I can't remember what that means for the south of France. It's not yet eleven. Tonio can be quite stealthy: suddenly he's standing beside me.

'Adri, have you ever seen a total solar eclipse?'

'I don't know if it was total or not, but it was in the early sixties … I was as old as you are now … there was a big fuss about it. The world would come to an end, I think it was. The only thing I can remember is the sun with a nibble taken out of it.'

'Did you have eclipse glasses back then?'

'We had to make do with the lid to a *hagelslag* jar. It was made of dark-brown hard plastic. If I didn't go blind, it was thanks to the points you could save up to get yourself one of those jars.'

'I'm gonna go look.'

Movo is trying, quite deliberately, to mislead the nurse. His dive into the deep-fry oil was intended to blind him completely. That did not entirely succeed. Now he will try again. Twelve seconds of looking directly at the eclipsed sunlight will damage the cornea sufficiently to finish off the job. What the nurse does not know is that Movo's stitched-on eyelids still show little-to-no capacity for reaction …

It's how it is, and always has been: I ruin every idyll by grinding it up into material for fiction. May I, for that reason, burn in a hell too far away to convey me in an ambulance to Beverwijk.

'It's starting,' Tonio calls from his lawn chair. He even sits up extra straight.

I look at the watch next to my typewriter. Just past eleven.

'So soon?' asks Miriam. She raises her sunglasses and looks at Tonio, but not at the sun (fortunately).

'See for yourself.' Tonio brings his mother the eclipse glasses.

'A nibble,' she says. Tonio yanks the glasses back off her nose, casts a quick glance through them, and then brings them over to me. A small but unmistakable nibble.

6

When Tonio returns to the lawn chair wearing the cardboard glasses, I'm barely able to continue working. My eyes are repeatedly drawn to my beautiful boy, who sits there with such diligence, following with his tense little body this exceptional occurrence he so clearly explained to me the previous day. In turn, I wowed him with the report (which I'd got out of the newspaper) that the next total solar eclipse, in the Netherlands at least, won't be until 7 October 2135.

'136 years from now,' I said. 'I won't be here for that one.'

'Will I be?' He asked it with a laugh.

'The scientists claim that, in the not-too-distant future, people could easily live to be a hundred and fifty. You're eleven now.'

'I'll make it!' he cheered. 'With three years to spare!'

'So you'll have those three extra years to reminisce about that eclipse on 7 October … and the one from 136 years earlier, when you were on vacation with your parents in France.'

He beamed at me, wanting to say something, but I could tell he was completely occupied with the thoughts and images somersaulting over one another in his mind.

There is certainly something comfortable about it, Movo thinks: being able to look straight at the sun, which always used to make you lower your eyes the moment you looked at it.

Every now and then, I get up and go crouch next to Tonio. He hands me the eclipse glasses without being asked. The black bite the moon has taken out of the sun keeps on growing. Occasionally, Tonio brings the glasses over to his mother. 'You watch for me, honey,' she says.

'Suit yourself,' says Tonio. 'The next one is in a hundred and thirty-six years and two months.'

'You can watch for me then, too.'

By around noon, it's clear that the premature dusk has spread an exanimate light over everything. The sun, or what's left of it, casts a velvety shadow, but it no longer warms one's exposed body parts. A hush falls over the surrounding land, disrupted only by barking dogs at a nearby farm and the tinny voices of children at the campground. Then the birds begin to chirp, at first hesitantly, questioningly, a few hours after the early heat has silenced them. They sing like they do at twilight — melancholy and resigned, less shrill than at sunrise.

'In a minute, honey,' Miriam says as Tonio offers her the glasses again. 'I'd rather wait until it's totally eclipsed.'

'Here in the south,' I say, 'it won't be more than 80 per cent.'

'Don't shout so,' Miriam whispers, so quietly that I almost can't make out what she said. 'I want to hear this special calm.'

I didn't shout, didn't even raise my voice, but the atmosphere is now so fragile and intimate and lonely that *every* human noise sounds too loud. Through the eclipse glasses, one observes a starless night sky, with a waning moon.

'This is what's great about an eclipse,' I whisper to Tonio, handing him back the glasses. 'The sun masquerades as a crescent moon, just for the occasion. Welcome to the masked ball of the heavenly bodies.

The carnival of the solar system.'

Tonio puts on his 'what a bore' face and responds with the standard phrase he has plagiarised from his mother: 'Good day at work, apparently.'

Except for a few thin cloud banks just above the horizon, the sky is clear, but it nevertheless does not look blue, more like colourless: a grainy light-grey, like ground ice covered with a thin layer of powdery snow. I wonder if the fresh lines of condensation, not far from the largely eclipsed sun, weren't put there in purpose at that hour by a pair of vain fighter-jet pilots. All of France is looking upward at this moment. While scratching your initials into an Egyptian pyramid stone might last longer, writing with smoke in the sky has more effect. Ever since I could throw back my head and gaze upward toward the sky as a child, I have been trying to decipher the script of vapour lines. Sometimes I convince myself that I've got the message. Today, I can't make heads or tails out of them, dulled by the overshadowed sun.

The hush is suddenly broken by an unseen car racing along the hardened dirt road that runs past our yard. Bits of gravel are thrown into the hedges, and rustle as they fall through the dry leaves.

'Sheesh,' Miriam says. 'Bet he promised to be home before dark.'

The eclipse approaches its French maximum of 80 per cent. In our yard, it's definitely dusk now, but without the backlight that makes the tree branches look like they were snipped out of black paper. Contrary to a normal Dordogne twilight, this one is deathly, soulless, devoid of ambience. Tonio hands me the cardboard glasses.

'I think it's as far as it's going to get,' he says.

I put on the glasses. There is still a thick toenail of sun left. I look at it at length, hoping to see the arc of light get smaller. The process seems to be standing still. Tonio grabs the glasses from my nose and puts them on. He stands on the lawn chair.

'It's over,' he says after a few seconds. 'Here, keep 'em.' He nonchalantly tosses the glasses at me. 'I've seen enough.'

He runs up the few stone steps to the front door, and disappears into the dark house.

'What's with him?' Miriam asks. She is still lying there reading, but with the sunglasses on her forehead and the book close to her eyes.

'He's had enough.'

Typical Tonio. Once he's figured out how something — whether it's a machine or a natural event — works, he loses interest in it. There is more going on in the world that needs his attention.

My diary tells what comes next. At the height of the eclipse, the birds go silent. As the light gradually returns, they start up again, one by one, now cautiously cheerful, like at dawn. It is a quarter past one. I haven't seen Tonio again. Little by little, the sky takes on a blue tint. If I raise my face toward the sun, I do not yet really feel its warmth. Miriam offers to warm up yesterday's two leftover quails for me.

If I put the eclipse glasses back on, it's only to check the progress of the Return of Light, as though, taking after Tonio, I want to it to be over and done with already.

'He's sitting there reading, half in the dark,' Miriam says when she comes out of the kitchen with the food. 'With a clip-on bedside lamp, the goofball.'

I enjoy my quails, but there is something disconcerting about eating a meal in such deadened light. I feel liberated when, at a quarter to two, the eclipse is over.

It's all there in black and white, an account of the rest of the day, too. But since Black Whitsun almost eleven years later, my recollection of the eclipse stalls at the point that Tonio called it quits. 'I've seen enough.' In moments when the reality of his death *truly* hits me, and my heart constricts with cold and shock, that soulless image of the eclipse once again blankets the whole world, which, like back then, holds its breath, birdcalls and all. Everything else (the dawn, the burning sun in the cloudless blue sky, the twilight with its many contrasts) is illusion, a memory of how it might once have been. A shadow has fallen over it — not the vibrant shadow, which indicates the motility and vitality of the sun, but the perfidious, poisonous shadow of the eclipse, permeating and tainting everything.

7

After finishing the quails, I go back inside. There's so much bright sunlight outside again that in the semi-darkness of the house, the sun-flecks dance about in front of me. The door to Tonio's room is wide open. He is sitting cross-legged on the bottom mattress of the bunk bed (he sleeps on top). A magazine lies open across his thighs. The shutters are closed. Tonio is reading by the dim light of a pinecone-shaped lamp affixed to one leg of the bed. His eyes dart over the pages, one after the other. There is a huge stack of Donald Duck comic books on the floor; Miriam had bought out the entire stock of old issues at Lambiek on the Kerkstraat. Judging from the speed with which he turns the pages, you might conclude that he's only looking at the pictures, but when I once decided to test out my theory and quizzed him on one of the stories, it appeared he had not missed a single text balloon.

The occasional brief sniff: his way of laughing when he thinks he's not being watched; with us around, he guffaws with generous hilarity. Just a normal eleven-year-old boy, who devours a comic book as though it were a hamburger or a Mars bar. He has still not noticed my presence, or if he has, he hides it well. I observe him, and melt. When I think back on the scene, I count myself lucky that I did not know then what I do now: that there, eleven years old, he was already halfway through his allotment of years. A bit more than halfway.

8

Sometimes I want to hold him really tightly. The thought usually hits me when I'm in bed reading, and just happen to lay my book aside. Come, Tonio, I say soundlessly. Come, Tonio, climb under the blankets. I'll keep you warm.

His body is unresisting, limp, but not cold. It is the Tonio who lay on the asphalt after the collision, half a day before his death. The occupants of the red Suzuki Swift are standing outside the car, and do not dare go look at the body that's been chucked a ways further up. The police and ambulance sirens are not yet audible. The blue flicker of the rotating lights hasn't arrived yet. It is right then that I pick him up and carry him to my bed, and pull back the blanket.

Come. Come lie close to me. It'll keep you warm. They're coming, they'll be here soon, to make you better.

9

I think Miriam will agree with me if I allow Jenny to have the last word.

Jenny had asked, before going home, if she could have a look at Tonio's room. 'Of course, go ahead.' I understood. That's where most of the photo shoot had taken place. Miriam offered to accompany her, but Jenny preferred to go up alone.

'I know the way.'

We heard her gentle treads as she went up the stairs to the second floor — and then, silence. No creaking footsteps on the parquet floor above overhead, as we were accustomed to until two years ago. No, just a very present silence, nothing more.

She stayed up there a long time, Jenny. Miriam and I looked at each other a couple of times without saying anything. We were thinking the same thing. For God's sake, get that girl out of the house so we can unleash our tears. We hadn't truly appreciated it: a glimpse at a budding romance was the most awful thing that could happen to us, precisely *because* there would never, for all eternity, be the chance of seeing it through.

Jenny did not come back down, nor did she make any sound upstairs.

'Maybe she just snuck out,' Miriam said. 'Did you hear the downstairs hall doors? They haven't been closing so well recently. When the front door shuts, they rattle.'

'I haven't heard anything,' I said. 'She must still be up there.'

We whispered.

'Shall I go have a look?' Miriam asked.

'I'll go have a listen at the bottom of the stairs.'

I held my breath as I walked out onto the landing. I listened. Not a peep. The curve in the staircase blocked any view of what was going on up on the next floor. The dim light of the wall lamp on the second floor did not betray any motion, not even a shadow. Afraid to disturb something intimate, I dared not go any further. At the same time, I was anxious.

I went down to the ground floor, where the cats stopped their horseplay on the marble floor and looked inquisitively up at me. To keep them from escaping, I closed the double inner doors tightly. This was how I used to sneak out to Café Welling, but that was no longer necessary. I twisted the bolt so that the lock wouldn't click shut, and walked backwards between the parked cars onto the street, far enough to look into Tonio's room.

The curtains were open. There were no lights on. From the right, though, where the door led to the landing, a minimally faint light shone into the room. I waited, in case I might see something move. A few times, I had to take a few steps forward, toward the parking spots, in order to let traffic pass. Soon the Concertgebouw would be opening its doors, so the neighbourhood was already crawling with patrons in search of a parking space.

Nothing happened, so I went back inside. The cats had nestled into the curve of the stairs, as though waiting for me: a moment later, they raced ahead of me into the living room, where Miriam sat on the sofa, fighting the urge to cry.

'There's no light,' I said.

We sat next to each other in silence, waiting resignedly for what was to come. The glasses were empty, but I did not ask for more to drink. It was some time before we heard soft footsteps on the stairs, and only then because I hadn't shut the living-room door all the way. There was a tentative knock at the door.

'Yes, Jenny?'

'I just wanted to say goodbye.'

Jenny hugged Miriam, and then me. Her face was not red from crying, but her lower eyelashes were stuck wetly together.

'Could you find the light switch?' I asked, just to break the silence.

'Oh, I didn't go in the room.' She sounded slightly startled, as though she thought I suspected her of desecration. 'The door was open. I stood at the threshold for a long time. To say goodbye.' And as she turned to go, she said: 'You know, I really believe that the dead leave a kind of energy behind for us.'

Amsterdam, June 2010–March 2011

Translator's note

The translator wishes to thank Ruud van Odenhoven for his invaluable and unstinting assistance in matters pertaining to Dutch culture.

The English translation published here of Gerrit Kouwenaar's poem 'there are still' (originally published in Dutch as '*Men moet*' by Querido) is copyright © David Colmer.

Hans Faverey (1933–1990) wrote his collection of poetry *The Missed* on his deathbed, after a lengthy illness. It was originally published in Dutch as *Het ontbrokene* by De Bezige Bij. The English translation published here is copyright © Francis R. Jones.

All footnotes have been written by the translator, with the exception of one provided by the author and identified as such.

The following works are cited in *Tonio*:

by Adri van der Heijden:
Advocaat van de Hanen (*Lawyer to the Punks*)
Asbestemming (*Ash Destination*)
De Tandeloze Tijd (*The Toothless Time*)
De Draaideur (*The Revolving Door*)
Een gondel in de Herengracht (*A Gondola in the Herengracht*)
Het schervengericht (*Judgement by Shards*)
De slag om de Blauwbrug (*The Battle of the Blue Bridge*)
Vallende Ouders (*Falling Parents*)
Homo duplex (*Homo duplex*)
Het Hof van Barmhartigheid (*The Court of Mercy*)
Onder het plaveisel het moeras (*Under the Pavement the Morass*)

De Movo Tapes (The Movo Tapes)
De gevarendriehoek (The Danger Triangle)
Reis in een boom (Travels in a Tree)
Weerborstels (Cowlicks)
Het bankroet dat mijn goudmijn is (The Bankruptcy That is My Goldmine)
Kwaadschiks (Unwillingly)

To date, none of Van der Heijden's works, aside from *Tonio*, has been translated into English. The English equivalents given above are provisional working titles that have been assigned by the Dutch Foundation for Literature.

by Alfred Kossmann:
Geur der droefenis (Smell of Sadness)

by Jan Wolkers (film by Paul Verhoeven):
Turks Fruit (Turkish Delight)

by Louis van Gasteren (film):
Hans, het leven voor de dood

Author's note

This requiem memoir is based in part on my diary entries, some of which were published earlier in their original form in *Engelenplaque* (2003) and *Hier viel Van Gogh flauw* (2004). The incident of the replaced front-door lock appeared, in modified form, in the novella *Sabberita* (1998) and the collection of short stories *Gentse lente* (2008).